Webster's

NEW WORLD
DICTIONARY®
OF
COMPUTER
TERMS

Webster's

NEW WORLD DICTIONARY®

OF

COMPUTER TERMS

FIFTH EDITION

Compiled by
Donald Spencer

MACMILLAN • USA

Macmillan General Reference
A Prentice Hall Macmillan Company
15 Columbus Circle
New York, NY 10023

A Webster's New World™ Book

Dictionary Editorial Offices:
New World Dictionaries
850 Euclid Avenue
Cleveland, Ohio 44114

Library of Congress Cataloging-in-Publication Data

Spencer, Donald.

ISBN: 0-671-89993-7

Manufactured in the United States of America

10 9 8 7 6 5 4 3 2 1

Fifth Edition

Introduction

It is unlikely that any field has contributed more new terms (or new meanings of old ones) to the language in the last few years than has computer technology. This is largely because computer technology is itself a new and changing field. As it evolves, fresh terminology must be developed to communicate, describe, and define the heretofore unknown concepts, components, and techniques. This book provides a glossary of over 7,000 words, phrases, acronyms, and abbreviations used in connection with computers.

When a business installs its first computer, not only are the owners and managers apprehensive; the majority of the office and administrative personnel are also involved in the change that has taken place. Managers must know something about the current computer jargon in order to assist the staff with knowledgeable explanations of what is happening. Filling the need for this information is the purpose of this book.

This new edition offers up-to-date coverage of terms used in reference to hardware, software, programming, logic, and computer graphics, as well as those used in ancillary fields such as data communications and artificial intelligence. Areas of frequent application are also covered, particularly mathematics and business administration.

The terms in this book have been selected as those most likely to confront the beginning computer-user, and they are defined in a way that any lay person can understand. Wherever possible, technical terms have been avoided so that the definitions might be easily read and understood. Where a proper understanding of a term depends upon the comprehension of another term, the reader is directed to it by a cross-reference (in SMALL CAPITALS).

All terms are entered in a strict alphabetical listing, so spaces and dashes are to be ignored in looking up a particular word or phrase; for example, *programming language* comes between *program* and *program storage*. The terms normally appear in boldface lowercase characters. Acronyms are capitalized and the appropriate letters are amplified in the text; for example, RAM stands for **r**andom **a**ccess **m**emory.

The most common meaning has been provided for most terms. Frequently, the same term will have other, more specific meanings when used in specialized fields within the computer industry. If a term has more than one commonly accepted meaning, or is used as more than one part of speech, each sense is preceded by a number. Wherever possible, the more general sense of the term appears first.

This book is intended to be a useful reference for anyone with an interest in computer technology.

A

A:drive A designation for the first floppy disk drive in IBM-compatible microcomputers. B:drive is the second floppy disk drive; C:drive is the hard disk drive.

AAAI Abbreviation for **A**merican **A**ssociation for **A**rtificial **I**ntelligence, a professional organization concerned with advancing artificial intelligence.

abacus An ancient device for doing simple calculations that uses movable beads threaded on a grid of wires. First used in ancient Mediterranean cultures and ancient China, it is still used in several Asian countries.

ABC See ATANASOFF-BERRY COMPUTER.

abend Acronym for **ab**normal **end**ing. Early termination of a program due to an error condition (erroneous software logic or hardware failure).

abnormal end See ABNORMAL TERMINATION.

abnormal termination The stopping of a program before it has finished running because of a problem.

abort The procedure for terminating a program when a mistake, malfunction, or error occurs.

abscissa The X-AXIS of a graph or chart. Contrast with ORDINATE.

absolute address An address that is permanently assigned by the machine designer to a particular storage location. Addresses 0000, 0001, 0002, and 0003 might be assigned to the first four locations in a computer's storage. Also called machine address.

absolute addressing   A method of machine addressing in which the address part of an instruction contains an absolute address.

absolute coding   Coding that uses machine instructions and absolute addresses. It can be directly executed by a computer without prior translation to a different form. Contrast with SYMBOLIC CODING.

absolute coordinates   A location relative to a coordinate system's origin. In Cartesian coordinates, a two-dimensional point is identified by its distance from the origin along the X- and Y-axes; a three-dimensional point is identified by its distance from the origin along the X-, Y-, and Z-axes.

absolute error   The magnitude of an error without regard for its algebraic sign.

absolute instruction   An instruction in its final, executable form.

absolute value   The magnitude of a number, regardless of its algebraic sign, equal to the positive value of the number. The absolute value of −82, for example, is 82.

absolute vector   In computer graphics, a vector with end points designated in ABSOLUTE COORDINATES.

abstract art   Art not primarily concerned with the representation of nature. The artist or computer graphicist selects and exaggerates certain aspects of reality in order to provide a visual experience by means of line, color, and form.

abstract class   In OBJECT-ORIENTED PROGRAMMING, a class that has no instances.

abstraction   In OBJECT-ORIENTED PROGRAMMING, the process of creating a superclass by extracting common qualities or general characteristics from more specific classes or objects.

AC   Abbreviation for ALTERNATING CURRENT.

ACC   Abbreviation for ACCUMULATOR.

accelerator   A device to speed up either the computer or monitor. Typically a circuit card with an extra processing chip and/or additional RAM.

acceptance test   A test used to demonstrate the capabilities and workability of a new computer system. Usually conducted by the manufacturer to show the customer that the system is in working order.

access   **(1)** Generally, to obtain data. **(2)** To locate desired data.

access arm   A mechanical device in a disk file storage unit that positions reading and writing mechanisms.

access code   A group of characters or numbers that identifies a user to the computer system.

access control   The process whereby use of a computer is restricted to authorized individual users.

access level   In COMPUTER SECURITY, the level of authority a subject has when using a protected resource.

access light   The light on the front of a system unit that signals when the computer is reading from or writing to a disk.

access lock   Same PRIVACY LOCK.

access mechanism   The mechanical device in the disk storage unit that positions the read/write heads on the proper tracks.

access method   Any of the data management techniques available to users for transferring data between storage and an input/output device.

access mode   The manner in which files are referred to by a computer.

access monitoring   A method of giving a system user only a certain number of attempts to provide the correct password.

access name   In a database system, a name that identifies an entity by the correct password.

accessor   In COMPUTER SECURITY, any user of a protected resource.

accessory   A basic part or assembly used with another assembly, device, or unit.

accessory card   An additional circuit card that can be mounted inside a personal computer and connected to the system bus.

access path   The procedure used by a DATABASE MANAGEMENT SYSTEM to access data stored in a DATABASE.

access time   The time a computer takes to locate and transfer data to or from storage. Composed of SEEK TIME and TRANSFER RATE.

accountability   In COMPUTER SECURITY, the property that enables activities on a computer system to be traced to individuals who may then be held responsible for their actions.

accounting   A process that tracks the financial health of a company or individual.

accounting information system (AIS)   A subsystem of the management information system that processes primarily economic and financial data.

accounting package   A group of programs that allows a business to keep track of its financial affairs.

account number   A unique number assigned to an individual or group that is used to gain access to the system. After entering the account number, the operator enters a password, which is checked by the operating system software.

accounts receivable   A module of a business accounting software package that keeps track of money owed to a firm and when payments are due.

accreditation   In COMPUTER SECURITY, the authorization that is granted to an information system to process sensitive information in its operational environment.

accumulate   To collect.

accumulator   A register or storage location that temporarily holds the result of an arithmetic or logic operation. Commonly used when a series of calculations is to be totaled.

accuracy   The degree of exactness of an approximation or measurement. *Accuracy* normally denotes absolute quality of computed results; *precision* usually refers to the amount of detail used in representing those results. Four-place results are less precise than six-place results, yet a four-place table could be more accurate than an erroneously computed six-place table.

accuracy aids   In CAD, preprogrammed techniques that allow a designer to achieve positioning accuracy on an interactive display, such as a grid constraint.

ACD   Abbreviation for **a**utomatic **c**all **d**istribution, a service that allows incoming telephone calls directed to the same dialed number to be routed to one of multiple agents, all of whom can provide the same service to the calling party.

achromatic   Having no color; being a neutral such as black, white, or gray.

ACK   Abbreviation for **ack**nowledge, an international transmission control code that is returned by a receiving terminal to a transmitting terminal to acknowledge that a frame of information has been correctly received.

acknowledge   To answer.

acknowledged mail   In ELECTRONIC MAIL, a function that allows a user to request and receive an acknowledgement that the mail item he or she sent was received.

acknowledgement   An indication that an item sent was received.

ACM   See ASSOCIATION FOR COMPUTING MACHINERY.

acoustical sound enclosure   A device that fits over a printer or other machine to reduce noise. It is most noticeable when absent.

acoustic coupler   A type of modem that translates computer signals into telephone tones and the reverse. This allows computers to communicate with each other by the telephone network. An acoustic coupler looks like a plastic box in which a telephone handset is placed.

acoustic radar   The use of ultrahigh-frequency sound waves to determine the position of an object in space. Acoustic radar techniques have been used in the design of graphic input data tablets.

acronym   A word formed from the first letter (or letters) of each word in a phrase or name (for example, DOS stands for **d**isk **o**perating **s**ystem and RAM stands for **r**andom **a**ccess **m**emory).

action   The activity resulting from a given condition.

action diagram   A programming tool that facilitates the coding of structured programs.

action entry   One of the four sections of a decision table. Specifies what actions should be taken.

action lines   In computer graphics, extraneous lines used to suggest action.

action message   A message issued because of a condition that requires an operator response.

action-oriented management report   An exception report used to alert management to abnormal situations that require special attention.

action statement   A statement that tells the computer to perform an action.

action stub   One of four sections of a decision table. Describes possible actions applicable to the problem to be solved.

activate   To put a unit or device into an operational state.

activating   Making a device, unit, program, or system available for use.

active   Operational.

active cell   In an ELECTRONIC SPREADSHEET, the cell on the matrix that is highlighted by the cursor. Information may be entered, altered, or deleted by the user when the cell is active. Also called current cell.

active display   A display, such as a cathode ray tube, electroluminescent display, or plasma panel, that presents information by emitting light.

active file   A file currently being used.

active line   In DATA COMMUNICATIONS, a line that is currently available for transmission of data.

active object   In OBJECT-ORIENTED PROGRAMMING, an object that monitors events occurring in an application and takes action autonomously; an object that encompasses its own thread of control.

active page   A page in main storage that can be displayed or modified.

active program   Any program that is loaded into computer memory and ready to be executed.

active record   A record available for processing.

active station   A station that is currently available for accepting messages.

active storage   See INTERNAL STORAGE.

active window   In a window environment, the window in which the user is currently working.

activity   One of the subunits of work that comprise a task.

activity ratio   When a file is processed, the ratio of the number of records in the file that have activity to the total number of records in that file. Sometimes confused with volatility.

actor   In OBJECT-ORIENTED PROGRAMMING, an object that can operate upon, but is never operated upon by, other objects.

ACTOR   An object-oriented programming language with a PASCAL-like syntax.

actual address   Same as ABSOLUTE ADDRESS.

actuator   In a disk drive, the mechanism that moves the read/write head to the desired position over the disk surface.

ACU   See ASSOCIATION OF COMPUTER USERS.

Ada   An extremely powerful high-level structured programming language designed by the United States Department of Defense to ensure transportability of programs. It was derived from the Pascal language but has major semantic and syntactical extensions. Ada was named after the first programmer, Augusta Ada Byron, Countess of Lovelace (1815–1852). It was she who suggested to Charles Babbage (1792–1871), an English mathematician who invented the forerunner of the modern computer, several programming principles that remain valid to this day.

adapter   **(1)** A device that allows compatibility of different types of equipment. **(2)** A device that changes alternating current to direct current.

adapter boards   Printed circuit boards that connect a system board to peripheral I/O devices or add specialized functions to the system.

adaptive sampling   Adjusting the sampling density for a graphics calculation in response to characteristics of the object being rendered.

adaptive system   **(1)** A system demonstrating the ability to learn, change its state, or otherwise react to a stimulus. **(2)** Any system capable of adapting itself to changes in its environment.

addend   In an addition operation, a quantity added to the AUGEND.

adder   A device capable of forming the sum of two or more quantities.

add file   A file to which records are being added.

add-in   A component that can be placed on a printed circuit board already installed in a computer, such as memory chips inserted in empty slots in a microcomputer.

add-in board   A board that may be inserted into a computer's system unit to perform one or more functions.

additive color mixing   In computer graphics, producing colors by mixing colors of light (red, green, and blue) rather than mixing pigments (such as cyan, magenta, yellow, and black used in printing).

additive primary colors   In computer graphics, red, blue, and green colors that produce white when projected onto a single area.

add-on   A component or device added to a computer system to increase its storage capacity, modify its architecture, or upgrade its performance.

add operation   An operation generated by an add instruction.

address   Identification—such as a label, number, or name—that designates a particular location in storage or any other data destination or source.

addressability   The ability to locate an item in online storage.

addressable point   In computer graphics, the smallest coordinate point on a raster display screen that can be addressed; usually refers to a PIXEL.

address bus   A bus that conveys address data from one system component to another.

addressee   The intended recipient of a message.

address field   In DATA COMMUNICATIONS, the part of a packet containing addressing information.

address format   The arrangement of the address parts of an instruction.

addressing   (1) Locating a required piece of data by specific techniques. (2) A data communications control method whereby the host computer specifies the particular terminal for which it has data.

address modification   Any arithmetic, logic, or syntactic operation performed on an address.

address register   A register containing the address of the instruction currently being executed.

address translator   A functional unit that changes virtual addresses to real addresses.

add time   The time required for a computer to perform an addition, exclusive of the time required to obtain the quantities from storage and put the sum back into storage.

adjust   In DESKTOP PUBLISHING, to move text into alignment between the defined left and right margins.

administrative data processing   The field of data processing concerned with the management or direction of an organization.

Adobe Illustrator   See ILLUSTRATOR.

Adobe Photoshop   See PHOTOSHOP.

Adobe Systems, Inc.   Founded in 1982, a company that has introduced several powerful software products, including the PostScript page image description language for text/graphics systems, Adobe Illustrator, and Adobe Photoshop.

Adobe Type Manager™   A font generator and utility for the Apple Macintosh computer from Adobe Systems, Inc.

ADP   Abbreviation for **a**utomatic **d**ata **p**rocessing.

ADP system   Same as COMPUTER SYSTEM.

ADU   Abbreviation for AUTOMATIC DIALING UNIT.

advanced BASIC   A generic term used to describe versions of the BASIC programming language that include features and operators not found in standard BASIC.

advisory system   An EXPERT SYSTEM that gives advice rather than dictating to the user.

AEC   Abbreviation for **a**rchitecture, **e**ngineering, and **c**onstruction, a computer graphics market requiring specialized applications that facilitate efficient planning, design, drafting, and analysis.

aesthetics   A branch of philosophy having to do with the nature of beauty and art and its relation to human experience.

affine map   In computer graphics, any transformation composed only of translations, rotations, scalings, and shears.

AFIPS   Acronym for AMERICAN FEDERATION OF INFORMATION PROCESSING SOCIETIES, the U.S. representative of IFIP from 1961 to 1990. Dissolved in 1990.

aftermarket The market for peripherals and software created by the sale of a large number of a specific brand of computer.

agenda A prioritized list of pending activities.

agent In OBJECT-ORIENTED PROGRAMMING, an object that can both operate upon and be operated upon by other objects. An agent is usually created to do work on behalf of an actor or another agent.

aggregate A structured collection of data objects that forms a data type.

aggregate class In OBJECT-ORIENTED PROGRAMMING, a class that is constructed primarily by inheriting from other classes and rarely adds its own structure and behavior.

AI Abbreviation for ARTIFICIAL INTELLIGENCE, the study of how to make computer systems behave more as if they were bright and helpful humans.

AIA See AUTOMATED IMAGING ASSOCIATION.

aiming symbol A movable screen cursor on a display screen.

AIP Abbreviation for **a**verage **i**nstructions **p**er second.

airbrush A fine paint spray gun. In graphics, a term denoting a soft, diffused treatment of an image. Computer paint systems have various "brush styles" that can pick up color from a palette to apply to the image.

aircraft simulator A computer-controlled device that is used to train pilots. All of the instruments of a modern jet cockpit are there to make the simulation as close to reality as possible. The simulator includes a large screen, like a windshield, on which a mind-boggling array of graphics is generated. These sophisticated simulators are so realistic that the Federal Aviation Administration equates them with flying an actual aircraft.

airline reservation system An application in which a computer system is used to keep track of flight schedules, passenger seat inventories, and other related information required to run an airline.

AIS Abbreviation for **a**ccounting **i**nformation **s**ystem.

Aldus PageMaker   See PAGEMAKER.

alert box   A screen display, usually in a small window, that asks a question or warns the user of impending doom if his or her next move is the wrong move. The user answers by clicking a mouse button on a choice or giving a key command.

alert messages   Messages that inform the user that the operation being performed is improper or impossible.

algebra   A form of mathematics in which letters representing numerical values can be operated upon according to basic rules of arithmetic.

algebraic language   An algorithmic language, such as ALGOL, APL, BASIC, and FORTRAN, many of the statements of which are structured to resemble algebraic expressions.

algebraic manipulation   The processing of mathematical expressions without concern for the numerical values of the symbols used.

algebra of logic   A system of logical relations expressed as algebraic formulas first introduced by George Boole. See BOOLEAN ALGEBRA.

ALGOL   Acronym for **algo**rithmic **l**anguage, an international high-level programming language used to code problem-solving algorithms. ALGOL was the first structured procedural programming language; it was developed from 1957 to 1960 during conferences attended by computer scientists from the United States and several European countries. Although it never gained widespread use commercially, ALGOL had an important influence on three other languages: Pascal, C, and Ada.

algorithm   A prescribed set of well-defined, unambiguous rules or processes for the solution of a problem in a finite number of steps. Commonly used as integral parts of computer programs; thus, the study of computers and that of algorithms are closely related.

algorithmic   Based on algorithms.

algorithmic language   An ARTIFICIAL LANGUAGE for expressing algorithms.

alias   An alternate label or name.

aliasing   Undesirable visual effects in computer-generated images caused by improper sampling techniques. The most common effect is a jagged edge along object boundaries.

alias name   An alternate name.

align   To arrange in line with one or more reference points.

aligning edge   The edge of a form that, in conjunction with the leading edge, serves to correctly position a document to be scanned by an OCR device. Also called reference edge.

alignment   Adjustment of tolerances within the mechanism of a device so that it will operate properly.

allocate   To assign a resource.

allocation   The process of reserving computer storage areas for instructions or data, done by a programmer or automatically by a program.

allowance   The downward adjustment in retail selling price of merchandise because of trade-in, damage, age, or promotion.

all points addressable   A graphics mode in which each pixel on the display screen can be accessed directly by a program.

alphabet   An ordered set of characters or symbols.

alphabetic character   Any one of the letters a through z, or A through Z.

alphabetic string   A string in which the characters are letters or pertain to an agreed alphabet set.

alphameric   Same as ALPHANUMERIC.

alphanumeric   A general term for alphabetic letters A through Z, numerical digits 0 through 9, and special characters—such as –, /, *, $, ( ), #, and +—that are machine processable.

alphanumeric code   A code the application of which results in a code element set with elements formed from an alphanumeric character set.

alphanumeric data Data represented by digits, letters, and special characters.

alphanumeric display A device that only displays letters, numbers, and punctuation symbols.

alphanumeric field A field that can contain any alphabetic, numeric, or special character.

alphanumeric keyboard A keyboard used to enter letters, numbers, and special characters.

alphanumeric sort The process in which a computer system puts a list into alphabetical or numerical order, or both.

alpha test The product test stage during the research and development of a new product in which the first manufactured version of a system is tested with application software. The preliminary testing stage of software development.

Altair 8800 The first microcomputer system to achieve a degree of commercial success.

alternate function key A key that normally produces a character but that performs a special function when another key is held down simultaneously.

alternate name An alternate label.

alternate route A secondary route that is used if normal routing is not possible.

alternate track A space track on a hard disk that is used if a regular track is determined to be damaged or unusable.

alternating current (AC) An electric current that reverses its direction at regularly recurring intervals.

Alto A personal computer, designed by Xerox Corporation in 1973, that pioneered the icon operating system environment and the use of a mouse. The Alto was the progenitor of the Xerox Star and the Apple Macintosh.

ALU   Abbreviation for ARITHMETIC LOGIC UNIT, the portion of the central processing unit where arithmetic and logical operations are performed.

ambient conditions   Environmental conditions that surround a computer system, such as light, temperature, and humidity.

ambient light   Nondirectional illumination or surrounding light.

ambient noise   In acoustics, the noise associated with a particular environment.

ambient temperature   The temperature surrounding a piece of equipment.

Amdahl Corporation   A computer manufacturer founded in 1970 by Gene Amdahl. Its purpose was to build IBM-compatible mainframes with better performance, the first of which was the 470/V6 computer, released in 1975.

American Federation of Information Processing Societies (AFIPS)   An organization representing computer science and data processing organizations. Founded in 1961, its activities include committee work on education, research, government activities, standards and practices, and the history of computing. It was the American representative of IFIP from 1961 to 1990. Dissolved in 1990.

American National Standards Institute (ANSI)   An organization that acts as a national clearinghouse and coordinator for voluntary standards in the United States. It was founded in 1918 and is supported by more than a thousand professional societies, trade organizations, and companies.

American Society for Information Science (ASIS)   A professional organization that provides a forum for librarians, information specialists, and scientists who seek to improve the communication of information. Members are highly educated, involved administrators, managers, coordinators, information technologists, and scientists who work in systems analysis and design; manage information programs and services; search, prepare, and analyze information; market information programs, services, and databases; consult; and program.

American Standard Code for Information Interchange See ASCII.

Amiga™ The brand name for a family of microcomputers manufactured by Commodore Business Machines, Inc. Used extensively in the areas of computer graphics and animation, the Amiga personal computers are based on the Motorola 68000 family of microprocessors.

ampere The base SI unit of electric current. A current of 1 ampere means that 6.25×10^{18} electrons are flowing by a point each second; 1 ampere equals 1 coulomb per second.

amplifier An electronic circuit that increases the voltage, current, or power of an input signal, or that isolates one part of a system from another.

amplitude The height of the carrier wave in analog transmission, which indicates the strength of the signal.

analog Pertaining to data that consist of continuously variable physical quantities. Contrast with DIGITAL.

analog computer A computer that measures continuously changing conditions, such as temperature and pressure, and converts them into quantities.

analog data The physical representation of information such that the representation bears an exact relationship to the original information. Electrical signals on a telephone channel are analog data representations of the original voice data.

analog model A model that relates physical similarity to the actual situation.

analogous colors In COMPUTER GRAPHICS, hues that are close to each other on the color wheel, such as violet-blue, blue, and blue-green.

analog representation A representation that does not have discrete values but is continuously variable.

analog signal A signal that varies continuously in wave form, such as the human voice.

analog sound A sound that must be converted to digital form before it can be processed by a computer.

analog-to-digital converter (A-D converter) A mechanical or electrical device used to convert continuous analog signals to discrete digital numbers.

analog transmission The transmission of data as continuous wave patterns.

analog video Video in which the information that represents images is in a continuous-scale electrical signal for amplitude and time.

analysis **(1)** The investigation of a problem by a consistent, systematic procedure. **(2)** In program and systems development, the process of studying a problem area to determine what should be done.

analysis graphics Types of graphics programs that are designed to allow users to more clearly examine and analyze data, making it easier for them to develop conclusions about what the data itself means. The major component of business graphics, analytical graphics programs consist basically of bar, area, line, and pie charts.

analyst A person skilled in the definition and development of techniques for solving a problem, especially those techniques for solutions on a computer.

analytical engine A device conceived by Charles Babbage in the 1800s to perform computations. This machine is considered the forerunner of today's modern electronic computer.

analytical graphics Traditional line graphs, pie charts, and bar charts used to illustrate and analyze data. A type of presentation graphics built into a spreadsheet, database, or word processing program.

anamorphic A change in size of an object such that it is stretched or compressed more in one dimension than another.

anchor point   In computer graphics, the starting and ending points of a Bezier curve. By moving the anchor points, the position and shape of a Bezier curve can be controlled.

ancillary equipment   Same as auxiliary equipment. Equipment not under direct control of the processing unit.

AND   A logical connector, as in the statement A AND B, which means that the statement is true if, and only if, both A and B are true simultaneously. Also called logical multiply.

AND gate   (**1**) A binary circuit with two or more inputs and a single output, in which the output is logic 1 only when all inputs are logic 1, and the output is logic 0 if any one of the inputs is logic 0. (**2**) In a computer, a gate circuit with more than one input terminal. No output signal will be produced unless a pulse is applied to all inputs simultaneously.

androids   Robots that have built-in microprocessors.

angstrom   A unit of measurement, $\frac{1}{250}$ millionth of an inch (10^{-8} cm). Used to measure the elements in electronic components on a chip. There are 10,000 angstroms in one micron.

animate   To cause to appear lifelike and to have movement, as in animated cartoons. See COMPUTER ANIMATION.

animated graphics   Moving diagrams or cartoons often found in computer-based courseware.

animation   The process of making an object appear to move by rapidly displaying a series of pictures of it, each one in a slightly different position; a technique used for producing computer-generated movies.

animator   (**1**) In animation production, the person who brings the designs and characters to life through animation. (**2**) The operator of a computer animation system.

annotation   The process of inserting text or a special note of identification on a drawing, map, or diagram constructed on a graphics system.

annotation symbol　A symbol used to add messages or notes to a flow-chart, attached to other flowcharting symbols by dashed lines.

ANS-COBOL　A version of COBOL standardized in 1974 by the American National Standards Institute.

ANSI　Acronym for AMERICAN NATIONAL STANDARDS INSTITUTE, the organization that publishes standards for various aspects of the computer industry.

answer　To respond to a call to complete the connection between data stations.

answerback　The response of a terminal to remote control signals.

answering　The process of responding to a calling station to complete the establishment of a connection between data stations.

answer mode　The ability of a modem to accept an incoming call from another modem.

answer/originate　In telecommunications, the alternatives of receiving (answering) or sending (originating) a phone call.

anthropomorphism　A figure of speech used to describe computers, and devices controlled by computers, as though they were persons.

anti-aliasing　The smoothing or removal of "jaggies," diagonal lines in digitized images at low resolutions that appear as stair-steps, to re-create smoother diagonal lines.

antistatic mat　A floor mat placed in front of a device, such as a disk unit, that is sensitive to static, to prevent shocks that could cause loss of data during human handling of the unit.

antivirus program　See VACCINE.

AO　Abbreviation for AUTOMATED OFFICE.

AP　Abbreviation for **a**lternate **p**rinter.

aperture　An opening in a DATA MEDIUM.

aperture card　A card into which microfilm frames may be inserted.

APF   Abbreviation for **a**uthorized **p**rogram **f**acility.

APL   Abbreviation for **A P**rogramming **L**anguage, a mathematically structured programming language. The power of this language is demonstrated by its extended single operators that allow a user to perform directly such calculations as taking the inverse of a matrix or solving a set of linear equations. APL was developed by Kenneth Iverson in the mid-1960s and originally designed for use on IBM mainframes. It is a very compact, hard-to-read, scientific programming language that is used on a wide variety of computers from microcomputers to supercomputers.

Apollo   A manufacturer of high-performance workstations. Apollo was founded in 1980 and pioneered the concept of networked workstations. In 1989, it became a division of the Hewlett-Packard Company.

apothem   A perpendicular line from the center to one side of a regular polygon.

append   To add on, such as to add new records to a database or to add to the end of a character string or list.

Apple Computer, Inc.   One of the first and certainly the most influential of the microcomputer manufacturers. Founded in 1976 by Steven P. Jobs and Stephen G. Wozniak, using the family garage as a base and $100 in capital, Apple made computers that became wildly successful. Because of excellent design principles, the early Apple II™ family of microcomputers is still useful, and later machines, such as the Macintosh™ family of microcomputers, have become extremely popular and have greatly affected the design of other machines and of software. The Macintosh computer, with its innovative software, is in a class by itself. Apple Computer, Inc. is a leader in high-performance personal computing.

Apple key   On keyboards produced by Apple Computer, Inc., a special key identified by the Apple™ logo symbol. The key is used by the operating system and certain applications programs.

Apple Macintosh   See MACINTOSH.

Applesoft BASIC   An extended version of the BASIC programming language used with the Apple II family of computers and capable of processing numbers in floating-point form. An interpreter for creating and executing programs, Applesoft BASIC is built into the computer.

AppleTalk™   A network scheme designed primarily for the Apple Macintosh computer. The system often uses the relatively slow LocalTalk hardware, but has grown in popularity because of its low cost, ease of use and installation, and general reliability. It allows computers to share files and peripherals.

Apple II   A family of personal computers from Apple Computer, Inc. The first Apple II was introduced in 1977. The computer family now includes several models widely used in secondary schools, businesses, and homes. The Apple II computers are based on the MOS Technology 6502 microcomputer.

AppleWorks™   An integrated software package that runs on the Apple II family of microcomputers. The program combines word processing, spreadsheet, and database management, and was introduced in 1983.

application   A task to be performed by a computer program or system. Broad examples of computer applications are engineering design, numerical control, airline seat reservations, business forecasting, and hospital administration. Accounts receivable, mailing list, or electronic spreadsheet programs are examples of applications that run on small business computers.

application developer   The person, business, or organization creating an application for a particular user need.

application generator   A very-high-level language that allows the user to give a detailed explanation of what data are to be processed, rather than how to process the data.

application-oriented language   A problem-oriented programming language whose statements contain or resemble the terminology of the computer user.

application package   A product that, when the user sets a few parameters, becomes a finished applications program ready to meet specific end-user needs.

application problem   A problem submitted by an end user and requiring information processing for its solution.

applications programmer   A computer programmer who develops applications programs.

application programmer's interface (API)   The interface to a library of language-specific subroutines (graphics library) that implement higher-level graphics functions.

applications programming   The preparation of programs for application to specific problems to find solutions.

applications programs   Programs normally written by programmers within an organization that enable the computer to produce useful work such as specific inventory control, attendance accounting, linear programming, or medical accounting tasks.

applications software   Software that is specific to the solution of an applications problem. Some examples are word processing programs, electronic spreadsheets, games, educational programs, drawing programs, etc.

application-specific integrated circuit   An integrated circuit designed to fill the specific requirement of an application.

applied mathematics   Mathematics put to practical use as in mechanics, physics, or computer science.

approximation   A number that is not exact, but has been rounded off to a prescribed decimal place; for example, 3.14 and 3.14159 are both approximations of *pi*.

APT   Acronym for **a**utomatic **p**rogrammed **t**ool, a programming system used in numerical control applications for the programmed control of machine functions. APT allows a user to define points, lines, circles, planes, and conical and geometric surfaces.

Arabic numbers   The numerals used for depicting decimal numbers: 0, 1, 2, 3, 4, 5, 6, 7, 8, and 9.

arc   A portion or section of a circle or curved line.

arcade game   A computer video game popularized by coin-operated machines, characterized by high-resolution color graphics, high-speed animation, and sound. Players often use joysticks to control a screen object, and the computer scores points based on the game's rules.

architecture   **(1)** The physical structure of a computer's internal operations, including its registers, memory, instruction set, and input/output structure. **(2)** The special selection, design, and inter-connection of the principal components of a system.

archival   Pertaining to long-term storage of data.

archival database   A historical copy of a DATABASE.

archival storage   **(1)** Refers to memory (on magnetic disks, optical discs, or magnetic tape) used to store data outside of the main memory. **(2)** Saving digital data for future reference.

archive   **(1)** To copy programs and data onto an auxiliary storage medium, such as a disk or tape, for long-term retention. **(2)** To store data for anticipated normal long-term use. **(3)** A procedure for transferring image information from an online optical storage medium to an offline medium.

Arcnet   A computer networking scheme.

area chart   Usually, a combination of two line charts with the differences between them highlighted for emphasis.

area fill   In a painting system, the process of flooding a defined area of the display screen with a specific color or pattern.

area sampling   The determination of a pixel's color and intensity based upon the color and intensity of the pixels surrounding it.

area search   Examination of a large group of documents to select those that pertain to one group, such as a specific category or class.

argument   A variable to which either a logical or a numerical value may be assigned.

argument list   A string of arguments.

arithmetic   **(1)** The branch of mathematics concerned with the study of the positive real numbers and zero. **(2)** Pertaining to such operations as addition, subtraction, multiplication, and division, or to the section of the computer hardware that performs these operations.

arithmetic expression   One or more numbers, variables, functions, symbols, or any combination of these that represents a single value in an arithmetic operation or function. $(3 + 48)/17$, $A + 10$, $X * Y - 82$, and 6 are all arithmetic expressions.

arithmetic function   A function that represents one of the basic arithmetic operations: addition, division, multiplication, and subtraction.

arithmetic-logic unit   The basic element of the central processing unit where arithmetic and logical operations are performed.

arithmetic operations   Various manipulations of numerical quantities, including the fundamental operations of addition, subtraction, multiplication, and division, as well as aggregation, exponentiation, and extraction of roots.

arithmetic operator   A symbol that tells a computer to perform addition, subtraction, multiplication, division, aggregation, or raising to a power—which, with negative powers, is tantamount to extracting roots.

arithmetic overflow   In an ARITHMETIC OPERATION, the generation of a quantity beyond the capacity of the register or storage location that is to receive the result.

arithmetic register   A REGISTER that holds operands, or the results of arithmetic or logic operations.

arithmetic relation   Two arithmetic expressions separated by a RELATIONAL OPERATOR.

arithmetic shift   To multiply or divide a quantity by a power of the number base. For example, if binary 1101, representing decimal 13, is arithmetically shifted twice to the left, the result is 110100, representing 52, which is also obtained by multiplying 12 by 2 twice; however, if decimal 13 is shifted to the left twice, the result will be the same as multiplying by 10 twice, or 1,300.

arithmetic statement   In a PROGRAMMING LANGUAGE, a statement that causes an arithmetic operation to be executed.

arithmetic underflow   In an ARITHMETIC OPERATION, a result smaller than the smallest possible quantity the computer is capable of storing.

arithmetic unit   Same as ARITHMETIC-LOGIC UNIT.

arrangement   The order of index terms or items of data in a system.

array   (1) A series of related items. (2) An ordered arrangement or pattern of items or numbers, such as a determinant, matrix, vector, or table of numbers.

array element   A data item in an ARRAY.

array expression   An expression that represents an array of values.

array name   The name, or identification label, of an ordered set of data items.

array processing   A type of PARALLEL PROCESSING that allows supercomputers to perform the same operation on a list of values simultaneously.

array processor   A processor that performs matrix arithmetic much faster than standard computers. Capable of performing operations on all the elements in large matrices at one time. Also called a vector processor.

arrival rate   The number of characters or messages arriving over a data communications medium per unit of time.

ART   A PFS First Publisher graphics format used for clip art.

artifact   A visible error or oddity in a displayed image. Aliasing, for instance, is an artifact resulting from producing graphics images on a raster grid.

artificial intelligence (AI) A group of technologies that attempt to emulate certain aspects of human behavior, such as reasoning and communicating, as well as to mimic biological senses, including seeing and hearing. Specific technologies include expert systems (also called knowledge-based systems), natural language, neural networks, machine translation, and speech recognition. AI is the branch of computer science that is concerned with developing computer systems capable of simulating human reasoning and sensation. It involves using computers and software that, like the human mind, use stored knowledge to make decisions involving judgment or ambiguity. See ROBOTICS.

artificial language A language based on a set of prescribed rules that are established prior to its usage.

artificial reality A computer-generated simulation of reality with which users can interact using specialized peripherals such as data gloves and head-mounted computer graphics displays.

Artline An illustrative graphics program for use with IBM-compatible microcomputers. Features include multilayer editing, an autotrace facility, scalable fonts, 3-D shading effects, a blending function to change one image into another, and access to a large supply of clip art images.

art nouveau In computer graphics, a decorative design style of the 1890s, based primarily on flowing, curvilinear plant and animal forms.

Arts & Letters™ Graphics Editor An illustrative graphics program that runs on Windows and OS/2. A special effect function allows text, clip art, and freeform graphics to be warped, bent, stretched, and twisted by specifying the shape into which the object is to fit. A Graduated Fill function allows colorful blends and the 3-D illusion of depth by a variety of linear and radial fill for text and graphic artwork. The program has several thousand files of clip art and an autotrace feature.

artwork Visual and graphic elements on a page, such as line drawings, halftones, or solids.

ARU Acronym for **a**udio **r**esponse **u**nit, an output unit that provides a spoken response to digital inquiries from a device.

AS/400 IBM Application System/400 computer system.

ascender The portion of a lowercase letter that extends above the main portion of the letter, such as the top of b, d, or h.

ascending order An order that ranges from smallest to largest or first to last. Alphabets and counting numbers are in naturally ascending order. Contrast with DESCENDING ORDER.

ASCII Acronym for American Standard Code for Information Interchange, pronounced "ass-key." A seven-bit standard code adopted to facilitate interchange of data among various types of data processing and data communications equipment. Compare EBCDIC.

ASIS See AMERICAN SOCIETY FOR INFORMATION SCIENCE.

ASM See ASSOCIATION FOR SYSTEMS MANAGEMENT.

aspect A nongeometric property of a graphics primitive, such as its color.

aspect ratio In computer graphics, the relationship of the height and width of the video display screen frame or image area.

ASR Acronym for automatic send/receive.

assemble To load a symbolic program into a computer together with an assembler. The assembler translates the symbolic program into a machine language program that can then be executed on the computer.

assembler A computer program that takes nonmachine-language instructions prepared by a computer user and converts them into a form that may be used by the computer; a computer program that assembles.

assembler language Same as ASSEMBLY LANGUAGE.

assembling The automatic process by which a computer converts a symbolic source-language program into a machine language, usually on an instruction-by-instruction basis.

assembly language A low-level programming language that allows a computer user to write a program using mnemonics instead of numeric instructions. Closely resembles machine-code language.

assembly listing   Printed output produced by an assembler. Lists the original assembly-language program, the machine-language version of the program, storage assignments, error messages, and other information useful to the programmer.

assembly program   Same as ASSEMBLER.

assembly time   The time at which an assembler translates symbolic machine-language statements into their object code form (machine language).

assertions   A concept referring to the storage of procedures as a part of an object-oriented database. An assertion is a property of the object with which it is associated, typically some condition that the object must satisfy. Assertions are like methods, but are not encapsulated along with the local data on which they operate.

assign   To redirect a local device name to a shared resource on a network.

assignment   The process of giving values to variables.

assignment statement   A source language statement that makes an assignment.

Association for Computing Machinery (ACM)   The world's largest educational and scientific society committed to the development of technical skills and professional competence of computer specialists. Founded in 1947, ACM has earned a reputation for technical excellence by publishing prestigious journals and sponsoring numerous conferences that promote an ongoing dialogue among students, educators, and practitioners. The association is dedicated to the development of information processing as a discipline and to the responsible use of computers in an increasing diversity of applications.

Association for Systems Management (ASM)   An international organization engaged in keeping its members abreast of the rapid growth and change occurring in the field of systems management and information processing. Founded in 1947, it has five technical departments: Data Communications, Data Processing, Management Information Systems,

Organization Planning, and Written Communications. Members can belong to one or more of these departments.

Association for Women in Computing (AWC)   A nonprofit professional organization comprising people who have an interest in the field of computer data processing. Its main goals are to promote communication among, further the professional development and advancement of, and promote the education of women in computing.

Association of Computer Users (ACU)   An organization founded in 1979 whose members are interested in the use of small computers for business purposes.

Association of Data Processing Service Organizations (ADAPSO) An association of commercial institutions that offers data processing services through systems that its members operate on their own premises. Founded in 1960, ADAPSO is oriented toward improving management techniques and defining performance standards for computer services.

Association of Information Systems Professionals (AISP)   An organization of professionals involved in all aspects of information systems. Founded in 1972 as the International Word Processing Association, AISP now has members worldwide with organized chapters in more than 100 metropolitan areas of the United States and Canada.

associative dimensioning   A CAD capability that links dimension entities to geometric entities being dimensioned, allowing the value of a dimension to be automatically updated as the geometry changes.

associative storage   A storage device whose storage locations are identified by their contents (rather than by names or positions, as in most computer storage devices).

associativity   Any logical linking of geometric entities in a CAD/CAM database with their nongraphic attributes or with other geometric entities.

assumed value   Same as DEFAULT VALUE.

asterisk A symbol (*) used in many programming languages to represent a multiplication operator.

asterisk fill Numeric editing that places asterisks to the left of a number to fill unused positions; for example, "****28.14."

asynchronous Pertaining to a mode of data communications that provides a variable time interval between characters during transmission.

asynchronous computer A computer in which each operation starts as a result of a signal generated by the completion of the previous operation or by the availability of the equipment required for the next operation.

asynchronous input Input data having no time-dependable pattern or cycle when related to the computer system.

asynchronous transmission A method in which data characters are sent at random time intervals. Limits phone-line transmission to about 2,400 bps.

AT The first 80286-based personal computer, introduced by IBM Corporation in 1984. AT stands for **A**dvanced **T**echnology.

Atanasoff-Berry Computer (ABC) The world's first electronic digital computer, built in the early 1940s by John V. Atanasoff and his assistant, Clifford Berry.

Atari Corporation The manufacturer of a popular line of personal computer systems. Atari produced several older home computers and in 1985 introduced the Atari ST family of microcomputers, high-performance personal computers with capabilities for computer graphics in color.

Atari ST A personal computer series from Atari Corporation.

ATM Abbreviation for AUTOMATIC TELLER MACHINE.

atom (1) The elementary building block of data structures. Corresponds to a record in a file and may contain one or more fields of data. (2) In list processing programming languages, a basic element in a list. For example, in the list, "This is a list," each word is an atom.

atomic operation An operation that cannot be divided into smaller operations.

attach To connect a peripheral to a computer to increase its capacity.

attachment A device or feature attached to a processing unit.

attack In COMPUTER SECURITY, an attempt to violate data security.

attention key A terminal function key that, when pressed, causes an input-output interruption in the processing unit.

attenuation A decrease in the strength of a signal as it passes through a control system.

atto A prefix meaning one quintillionth, or a billionth of a billionth, as in 10^{-18}. Abbreviated as a.

attribute (1) The manner in which a variable is handled by the computer. (2) A characteristic quality of a data type, data structure, element of a data model, or system. (3) A feature of a device. (4) A column of a relation in a relational database.

audio Sound that can be heard by a human (15 to 20,000 Hz).

audio device Any computer device that accepts and/or produces sound.

audio output Computer output generated through voice synthesizers that create audible signals resembling a human voice.

audio-response device A device that converts data in internal storage to vocalized sounds understandable to humans. Also called a voice output unit or voice synthesizer.

audiovisual Pertaining to nonprint materials—such as films, tapes, and cassettes—that record information by sound and/or sight.

audiovisual program A COMPUTER PROGRAM that makes use of both images and sound.

audit (1) An inspection used to determine whether a system or procedure is working as it should or if a claimed amount is correct. (2) To review the activities of a DATA PROCESSING SYSTEM.

audit trail A means for identifying the actions taken in processing input data or in preparing output. By use of the audit trail, data on a source document can be traced to a specific output, and an output can be traced to the source items from which it was derived. For example, it could reveal that Nancy Wilson changed the inventory figures in the Auto Supply account at 2:32 p.m. on October 8.

augend In an addition operation, a quantity to which quantities are added.

authentication A process for verifying the correctness of a piece of data.

authenticity The integrity of a message.

author (1) A person who designs instruction material for computer-assisted instruction systems. (2) A person who creates a HYPERTEXT document.

authoring language A PROGRAMMING LANGUAGE that enables a nonprogrammer to create courseware.

authoring system standard A computer system capable of executing an author language.

authority The right to access functions, objects, or resources.

authorization A system control feature that requires specific approval before processing can take place.

authorize To permit a user to communicate with or make use of a function, object, or resource.

authorized library A library that may contain authorized computer programs.

authorized program A computer program capable of altering the fundamental operation or status of a computer system.

author language A PROGRAMMING LANGUAGE used for designing instructional programs for computer-assisted instruction systems.

auto-answer   A modem that can automatically answer incoming telephone calls from computers and pipe the data into another computer.

autochart   A type of documentor used for the automatic production and maintenance of charts, principally flowcharts.

auto-dial   A modem capable of connecting to the telephone system and dialing a number. The modem and communications software perform the proper communications procedures so that computers can exchange data.

autodimensioning   In a drafting program, a feature that computes and annotates the size of drawn elements.

AUTODIN   Acronym for **Auto**matic **Di**gital **N**etwork, the data-handling portion of the military communications system.

auto-disconnect   Automatic disconnecting by one modem when it receives a disconnect message or when the other party hangs up.

autoflow   A setting found in many page layout programs that allows for continuous placement of blocked text from page to page without operator intervention.

autofont   A self-training OCR system that automatically adjusts to the type designs of different typefaces in order to read a wide range of documents quickly and accurately.

autoindex   To prepare an index by a machine method.

auto indexing   A system of indexing that superimposes additional information at any of several given addresses.

autointeractive design (AID)   A combination of DESIGN AUTOMATION, where the computer executes programs or routines with no operator intervention, and computer-aided design, where the operator interacts with the computer in the design process.

auto key   In WORD PROCESSING, a control that starts the continuous printing or scanning of selected recorded text.

autoleading   Automatically increasing or decreasing the space between lines of text to allow for the appropriate leading for the largest font on the lines. The space added is about 20 percent of the type size under each line of text.

auto-load   A key on some computer keyboards that activates the computer, essentially booting the operating system into internal storage and starting execution of the system.

autologon   Same as automatic logon.

automata   A theory related to the study of the principles of operation, behavioral characteristics, and application of automatic devices.

automate   To convert a process or piece of equipment to automatic operation.

automated data processing   Largely self-regulating process in which information is handled with a minimum of human effort and intervention.

automated design system (ADS)   Another term for a computer-aided design system.

automated drafting system   A computer-based system designed primarily to automate the process of drafting.

automated flowchart   A flowchart drawn by a computer-controlled printer or plotter.

automated graphics   The method of drawing geometric figures using computers.

Automated Imaging Association (AIA)   A trade group dedicated to promoting the acceptance and productive use of image processing, image analysis, and machine vision technologies. The use of these technologies will include both scientific and industrial applications from all areas of product manufacturing, physical science, and governmental and research communities. The association's membership includes manufacturers of both related and peripheral products, integrators, end-users, consultants, and research groups directly involved with these technologies. Key AIA activities include an annual financial forum, standards development, user-supplier meetings, market studies, and trade shows and conferences. AIA was founded in 1984.

automated office   The result of the merger of computers, office electronic devices, and telecommunications technology in an office environment.

automated teller machine (ATM)   A banking terminal that provides customers with 24-hour deposit-and-withdrawal service; a special-purpose device connected to the bank's computer system. To use the automatic teller, the customer inserts a plastic identification card, enters a special password code, and communicates with the system by using a numeric keypad and visual display.

automatic   Pertaining to a process or device that, under specified conditions, functions without intervention by a human operator.

automatic calling unit (ACU)   A dialing device that permits a computer to automatically dial calls over a computer network.

automatic carriage   A printer mechanism that can automatically control the feeding, spacing, skipping, and ejecting of paper or preprinted forms.

automatic check   An equipment check built in specifically for checking purposes.

automatic coding   Machine-assisted preparation of machine-language routines.

automatic controller   A device or instrument capable of measuring and regulating by receiving a signal from a sensing device, comparing this data with a desired value, and issuing signals for corrective action.

automatic data processing (ADP)   Same as DATA PROCESSING.

automatic decimal alignment   In WORD PROCESSING, a feature that automatically aligns columns of numbers on either side of a decimal marker.

automatic dialing unit (ADU)   A device capable of automatically generating dialing digits.

automatic digitizing   The automatic scanning and encoding of graphic elements contained in engineering drawings, entering their coordinate positions into computer memory.

automatic dimensioning   A CAD capability that computes the dimensions in a displayed design, or in a designated section, and automatically places dimensions, dimensional lines, and arrowheads where required.

automatic error correction   A technique for detecting and correcting errors that occur in data transmission or within the system itself.

automatic function   Work done by a computer that a user does not have to request explicitly.

automatic hyphenation   A feature that hyphenates words automatically; often found in word processor and page layout programs.

automatic loader   A hardware loader program, usually implemented in a special ROM, that allows loading of an auxiliary storage unit (a hard disk or floppy disk).

automatic page numbering   In WORD PROCESSING, the ability to automatically generate page numbers to the successive pages of a document.

automatic pagination   A feature that automatically breaks text into pages; often found in word processing and page layout programs.

automatic programmed tool (APT)   A PROGRAMMING LANGUAGE used in COMPUTER-AIDED MANUFACTURING to program numerically controlled machine tools.

automatic programming   (1) The process of using a computer to perform some stages of the work involved in preparing a program. (2) The production of a machine-language computer program under the guidance of a symbolic representation of the program.

automatic reformatting   In word processing, automatic adjustment of text to accommodate changes.

automatic shutdown   The ability of some systems software to stop a network or a computer system as a whole in an orderly fashion.

automatic teller machine   See AUTOMATED TELLER MACHINE.

automation   **(1)** The implementation of processes by automatic means. **(2)** The automatically controlled operation of an apparatus, process, or system by mechanical or electronic devices that take the place of human observation, effort, and decision.

automaton   A machine designed to simulate the operations of living things.

automonitor   **(1)** A computer's record of its functions. **(2)** A computer program that records the operating functions of a computer.

autopolling   Contraction of automatic polling, a process whereby terminals in a computer network are scanned periodically to determine whether they are ready to send information; a combination of hardware and software that polls the terminals in a computer network.

auto-redial   A modem feature for redialing a number until contact is established.

auto-repeat   A feature of some keyboards that allows a key to repeat automatically when held down.

auto-restart   The capability of a computer to perform automatically the initialization functions necessary to resume operation following an equipment or power failure.

autoscore   In word processing, an instruction that causes text to be underlined.

auto scroll   On some drawing and graphics programs, a feature that appears to move a large document to make more of it visible on the screen when the mouse pointer or a tool reaches the edge of the visible region.

autotrace   A feature of many drawing programs that draws lines along the edges of a bit-mapped image in order to convert the image into an object-oriented one. Using the autotrace tool users can transform low-resolution graphics (72 dots per inch of bit-mapped image) into art that can print at substantially higher resolution (OBJECT-ORIENTED GRAPHICS can print at the printer's maximum resolution).

auxiliary equipment   Equipment not under direct control of the central processing unit.

auxiliary operation   An operation performed by equipment not under control of the central processing unit.

auxiliary storage   Storage that supplements the main storage of a computer, such as hard disks, floppy disks, magnetic tapes, and optical discs.

availability   The ratio of the time that a hardware device is known or believed to be operating correctly to the total hours of scheduled operation.

available memory   In a COMPUTER SYSTEM, the number of bytes of memory that can be used for application programs.

available time   The time that a computer is available for use but is not being used.

Avant Garde   A modern sans serif typeface design owned by the International Typeface Corporation (ITC) and included as a built-in font with many POSTSCRIPT LASER PRINTERS.

average access time   The average time between the instant of request and the delivery from a storage device.

axes   In a two-dimensional coordinate system, lines used as references for vertical (Y) and horizontal (X) measurement. See CARTESIAN COORDINATE SYSTEM.

axonometric view   In computer graphics, a view that shows three sides of an object to provide a 3-D view. Horizontal and vertical distances are drawn to scale, but diagonal lines are distorted.

AZERTY   The key layout of keyboards used in some European typing machines.

b Abbreviation for BIT or BINARY; for example, bps for bits per second and 1101b for the binary number 1101.

B Abbreviation for BYTE or BAUD. Used for bytes when referring to storage, or BAUD RATE when referring to communications; for example, KB means 1 kilobyte (1,024 bytes).

babble The cross-talk from a large number of channels in a system.

backbone A wire that connects nodes.

back clipping plane **(1)** In COMPUTER GRAPHICS, a specified plane that cuts across the view volume, making it finite. Graphic entities straddling this boundary are clipped in the Z-axis. A plane perpendicular to the line of sight for clipping out distant objects. **(2)** The YON PLANE.

back-face culling In COMPUTER GRAPHICS, omitting the drawing of one or more back-facing polygons, thus increasing drawing speed.

background **(1)** In multiprogramming, the environment in which low-priority programs are executed. **(2)** That part of a display screen not occupied with displayed characters or graphics (foreground). **(3)** In large computers, the memory area for programs with low priorities.

background activity A process that does not require operator intervention but can be run by the computer while the system is used to do other work.

background color In computer graphics, a default color to which every pixel on the display is to be initialized.

background noise In optical scanning, electrical interference caused by such things as ink tracking or carbon offsetting.

background processing Execution of lower-priority computer programs during periods when system resources are not required to process high-priority programs.

background program A program that can be executed whenever the facilities of a multiprogramming computer system are not required by other programs of higher priority. Contrast with FOREGROUND PROGRAM.

backing store The backup memory to the computer's main memory; more commonly called auxiliary storage.

backing up Making backup copies of files to prevent loss of their contents in the event the originals are damaged or lost.

backlash In a mechanical operation, the "play" between interacting parts, such as two gears, as a result of tolerance.

backlight Light coming from behind a subject.

backlog In an MIS department, jobs that have been submitted for systems analysis and design but have not been completed.

back margin The margin of a page that is closest to the binding edge.

back matter The parts of a book that are located after the main chapters or sections, such as the appendix, glossary, or index.

back panel The back of a computer case, with a number of sockets for connecting peripheral devices to the computer.

backplane (1) The circuitry and mechanical elements used to connect the boards of a system. (2) The main circuit board of a computer into which other circuit boards are plugged.

backslash Used to separate directory names and filenames in a DOS system.

backspace The keyboard operation that moves the cursor one place to the left. It allows for modification of what has already been typed before it is entered into the computer.

backspace key A control for effecting the backspace function.

backspace tape The process of returning a magnetic tape to the beginning of the preceding record.

backtracking The operation of scanning a list in reverse.

backup **(1)** A term pertaining to procedures or standby equipment available for use in the event of failure or overloading of the normally used procedures or equipment. **(2)** To make a copy of a program or data in case the original is lost, damaged, or otherwise inaccessible.

backup copy A copy of a file or data set kept for reference in case the original file or data set is destroyed.

backup disk A duplicate copy of a floppy disk that preserves files in case of a disaster.

backup file A copy of a FILE made for possible later reconstruction of the file.

backup hierarchy A policy of backing up information on diskettes that rotates three or four diskettes to generate the most recent backup copy.

backup plan See CONTINGENCY PLAN.

backup programmer A programmer who is an assistant to the chief programmer.

backup storage An AUXILIARY STORAGE DEVICE that retains information copied from a recording medium; for example, a high-capacity diskette or a magnetic tape. Same as backing store.

Backus Normal Form (BNF) The notation for describing the syntax of programming languages. The first metalanguage to define programming language, it was developed by John Backus and Peter Naur in 1959. Also called Backus-Naur Form.

backward chaining A goal-driven method of reasoning that proceeds from the desired goal to the facts already known. Contrast with FORWARD CHAINING.

backward compatible Compatible with earlier versions of a product.

backward read A feature available on some magnetic tape systems whereby magnetic tape units can transfer data to computer storage while moving in reverse.

backward search   Searching from the cursor's current position to the beginning of a document.

backwards ray tracing   In computer graphics, ray tracing in which the computations are performed as if the rays traveled from the viewpoint to the light sources.

badge reader   A terminal equipped to read credit cards or specially coded badges.

bad sectors   Unusable sectors "flagged" as bad during formatting of disks and not used by the operating system. The remaining areas can still be used. Bad sectors are sometimes used by viruses to store the code outside the reach of the users and the operating system.

BAL   Abbreviation for **b**ranch **a**nd **l**ink.

balance   In COMPUTER GRAPHICS, the visual arrangement of colors, shapes, or masses to create a sense of equilibrium.

balloon   (1) A box containing descriptive data (usually text) connected to a reference location in a drawing; commonly used in cartoons. (2) A descriptive message box in some graphic user interfaces.

ball printer   A printer that has the printing elements on the face of a ball-like replacement element. Type fonts can easily be changed by changing the typeball.

band   A group of tracks on a recording medium, all of which are read or written in parallel.

band printer   An impact printing device that uses a steel band or polyurethane belt to carry the character set. It can produce multiple carbon copies at speeds ranging from 300 to 2,000 lines per minute.

bandwidth   In data communications, the difference between the highest and lowest frequencies of a band. Used as a measure of the capacity of a communication channel, bandwidth is expressed in bits per second, or bauds.

bank   (1) In communications, a range of frequencies, as between two specified limits. **(2)** The range, or scope, of operation. **(3)** A group of circular recording tracks on a storage device such as a disk.

bar chart   A widely used chart in business graphics.

bar code   A code made up of a series of variable-width vertical lines that can be read by an optical bar reader. Bar codes are used to identify retail sales items, including books.

bar code reader   A photoelectric scanner that reads bar codes by means of reflected light.

bare board   A printed circuit board with no electronic components on it.

bar graph   A graph made up of filled-in columns or rows that represent the change of data over time.

bar printer   An impact printing device that uses several type bars positioned side by side across the line.

barrel distortion   Image distortion in an optical or video system, characterized by its bending of the edges of a displayed grid into a barrel shape with convex sides and compressed corners. This can be corrected by image processing techniques.

base   **(1)** The radix of a number system. **(2)** The region between the emitter and collector of a junction transistor that receives minority carriers ejected from the emitter. **(3)** On a PRINTED CIRCUIT BOARD, the portion that supports the printed pattern.

base address   A specified address that is combined with a relative address to form the absolute address of a particular storage location.

baseband transmission   A method of using low-frequency transmission of signals across coaxial cables for short-distance, LOCAL AREA NETWORK transmission.

base class   In OBJECT-ORIENTED PROGRAMMING, the most generalized class in a class structure. Most applications have many such base classes. Some languages define a primitive base class, which serves as the ultimate superclass of all classes.

base 8   See OCTAL.

baseline   An imaginary horizontal line with which the base of each character, excluding descenders, is aligned.

baseline document   The reference document for changes to a data processing system.

base shape   The shape that identifies a character but not its presentation shape.

base 16   See HEXADECIMAL.

base 10   See DECIMAL.

base 2   See BINARY.

BASIC   Acronym for **B**eginner's **A**ll-purpose **S**ymbolic **I**nstruction **C**ode, an easy-to-learn, easy-to-use algebraic programming language with a small repertory of commands and simple statement formats. Developed at Dartmouth College by John Kemeny and Thomas Kurtz, BASIC is widely used in programming instruction, in personal computing, and in business and industry. The language has changed over the years: early versions are unstructured and interpreted; later versions are structured and often compiled. Implementations of BASIC include APPLESOFT BASIC, BASICA, CBASIC, GW-BASIC, MICROSOFT BASIC, TURBO BASIC, and QUICKBASIC.

BASICA   A version of the BASIC programming language developed by Microsoft Corporation for the IBM PC family of computers.

basic format   Same as DEFAULT FORMAT.

basic input-output system (BIOS)   A set of programs encoded in read-only memory (ROM) in IBM-compatible microcomputers. These programs facilitate the transfer of data and control instructions between the computer and peripherals.

basic linkage   The linkage used repeatedly in one routine, program, or system that follows the same set of rules each time.

batch   (**1**) The group of records or programs considered as a single unit for processing on a computer. (**2**) To use BATCH PROCESSING.

batch compilation   A method of compiling programs without the continual attention of an operator.

batched communication   The sending of a group of data from one network station to another without intervening responses from the receiving unit.

batched execution   The execution of programs and data that have been accumulated as batched input.

batched job   A job that is grouped with other jobs as input to a computing system.

batch file   A FILE that contains a series of commands to be processed sequentially.

batch job   A job submitted as a predefined series of actions to be performed with little or no interaction between the user and the system.

batch mode   A job entry mode in which the entire job is entered at one time from a disk drive, tape drive, or card reader.

batch package   A SOFTWARE PACKAGE that has all data submitted at one time in a batch.

batch printing   Queuing one or more documents to print in a separate job as a background process.

batch processing   **(1)** The technique by which programs to be executed are coded and collected for processing in groups or batches. The user gives the job to a computer center, where it is put into a batch of programs, processed, and then returned. The user has no direct access to the machine. See REMOTE BATCH PROCESSING. **(2)** The processing as a group of data that has been accumulated over a period of time or must be done periodically, as in payroll and billing applications.

batch session   A session established to transmit batches of messages or records.

batch total   The sum of a set of items in a batch of records; used to check the accuracy of operations involving the batch.

BAT file   Short for BATCH FILE.

battery   A source of DIRECT CURRENT.

battery backup   Auxiliary power provided to a computer so that volatile information is not lost during a power failure.

Baudot code   A code for the transmission of data in which five bits represent one character. The term is usually applied to the code used in many teleprinter systems and is also called International Telegraph Code Number 1. By 1950, this code had become one of the standards for international telegraph communications.

baud rate   The speed at which telecommunicated data is transmitted, measured in bits per second. Common baud rates are 300, 1,200, and 2,400.

bay   The cabinet or rack in which electronic equipment is installed; also called equipment bay.

BBS   Abbreviation for **b**ulletin **b**oard **s**ervice, which enables users to log into another computer system from remote terminals. Many of these BBSs can be used free of charge and can be reached by modem.

BCD   Abbreviation for **B**INARY **C**ODED **D**ECIMAL.

beacon   In a network, a special message sent by a node indicating a serious network problem.

beam penetration CRT   A vector display system that produces color by varying the strength of an electron beam directed at a screen coated with (typically) both red and green phosphor layers.

beam tracing   In computer graphics, a variation of ray tracing using a polygonal cone for the intersection computations rather than a single line (ray).

bebugging   The intentional seeding of a program with known mistakes to measure the rates of debugging by student programmers.

beep   An audible sound produced by a computer's speaker. Also a command in some programming languages that causes the computer's speaker to emit a sound.

beginning-of-file label   Same as HEADER LABEL.

beginning-of-tape marker   A marker on a magnetic tape used to indicate the beginning of the recordable area. Contrast with END-OF-TAPE MARKER.

behavior   In OBJECT-ORIENTED PROGRAMMING, how an object acts and reacts in terms of its state changes and message passing.

BEL   An abbreviation for BELL character, a control character that is used to activate an alarm device.

Bell Laboratories   The research and development center of AT&T Company and one of the most renowned scientific laboratories in the world. Many computer hardware developments, software concepts, and programs were generated at Bell Laboratories.

bell 103   The standard for 300-baud modems.

bells and whistles   An informal description of the special or extra features of a computer system, including graphics, color displays, sound, and many peripherals.

bell 212A   The standard for 1,200-baud modems.

belt-bed plotter   A pen plotter that uses a wide continuous belt for holding the paper.

belt printer   An impact printer in which the character set available for printing is carried on a belt.

benchmark   A point of reference from which measurements can be made, such as use of a program to evaluate the performance of a computer; any standard against which products can be compared.

benchmark problem   A problem designed to evaluate and compare the performance of digital computers.

benchmark tests   Tests used in the measurement of computer equipment performance under typical conditions of use, such as a computer program run on several different computers for the purpose of comparing execution speed, throughput, and so forth.

benday   A process using screens of different dot patterns to mechanically produce shading effects; named for its inventor, Benjamin Day (1838–1916). Benday screen patterns are available in almost all paint programs.

Benson, Inc.   A major manufacturer of hard-copy technology, especially in electrostatic printers. Benson introduced the first electrostatic plotter in 1967.

Bernoulli™ box   A removable hard disk system for microcomputers, manufactured by Iomega Corporation. The main advantage of this cartridge system is that one hard disk system can be used for multiple libraries of hard disk data.

beta site   Where a COMPUTER PROGRAM is tested.

beta test   **(1)** The product test stage following alpha test during which a new product is tested under actual usage conditions in a customer environment. **(2)** Software testing by first-time users.

between failures   See MEAN TIME BETWEEN FAILURES.

Bezier curve   A type of curve generated by an algorithm. Named after French mathematician Pierre Bezier, it is used to display nonuniform curves based upon a fitting algorithm. Bezier curves need only a few points to define a large number of shapes, hence their usefulness over other mathematical methods for approximating a given shape. Within drawing programs, they are typically reshaped by moving the handles that appear off the curve.

Bezier patch   A portion of a three-dimensional surface generated using the Bezier curve algorithm. Two-dimensional Bezier curves are drawn through selected control points, and the three-dimensional curve is interpolated between them.

BG   Abbreviation for BACKGROUND.

bias The amount by which the average of a set of values departs from a reference value.

bias error An error that is due to bias.

bibliography (1) An annotated catalog of documents. (2) An enumerative list of books. (3) A list of documents pertaining to a given subject or author. (4) The process of compiling catalogs or lists.

bidirectional A term describing data flow that may go in either direction on a wire. Transceivers at each end both receive and transmit. Common bidirectional buses are tristate or open collector transistor–transistor logic.

bidirectional printer A printer that prints from left to right, as well as from right to left, avoiding carriage-return delay.

bidirectional transmission DATA TRANSMISSION that may occur in either direction along a transmission medium.

biform In typography, a typeface that combines lowercase and small capital characters to form the lowercase alphabet.

bifurcation A condition whereby two, and only two, outcomes can occur, such as on or off, 1 or 0, and true or false.

Big Blue Nickname for International Business Machines Corporation (IBM), derived from the company's use of a distinctive blue paint on its mainframes and other equipment.

bilinear patch A two-dimensional surface patch that can be warped into a three-dimensional surface.

bill of materials A listing of all the subassemblies, parts, materials, and quantities required to manufacture one assembled product or part, or to build a plant. A bill of materials can be generated automatically on a CAD/CAM system.

binary The mathematical representation of a number to the base 2, i.e., with only two states: 1 and 0, ON and OFF, or HIGH and LOW. It requires a greater number of digits than base 10; for example, $254 = 11111110$.

binary arithmetic   (**1**) A mathematical numeration system equivalent to our decimal arithmetic system but involving only two digits: 1 and 0. (**2**) An expression recognizing that all arithmetic calculations are done with two values at a time.

binary character set   A character set that consists of two characters.

binary code   A coding system in which the encoding of any data is done through the use of bits, 0 or 1, in which 0 represents off and 1 represents on. ASCII and EBCDIC are two such systems.

binary coded character   One element of a notation system representing alphanumeric characters—such as decimal digits, alphabetic letters, and special symbols—by a predetermined configuration of consecutive binary digits.

binary coded decimal (BCD)   A computer coding system in which each decimal digit is represented by a group of four binary 1's and 0's.

binary coded decimal number   Any number, usually consisting of successive groups of figures, in which each group of four figures is a binary number that represents, but does not necessarily equal arithmetically, a particular figure in an associated decimal number; for example, the decimal number 264 is represented as the binary coded number 0010 0110 0100.

binary coded notation   A binary notation in which each character is represented by a binary numeral.

binary device   (**1**) A device that can register two conditions, such as an electrical switch that can be on or off. (**2**) In computer science, equipment that records data in binary form or that reads the data so coded.

binary digit   Either the character 0 or 1. Abbreviated as BIT.

binary file   A file containing programs in machine code.

binary notation   A numeral system written in base 2 notation.

binary number   Any numeral, usually of more than one digit, expressing a sum in which the quantity represented by each digit is based on a radix of 2. The digits used are 0 and 1.

binary point   The radix point in a mixed binary numeral, separating the fractional part from the integer part. In the binary numeral 110.011, the binary point is between the two 0's.

binary search   A search method in which a series of items is divided into two parts, one of which is rejected, with the process repeated on each unrejected part until the item with the desired property is found. It is often the best method when the list to be searched is known to be in order and relatively uniform. Many database systems use this method for locating items in their indexes.

binary system   A numeral system with a base or radix of 2. The numeral 111 in the binary system represents the quantity 1, plus 1×2^1, plus 1×2^2—that is, 7 in the decimal system.

binary-to-decimal conversion   The process of converting a numeral written in base 2 to the equivalent numeral written in base 10.

binary-to-hexadecimal conversion   The process of converting a numeral written in base 2 to the equivalent numeral written in base 16.

binary-to-octal conversion   The process of converting a numeral written in base 2 to the equivalent numeral written in base 8.

binary tree   A data structure in which each node contains one parent and no more than two children.

binding   In OBJECT-ORIENTED PROGRAMMING, the process of weaving a program together to resolve all the connections among its components. Static, or early, binding resolves these connections before the program is run. Dynamic, or late, binding occurs while the program is running.

binding edge   The edge of a page to be bound.

binding time   The stage at which a compiler replaces a symbolic name or address with its machine-language form.

biochip   An organic device that assembles itself and requires no electricity to operate. If biochip research proves to be successful, one billion times as much data as is now stored on a silicon chip will be able to be stored on a biochip.

biocomputer   A computer that will have its central processor and memory stored on BIOCHIPS.

biometrics   The science of measuring individual body characteristics; used in some security systems.

bionics   The study of living systems for the purpose of relating their characteristics and functions to the development of mechanical and electronic hardware.

BIOS   Acronym for **b**asic **i**nput/**o**utput **s**ystem. In some operating systems, the part of the system that customizes it to a specific computer.

bipolar   Pertaining to the most popular fundamental kind of integrated circuit, formed from layers of silicon with different electrical characteristics; literally "having two poles," unlike the earlier MOS Field Effect Transistor (MOSFET), which is unipolar. As in MOSFET, the current flow of majority carriers goes in one direction only, such a from source to drain. In a bipolar transistor, the current in the emitter region splits and flows toward two terminals (poles), the base and the collector.

bipolar read-only memory   See BROM.

biquinary code   A seven-bit weighted code used primarily to represent decimal numbers; a redundant code that may be used to provide error-checking features. A pair of bits represents the decimal number 5 or 0, and the remaining 5 bits are used to represent the decimal numbers 0 through 4.

bistable device   A device with only two stable states, such as on and off.

bi-state   A situation in which a computer component takes on one of only two possible conditions.

bit   **(1)** A binary digit; a digit (1 or 0) in the representation of a number in binary notation. **(2)** The smallest unit of information recognized by a computer and its associated equipment. Several bits make up a BYTE, or a COMPUTER WORD.

bit control   The means of transmitting serial data in which each bit has a significant meaning and a single character is surrounded with start and stop bits.

bit density   The measure of the number of bits recorded per unit of length or area on MAGNETIC TAPE or DISK.

bit-flipping   The process of inverting bits—changing 1's to 0's and vice versa. For example, in a graphics program, to invert a black-and-white BIT-MAPPED IMAGE (to change black to white and vice versa), the program could simply flip the bits that make up the bit map.

bit image   A collection of bits stored in a computer's memory, arranged into a rectangular matrix. The computer's display screen is a bit image that is visible to the user.

bit manipulation   The act of turning bits on and off, sometimes called BIT-FLIPPING.

bit map   A data structure that describes a bit image being held in computer storage. Each picture element (pixel) is represented by bits stored in the memory. BIT-MAPPED GRAPHICS are notorious for using lots of memory. Up to one million bytes of memory may be required to store a bit map for a high-resolution screen display or to store a full-page scanned image.

bitmap file formats   See ART, CUT, GIF, IFF, IMG, MACPAINT, NEO, PCX, TGA, and TIFF. Contrast with OBJECT FILE GRAPHIC FORMATS.

bit-mapped font   A set of characters in a particular size and style, in which each character is described in a unique bit map (pattern of dots). Bit-mapped screen or printer fonts represent characters with a matrix of dots. To display or print bit-mapped fonts, the computer or printer must keep a full representation of each character in memory.

bit-mapped graphics   A method of generating screen images by creating a one-for-one correspondence between bits in memory and pixels on the screen. In color graphics, three or more bits are required in the bit map to represent the red, green, and blue values of an individual pixel. Bit-mapped graphics are created by paint programs and some scanners.

BITNET   One of the largest wide-area networks. Links colleges and universities in the United States, Canada, and Europe.

bit plane   In computer graphics, the hypothetical two-dimensional plane containing a bit in memory for each pixel on the raster. For any raster image, there is at least one bit plane in frame buffer memory; each bit plane has a one-to-one correspondence of bits to pixels.

bit position   A digit position in a BINARY NUMBER.

bit rate   The rate at which binary digits, or pulse representations, appear on communication lines or channels.

bits per pixel   In a digitized image, a measure of the color value of a given pixel.

bit stream   A binary signal without regard to groupings by character.

bit test   A program check to determine whether a specific bit is on (1) or off (0).

bit transfer rate   The number of bits transferred per unit of time, usually expressed in bits per second.

bit twiddler   (1) A HACKER. (2) A person who enjoys working with computers.

black box   An electronic or mechanical device that alters input signals in a predictable manner but whose inner workings are often a mystery to the user.

blank   (1) Part of a medium in which no characters are recorded. (2) In electronic spreadsheets, a command that will erase the contents of a cell or range of cells. (3) An empty space with a dimension of one character of data.

blank cell   In a DATABASE or SPREADSHEET, a cell that contains no values, labels, or formatting.

blank character A graphic representation of the space character.

blanking On a display screen, not displaying a character although it is present; leaving a space.

bleed In a printed document, any element that runs off the edge of the page.

blend A feature on many digital painting programs that allows the user to soften the edges or mix colors where two objects or regions meet.

blessed folder An Apple Macintosh system folder that contains files loaded at the beginning of an operating session.

blind search A time-consuming type of search that uses an orderly scheme, but no prescience, to exhaust all possibilities.

blinking A graphics aid that causes a predefined graphic entity to blink on the CRT to attract the designer's attention.

block A string of data elements recorded or transmitted as a unit.

block-action command In word processing, the definition and subsequent movement, deletion, or other action on a block of text.

block device A device such as a disk drive that can read and write data only in chunks at a time, rather than byte by byte or bit by bit. The number of bytes in each chunk is normally called the block size. Almost all mass-storage devices are either inherently block devices or made in software to appear as if they were.

block diagram The graphic representation of the logical sequence by which data is processed.

blocked records A combination of logical records into a physical record that is read by the tape drive.

block graphics Graphics images created by using block graphics characters. Because these characters are handled the same way as ordinary characters, the computer can display block graphics considerably faster than BIT-MAPPED GRAPHICS.

block header   A brief record of data that describes a block of memory and its contents.

blocking   The process of grouping a specified number of logical records into one contiguous unit of storage called a block, usually to increase the efficiency of computer input and output operations.

blocking factor   The number of logical records per physical record on a MAGNETIC TAPE or DISK.

blocking object   In OBJECT-ORIENTED PROGRAMMING, a passive object whose semantics are guaranteed in the presence of multiple threads of control.

block length   The measure of the size of a block, usually specified in units such as records, words, characters, or bytes. Same as BLOCK SIZE.

block move   (1) The process by which a block of text is moved from one part of a document or file to another, or from one document or file to another. (2) In word processing, a feature that allows the user to identify a block of text and move it anywhere in a file; the electronic equivalent of CUT AND PASTE.

block size   The number of data elements in a BLOCK.

block sorting   A sorting technique used to break down a file into related groups.

block structure   A hierarchy of program blocks.

blocks world   An artificially created environment of blocks used in the study of ROBOTICS and NATURAL LANGUAGE.

block transfer   The relocation of an entire block of data from one area of storage to another.

blow up   (1) The unexpected halt to a program due to a bug or because it encounters data conditions it cannot handle. (2) To enlarge a picture.

blue print style   A visual style using line drawings to produce either two-dimensional or three-dimensional images and models.

blue ribbon program A computer program that executes properly on the first try and does not require any debugging.

blurring A technique used to model objects as they present the idea of motion to the viewing eye.

BMP A standard file format that stores OBJECT-ORIENTED GRAPHICS in device-independent form, enabling them to work in different systems and programs.

BNF Abbreviation for BACKUS NORMAL FORM.

board Short for printed circuit board, a flat, thin, rectangular component of a computer or peripheral that includes one or more layers of printed circuitry and to which chips and other electronic parts are attached; sometimes called card.

board computer A computer in which all electronic components are laid out on a single CIRCUIT BOARD.

board exchange warranty A warranty that provides a customer with a new replacement board when the original needs repair.

body On a printed page, the area between the top and bottom margins that contains the text.

body of loop The part of a loop that is repeated.

body text The type used for the body of copy, or the main text, of a document. Usually 12 points or less in size, and distinguished from headings, captions, and display lettering.

BOF Acronym for **b**eginning-**o**f-**f**ile.

boilerplate Pieces of text that are used over and over again, word for word, in different documents.

boilerplate document A document created by combining selected paragraphs from a set of standard paragraphs with only a small amount of original information.

boldface   Describing printed characters in darker type than the surrounding characters.

boldface font   A set of type characters that are darker and heavier than normal type.

bold printing   The ability to make certain letters darker than the surrounding text. Some printers produce bold characters by OVERSTRIKING or SHADOW PRINTING.

bomb   (**1**) A concealed fault that can cause a system to crash. (**2**) To sabotage a system by deliberately writing a program that will disrupt it.

bookkeeping   See HOUSEKEEPING.

Bookman   A serif typeface frequently used for body type. Bookman, a design owned by the International Typeface Corporation (ITC), is included as a built-in font with many PostScript laser printers.

Boolean algebra   A branch of symbolic logic similar in form to algebra but dealing with logical relationships instead of numerical relationships. It lay dormant until it could be usefully applied to the fields of relay switching and electronic computers. Boolean algebra has now become an important subject in logic design of electronic computers. It was developed by English mathematician and logician George Boole (1815–1864).

Boolean function   A switching function in which the number of possible values of the function and each of its independent variables is two.

Boolean operation   Any operation in which each of the operands and the result take one of two values.

Boolean operator   A logic operator each of whose operands and whose result has one of two values.

boot   To start up a computer. Microcomputers have a bootstrap routine in a ROM chip that is automatically executed when the computer is turned on or reset. It searches for the operating system, loads it, and then passes control over to it.

bootstrapping Starting up a computer system. *Cold boot* refers to complete restarting after switching the power on, while *warm boot* means partial restarting under operating system control.

boot virus A type of computer virus that modifies one or more of those parts of the operating system that are read in during the bootstrapping process.

border (**1**) In on-screen windows, the edge surrounding the user's workspace. Window borders provide a visible frame around a document or graphic. (**2**) In printing, a decorative line or pattern along one or more edges of an illustration or page.

bore The diameter of a hole, such as on a FLOPPY DISK or MAGNETIC TAPE REEL.

Borland International, Inc. A leading microcomputer software company. Founded in 1983 by Philippe Kahn, Borland introduced TURBO PASCAL, which instantly became a popular commercial product. Borland has continued to develop popular software products.

borrow An arithmetically negative carry that occurs in direct subtraction by raising the low-order digit of the minuend by one unit of the next-higher-order digit.

BOT Acronym for **b**eginning **o**f **t**ape, a mark that shows where to start recording on a magnetic tape.

bottleneck See LIMITING OPERATION.

bottom-up technique An implementation technique wherein the bottom-level modules are written and tested, after which the next-lowest level modules are written and tested. This process continues until all the modules have been completed. Contrast with TOP-DOWN DEVELOPMENT.

bounce The reflection of a transmission on a telecommunication line.

bound Pertaining to whatever limits system performance. *Processor bound* or *I/O bound* indicates the component of a system that is the bottleneck preventing faster performance.

boundary   The delineation between a system and its environment.

boundary fill   The process of filling a region with color by switching to a new value all pixels that are bounded by other pixels having boundary values.

boundary representation   In computer graphics, one of the main methods of solid modeling, in which the object is described by its geometry and topology.

bounding box   In computer graphics, a rectangular box aligned with the axes drawn around the smallest area that entirely contains a particular polygon or object.

boxing   The use of bounding boxes to select particular entities on a computer graphics display.

bozo bit   Simple copy protection on an Apple Macintosh computer system.

bpi   Abbreviation for **b**its **p**er **i**nch; sometimes BYTES PER INCH, which is also abbreviated bpi.

bpp   Abbreviation for BITS PER PIXEL.

bps   Abbreviation for **b**its **p**er **s**econd; sometimes bytes per second, which is also abbreviated bps. 1 bps = 1 baud.

braces   The characters { and } (left brace and right brace, respectively).

brackets   The characters [and] (left bracket and right bracket, respectively).

brain-damaged   A term describing a program that performs in an ill-behaved or destructive manner. For example, a program that fails to respond predictably to commands is said to be a brain-damaged program.

brain-wave interface   A capability of hardware and software that enables the computer to read and act upon the thoughts of humans.

branch   The selection of one or more possible paths in the flow of control, based on some criterion; programming instruction that causes transfer of control to another program sequence.

branching   Performing a statement other than the next one in sequence.

branch instruction   Instruction to a computer that enables it to choose between alternative program paths, depending upon the conditions determined by the computer during the execution of the program.

branchpoint   The place in a program where a branch is selected.

breadboard   An experimental or rough construction model of a process, device, or construction.

break   (1) The interruption of a transmission. (2) To interrupt execution of a program.

break-even analysis   A process that calculates the number of units of a given product that must be produced and sold before a profit is realized.

break key   On some computers, a keyboard key that will interrupt what the computer is doing.

breakpoint   A specified point in a program at which the program may be interrupted by manual intervention or by a control routine. Generally used as an aid in testing and debugging programs.

bridge   A device that connects networks of the same type, allowing equipment on one LOCAL AREA NETWORK (LAN) to communicate with devices on another.

bridgeware   Computer programs used to translate instructions written for one type of computer into a format that another type of computer understands.

briefcase computer   A portable computer that will fit inside a briefcase.

brightness   (1) In the HSB color model, one of the three characteristics used to describe a color. Brightness refers to the color's percentage of black. (2) In computer graphics, the relative presence or absence of shading (whiteness to grayness to blackness). (3) On some CRT terminals, the ability to vary the intensity of the screen display. Especially useful in highlighting selected segments.

brilliant   In computer graphics, having both high color value and high color saturation.

bring-up   The process of starting a COMPUTER SYSTEM.

broadband   Data communications transmission facilities that are capable of handling frequencies greater than those required for voice-grade communications. Broadband communication channels—such as microwaves, fiber optics, laser beams, and satellite transmission—can transmit data at rates of up to five million bauds.

broadcast   In data communications, the dissemination of information to a number of stations simultaneously.

broadcast message   A message transmitted to two or more network stations.

BROM   Acronym for **B**IPOLAR **R**EAD-**O**NLY **M**EMORY, a read-only memory with no write function that uses BIPOLAR semiconductor devices.

brownout   A period of low-voltage electrical power caused by unusually heavy demand. Brownouts can cause computers to operate erratically or to crash.

browse   To look at information without changing it; to view data.

browser   A tool supplied with the programming language that lets the programmer view the HIERARCHY and edit code in OBJECT-ORIENTED LANGUAGES.

browsing   Looking at files or computer listings in search of something interesting, often without authorization to do so.

brush   In computer paint programs, a tool used to produce brushstrokes of varying width, and in some cases calligraphic or shadowing effects.

brute-force technique   Any mathematical technique that depends on the raw power of a computer to arrive at an inelegant solution to a mathematical problem. Most computer users try to avoid brute-force techniques unless they have no practical alternative.

BSC   Abbreviation for **b**inary **s**ynchronous **c**ommunication, a procedure used for DATA TRANSMISSION.

B-spline curve   In computer graphics, a sequence of parametric polynomial curves (typically quadratic or cubic polynomials) forming a smooth fit between a sequence of points in 3-D space. The curve is defined by a series of control points, which in turn define a series of continuous Bezier curves. The piecewise-defined curve maintains a level of mathematical continuity dependent upon the polynomial degree chosen. It is used extensively in mechanical design applications in the automotive and aerospace industries.

BTAM   Abbreviation for **B**asic **T**elecommunications **A**ccess **M**ethod, an access method that permits read/write communications with remote devices.

B-tree   Short for balanced tree, a way of organizing the pointers to information in databases that allows quick retrieval of any single specified record.

bubble chart   A type of chart in which annotated circles (bubbles) connected by lines represent connections between concepts or parts of a whole without emphasizing a structural, procedural, or sequential relationship between the parts.

bubble memory   A method by which information is stored as magnetized dots (bubbles) that rest on a thin film of semiconductor material. It offers a compact, nonvolatile storage capability.

bubble sort   A sort achieved by exchanging successive pairs of keys until the list is ordered; also called RIPPLE SORT.

bucket   A specific portion of storage used to hold a group of records that are addressed jointly; could be hardware-related or determined by HASHING.

budgeting   A process that compares anticipated expenses with anticipated income.

budgeting and control   An accounting information system function for first planning and then monitoring income and expenditures.

buffer A temporary storage area used to equalize or balance different operating speeds. A buffer can be used between a slow input device, such as a terminal keyboard, and the main computer, which operates at a very high speed.

buffered computer A computer that provides for simultaneous input/output and process operations.

buffering The delaying and temporary storing of data in a data communications path.

bug A mistake in a computer program or system, or a malfunction in a computer hardware component. To DEBUG means to remove mistakes and correct malfunctions.

build-in In PROGRAMMING LANGUAGES, pertaining to a language object that is declared by the definition of the language.

build-in check Same as AUTOMATIC CHECK.

building block principles A system design that permits addition of other equipment units to form a larger system. See MODULARITY.

built-in check See AUTOMATIC CHECK.

built-in font A printer font encoded permanently in the printer's READ-ONLY MEMORY (ROM).

bulk annotation A computer graphics feature that enables the designer to automatically enter repetitive text or other annotation at multiple locations on a drawing or design.

bulk eraser A device used to erase information from a storage medium such as a FLOPPY DISK or TAPE.

bulk storage Large-capacity data storage, generally long-term.

bullet An open or closed circle used to set off items in a list.

bulletin board service (BBS) A service that permits individuals who have personal computers to communicate with others who have similar interests. Individuals who subscribe to the service can retrieve information from a common database.

bundle To include software, peripherals, and services as part of the purchase price of a computer system.

bundled software The software included with a computer system as part of the system's total price. Contrast with UNBUNDLED.

bunny suit The protective clothing worn by an individual in a clean room that keeps human bacteria from infecting the computer chip-making process.

burn To ruin circuitry by subjecting it to excessive current or heat.

burn-in The process of testing electronic circuits and components by running the circuits at elevated temperatures in an oven. A typical test might be to run components continuously for a week at 50°C (122°F). This testing process causes weak links in the circuit to burn out, so that the failed circuitry can be replaced with components that will withstand the test.

burning The process of programming a READ-ONLY MEMORY chip.

burst (1) In computer operations, to separate continuous-form paper into discrete sheets. (2) In data transmission, a sequence of signals counted as one unit.

burster A mechanical device that takes apart a multipage computer printout, separates copies, and removes carbon paper.

burst mode A method of reading or writing data that does not permit an interrupt to occur.

bus A channel or path for transferring data and electrical signals.

business area An application area where business is performed.

business data processing Data processing for business purposes such as payroll, scheduling, and accounting.

business graphics (1) Pie charts, bar charts, scattergrams, graphs, and other visual representations of the operational or strategic aspects of a business, such as sales vs. costs, sales by department, comparative product performance, and stock prices. **(2)** Applications programs that allow the user to display data as visual presentations.

business-oriented programming language   A language designed for handling large data files in business applications. See COBOL.

business programming   The branch of computer programming in which business problems are coded for computer solution. This usually involves relatively few calculations but extensive files with a large number of data inputs and outputs.

business software   Programs specifically designed for business applications. Examples include electronic spreadsheets, database management systems, business graphics packages, payroll programs, and accounting programs.

bus mouse   A mouse connected to the computer with an adapter or expansion board.

bus network   A TELECOMMUNICATIONS NETWORK in which all stations, or computer devices, communicate by using a common distribution channel, or BUS. The network is so named because data are picked up and dropped off at devices in a manner similar to the way passengers are picked up and dropped off at bus stops.

bus system   A network of paths inside the computer that facilitate data flow. Important buses in a computer are identified as DATA BUS, CONTROL BUS, and ADDRESS BUS.

button box   A keyboard function keep that can provide additional programmable features to a system.

buzzwords   Words or phrases that happen to be the popular clichés of a group of people.

bypass   A parallel path around one or more elements of a circuit.

bypass capacitor A CAPACITOR used to reduce electrical noise from the power supply.

byte **(1)** Several (usually eight) binary bits of data grouped together to represent a character, digit, or other value. **(2)** Eight bits treated as a unit for purposes of machine operations.

bytes per inch (BPI) The number of bytes that can be contained on one inch of magnetic tape. A common measure of recording density.

— C —

c   Centi. One hundred.

C™   The full name of a programming language designed for use on microcomputers. Combines high-level statements with low-level machine control to deliver software that is both easy to use and highly efficient. C is very popular with system programmers because of its transportability between computer systems.

C++   An object-oriented version of the C programming language that has been chosen by several large software publishers for major development projects. The term C++ means "more than C."

C4   Represents CAD, CCM, CAE, CIM; the disciplines related to the use of computers and computer graphics to automate design and production processes.

©   The copyright symbol, indicating the exclusive right granted by law to sell, distribute, or reproduce a graphic image or document.

cable   The electrical wire or bundle of wires used to connect two parts of a system. Carries electrical power of electrical signals.

cable connector   The male/female plug used for connecting cables between a computer and peripherals.

cabling diagram   A diagram showing connections and physical locations of system or unit cables, and used to facilitate field installation and repair of wiring systems. Can be generated by a computer-aided design.

cache   A memory in which parts of the information in the main (slower) memory or disk are copied. Information that is likely to require reading or alteration goes to the cache, where the system can access it more quickly. Caching can significantly speed processing of some programs, especially if floppy disks are used for mass storage.

cache disk   A disk management scheme whereby more data than are necessary are read from disk during each time-consuming disk fetch and stored in internal memory, minimizing the number of fetches.

caching Retaining data in cache memory for rapid access.

caching disk On microcomputers, a diskette that simulates the operation of cache memory.

CAD Acronym for cOMPUTER-aIDED dESIGN, a term applied to programs and computer systems used in designing engineering, architecture, and scientific models. The process involves direct, real-time communication between a designer and a computer, generally by the use of a CRT display and a light pen, mouse, or graphics tablet. Some CAD applications create objects in two or three dimensions, presenting the result as wire-frame "skeletons," models with shaded surfaces, or as solid objects.

CADAM Acronym for cOMPUTER-aUGMENTED dESIGN aND mANUFACTURING, the process of, or methods for, using computer systems as tools in design and manufacturing applications.

CAD/CAM Acronym for cOMPUTER-aIDED dESIGN/cOMPUTER-aIDED mANU-FACTURING.

CADD See cOMPUTER-aIDED dESIGN AND dRAFTING.

CAE Abbreviation for cOMPUTER-aIDED eNGINEERING, which can analyze a design for basic error-checking or to optimize manufacturability, performance, and economy. Information drawn from the CAD/CAM design database is used to analyze the functional characteristics of a part, product, or system under design, and to simulate its performance under various conditions.

cage See cARD cAGE.

CAI Abbreviation for cOMPUTER-aSSISTED iNSTRUCTION.

CAL Acronym for cOMPUTER-aUGMENTED lEARNING.

CalComp Abbreviation for **Cal**ifornia **Comp**uter Products, one of the first pen plotter manufacturers and an early leader and supporter of computer graphics. Almost all of the early (1960s) hard-copy computer graphics images were drawn on CalComp plotters. Today, the company has grown to become one of the most versatile in the business, offering displays, plotters, digitizers, and other equipment.

calculated field   A DATA FIELD that contains the results of calculations.

calculating   Reconstructing or creating new data by compressing certain numeric facts.

calculations   Any mathematical processes performed on data.

calculator   Any mechanical or electronic machine used for performing calculations. Calculators, as distinguished from computers, usually require frequent human intervention.

calculator mode   The operating mode on some interactive computer systems that allows the terminal (or keyboard/display, in the case of microcomputer systems) to be used as a desk calculator. The user types an expression; the computer then evaluates it and returns the answer immediately.

calibration   The process of determining by measurement or by comparison with a standard the correct value of each scale reading on a meter or the correct value of each setting of a control knob.

call   (1) To transfer control to a specific closed subroutine. (2) In communications, the action performed by the calling party, or the operations necessary in making a call, or the effective use made of a connection between two stations.

callback device   A device on the receiving end of a communications network that ascertains the authenticity of the sender by calling the sender back.

callback PPD   A PORT PROTECTION DEVICE that screens incoming calls.

calligraphic graphics   A method of forming an image from scan lines oriented in arbitrary directions and drawn in an arbitrary order. Expensive electronics are required, but spatial anti-aliasing is not. Typical of this style of graphics are the "wire-frame" models that were considered synonymous with computer graphics in the early days.

calling   The process of transmitting selection signals in order to establish a connection between data stations.

calling program   A PROGRAM that requests execution of another program.

calling sequence   The specified set of instructions and data necessary to call a given subroutine.

call instruction   An instruction that, after diverting execution to a new sequence of instructions, permits return to the program's original sequence.

callout   Text that identifies parts of an illustration.

Calma Company   A pioneer of computer graphics hardware for CAD/CAM applications since 1964.

CAM   Acronym for **c**omputer-**a**ided **m**anufacturing, the use of computers to assist in any or all phases of manufacturing.

cameo type   Describing a typeface in which characters are reversed white out of a solid or shaded ground.

camera cone   A device that allows a user of a graphics system to take a "snapshot" directly off a CRT monitor by shielding the display from incident light.

camera-ready   In publishing, a final copy that is photographed to create a printed copy.

CAMM   Acronym for **c**omputer-**a**ided **m**aintenance **m**anagement, the use of computers to reduce the time needed to find and correct the causes of breakdowns in automated manufacturing systems.

Canadian Information Processing Society (CIPS)   The organization formed to bring together Canadians with a common interest in the field of information processing. It has a membership of scientists, business people, and others who make their careers in computing and information processing.

cancel **(1)** A keyboard operation that deletes the line currently being typed. **(2)** To end a task before it is completed.

cancel key Same as STOP KEY.

candidates Any of the alternative plans offered in the preliminary design phase of a project.

canned software Programs prepared by computer manufacturers or software developers and provided to a user in ready-to-use form that are general enough to be used by many businesses and individuals. Contrast with CUSTOM SOFTWARE.

Canon engine The internal mechanism of a Canon office photocopier, used in many LASER PRINTERS.

Canvas™ A power-packed multi-purpose drawing and painting program for the Apple Macintosh computer. With 24-bit color, unlimited layers, Bezier curves, precision tools, bit-mapped editing at high resolutions, and full-color separation, it combines color capabilities and powerful object-editing options with a friendly interface and ease of use.

CAP Acronym for COMPUTER-AIDED PUBLISHING.

capacitance The measure of the ability to store electric charge, the basic unit of measurement being a FARAD.

capacitor The electronic component that stores a charge of static electricity and, when properly stimulated, releases this charge. This is the way bits are written to and read from computer storage.

capacitor storage A storage device that utilizes the capacitance properties of materials to store data.

capacity The number of items of data that a storage device is capable of containing. Frequently defined in terms of computer words, bytes, or characters.

cap height The height of a capital letter from the baseline.

capline In DESKTOP PUBLISHING, the hypothetical line that connects the tops of capital letters.

caps   Capital letters. All caps means that all letters are capitalized; initial caps refers to the capitalization of the first letter of each significant word.

capstan   The rotating shaft within a magnetic tape drive that pulls the tape across the recording heads at a constant speed.

caption   (1) A title or subtitle identifying what is being displayed on the screen. (2) Text associated with, and describing, a figure or table.

capture (of data)   The recording of data on a form or its entry into a COMPUTER.

carbon ribbon   A ribbon used with printers to produce extremely sharp characters with excellent definition.

card   (1) A printed circuit board. (2) A storage medium in which data are represented by means of holes punched in vertical columns in a 7.37-inch-by-3.25 inch (18.7-cm-by-8.3-cm) paper card.

card cage   The chassis inside the computer housing on which printed circuit boards are mounted.

card code   The combinations of punched holes that represent characters in a PUNCHED CARD.

card column   One of the vertical lines of punching positions on a punched card.

card field   The fixed number of consecutive PUNCHED CARD columns assigned to a unit of information.

card hopper   A device that holds PUNCHED CARDS and makes them available for the feeding mechanism of card handling equipment.

cardinality   In OBJECT-ORIENTED PROGRAMMING, the number of instances that a class may have; the number of instances that participate in a using class relationship.

cardinal number   A number that indicates how many items there are in a set. For example, if "file 21 contains 10 graphic images," 21 is ordinal; 10 is cardinal. See ORDINAL NUMBER.

card punch An output device that accepts information from the computer's memory and punches it into cards.

card reader (**1**) An input device that reads information punched into cards and transfers it into the computer's memory. (**2**) A device designed to read the magnetic strip on the back of credit cards.

card row One of the horizontal lines of punching positions on a PUNCHED CARD.

caricature In computer graphics, an amusing distortion or exaggeration of something so familiar that it would be recognized even in the distortion. A caricature captures the likeness of a person. Used to create a humorous or satirical portrait.

carriage A control mechanism for a printer that automatically feeds, skips, spaces, and ejects paper forms.

carriage return (CR) In a character printer, the operation that causes the next character to be printed at the left margin.

carrier frequency A constant signal transmitted between communicating devices that is modulated to encode binary information.

carrier signal A signal with a constant frequency that can be modulated to carry a data signal.

carrier tone An audio tone that is modulated to send signals between computers.

carry (**1**) The process of bringing forward. The special condition that occurs when the sum of two digits in a single column is equal to or greater than the number base. (**2**) A carry digit, or the digit to be added to the next higher column.

CARS Acronym for computer-assisted retrieval system, a system locating offline archival document storage on microfiche cartridges or microfilm rolls.

Cartesian coordinate system The system named for French mathematician Rene Descartes (1596–1650) whereby, in a flat plane, a point can be located by its distances from two intersecting straight lines, called the AXES, the distance from one axis being measured along a parallel to the other axis. The numbers associated with the point are called the coordinates of the point.

cartoon (1) A drawing, usually humorous, that stands by itself as a work of art and is designed for publication. Today, cartoons can be prepared using a computer and a drawing software package. Computer-produced cartoons are beginning to appear in publications, generally accompanied by captions. (2) An animated film, usually with various characters and a set story line. (3) A satirical drawing or caricature. (4) A comic strip.

cartridge A generic term that can refer to any of several devices that are self-contained, usually in some kind of plastic housing; for example, ROM CARTRIDGE, DISK CARTRIDGE, TONER CARTRIDGE, MEMORY CARTRIDGE, TAPE CARTRIDGE, or FONT CARTRIDGE.

cartridge disk A magnetic disk in which a single disk platter is contained in a sealed plastic case that is mounted onto a disk unit when data are to be read from or written to the disk inside.

cartridge font A series of typefaces contained in ROM chips mounted within a plastic module called a CARTRIDGE. The cartridge is placed in a compatible laser printer to allow it to use the typefaces.

cartridge tape A form of magnetic tape that is stored in a cartridge; cartridge tape stores data using a magnetic bit pattern.

cascade connection Two or more similar component devices arranged in tandem, with the output of one connected to the input of the next.

cascade control An automatic control system in which the control units are linked in chain fashion, each feeding into, as well as regulating, the next stage.

cascade sort An external tape sort that sorts by merging strings from all but one tape onto the remaining tape. Subsequent passes merge fewer tapes until one tape contains all items.

cascading windows Overlapping on-screen windows.

CASE Acronym for **c**omputer-**a**ided **s**oftware **e**ngineering, a combination of techniques and tools aimed at building and maintaining software systems of all types—large and small, commercial and scientific, online and real-time. CASE tools provide coverage of the software life cycle by providing auto analysis, design, implementation, and maintenance, as well as project management of software systems.

case control structure A control structure that can be formed by nesting two or more selection control structures.

case sensitivity A program's ability to distinguish between upper- and lowercase letters.

cashless society A computerized system in which purchase transactions would be settled instantaneously by transferring credits from the buyer's bank account to the seller's account. No cash would ever be exchanged, with EFT deposits replacing paychecks as well as payments for goods and services.

cassette recorder A device designed to use cassettes to record and store digital data and, at a later time, reload this data into the computer's internal storage. It was used with early microcomputer systems.

cast (**1**) A tint or overemphasis of one color in a color image, particularly if unintended. (**2**) In some animation programs, the elements that can be moved around the screen.

CAT Acronym for **c**omputer-**a**ssisted **t**ypesetting, the arrangement of type on a page for printing.

catalog (**1**) An ordered compilation of item descriptions and sufficient information to afford access to the items, such as a listing of programs or data file names that are stored on a diskette. (**2**) To instruct the computer to print out a list of all of the files on a disk.

catalog directory A table in a catalog that identifies the items it contains.

catena A connected series.

cathode ray tube (CRT) An electronic tube with a screen upon which information can be displayed.

cavalier projection In computer graphics, a type of oblique projection in which the direction of projection is at 45 degrees to the projection plane.

CBASIC A compiler BASIC programming language. A CBASIC program is translated into object code before it is executed. Program execution time is much faster than the more popular interpreter BASIC.

CBEMA See COMPUTER AND BUSINESS EQUIPMENT MANUFACTURERS ASSOCIATION.

CCP Abbreviation for **C**ertificate in **C**omputer **P**rogramming. CCP examinations are given annually at test centers in colleges and universities in the United States, Canada, and several international locations. Three separate full-day examinations test a common core of programming knowledge and an area of specialization: business programming, scientific programming, or systems programming. The common core of knowledge emphasizes such areas as data and file organization, techniques of programming, programming languages, interaction with hardware and software, and interaction with people. The certificate is awarded by the INSTITUTE FOR CERTIFICATION OF COMPUTER PROFESSIONALS.

CCU Abbreviation for **c**entral **c**ontrol **u**nit.

C-curve A type of line fractal, made by applying a fractal generator to a line.

CD Abbreviation for COMPACT DISC, a 4⅝-inch silver platter used for audio recordings. Compact, durable, and capable of extraordinary fidelity, the CD is an excellent long-lasting recording medium. See CD-ROM.

CD-I Abbreviation for **C**ompact **D**isc-**I**nteractive, a small optical disc system that is under the interactive control of the user.

CDP Abbreviation for **C**ertificate in **D**ata **P**rocessing. CDP examinations are given annually at test centers in colleges and universities in the United States, Canada, and several international locations. This broad-based examination consists of five sections and requires half a day to complete.

In addition to meeting experience requirements and espousing the Code of Ethics, CDP candidates must successfully complete all five sections of the examination to receive the certificate. The certificate is awarded by the INSTITUTE FOR CERTIFICATION OF COMPUTER PROFESSIONALS.

CD player A device that reads the information stored on a COMPACT DISC.

CDR A COREL DRAW object file format.

CD-ROM Acronym for **c**ompact **d**isc **r**ead-**o**nly **m**emory, a type of optical disc that uses the same basic technology as do the popular CD audio discs. Although a CD-ROM drive can only read data (the data is permanently stamped onto the discs during manufacturing), the discs are inexpensive to make and can each hold about 650 megabytes of data. Contents are typically an entire encyclopedia on a single CD, a set of reference works, a clip-art library, a collection of fine art, or any other publication that is for reading only.

CE Acronym for **c**ustomer **e**ngineer, an individual who performs maintenance services for computer equipment or systems.

cel **(1)** Thin sheets of clear acetate on which conventional animation is painted (also, cell). Computer graphics systems are now used to produce cels. **(2)** In COMPUTER ANIMATION, a single-frame image. **(3)** In computer graphics, a pattern of an image including both color and transparency values for each pixel that is mapped as a texture into a scene.

cel animation An animation technique in which a background painting is held stationary while animated images are moved over the painting, producing the illusion of movement. Animation programs that perform cel animation are available.

cell **(1)** Storage for one unit of information, usually one character, one byte, or one word. A binary cell is a cell of one binary digit capacity. **(2)** A single coordinate location within the grid, or matrix, that constitutes the basic form of an electronic spreadsheet.

cell address In a spreadsheet, the column and row coordinates of a cell.

cell animation An animation technique in which a background painting is held stationary while animated images are moved over the painting, producing the illusion of movement. Animation programs that perform cell animation are available.

cell contents   The label, value, formula, or function contained in a SPREADSHEET cell.

cell definition   In ELECTRONIC SPREADSHEETS, the contents of a cell.

cell format   The way a spreadsheet program displays the contents of cells on the display screen.

cell pointer   A special cursor that designates the cells into which information is entered in an electronic spreadsheet.

centering   The WORD PROCESSING and PAGE LAYOUT PROGRAM feature that places a line of text midway between the left and right margins.

center of perspective   The position at which an image subtends the same angle to the viewer as the object subtended to the camera (in photography) or to the "synthetic camera" (in computer graphics).

centimeter   One-hundredth of a meter (0.39 inch).

centralized data processing   The concept by which a company has all its computing equipment located at the same site and field-office operations have no effective data processing capability. Contrast with DISTRIBUTED COMPUTING.

centralized network configuration   The structure of a computer network whose dominating feature is a central computer that, one way or another, is involved in everything that happens in the system.

centralized system   A processing system with a single database that users access from terminals.

central processing unit (CPU)   The major component of a computer system with the circuitry to control the interpretation and execution of instructions.

central processor   A processor that contains the sequencing and processing facilities for instruction execution, timing functions, initial program loading, and other machine-related functions.

central storage   Storage that is an integral part of the processing unit.

central structure store (CSS)   An editable hierarchy of structures composed of attributes, elements, and transformations. CSS attributes are qualities such as color and style, and CSS elements are drawing primitives such as lines and polygons.

Centronics Interface   A de facto standard for parallel data exchange paths between computers and peripherals. Centronics Corporation was one of the original printer manufacturers to use the parallel scheme for communications between computers and printers. The 36-pin parallel interface was introduced in 1970.

Certificate in Computer Programming   See CCP.

Certificate in Data Processing   See CDP.

certification   (1) The acceptance of software by an authorized agent, usually after the software has been validated by the agent, or after its validity has been demonstrated to the agent. (2) A voluntary system of attesting that a person has achieved a certain professional status, usually by passing a rigorous examination. See CCP and CDP.

CG   Abbreviation for **C**OMPUTER **G**RAPHICS, any graphical element created with the aid of a computer.

CGA   Abbreviation for **C**olor/**G**raphics **A**dapter, the original low-resolution color standard for IBM-compatible microcomputers, introduced by IBM Corporation in 1981. CGA is capable of several character and graphics modes. It has been superseded by EGA and VGA.

CGA monitor   A monitor capable of showing graphics in four colors and medium-quality text.

CGI   (1) Abbreviation for **c**omputer-**g**enerated **i**magery, images generated using computer graphics techniques. (2) Abbreviation for **C**omputer

Graphics Interface, a standard for direct communication of drawing primitives to graphics devices.

CGM   Abbreviation for COMPUTER GRAPHICS METAFILE, a standard object-oriented graphics file format. CGM stores images primarily in vector graphics, but also provides a raster format.

chain   (1) The linking of records by means of pointers in such a way that all like records are connected, the last record pointing to the first. (2) A set of operations that are to be performed sequentially.

chained files   Data files where data blocks are chained together by using POINTERS.

chained list   A list in which each item points to the next item and the order of retrieval need not have any relation to the storage order.

chain field   The field in a record that defines the location and storage device of other data items logically related to the original record but not physically attached.

chaining   (1) The process of linking a series of records, programs, or operations together. (2) The method of allowing the execution of programs larger than the main memory of a computer by loading and executing modules of the same program sequentially.

chaining search   A technique used for retrieving data from a file by using addresses in the records that link each record to the next in the chain.

chain list search   A search that uses a chained list.

chain printer   An impact LINE PRINTER that has its character set assembled on a chain revolving horizontally past all print positions. It prints when a print hammer (one for each column on the paper) presses the paper against an inked ribbon that in turn presses against the appropriate characters on the aligned print chain.

chained printing   Printing separate files as a unit.

chamfer   A beveled edge between two intersecting lines.

change agent   The role of the systems analyst in overcoming resistance to change within an organization.

change sign   The reversal of a sign of a number held in a computer.

channel   (**1**) A path for electrical or electronic transmission between two or more points. Also called path, link, line, facility, or circuit. (**2**) The transmission path that connects auxiliary devices to a computer.

channel adapter   A device that enables data communications between channels on different hardware devices.

channel capacity   In DATA COMMUNICATIONS, an expression of the maximum number of bits per second that can be accommodated by the channel. This maximum number is determined by the bandwidth modulation scheme and certain types of noise. The channel capacity is most often measured in bauds, or bits per second.

chaos   A topic that has connections with fractal geometry. Chaotic systems have the appearance of unpredictability but are actually governed by precise, deterministic laws, as are many fractal images. The rise of chaos theory has been meteoric. During the 1980s, it received widespread prominence, and some scientists have even placed it alongside two other great revolutions of physical theory in the twentieth century, relativity and quantum mechanics. The growth of chaos theory is linked with the rapid development of powerful computers. Within the last 15 years, successful innovation in computer graphics is one of the factors that has enabled scientists and mathematicians to make progress in nonlinear systems from which chaos theory is derived.

character   Any symbol, digit, letter, or punctuation mark—including the blank character—stored or processed by computing equipment.

character array   A named matrix of character data items.

character checking   The checking of each character by examining all characters as a group or field.

character code   A code designating a unique numerical representation for a set of characters.

character data Data in the form of letters and special characters.

character density See DENSITY.

character display A display device that provides a representation of data only in the form of graphic characters.

character generator A circuit that forms the letters or numbers on a screen or printer.

character graphics A set of special symbols that are placed together to create GRAPHICS.

character identifier A symbol that represents a character.

characteristic That part of a floating-point number that represents the size of the exponent. See MANTISSA.

character outline The graphic pattern established by the stroke edges of a character.

character pitch In a line of text, the number of characters per inch.

character printer A printer in which only a single character is composed and determined within the device prior to printing.

character reader An input device that performs character recognition.

character recognition The technology of using machines to identify human-readable symbols automatically, and then to express their identities in machine-readable codes. This operation of transforming numbers and letters into a form directly suitable for electronic data processing is an important method of introducing information into computing systems.

character set (1) All the numbers, letters, and symbols associated with a given device or coding system. (2) All the characters recognized by a COMPUTER SYSTEM.

characters per inch The method of expressing the output from dot matrix and daisy wheel printers as determined by type size and style. Abbreviated cpi.

characters per second   A unit for measuring output of low-speed SERIAL PRINTERS. Abbreviated cps.

character string   A string of alphanumeric characters.

charge coupled device (CCD)   A semiconductor memory device within which stored information circulates rather than remaining in fixed locations.

Charles Babbage Institute   An organization for the study of the information revolution from a historical perspective, intended as a clearinghouse for information about research resources related to this history and a repository for archival materials.

chart   The visual representation of quantitative information, such as a bar graph, in which the information is made visual by heavy horizontal or vertical lines, or a circle graph or pie chart, in which the information is pictured as slices of an imaginary pie. See FLOWCHART and STRUCTURE CHART.

chartbook   In business and presentation graphics, a collection of chart formats from which a user may select an appropriate application format.

charting package   A PRESENTATION GRAPHICS package that shows the relationship between sets of numerical information.

chassis   The metal frame upon which the wiring, sockets, and other parts of an electronic assembly are mounted.

check bit   A bit added to each byte to alert the computer to an error in data transmission. Also called PARITY BIT.

check digits   One or more digits carried within a unit item of numerical data to provide information about the other digits in the unit in such a manner that, if a transcription or transposition error occurs in subsequent data entry, the check fails, and an indication of error is given.

checkout   See DEBUG.

check plot   In computer graphics, a pen plot generated automatically by a CAD system for visual verification and editing prior to final output generation.

checkpoint A specified point at which a program can be interrupted, either manually or by a control routine. Used primarily as an aid in debugging programs.

check problem A testing problem designed to determine whether a COMPUTER or a COMPUTER PROGRAM is operating correctly.

check sum The summation of digits or bits used primarily for checking purposes and summed according to an arbitrary set of rules. Used to verify the integrity of data.

chiaroscuro Shading.

chiclet keyboard A type of microcomputer keyboard. The name was derived from the chewing gum because the keys are small and square, resembling the gum pieces. Chiclet keys are very small and typically spread out, so that touch typing is more difficult than on a conventional keyboard. An undesirable keyboard used in older low-cost microcomputers; however, a useful keyboard in systems for children and handicapped people.

chief information officer The manager of an MIS department.

chief programmer team A software development team structure in which one programmer is assigned overall responsibility for the project.

child A data record that can be created only based upon the contents of one or more other records (parents) already in existence.

children In hierarchical databases, those data elements that are linked in a subordinate fashion to a parent element.

chip A small component that contains a large amount of electronic circuitry; a thin silicon wafer on which electronic components are deposited in the form of integrated circuits. Chips are the building blocks of a computer and perform various functions, such as doing arithmetic, serving as the computer's memory, or controlling other chips.

chip-carrier   The intermediate physical package into which the die is mounted.

chip family   A group of related chips, each of which (except the first) evolved from an earlier chip in the family; for example, the Intel Corporation's family of 80 x 86 microprocessors: 80286, 80386, and 80486.

chooser   In the Apple Macintosh environment, a desktop accessory that allows the user to select a device driver to be used by the system.

chop   To discard unneeded data.

chord   In computer graphics, a short line segment whose end points lie on a circle.

chroma   Color attributes, such as saturation, shade, and hue.

chromaticity   The dominant wavelength and purity of a color as objectively measured; corresponds to hue and saturation of the color without regard to brightness.

chrominance   Those portions of a composite video signal controlling color.

chunking along   A slang term referring to the operation of a long-running, dependable program.

churning   See THRASHING.

CIM   Abbreviation for **C**OMPUTER **I**NPUT **M**ICROFILM.

cipher   A secret method of representing information to ensure computer security.

ciphertext   Data that has been encrypted.

circle   A collection of points equally distant from a fixed point, the center. See CONIC SECTION.

circuit   (**1**) A pathway designed for the controlled flow of electrons. (**2**) A system of conductors and related electrical elements through which electrical currents flow. **(3)** A communication link between two or more points.

circuit board The thin insulating board used to mount and connect various electronic components and microchips in a pattern of conductive lines. This circuit pattern is etched into the board's surface.

circuit capacity The number of channels in a circuit that can be dealt with simultaneously.

circuit card See CIRCUIT BOARD.

circuit load Usually a percentage of maximum circuit capability to reflect actual use during a span of time.

circuitry A complex of circuits describing the interconnection within or between systems.

circuit switching A physical connection between two nodes in a communication network that dedicates bandwidth of that circuit until the connection is dropped.

circular graph In computer graphics, a graph in which the values are plotted from a central point along radiating axes.

circular list A linked list, usually of data elements, in which the last element points to the first one.

circular shift A shifting operation whereby bits or characters shifted off one end of a register enter the register on the opposite end.

CISC Acronym for **c**omplex **i**nstruction **s**et **c**omputer, a central processing unit that recognizes as many as 200 instructions.

CIU Abbreviation for COMPUTER INTERFACE UNIT.

cladding A glass or plastic sheath that surrounds the core of an optical fiber. It keeps the light waves inside the core by bouncing them back into the core of the unit.

Claris CAD™ A full-featured, easy-to-use, two-dimensional COMPUTER-AIDED DESIGN program for the Apple Macintosh computer from Claris

Corporation. Claris CAD gives users the power to create accurate, professional illustrations and drawings.

class   In OBJECT-ORIENTED PROGRAMMING, the description of a set of nearly identical objects that share common methods and general characteristics. The terms *class* and *type* are usually interchangeable; however, a class is a slightly different concept than a type in that it emphasizes the importance of hierarchies.

class category   In OBJECT-ORIENTED PROGRAMMING, a collection of classes, some of which are visible to other class categories and others of which are hidden.

class diagram   In OBJECT-ORIENTED PROGRAMMING, part of the notation of OBJECT-ORIENTED DESIGN, used to show the existence of classes and their relationships in the logical design of a system. A class diagram may represent all or part of the class structure of a system.

classify   To categorize or place data with similar characteristics into the same category.

class library   In OBJECT-ORIENTED PROGRAMMING, a collection of generic classes that can be adapted and tailored for a particular application.

class structure   In OBJECT-ORIENTED PROGRAMMING, the "kind of" hierarchy of a system; a graph whose vertices represent classes and whose arcs represent relationships among these classes. The class structure of a system is represented by a set of class diagrams.

class variable   In OBJECT-ORIENTED PROGRAMMING, a placeholder for part of the state of a class. Collectively, the class variables of a class constitute its structure. A class variable is shared by all instances of the same class.

clean room   A room in which dust and other small particles are filtered from the air and in which protective clothing is worn to avoid contaminating electronics components and other delicate, sensitive equipment.

clear   **(1)** The keyboard function that removes the contents from the display screen. **(2)** Same as ZAP.

clear display   The action of deleting all information from a display.

clearing   Replacing the information in a register, storage location, or storage unit with zeros or blanks.

cleartext   A readable form of information.

click   To point a mouse pointer at a word or icon on the screen, press the mouse button, and then release it quickly. Clicking is usually performed to select or deselect an item or to activate a program or program feature.

click art   Clip art on a DISKETTE or CD-ROM; a floppy disk or CD-ROM of professionally drawn pictures that are ready to copy and use in computer-produced documents.

clicking   The term used to describe the pressing of a button on the top of a mouse.

client   **(1)** In OBJECT-ORIENTED PROGRAMMING, an object that uses the resources of another, either by operating upon it or by referencing its state. **(2)** An individual or organization contracting for systems analysis.

client-based application   An application that can be used only by certain workstations in a local area network.

client/server   A relationship between machines in a communications network. The client is the requesting machine; the server is the supplying machine.

clip   To select a part of a graphic to show on the screen or place into a document. Clipping is used to select a region of interest rather than scaling the entire image.

clip art   Collections of pictures and design elements (such as borders, symbols, and drawings). The collections may be in printed form or stored on DISKETTES or CD-ROM. This predrawn artwork can be used in designing newsletters, brochures, flyers, books, and magazines, or incorporated into other documents.

clipboard   A temporary holding place that facilitates the cutting and pasting of text and graphics. Clipboard information is held in memory only while the computer is turned on. A clipboard allows information to be transferred from one program to another and stores a copy of the last information that was copied or cut. A PASTE operation passes data from the clipboard to the current program.

clip boundary   The defining boundary of display space outside of which display elements will not be visible.

clipping   Removing portions of an image that are outside the boundaries of the edge of a window or display screen. Certain graphics programs also support clipping as a means of masking everything but a certain object so that painting tools, for example, can be applied to the object alone.

clipping path   A curve or polygon that is used to mask an area in a document. Only what is inside the clipping path appears when the document is printed.

clipping plane   In graphics programs, a plane perpendicular to the line of sight that can be applied anywhere between the viewer's position and the target, blocking anything behind or in front of it. It is used to constrain the amount of memory required by a drawing. Any object, or portion of an object, beyond the clipping plane is discarded. Often there is both a front clipping plane and a back clipping plane.

clobber   To write new data over the top of good data in a file or otherwise damage a file so that it becomes useless; to wipe out a file.

clock   **(1)** A timing device that generates the basic periodic signal used to control the timing of all operations in a computer. **(2)** A device that records the progress of real time, or some approximation of it, and whose contents are available to a computer program.

clocking   The technique used to synchronize a sending and receiving data communications device. Permits synchronous transmission at high speeds.

clock pulse   The synchronization signal provided by a clock.

clock rate   The time rate at which pulses are emitted from a clock.

clock speed The rate at which a microprocessor executes instructions.

clock track The track on which a pattern of signals has been recorded to provide a time reference.

clockwise Moving from left to right.

clone In nonbiological terms, a product or idea that is an exact duplicate or copy of another, including a computer or software program that duplicates another program exactly (such as a personal computer that closely imitates the operation and architecture of the IBM PS/2 computer).

CLOS Acronym for COMMON LISP OBJECT SYSTEM, a system wherein the user can experiment not only with OBJECT-ORIENTED PROGRAMMING, but also with the design of object-oriented programming systems.

close To finish and save.

close box A small box at the upper left-hand corner of a window used to close the window.

closed architecture A personal computer design that limits add-ons to those that can be plugged into the back of the machine.

closed broken line In computer graphics, a figure formed when the starting point of a broken line intersects its endpoint.

closed bus system A system in which a computer's internal data bus does not contain receptacles and is not easily upgradable.

closed file A file that cannot be accessed for reading or writing. Contrast with OPEN FILE.

closed loop A loop that is completely circular.

closed plane figure In computer graphics, a figure that starts at and comes back to the same point.

closed routine See CLOSED SUBROUTINE.

closed shop The operation of a data processing center only by professional operators. Programs and data are carried by messengers or transmitted over telephone lines, avoiding the necessity of users entering the computer room and enabling a much more efficient use of the computer. Contrast with OPEN SHOP.

closed subroutine A subroutine stored at one place and linked to one or more calling routines. Contrast with OPEN SUBROUTINE.

closed surface In computer graphics, a solid surface with no holes, so that none of the interior is visible.

CLS An internal command in DOS and OS/2 operating systems that clears the screen and places the cursor in the upper left-hand corner.

cluster A station that consists of a control unit and the terminals connected to it.

cluster controller A down-line processor that collects data from a number of low-speed devices, then transmits concentrated data over a single communications channel.

cluster configuration A dedicated word processing system in which several word processors are tied together by cable and share storage and printers.

clustered devices A group of terminals connected to a common controller.

clustering (1) In OBJECT-ORIENTED PROGRAMMING, the storing of objects contiguously on a disk for efficient accessing. (2) Grouping things with similar characteristics.

CLV Abbreviation for constant linear velocity, a method of packing more data onto a disk by making sure the rate at which the disk passes the head stays the same on the outer tracks as on the inner tracks. In practice, that means changing the disk's rotation speed as the head moves in and out.

CMI Abbreviation for COMPUTER-MANAGED INSTRUCTION.

CML Abbreviation for CURRENT MODE LOGIC.

CMOS Abbreviation for complementary metal-oxide semiconductor, a technology for making integrated circuits that use very little power. This technology is popular both for portables and for desktop computers, partly because it produces less heat than other integrated circuits. Invented by Frank Wanlass in the mid-1960s.

CMY   Abbreviation for CYAN, MAGENTA, YELLOW, a color-mixing system used to print colors.

CMYK   Abbreviation for CYAN, MAGENTA, YELLOW, KEY/BLACK, the color model used in the printing color separation process. The colors of this model are also known as process colors and are based on the three main tones of printing inks used in much color reproduction.

CO   Abbreviation for central office.

coalesce   To combine two or more sets of items into one set.

coaxial cable   A special type of communications cable that permits transmission of data at high speed. Usually employed in local networks.

COBOL   Acronym for Common Business-Oriented Language, a high-level language developed for business data processing applications. Every COBOL source program has four divisions: (1) Identification Division, which identifies the source program and output of a compilation; (2) Environment Division, which specifies those aspects of a data processing problem that are dependent upon the physical characteristics of a particular computer; (3) Data Division, which describes the data that the object program is to accept as input, manipulate, create, or produce as output; and (4) Procedure Division, which specifies the procedures to be performed by the object program, using English-like statements.

CODASYL   Acronym for Conference On Data Systems and Languages, a federally sponsored industry committee that developed standards that led to the COBOL language and many of the more complex types of databases. Founded in 1959, it is made up of individuals and institutions that contribute their own time and effort.

code   (1) A set of rules outlining the way in which data may be represented.
(2) The rules used to convert data from one representation to another.
(3) To write a program or routine; same as ENCODE.

code breaking   Same as CRYPTANALYSIS.

code conversion   The process for changing the bit groupings for characters in one code into the corresponding character bit groupings for a second code.

coded decimal number   A number consisting of successive characters or a group of characters that usually represents a specific figure in an associated decimal number.

Code of Fair Information Practices   The code published in a report prepared by the Department of Health, Education, and Welfare that resulted in the passage of the Privacy Act of 1974.

coder   One who expresses a problem design, or part of a problem, in a computer language. The term is often used in a derogatory sense to refer to a person who does little analysis and planning, merely expressing someone else's design in a computer language.

code set   A complete set of representations defined by a code; for example, all the two-letter post office identifications for the 50 states constitute a code set.

coding   (1) Writing a list of instructions that will cause a computer to perform specified operations. (2) An ordered list or lists of the successive instructions that will cause a computer to perform a particular process.

coding form   A form on which the instructions for programming a computer are written. Each programming language has its own coding form.

coercion   In programming-language expressions, an automatic conversion from one data type to another.

COGO   Acronym for **Co**ordinate **Geo**metry, a problem-oriented programming language used primarily by civil engineers to solve geometric problems.

coherence   An assumption used in raster scan display technology that attributes the same value of an individual pixel to its adjacent pixel.

cohesion   A measure of the inner strength of a program module.

cold boot The act of turning a computer on and loading an operating system into it.

cold fault A computer fault that is apparent as soon as the machine is switched on.

cold site An environmentally suitable empty shell in which a company can install its own computer system.

cold start Restart activity used when a serious failure has occurred in a system, making the contents of the direct access storage inaccessible so that no trace of the recent processing can be used. The system must be reloaded and activity restarted as though at the beginning of a day. More simply, restarting the computer by turning it off and then on again—all programs and data in memory are lost.

collage (**1**) A composition of flat objects, such as paper and cloth, pasted together on a surface and often combined with drawings and colors for artistic effect. A similar effect can be created with computers using images input via a digitizer. (**2**) The combination of graphics and/or effects; the production of images with a mixture of media and textures, typography and/or photography.

collate To merge two or more sequenced data sets to produce a resulting data set that reflects the sequencing of the original sets.

collating sort A sort that uses a technique of continuous merging of data until one sequence is developed.

collation sequence The order that the computer uses when it arranges items from first to last, typically alphabetical for words and numerical for numbers. The issue becomes complex when taking into account uppercase and lowercase, mixed numbers and words, punctuation, numbers that are not filled to the same length with leading zeros, and other factors.

collection The process of gathering data from various sources and assembling it at one location.

collector   The section of a semiconductor device towards which electricity flows.

collision   **(1)** The result of keys colliding at the same address when two keyboard operations are ordered simultaneously. Programming in the computer's operating system defines which operation will be performed. **(2)** The problem that occurs when two records have the same disk address.

collision detection   **(1)** In computer graphics, particularly in arcade-type games, the determination of when objects have collided. Several programming techniques may be used to detect a collision. **(2)** A task performed in a MULTIPLE-ACCESS NETWORK to prevent two computers from transmitting at the same time.

color   The hue perceived for different wavelengths in the portion of the electromagnetic spectrum to which the human eye responds. It is possible to create almost all visible colors using two systems of primary colors. Transmitted colors use red, green, and blue (RGB), and reflected colors use cyan, magenta, and yellow (CMY). Color displays use RGB and color printers use CMY.

color bits   A predetermined number of adjacent bits assigned to each displayable pixel that determines its color when it is shown on a display screen. For example, two color bits are required for four colors, four color bits are required for 16 colors, eight color bits are required for 256 colors, and 24 color bits are required for over 16 million colors.

color burst signal   The signal present in composite video output that provides color information. Sometimes turning off the color burst signal improves the quality of pictures on black-and-white monitors.

color coding   The process of identifying records by using different colors for different types of records.

color correction   The process of changing the color balance of an image to more closely approach the desired values.

color display   A display unit that can display more than two colors and the shades produced by combinations of two colors.

color graphics   Any type of computer graphic in which the images displayed on a visual display screen, printed copy, or other type of display are shown in more than one color.

color graphics adapter (CGA)   An adapter that simultaneously provides four colors. It allows a computer to show color graphics as well as text.

colorizing   (1) The capacity of certain computers and software programs to modify the colors in images. (2) Pseudocoloring. (3) Adding color to a black-and-white graphic image.

color look-up table   A small section of computer memory that contains color content values.

color map   The color options in a graphics system arranged by index number.

color map animation   An animation method in which an object or character is made to appear as if it is moving. Consecutive images are drawn on subsets of the bit planes in the frame buffer in different stages of movement. The color map is used to cycle through this animation sequence on the bit planes, all of which are visible simultaneously, illuminating only one of the duplicate images at a time in the object color and the remainder of the objects in the background color. This method is advantageous because it is faster to change the colors in the color map than it is to redraw an image again and again.

color model   Any method for representing color in graphic arts and desktop publishing. In the graphic arts and printing areas, colors are often specified with the Pantone system. In computer graphics, colors can be described using any of several different color systems: RGB (red, green, blue), CMY (cyan, magenta, yellow), and HSB (hue, saturation, brightness).

color monitor   A computer display designed to work with a video card or adapter to produce text or graphics image in color. A color monitor has a screen coated internally with three phosphors—one each for red, green, and blue. To light the phosphor and produce a spot of color, such a monitor also usually contains three electron guns—again, one for each of the three colors.

color palette   A set of colors that can be displayed on a screen at one time.

color printer   An output device that can produce text, charts, graphics, and artwork in several colors. DOT MATRIX, INK-JET, THERMAL WAX-TRANSFER, and LASER PRINTERS can print full-color output.

color resolution   The number of different colors or gray-scale values a system can produce or work with. A value is usually given in bits.

ColorRIX   A draw/paint program for IBM-compatible microcomputers. In addition to the usual draw/paint tools, the program includes several scalable bit-mapped fonts, a printing/screen capture feature, a presentation slide show, an application/language independent screen loader, and sophisticated animation effects.

color saturation   The amount of a hue contained in a color; the more saturation, the more intense the color.

color scanner   An INPUT UNIT for converting color photographs and drawings to digital data for use in computer systems.

color scanning   The analysis of full-color images into the subtractive primary colors (cyan, magenta, and yellow) and black.

color separation   The creation of a multicolor graphic by creating several layers, with each layer corresponding to one of the colors that will be printed when the graphic is reproduced by a commercial printer.

color space   An imaginary area or volume containing all the points whose positions represent the available colors in a system when those points are graphed on a set of axes.

color spectrum   The range of colors available on a particular device or system, usually presented in the same order as the colors in the normal visible spectrum.

ColorStudio™   An Apple Macintosh 24-bit true color imaging program for graphics arts professionals. It allows for merging high-resolution color photos, video captures, pixel artwork, and PostScript type. Features include powerful paint and retouching tools, a full-density gray-scale mask, and six pressure tools: airbrush, charcoal, paintbrush, pencil, waterdrop, and finger tip. Painting and selection tools can be customized for photo-retouching, masking, and special effects. It allows for precise calibrating of its own color balance as well as that of other applications.

column (1) The vertical numbers of one line of an array. (2) One of the vertical lines of punching positions on a punched card. (3) The position of information in a computer word. (4) The horizontal division of an electronic spreadsheet. Together with rows, columns serve to form the spreadsheet matrix. Contrast with ROW.

COM Acronym for COMPUTER OUTPUT MICROFILM.

combination logic A circuit arrangement in which the output state is determined by the present state of the input; a digital system not utilizing memory elements.

combinatorial explosion A condition that occurs in problem solving when the possibilities to be examined become too numerous for the computer. It can occur even with very large computers.

combinatorics The study of combinations and permutations, or methods of counting how many objects there are of a given type or how many ways there are to do something.

COMDEX The largest computer trade show in the world, held in Atlanta, Chicago, and Las Vegas in the United States and in other locations throughout the world.

COM file An executable program file with a .COM filename extension that operates in a specific part of the base memory in DOS and OS/2 systems.

comic strip A popular art form, generally found in newspapers, characterized by continuing characters, a number of panels, and dialogue presented in balloons. Comic strips can be prepared with either pen and ink or computer graphics systems.

COMIT   One of the string processing languages.

command   **(1)** A control signal. **(2)** Loosely, a mathematical or logic operator. **(3)** Loosely, a computer instruction.

command-chained memory   A technique used in dynamic storage allocation.

command-driven software   Software that takes action as a result of the user typing single letter, word, or line commands.

command file   A file that will execute a program when the filename is entered.

command interpreter   Part of an OPERATING SYSTEM that interprets the user's keystrokes and sends a message to the appropriate utility or applications program to execute the command.

command key   Any keyboard key used to perform specific functions.

command language   The language used to give instructions to an operating system.

command language translator   SYSTEM SOFTWARE that translates instructions written in a command language into machine language instructions.

command menu   The list of commands in an applications software program.

command processing   The reading, analyzing, and performing of computer instructions.

command processor   The part of an operating system that accepts commands from the user for operating system tasks. Also called SHELL.

command tree   A hierarchical diagram that shows all the choices from a main command menu and the associated submenus.

comments   English prose that may be interspersed among the computer-language statements of a computer program to explain their action to human readers. Special markers on the comments cause the computer to ignore them. Properly done comments are a valuable form of internal documentation because they are embedded in the program itself and, therefore, they stay with the program. Comments provide helpful notes for future users who may later attempt to understand or alter the program.

comment statement   (1) In PROGRAMMING LANGUAGES, a source language statement that has no effect on the program other than that it is reproduced on an output listing. (2) A statement that explains the statements that actually execute program logic.

commercial art   Art that is created to serve a specific business purpose, such as selling a product; examples include advertising and fashion illustration.

Commodore Business Machines, Inc.   The manufacturer of the Amiga family of microcomputers and several older microcomputers, including the popular Commodore 64.

Commodore 64/128   The Commodore 64 is a home computer introduced in 1982 by Commodore Business Machines, Inc. Over 10 million of these machines have been sold worldwide. The Commodore 128 is an upgraded Commodore 64 that was introduced in 1986.

common carrier   A government-regulated private company that provides telephone, telegraph, and other telecommunications facilities for public use.

common language   A computer programming language intelligible to two or more computers with different machine languages. BASIC, COBOL, FORTRAN, and PASCAL are common languages.

Common Lisp Object System (CLOS)   An object-oriented version of the artificial intelligence language LISP.

common storage   The section of memory for each user that holds data or parameters that are accessible to all programs.

communicating   The process of transmitting information to a point of use.

communicating word processors   A network of word processors used to transmit electronic mail.

communication   (1) The flow of information from one point (the source) to another (the receiver). (2) The act of transmitting or making known. (3) The process by which information is exchanged between individuals through the use of a commonly accepted set of symbols.

communications channel   The physical means of connecting one location or device to another for the purpose of transmitting and receiving data. Coaxial cables, fiber optics, microwave signals, telephone lines, and satellite communications all serve as communications channels.

communications control unit   Usually, a small computer whose only job is to handle the flow of data communications traffic to and from a MAINFRAME computer.

communications link   The method by which information is transmitted between computer devices.

communications medium   The intervening substance, such as a telephone wire or cable, that connects two physically distant hardware devices.

communications processor   A computer that provides a path for data transfer between the computer system and the data communications network.

communications protocol   A set of communication rules that provides for error checking between devices and ensures that transmitted data are not lost.

Communications Satellite Corporation (COMSAT)   A privately owned U.S. communications carrier company operating under a mandate from Congress. The American representative in the INTELSAT organization, it provides technical and operational services for the global communications system. Traffic on the system is coordinated through an operations center in Washington, D.C.

communications satellites   Earth satellites placed in different spots in the geostationary orbit 22,250 miles (36,000 km) above the equator that serve as relay stations for communications signals transmitted from Earth stations. These satellites orbit Earth once every 24 hours, giving the impression that they are "parked" in one spot over the equator. Once in this orbit, a satellite is capable of reaching 43 percent of Earth's surface with a single radio signal.

communications server   A device that connects LOCAL AREA NETWORKS to WIDE AREA or TELECOMMUNICATIONS NETWORKS.

communications software   Programs that allow computers to communicate through a modem. Some communications programs are capable of automatic telecommunications such as auto-answering, auto-dialing, and even dialing another computer at a preset time to establish communication and send and receive information. Some programs allow operation of an unattended remote computer—accessing disk files, operating peripherals, and so forth.

communications system   A system that consists of senders, physical channels, and receivers of data communications.

comp   Abbreviation for **comp**rehensive, describing a layout showing what a printed page will look like.

compact disc   An optical disc, a nonmagnetic, shiny metal disk used to store digital information.

compaction   The packing of data structures to make room in storage.

compact keyboard   A keyboard with reduced-size keys or reduced spacing between keys.

Compaq Computer Corporation   A manufacturer of IBM-compatible microcomputers. Founded in 1982, Compaq has become an industry leader and is known for producing reliable computers.

comparative sort   A sort by comparison of two or more keys.

comparator   A device for checking the accuracy of transcribed data by comparing it with a second transcription, noting any variation between the two.

compare operation   An operation in which the computer compares two data items and performs alternative operations based on the comparison.

compart   Computer art.

compatibility   **(1)** A property of some computers that allows programs written for one computer to run on another (compatible) computer, even though it is a different model. **(2)** The ability of different devices, such as a computer and a printer, to work together. **(3)** The ability of specific software to work with a specific brand and model of computer. All software is not compatible with all computers.

compatible   **(1)** A term describing the degree of interworking possible between two devices or systems. If an element in a system is fully compatible with the functional and physical characteristics of that system, it can be incorporated into the system without modification. **(2)** A personal computer that can run software designed for the IBM PC and/or IBM PS/2 computers.

compatible software   Programs that can be run on different computers without modification.

COMP command   In DOS and OS/2, a command that compares two or more text files to see if they are identical.

compilation   One of two principal means of translating programs written in high-level languages into machine-language instructions that can be directly executed by the processor. Entails translating a complete program before any execution. Contrast with INTERPRETATION, in which each instruction is translated when it is to be executed.

compilation time   The time during which a SOURCE-LANGUAGE PROGRAM is translated (compiled) into an OBJECT PROGRAM (machine language).

compile   To prepare a machine-language program or a program expressed in symbolic coding from a program written in a HIGH-LEVEL PROGRAMMING LANGUAGE, such as COBOL or PASCAL.

compile-and-go   An operating technique by which the loading and execution phases of a program compilation are performed in one continuous run. Especially useful when a program must be compiled for a one-time application.

compiled program   The set of machine-language instructions that constitutes the output of the compilation of a SOURCE PROGRAM.

compiled statement   A high-level SOURCE LANGUAGE statement translated into MACHINE LANGUAGE.

compiler   A computer program whose purpose is that of translating high-level language statements into a form that can directly activate the computer hardware. Translates a complete program before any execution.

compiler-compiler   Same as METACOMPILER.

compiler language   SOURCE LANGUAGE that uses a COMPILER to translate the language statements into an OBJECT LANGUAGE.

compiler program   See COMPILER.

compile time   The time required to compile a program. The point in the processing of a program when it is being translated from SOURCE CODE to OBJECT CODE by a TRANSLATOR (compiler).

compile-time error   An ERROR that occurs while a program is being compiled, as opposed to run-time errors that occur while a program is being executed.

complement   A number used to represent the negative of a given number. Obtained by subtracting each digit of a number from the number representing its base and, in the case of two's complement and ten's complement, adding unity to the last significant digit.

complementary colors   The hues that appear opposite each other on the color wheel, such as orange and blue, red and green, or yellow and violet. When mixed in equal amounts, these hues form a neutral gray.

complementary constant current logic   See C^{3}L.

complementary MOS (CMOS)   A method of making METALLIC OXIDE SEMI-

CONDUCTOR (MOS) chips that uses almost no power and works faster than MOS. Not very good for LSI, but used in electronic watches and clocks where power has to come from a battery.

completion aid   A prompt that requires the user to enter information, such as a filename.

completion screen   A screen that requests information from the user.

completeness check   A procedure that establishes that none of a record's fields is missing and that the entire record has been checked.

complex number   A number consisting of an ordered pair of real numbers, expressible in the form a + bi, where a and b are real numbers and i^2 equals −1.

component   (1) A basic part; an element. (2) Part of a computer system. (3) A portion of an application.

composite   A type of video signal in which all three primary video color signals (red, green, blue) are combined, which limits the sharpness of the monitor image. Used in some monitors and TV sets that use only one electron gun to generate the three primary colors.

composite curve   A series of curves grouped together as a single entity so that they appear to be a single curve.

composite map   A single map created on a graphics system from a mosaic of individual adjacent map sheets.

composite symbol   A symbol consisting of more than one character, such as the composite symbol <>, which stands for "not equal to" in some software systems.

composite video   The color output from a computer color display described in terms of its hue and its brightness and encoded in a single video signal. The color control signal is a single data stream that must be decoded into three colors (red, green, and blue). Inexpensive color monitors called composite monitors use composite video and produce a slightly better picture than a TV set but not the high quality of RGB monitors.

composition The selection of type sizes and styles and the positioning of type on a page.

Composition and Make-up (CAM) terminal A CRT display device capable of showing and changing exact point sizes and character widths. Used for computer phototypesetting.

compound statement A single instruction that contains two or more instructions that could otherwise be used separately.

compress To save storage space by eliminating gaps, empty fields, redundancy, or unnecessary data in order to shorten the length of records or files.

compressed file A file that a file compression utility has written to a special disk format that minimizes the storage space required.

CompuServe The major information service network used by individuals as well as businesses. Carries timely news features, stock market reports, electronic mail, educational programs, legal advice, travel reservations, encyclopedia references, games, programming aids, and more. Personal computer owners can reference the CompuServe network via the common telephone system.

computability The property by which computational problems are classified.

computation The result of computing.

compute-bound Pertaining to a program or computer system that is restricted or limited by the speed of the central processing unit. Same as PROCESSOR BOUND.

computed field A file field that is based on the values of other fields.

computed radiography A diagnostic imaging technique that directs X-rays at a patient as conventional X-ray units do, but develops the image immediately by scanning with a laser beam, a process that also digitizes the image.

computed tomography   A diagnostic imaging technique that directs X-rays axially around a patient and computes a two-dimensional image of the body slice that is displayed on a CATHODE RAY TUBE.

computer   A device capable of solving problems or manipulating data by accepting data, performing prescribed operations (mathematical or logical) on the data, and supplying the results of these operations.

computer accessories   The equipment that can be attached to a computer, such as a MOUSE, DISK DRIVE, VISUAL DISPLAY device, KEYBOARD, or PRINTER.

computer-aided choreography   The use of computers, particularly computer graphics, to devise and score choreographic movements in ballet.

computer-aided design (CAD)   The computer systems and programs used in designing tools, automobiles, buildings, aircraft, molecules, farm equipment, integrated circuits, and thousands of other products. Computer-aided design has become a mainstay in a variety of design-related fields such as architecture, mechanical engineering, interior design, civil engineering, and electrical engineering. CAD applications are graphics- and calculation-intensive, requiring fast computers and high-resolution video displays.

computer-aided design and drafting (CADD)   The use of a computer system for industrial design and technical drawing.

computer-aided design/computer-aided manufacturing (CAD/CAM)   Efforts to automate design and manufacturing operations, a rapidly growing branch of computer graphics, currently relying primarily on calligraphic graphics but branching out to incorporate raster graphics. Wide-ranging uses include designing auto parts, buildings, and integrated circuits.

computer-aided factory management   A system for managing a production facility in which computers schedule operations, keep accurate accounts on parts inventories, and order new supplies as required from supply houses.

computer-aided manufacturing (CAM)   The use of computer technology in the management, control, and operation of manufacturing.

computer-aided publishing (CAP)   The use of software packages to facilitate the layout of text and graphics in publishing applications.

Computer and Business Equipment Manufacturers Association (CBEMA)   An organization for computer vendors, business equipment manufacturers, and suppliers. Founded in 1916, CBEMA is involved in the development of standards for the data processing and business equipment industries.

computer-animated graphics   In multimedia applications, graphics animated by means of a computer rather than film or videotape.

computer animation   Animation produced with the use of a software program and a computer. Computer animation makes possible an added dimension in which there are no rules for time and space, light and color, or for obeying the laws of physics as known to Newton or Einstein; no other medium has given artists such complete control and achieved such stunning results. Two-dimensional animation uses flat images for creating characters and/or backgrounds, while three-dimensional animation requires modeling or model design. Geometric models are stored in a computer and can be rotated, translated, and scaled as needed to create and manipulate images. More sophisticated three-dimensional systems allow the design and manipulation of complex scenes and characters for film-making. Most three-dimensional animation is used in advertising.

computer anxiety   Fear of computers.

computer architecture   The area of computer study that deals with the physical structure (hardware) of computer systems and the relationships among these various hardware components.

computer art   A broad term that can refer either to art created on a computer or to art generated by the computer, the difference being whether the artist is human or electronic. When created by human beings, computer art is done with painting and drawing programs that offer a range of drawing tools, brushes, pencils, patterns, shapes, and colors. The artist can dream lovely images and use the computer to bring them to vivid reality.

computer artist   A person who uses computers as tools in producing art.

computer-assisted   Same as COMPUTER-AIDED.

computer-assisted instruction (CAI)   The use of computers to augment individual instruction by providing students with programmed sequences of instruction under computer control. The manner of sequencing the materials permits students to progress at their own rate.

computer-assisted publishing   Same as ELECTRONIC PUBLISHING.

computer-augmented learning (CAL)   The use of a computer system to augment, or supplement, a more conventional instructional system, such as by using simulation programs to aid in problem-solving in a course of instruction.

computer awareness   Generally, an understanding of what a computer is, how it works, and the role and impact of computers in society.

computer-based learning (CBL)   A term used to embrace all the present forms of educational computing.

computer board   A board with chips and circuits that can increase the memory of functions of a computer.

computer camp   A camp, usually in session during the summer weeks, where campers learn how to use microcomputers in addition to participating in more traditional activities.

computer center   A facility that provides computer services to a variety of users through the operation of computer and auxiliary hardware, as well as through ancillary services provided by its staff.

computer center director The individual who directs the activities, operations, and personnel in a computer center.

computer chess A computer program that plays the game of chess. Since 1970, the ACM North American Computer Chess Championships have served both as a catalyst for progress and as a historical record of this most exciting area of artificial intelligence research. During these 20-plus years, programs have improved from the level of rank club players to among the best in the world. The names of some of the popular chess programs are: CHESS, RIBBIT, BELLE, CRAY BLITZ, HITECH, and DEEP THOUGHT.

computer circuits The circuits used in digital computers, such as gating circuits, storage circuits, triggering circuits, inverting circuits, and power amplifying circuits.

computer classifications The three classifications of digital computers: MAINFRAMES (which includes supercomputers), MINICOMPUTERS, and MICROCOMPUTERS.

computer competence The level of computer knowledge attained by an individual who can solve sophisticated problems in his or her field of expertise using a computer.

computer conferencing A method of sending, receiving, and storing typed messages within a NETWORK of users.

computer coordinator An educational professional who has the responsibility of teaching information technology in a specific school or school district.

computer crime The unauthorized use of computer systems, including software or data, for unlawful purposes.

computer curriculum The use of computers in schools to enhance the learning process.

computer-dependent language Same as COMPUTER-ORIENTED LANGUAGE.

computer disc-interactive (CDI)   Home entertainment and information technology that combines video, audio, and text and stores it on a compact disc, which can be played on a CDI video machine attached to a television monitor.

computer doctor   Jargon for a computer repairperson.

computer drawing   A graphic image prepared on a computer.

computer enclosure   The cabinet or housing for a computer's circuit boards and power supply.

computer engineering   The field of knowledge that includes the design of computer hardware systems. Offered as a degree program in several colleges and universities.

computer equity   Equal opportunity for computing for all social groups.

computerese   The jargon and other specialized vocabulary used by people working with computers and information processing systems.

computer family   A term commonly used to indicate a group of computers that have been built around the same central processing unit, the same microprocessor, or a series of related microprocessors and share significant design features. For example, the IBM PC and IBM PS/2 models represent a family designed by IBM Corporation around the Intel 80 x 86 series of microprocessors (80286, 80386, and 80486).

computer flicks   Movies made by a computer.

Computer Fraud and Abuse Act   A law passed by Congress in 1984 to fight COMPUTER CRIME.

computer game   Any interactive software or firmware in which the input data consists of a human player's physical actions and the output is an interactive graphics display.

computer-generated animation   Animation produced by using a computer to control the movements of an animation stand or camera. Makes possible a greater degree of accuracy, repeatability, sophistication, and speed of operation.

computer-generated surface   A computer graphics image representing a plot of three-dimensional data.

computer graphicist   A specialist who uses computer graphics systems to produce graphs, charts, animated diagrams, art forms, and graphics designs.

computer graphics   A general term for the appearance of pictures or diagrams, as distinct from letters and numbers, on a display screen or hard-copy output device. It encompasses different methods of generating, displaying, and storing information.

computer graphics artist   A person who uses computers as tools in producing fine art and commercial art. This is one of the hottest careers of the 1990s, according to a survey conducted by *Money* magazine; it appeared third on a list of the 15 fastest-growing and most lucrative, challenging, and prestigious professions for the next decade.

computer graphics magazines   Magazines that focus specifically on computer graphics and its applications, useful sources of the latest information on computer graphics hardware, software, and applications. Popular computer graphics periodicals include *Computer Graphics World*, *Computer Pictures*, *IEEE Computer Graphics and Applications*, and *ACM SIGGRAPH Newsletter*.

computer graphics metafile (CGM)   An international device-independent file format for storage of object-oriented graphics images. CGM files can be exchanged among users of different systems and different programs.

computer graphics peripherals   External devices added to a computer system to provide graphics capability, such as visual displays, graphics printers, plotters, and film recorders.

computer-independent language   A high-level language designed for use in any computer equipped with an appropriate COMPILER.

computer industry   The industry composed of businesses and organizations that supply computer hardware, software, and computer-related services.

tions that supply computer hardware, software, and computer-related services.

computer information system (CIS)   The coordinated collection of hardware, software, data, people, and support resources to perform an integrated series of functions that can include processing, storage, input, and output.

computer information systems curriculum   A course of study, normally offered by business schools, that prepares students for entry-level jobs as application programmers or systems analysts.

computer input microfilm (CIM)   The technology that involves using an input device to read the contents of microfilm or microfiche directly into the computer.

computer instruction   See INSTRUCTION.

computer instruction set   A complete set of the operators of a computer's instructions together with a description of the meanings that can be attributed to their operands.

computer integrated manufacturing (CIM)   The concept of a totally automated factory in which all manufacturing processes are integrated and controlled by a CAD/CAM system. CIM enables production planners and schedulers, shop/floor foremen, and accountants to use the same database as do product designers and engineers.

computer interface unit (CIU)   The device used to connect peripheral devices to a computer.

computerization   (1) The application of a computer to an activity formerly done by other means. (2) The actual reshaping of society by the widespread adoption and use of computers.

computerize   To automate by means of computer systems.

computerized axial tomography (CAT)   A computer-controlled X-ray technique that shows a picture of a site through the body at a given depth. The computer is used to bring out the details of this picture, recording

X-rays passing through the body in changing directions and generating an image of the body's structure.

computerized database   A set of computerized files on which an organization's activities are based and upon which high reliance is placed for availability and accuracy.

computerized game playing   The recreational use of computers that have been programmed to play a wide variety of games.

computerized mail   The technique of delivering mail in electronic form directly to homes and businesses through computer equipment. See ELECTRONIC MAIL.

computerized numerical control   See NUMERICAL CONTROL.

computer jargon   The technical vocabulary associated with the computer field. See COMPUTERESE.

computer language   See PROGRAMMING LANGUAGE.

computer leasing company   A company that specializes in leasing the computer equipment that it purchases from a computer manufacturer.

computer letter   A personalized form letter produced by a word processing system or a special form-letter program.

computer literacy   A broad knowledge of how to use computers to solve problems, general awareness of the functioning of the software and hardware, and an understanding of the societal implications of computers.

computer-managed instruction (CMI)   The application of computers to instruction in which the computer is used as a record keeper, manager, and/or prescriber of instruction.

computer mastery   The level of knowledge required of an individual who wants to be a success in the computer field.

computer matching   The process of matching records in two databanks to determine which records exist in both.

computer monitoring   Management's monitoring of an employee's use of a personal computer or computer terminal.

Computer Museum   An archive for computer history, located in Boston, Massachusetts, whose collection contains many early computer systems and taped presentations of computer pioneers.

computer music   Music employing computer equipment at any stage of its composition or realization as sound.

computer network   A complex consisting of two or more interconnected computer systems, terminals, or communication facilities.

computernik   An avid computer user who chooses to spend a large amount of time using computers.

computer numerical control   The technique by which a machine-tool control uses a computer to store numerical control instructions generated earlier by CAD/CAM for controlling the machine.

computer-on-a-chip   A complete MICROCOMPUTER on an INTEGRATED CIRCUIT chip.

computer operations   That part of a computer installation responsible for the day-to-day collection, production, distribution, and maintenance of data.

computer operations manager   The person who oversees the computer operations area in an organization. The manager is responsible for hiring personnel and scheduling work that the system is to perform.

computer operator   A person skilled in the operation of the computer and associated peripheral devices. This person performs other operational functions that are required in a computer center, such as loading a disk drive, removing printouts from the line printer rack, and sometimes bursting and decollating.

computer-oriented language   A LOW-LEVEL LANGUAGE.

computer output microfilm (COM)   The technology that involves recording computer output on MICROFILM or MICROFICHE.

computer output microfilm (COM) recorder   A device that records computer output on photosensitive film in microscopic form.

computer package   Commercially available software.

computer phobia   The fear of computers.

computerphiliac   A person who is totally involved with the computer to the exclusion of all other concerns.

computer process control system   A system that uses a computer connected to sensors that monitor a process in order to control that process and its modification so that a product can be produced at a profit.

computer processing cycle   **(1)** The steps involved in using a computer to solve a problem: write the program in a programming language; input the program into the computer; and compile and execute the program. **(2)** The basic processing cycle of input, process, and output.

computer program   A formal expression of the sequence of actions required for a data processing task; the programmer's specification of the task(s) to the computer in a formal notation that can be processed by the computer. Consists of a series of statements and instructions that cause a computer to perform a particular operation or task.

computer programmer   The person whose job is to design, write, and test programs that cause a computer to do a specific job.

computer resource   Any of the computer system elements needed to perform required operations, including software, data files, processing units, input-output units, storage units, and operating personnel.

computer revolution   See INFORMATION REVOLUTION.

computer science   A field of knowledge embracing all aspects of the design and use of computers. Aspects of computer science range from programming and computer graphics to artificial intelligence and robotics. Offered as a degree program in many colleges and universities.

computer science curriculum   A course of study that includes all technical aspects of the design and use of computers. Computer science is offered as a degree program in many institutions of higher learning.

computer security   The preservation of computing resources against abuse or unauthorized use, especially the protection of data from accidental or deliberate damage, disclosure, or modification.

computer services company   A company that provides computer services to other individuals and organizations.

computer simulation   The representation of a real or hypothetical system, constructed from a computer program.

computer specialist   An individual, such as a systems analyst or a programmer, who provides computer services to computer-using organizations, usually as an independent contractor or consultant.

computer store   A retail store where customers can select, from the shelf or the floor, a full computer system or just a few accessories. These stores typically sell software, books, supplies, and periodicals. In a broad-based computer store, users can examine and operate several types of microcomputer systems.

computer system   A system that includes computer hardware, software, and people. Used to process data into useful information.

computer typesetting   The use of a computer to process an input medium resulting in a justified, hyphenated, and formatted output medium. See DESKTOP PUBLISHING.

computer user   Any person who uses a computer system or its output.

computer users group   A group whose members share the knowledge they have gained and the programs they have developed on a computer or class of computers of a certain manufacturer. Most groups hold meetings and distribute newsletters to exchange information, trade equipment, and share computer programs.

computer utility   A service that provides computational ability, usually in the form of a time-shared computer system. Programs, as well as data, may be made available to the user. The user may also have her or his own programs immediately available in the central processing unit, have them on call at the computer utility, or load them by transmitting them to the computer prior to use. Certain data and programs are shared by all users of the service; other data and programs, because of their proprietary nature, have restricted access. Computer utilities are generally accessed by means of data communications subsystems.

computer vendor An organization that manufactures, sells, or services computer equipment.

computer virus A program that attaches itself to other programs or data. A virus's typical purpose is to disrupt the processing of information by infecting the system. When an infected program is executed, the virus reproduces and spreads by searching for other software that is not infected, and then attaching itself to previously "clean" software.

computer vision The processing of visual information by a computer.

computer word The fixed sequence of bits, bytes, or characters treated as a unit and capable of being stored in one storage location.

computer worktable A computer desk or work table, averaging about 30 inches (76 cm) from the floor. The chair height should be adjusted to leave a gap of at least 8 inches (20 cm) for the knees; the seat will then be about 16 inches (40 cm) from the floor.

Computerworld A weekly publication that provides articles and advertisements on topics of interest such as word processing, robotics, office automation, programming languages, computer equipment, computer personnel, and general computer information.

computing The act of using computing equipment for processing data; the art or science of getting the computer to do what the user wants.

computing power The relative speed of computing. One computer is described as being more powerful than another if it can handle more work at a faster speed.

computing system See COMPUTER SYSTEM.

COM recorder A device that records computer output on photosensitive film in microscopic form. See COMPUTER OUTPUT MICROFILM.

concatenate To link together or join two or more character strings into a single character string, or to join one line of a display with the succeeding line; to compress.

concatenated data set A collection of logically connected DATA SETS.

concatenated key More than one data item used in conjunction to identify a record.

concave In computer graphics, pertaining to a region or shape, such as a polygon, for which at least one straight line segment between two points of the region is not entirely contained within the region. Contrast with CONVEX.

concave polygon A polygon having at least one interior angle greater than 180 degrees.

concentrator A device that allows a number of slow-speed devices to utilize a single high-speed communications line. Also called multiplexer.

conceptual computer A simplified computer that can demonstrate the computer's major functions without involving its operational details.

conceptual tool Any tool for working with ideas instead of objects.

concordance An alphabetical list of words and phrases appearing in a document, with an indication of where those words and phrases appear.

concurrency In OBJECT-ORIENTED PROGRAMMING, the property that distinguishes an active object from one that is not active. Concurrency is one of the fundamental elements of the OBJECT MODEL.

concurrent Pertaining to the occurrence of two or more events for activities within the same specified interval of time.

concurrent access A term that refers to two or more users attempting to interactively access the same data at approximately the same time.

concurrent language   A language that supports the simultaneous execution of multiple objects, usually on PARALLEL architecture hardware.

concurrent object   In OBJECT-ORIENTED PROGRAMMING, an active object whose semantics are guaranteed in the presence of multiple threads of control.

concurrent processing   The performance of two or more data processing tasks within a specified interval.

concurrent program execution   Two or more programs being executed at the same time.

condensed type   Type narrowed in width so that more characters will fit a linear inch.

condition   (1) A given set of circumstances. (2) A definite state of being.

conditional branching   See CONDITIONAL TRANSFER.

conditional jump   A program transfer that takes place only when the instruction that specifies it is executed and specified conditions are satisfied. Contrast with UNCONDITIONAL JUMP.

conditional paging   A word processing feature that causes printing to begin on the next page if a specified block of text will not fit completely within the remaining space on a page.

conditional replace   A word processing function that asks the user whether to replace copy each time the program finds a particular item.

conditional statement   A statement that is executed only when a certain condition within the routine has been met.

conditional transfer   A instruction that may cause a departure from the sequence of instructions being followed, depending upon the result of an operation, the contents of a register, or the settings of an indicator. Contrast with UNCONDITIONAL TRANSFER.

condition code   A limited group of program conditions—such as carry, borrow, and overflow—pertinent to the execution of instructions.

condition entry   One of the four sections of a DECISION TABLE. Answers all questions in the CONDITION STUB.

conditioning   Improvement of the data transmission properties of a voice-band transmission line by correction of the amplitude phase characteristics of the line amplifiers.

condition stub   One of the four sections of a DECISION TABLE. Describes all factors (options) to be considered in determining a course of action.

conduit   A pipe for protecting cables.

CONDUIT   A nonprofit publisher of educational software. Reviews, tests, packages, and distributes instructional computer programs and related printed materials.

cone   A device used to eliminate reflections when photographing a computer display screen.

conference tree   A type of bulletin board structured around topics and user comments, with each main branch being a broad topic that the user can then elaborate on as the branch lengthens.

confidentiality   The quality of protection against unauthorized access to private or secret information.

CONFIG.SYS   Abbreviation for **config**uration **sys**tem, an ASCII text file for DOS and OS/2 operating systems that contains commands.

configuration   (1) The assembly of machines that are interconnected and are programmed to operate as a system. (2) The layout or design of elements in a hardware or information processing system.

configuration file   A FILE that contains information on the way a system is set up.

configuration management   The task of accounting for, controlling, and reporting the planned and actual design of a product throughout its production and operational life.

configure   To assemble a selection of hardware or software into a system and to adjust each of the parts so that they all work together.

conic generator   A function generator capable of drawing any conic section, such as an ellipse, hyperbola, or parabola.

conic sections   In computer graphics, a curve formed by the intersection of a plane and a right circular cone. Depending on where the plane cuts through, the conic section may be a circle, ellipse, parabola, or hyperbola.

connecting cable   The cable used to transfer electrical impulses between two pieces of equipment.

connectivity   **(1)** The ability to connect computers together. **(2)** A computer's or program's ability to link with other programs and devices.

connect node   In COMPUTER-AIDED DESIGN, an attachment point for lines or text.

connector   **(1)** A coupling device that provides an electrical and/or mechanical junction between two cables, or between a cable and a chassis or enclosure. **(2)** A device that provides rapid connection and disconnection of electrical cable and wire terminations.

connector symbol   A flowcharting symbol used to represent a junction in a line of flow. A small circle, possibly containing an identifier, connects broken paths in the line of flow on the same page. A pentagonal shape connects the flow on different pages of the same flowchart.

connect time   In time-sharing, the length of time a user is "on" the computer; the duration of the telephone connection. Usually measured by the duration between sign-on and sign-off.

consecutive   Pertaining to the occurrence of two sequential events without the intervention of any other such event.

consistency check   A check to ensure that specific input data fall within a predetermined set of criteria; a control method wherein like data items are checked for consistency of value and form.

console   That part of a computer system that enables human operators to communicate with the system.

console display A display at a system console on which an operator can use all control commands and display, reply, and send messages.

console operator Same as COMPUTER OPERATOR.

consortium A joint venture to support a complete computer facility to be used in an emergency.

constant A value that does not change during the execution of the program. Also called literal.

constraint Any condition that limits the solutions to a problem.

constructor In OBJECT-ORIENTED PROGRAMMING, an operation that creates an object and/or initializes its state.

consultant An expert in the use of computers in specific applications environments such as business data processing, education, military systems, or health care. Often helps to analyze and solve a specific problem.

container class In OBJECT-ORIENTED PROGRAMMING, a class whose instances are collections of other objects.

content-addressable memory Same as ASSOCIATIVE STORAGE.

contention A condition on a multipoint communications channel when two or more locations try to transmit at the same time. Also occurs when two CPUs attempt to control the same device at once.

contention system A system in which one or more stations compete for use of a line.

contents directory A series of queues that indicate the routines in a given region of internal storage.

context sensitivity A software feature that allows a user to access information about the application or command currently in use.

context switching The immediate activation of a program loaded into RAM.

contiguous Adjacent or adjoining.

contiguous data structure See SEQUENTIAL DATA STRUCTURE.

contiguous graphics Diagrams with certain characters that touch each other.

contingency plan In COMPUTER SECURITY, a plan for emergency response, backup procedures, and post-disaster recovery.

continuity check A check to verify that an electrical path exists.

continuous forms Fanfold paper or roll paper that has small holes on the outer edges for automatic feeding into printers. Can be blank sheets or preprinted forms such as checks, invoices, or tax forms.

continuous forms attachment A device that feeds continuous forms into a paper carrier.

continuous line A drawing produced without removing the drawing tool from the drawing surface until the image is complete.

continuous processing The input of transactions into a system in the order in which they occur and as soon after they occur as possible.

continuous scrolling Moving text, line by line, forward or backward, through a window.

continuous shading A smoothly varying shaded surface.

continuous tone Any photograph or artwork that is not yet screened for printing.

continuous-tone image A color or black-and-white image formed of combinations of separate areas made up of different color tones or gray tones.

contour (1) A single closed-loop boundary that encloses an area, as a contour on a map, which represents an area of equal elevation. (2) The outer limit of an object. (3) An outline.

contour characters Letters having a continuous, even-weight line drawn around the outside of the character but not touching it.

contour drawing   A line drawing using one continuing line or as few lines as possible.

contouring   (**1**) In computer graphics, the creation of the outline of a body, mass, or figure. For example, in a CAD model, the representation of the surface of an object—its bumps and crannies. (**2**) In image processing, the loss of detail that occurs in a shaded image when too few gradations of gray are used to reproduce a graphic such as a photograph.

contour map   A map that describes geographic terrain in the form of closed contours that define a three-dimensional path in space at a constant height.

contrast   In OPTICAL CHARACTER RECOGNITION, the differences on a document between color or shading of the printed material and the background on which it is printed.

contrast enhancement   The improvement of light-to-dark distinctions. A real digitizing process typically involves some kind of nonlinear detector that destroys the light-to-dark relationships of the object scanned. Correct contrast can be reintroduced if the characteristics of the detector are known. Contrast can even be heightened if desired.

control   The function of performing required operations when certain specific conditions occur or when interpreting and acting upon instructions. See CONTROL SECTION and CONTROL UNIT.

control ball   Same as TRACKBALL.

control block   A storage area through which a particular type of information required for control of the operating system is communicated among its parts.

control break   The point during program processing at which a special event takes place, based upon change in value of a control field.

control break reporting   A term that refers to "breaks" in the normal flow of information that periodically occur in a computer report for subtotals and totals.

control bus   In a computer, the path linking the CPU's control register to memory.

control character   A character whose occurrence in a particular context initiates, modifies, or stops a control operation.

control circuits   The electrical circuits within a computer that interpret the program instructions and cause the appropriate operations to be performed.

control clerk   The person who has responsibility for performing duties associated with the control over data processing operations.

control console   That part of a MAINFRAME system used for communication between the console operator or service engineer and the computer.

control data   One or more items of data used as a control to identify, select, execute, or modify another routine, record, file, operation, or data value.

Control Data Corporation (CDC)   One of the first major manufacturers of computer equipment. It was founded in 1957 by William Norris. CDC's first computer was the CDC 1604, introduced in 1957. Since then, CDC has produced many mainframes including several supercomputers. CDC is also the developer of the computer-based education system PLATO.

control field   The field in a data record used to identify and classify the record. Same as KEY.

control key   A special-function key on a computer keyboard. Used simultaneously with another key to enter a command instructing the system to perform a task.

control language   The set of all commands with which a user requests functions.

controlled variable   A variable that takes on a specific set of values in an iterative structure in a programming language.

controller   The electronic board or unit that regulates the operation of a peripheral device. There are disk controllers, printer controllers, tape controllers, and so on. The controller takes the general commands from the computer system, converts them into the actual signals for controlling the device, and brings the data and status signals from the device into the computer in the appropriate form.

control lever   Same as JOYSTICK.

control logic   The order in which processing functions are carried out by a computer.

control panel   That part of a computer control console that contains manual controls.

control points   The points that control the shape of a curve or curved surface.

control program   The operating system program responsible for the overall management of the computer and its resources.

controls   The methods and procedures for ensuring the accuracy, integrity, security, reliability, and completeness of data or processing techniques.

control section   That part of the central processing unit responsible for directing the operation of the computer in accordance with the instructions in the program.

control sequence   The normal order of selection of instructions by a computer wherein it follows one instruction order at a time.

control signal   A computer-generated signal for automatic control of machines and processes.

control statement   An operation that terminates the sequential execution of instructions by transferring control to a statement elsewhere in the program.

control station   The network station that supervises control procedures such as addressing, polling, selecting, and recovery. Also responsible for establishing order on the line in the event of contention or any other abnormal situation.

control structure   Same as INFERENCE ENGINE.

control structures   The facilities of a programming language that specify a departure from the normal sequential execution of statements.

control terminal   A terminal at which the user is authorized to enter commands affecting system operation.

control total   The accumulation of numeric data fields that are used to check on the accuracy of the input, processed data, or output data.

control unit   That portion of the central processing unit that directs the step-by-step operation of the entire computing system.

control words   A series of reserved character sequences that have a special meaning to the program that reads them.

convention   Standard and accepted procedures in computer program development and the abbreviations, symbols, and their meanings as developed for particular programs and systems; any programming style rule providing consistency among different programs.

conversational   Pertaining to a program or system that carries on a dialogue with a terminal user, alternately accepting input and then responding to the input quickly enough for the user to maintain his or her train of thought.

conversational interaction   Interaction with a computer that takes the form of a dialogue between the user and the machine.

conversational language   A programming language that uses a near-English character set that facilitates communication between the user and the computer. BASIC is a conversational language.

conversational mode   A mode of operation that implies a dialogue between a computer and its user in which the computer program examines the input supplied by the user and formulates questions or comments that are directed back to the user.

conversational system   See INTERACTIVE SYSTEM.

conversion   (1) The process of changing information from one form of representation to another, such as from the language of one type of computer to that of another or from a scanned image to magnetic disk. **(2)** The process of changing from one data processing method to another or from one type of equipment to another. **(3)** The process of changing a number written in one base to the base of another numeral system.

conversion table   A table comparing numerals in two different numeral systems.

convert   **(1)** To change data from radix to radix. **(2)** To move data from one type of storage to another, such as from CD-ROM to FLOPPY DISK.

converter   **(1)** A device that converts data recorded on one medium to another medium, such as a unit that accepts data from MICR documents and records it on magnetic disks. **(2)** A device that converts data in one form into data in another form, such as from analog to digital.

convex   Pertaining to a region or shape, such as a polygon, for which a straight line segment between any two points of the region is entirely contained within the region. Contrast with CONCAVE.

convolutions   Filtering techniques used to sharpen or soften an image for purposes of image enhancement.

cookbook   A step-by-step book or manual that describes a program, a system, or some other topic.

cool   A term describing color images that have a bluish tint. Those with a reddish tint are referred to as "warm."

cooling fan   A small fan that keeps circuit boards and ICs cool.

coordinate dimensioning   In computer graphics, a dimensioning system in which a point is defined in terms of a specified dimension and direction from a reference point measured with respect to defined axes.

coordinate graph   A GRAPH in which two variable quantities (in two-dimensional graphs) or three variable quantities (in three-dimensional graphs) are plotted as a series of points along coordinate axes.

coordinate graphics   Computer graphics in which display images are generated from display commands and coordinate data.

coordinate indexing   (**1**) A system of indexing individual documents by descriptors of equal rank so that a library can be searched for a combination of one or more descriptors. (**2**) An indexing technique whereby the interrelationships of terms are shown by coupling individual words.

coordinate paper   The continuous-feed graph paper used for graphs or diagrams produced on a DIGITAL PLOTTER.

coordinate points   Points at which axes converge in a Cartesian coordinate system. Specific coordinates can be selected by referring to the numbered points along the axes of a particular coordinate system. For example, the coordinates (2,5) in a two-dimensional coordinate system denote a coordinate point that is two points to the right of the origin along the X-axis and five points up the Y-axis. The coordinates (4,5,6) in a three-dimensional coordinate system denote a point that is four points along X, five points along Y, and six points along Z.

coordinates   (**1**) An ordered set of absolute or relative data values that specify a location in a Cartesian coordinate system. (**2**) In an electronic spreadsheet, the intersection of two numbers or letters that uniquely identify the column and row of a cell. (**3**) Any two numbers used to position the cursor, or pointer, on the screen.

coplanar   (**1**) A technique for building three-dimensional models from two-dimensional blueprints by using two coplanar views, a plan view and an elevation. (**2**) A term describing any two or more points, lines, line segments, or polygons that lie in the same plane.

coprocessor   A device that performs specialized processing in conjunction with the main microprocessor of a system. It works in tandem with another central processing unit to increase the computing power of a system. An extra microprocessor to handle some things faster than the main processor, such as a MATH COPROCESSOR or a GRAPHICS COPROCESSOR.

copy   (**1**) To reproduce data in a new location or other destination, leaving the source data unchanged, although the physical form of the result may differ from that of the source; for example, to make a duplicate of all the programs or data on a disk, or to copy a graphic screen image to a printer. **(2)** To reproduce text or a graphic image onto the clipboard.

copy buster   A program that is able to make copies of so-called copy-protected floppy disks.

copyfit   To get text to fit within the available area.

copy holder   A device used to hold papers so that the user can easily read them when typing on a keyboard. Its purpose is to reduce back, shoulder, neck, and eye strain.

copy program   **(1)** A program designed to duplicate one or more files to another disk. **(2)** A program that circumvents the copy-protection device on a computer program so that the software can be copied to another disk.

copy protection   The methods used by software developers to prevent any copying of their programs. To protect against illegal copying of software, many software developers build copy-protection routines into their programs. Copy-protection techniques are sometimes sophisticated, although several commercial programs exist that allow users to override many standard copy-protection techniques. Now that hard disks are common to many microcomputer systems, copy protection has been largely abolished.

copyright   The recognized ownership of creative work; protection against unauthorized use of the work.

copyright notice   A notification of copyright that is part of a computer program. It is often printed on the display screen at the start of the program, reminding the user that making copies for any purpose other than for backup is illegal.

copyrighted software   Software that costs money and must not be copied without permission from the software developer.

Corel Draw™   An illustrative graphics program that runs on WINDOWS. It has an advanced autotracing feature that quickly and easily builds a vector-based image from an entire bit-mapped black/white/gray scale, or color clip art, paint program, or scanned image file.

core storage A form of storage device that uses magnetic cores usually strung through wires in the form of an ARRAY; used in older computers.

corrective maintenance The activity of detecting, isolating, and correcting failures after they occur.

corrupted file A FILE with distorted data.

cost analysis A technique used to determine the overall costs of a given system and to compare them to cost factors estimated for a new design.

cost/benefit analysis A quantitative form of evaluation in which benefits are assessed and costs associated with achieving the benefits are determined.

cost-effectiveness The effectiveness of a system or an operation in terms of the relationship of the benefits received to the resources expended to attain them. A system in which the received benefits exceed the associated costs is considered to be cost-effective.

costing A method of assigning costs to a project, job, or function.

cottage key people People who work at home and transmit work to the company by telecommunications, diskettes, or other means.

count The successive increase or decrease of a cumulative total of the number of times an event occurs.

counter A device, such as a register or computer storage location, used to represent the number of occurrences of an event.

counting loop A program loop used to perform an action a fixed number of times.

coupling The interaction between systems or between properties of a system.

courier A monospaced typeface that resembles typewriter text. Commonly a built-in font on laser printers.

courseware   The name given to computer programs written especially for educational applications, such as teaching chemistry, history, mathematics, Spanish, or reading skills. See COMPUTER-ASSISTED INSTRUCTION.

cpi   Abbreviation for CHARACTERS PER INCH.

CPM   Acronym for CRITICAL PATH METHOD.

CP/M™   Abbreviation for Control Program for Microcomputers, an operating system for older microcomputer systems. Created by Gary Kildall of Digital Research, Inc., it was very popular in the early 1980s.

cps   Abbreviation for CHARACTERS PER SECOND.

CPU   Abbreviation for CENTRAL PROCESSING UNIT.

CR   Abbreviation for CARRIAGE RETURN.

cracker   A programmer who gains access to a system without authorization. See HACKER.

crash   A system shutdown caused by a hardware malfunction or a software mistake. When a computer fails to respond to any commands, it is said to have undergone a crash. This can be caused by human error, by incompatibility between the software and operating system, or even by static electricity.

crawl   A term describing the movement of text characters at an easily readable rate across the display screen, usually horizontally or vertically.

Cray   The brand name for a series of supercomputers manufactured by Cray Research, Inc.

Cray Research, Inc.   A manufacturer of supercomputers.

CRC   Abbreviation for CYCLIC REDUNDANCY CHECK, a method for checking for errors in transmitted data.

create   **(1)** To make a new file on a disk as opposed to modifying an existing file. **(2)** To define the fields for a database record, specifying field name, length, field type, and so on.

creative designer In DESKTOP PUBLISHING, the individual who lays out and designs a page.

credit An accounting term used in double-entry bookkeeping.

credit check Information from a credit bureau on the credit history of an individual.

creeping A type of scrolling in which text moves horizontally across the monitor in a manner similar to that of a news wire moving along the bottom of a television screen.

Cricket Draw An OBJECT-ORIENTED PostScript drawing program from Computer Associates International, Inc. The program offers extensive Bezier tools, object-to-Bezier path conversion, and comprehensive text manipulation.

Cricket Stylist A popular OBJECT-ORIENTED drawing program for the Apple Macintosh computer that allows the user to create drawings using the familiar line, rectangle, and oval tools.

crime, computer See COMPUTER CRIME.

critical path That path through a network that defines the shortest possible time in which the entire project can be completed.

critical path method (CPM) A management technique for control of large-scale, long-term projects involving the analysis and determination of each critical step necessary for project completion.

CROM Acronym for CONTROL ROM, an integral part of most CPU chips. Storage for the micro instructions that the CPU assembles into a sequence to form the complex macro instructions, such a Multiply or Branch-On-Negative Accumulator, available to the computer user.

crop To trim a graphics image for a better fit or to eliminate unwanted portions. In preparing an illustration for traditional printing, cropping is used to clean up a graphic for placement in a document.

crop marks Marks or indications on graphic images to be reproduced that give instructions on where to crop or cut.

cross-assembler   An assembler run on one computer for the purpose of translating instructions for a different computer.

cross-check   To check computing by two different methods.

cross-compiler   A compiler that runs on a machine other than the one for which it is designed to compile code.

cross-compiling/assembling   A technique involving the use of a mini-computer, mainframe, or time-sharing service to write and debug programs for subsequent use on microcomputers.

crossfade   Same as DISSOLVE.

cross-footing check   The process of cross-adding, or subtracting, and then zeroing-out the results.

cross-hair cursor   A digitizing device that is often moved over hard-copy images of maps and drawings to enter them into the computer system.

cross hairs   On an input device, two intersecting lines—one horizontal and one vertical—whose intersection marks the active cursor position of a graphics system.

crosshatching   In computer graphics, the shading of a portion of a drawing with a pattern of intersecting lines or figures repeated across the area being shaded. Crosshatching is one of several methods for filling in areas of a graphic.

cross-platform   Pertaining to applications that are operable with more than one operating system.

cross-reference dictionary   A printed listing that identifies all references of an assembled program to a specific label. In many systems, this listing is provided immediately after a source program has been assembled.

cross-section view   In computer graphics, a two-dimensional view that a user would see if he or she were to slice through an object and look at the area thus revealed. Three-dimensional construction can be shown using several cross-sectional views of the same object.

cross talk   The unwanted energy transferred from one circuit, called the disturbing circuit, to another circuit, called the disturbed circuit. Generally occurs when signals from one circuit emerge onto another circuit as interference.

crowbar A circuit that protects a computer system from dangerously high voltage surges.

CRT Abbreviation for CATHODE RAY TUBE, the picture tube of the standard computer display screen. A CRT display is built around a vacuum tube containing one or more electron guns whose electron beams rapidly sweep horizontally across the inside of the front surface of the tube, which is coated with a material that glows when irradiated.

CRT plot A computer-generated drawing or graph projected onto the screen of a CATHODE RAY TUBE.

CRT terminal **(1)** A visual display unit (VDU). **(2)** A display device with a keyboard used by an operator to communicate with a computer. As the operator types a message or text on the keyboard, the characters are displayed on the screen.

CRU Abbreviation for CUSTOMER REPLACEABLE UNIT.

crunch A nontechnical term used by computer people to refer to the computer's capacity to process numbers and perform routine arithmetic functions. Computers can process, or crunch, a lot of numbers quickly. See NUMBER CRUNCHING.

cryoelectronic storage A storage device consisting of materials that become superconductors at extremely low temperatures.

cryogenics The study and use of devices that utilize the properties assumed by materials at temperatures near absolute zero.

cryogenic storage A STORAGE DEVICE that uses the superconductive and magnetic properties of certain materials at temperatures near absolute zero.

cryosar A two-terminal semiconductor switching device that operates at very low temperatures.

cryotron   A current-controlled switching device based on superconductivity; used primarily in computer circuits.

cryptanalysis   The operation of converting encrypted messages to the corresponding plaintext without initial knowledge of the key employed in the encryption.

cryptographic system   In COMPUTER SECURITY, either a code system or a cipher system.

cryptographic techniques   Methods of concealing data by representing each character or group of characters by others.

cryptography   Any of various methods for writing in secret code or cipher. As society becomes increasingly dependent upon computers, the vast amounts of data communicated, processed, and stored within computer systems and networks often have to be protected, and cryptography is a means of achieving this protection. It is the only practical method for protecting information transmitted through accessible communications networks, such as telephone lines, satellites, or microwave systems.

cryptology   In COMPUTER SECURITY, the study of cryptanalysis and cryptography.

crystal   Quartz crystal that vibrates at a specific frequency when energy is supplied to it. These vibrations provide an accurate frequency by which to time the clock within a COMPUTER SYSTEM.

Crystal Paint   A drawing and graphics design tool for Apple Macintosh microcomputer. It can be used to produce intricate and ornate designs by repeating patterns.

CSG   Abbreviation for **c**onstructive **s**olid **g**eometry, one of the chief methods of solid modeling, using solid primitives and Boolean operators to construct complex solids.

CSMA   Abbreviation for **c**ARRIER-**s**ENSED **m**ULTIPLE-**a**CCESS, a protocol that controls access to a network's bus.

CSS   See CENTRAL STRUCTURE STORE.

CT   Abbreviation for **c**OMPUTED **t**OMOGRAPHY. See COMPUTERIZED AXIAL TO-MOGRAPHY.

CTRL   Abbreviation for CONTROL.

cube   A six-sided object in three-dimensional screen space.

cue   See CALL.

culling   The removal of unwanted representations in an image.

current   The flow of electrons through a conductor. Measured in amperes, where one ampere equals 6.25×10^{18} electrons per second.

current awareness system   A process whereby a user is notified periodically by a central file or library when selected items of information have been acquired.

current backup version   The latest backup copy of a data set, file, or computer program.

current cell   The cell currently available for use on a SPREADSHEET.

current document   A document that is being processed.

current drive   The disk drive currently being used by the COMPUTER SYSTEM.

current location counter   A counter kept by an assembler to determine the address that has been assigned to either an instruction or a constant being assembled.

current loop   A type of serial communication in which the presence or absence of an electrical signal indicates the state of the bit being transmitted.

current mode logic (CML)   A logic circuit that employs the characteristics of a differential amplifier circuit in its design.

current page box   In desktop publishing programs, an area that displays the current page being worked on.

current release   The latest available release of a software system or program.

cursive scanning   A scanning technique used with video display terminals in which the electrons being sent toward the screen are deflected to form the outlines of a picture one line at a time in the same way an artist might draw the same image.

cursor   (1) The moving, sliding, or blinking symbol on a CRT screen that indicates where the next character will appear. (2) The position indicator used on a video display terminal to indicate a character to be connected or a position in which data is to be entered. On graphic systems, it can take any shape (arrow, square, paintbrush, etc.) and is used to mark where the next graphic action is to take place.

cursor control   The ability to move a video display prompt character to any position on the screen.

cursor control keys   The keys that, when pressed, move the cursor in a designated direction. Cursor movement keys generally have directional arrows on their keytops.

cursor tracking   Positioning a cursor on a display screen by moving a stylus on a GRAPHICS TABLET connected to the computer.

curve fitting   A mathematical technique for finding a formula that best represents a collection of data points. Usually the formula is used to plot the best-fit line through the points.

curvilinear   Composed of curved lines.

custodian   The person or organization responsible for physical maintenance and safeguarding of data stored on disk packs, tape reels, diskettes, removable hard disks, and so forth. See LIBRARIAN.

customer engineer (CE)   A person who repairs or does preventive maintenance on a computer or on its input/output devices and other offline equipment. Also called field engineer.

custom IC   An INTEGRATED CIRCUIT (IC) manufactured to a specific customer's design and specification.

customize   To alter a piece of general-purpose software or hardware to enhance its performance, usually to fit a specific user's need.

customized form letters   Personalized form letters produced by word processing systems and special form-letter programs.

custom software   Programs prepared specifically for a business or organization and tailored to the business's needs.

cut   To remove text or graphics from a document. Compare PASTE.

CUT   A bitmap format used by DR. HALO and a few other graphics programs.

cut and paste   The method employed by some systems to move graphics and/or text from one location to another. Such systems usually permit the performance of other operations between the cut and the paste steps. Cut and paste enables compatible programs to share text and graphics.

cut form   A data-entry form, such as a utility bill, used by OCR devices.

cutout   (1) An image extracted from its original image for use in making up a third image. (2) An area deleted from a background image to allow for the printing of an overlay color.

cut plane   (1) A capability of graphics systems that enables the designer to define and intersect a plane with 2-D entities or 3-D objects in order to derive sectional location points. (2) A plane that intersects a 3-D object at a specific point, yielding a cross-section of the object.

cut-sheet feeder   A device that feeds sheets of paper to the printer one at a time. Usually a friction-feed device.

cutter path   A line described by the motion of a cutting tool controlled by a computer-aided manufacturing system.

cyan   The shade of blue frequently used on VDTS for color graphics.

Cyber™   The brand name for a line of mainframes and supercomputers manufactured by Control Data Corporation.

cybernetics   A branch of learning that seeks to integrate the theories and studies of communication and control in machines and living organisms.

cyberphobia   Fear of computers.

cycle   As related to computer storage, a periodic sequence of events occurring when information is transferred to or from the storage device of a computer; the time it takes to reference an address, remove the data, and be ready to select it again.

cycle sharing   The process by which a device uses machine cycles of another device or processing unit.

cycle stealing   The technique that allows a peripheral device temporarily to disable computer control of the I/O bus, thus allowing the device to access the computer's internal memory.

cycle time   (1) The minimum time interval between the starts of successive accesses to a storage location. (2) The time required to change the information in a set of registers.

cyclic overlays   The arrangement of a set of graphics objects that prevents their being prioritized in such a way that higher priority objects strictly occlude lower priority objects.

cyclic redundancy check (CRC)   An error-detection scheme often used in disk devices. When data are stored, a CRC value is computed and stored. Whenever it is reread, the CRC value is computed once again. If the two values are equal, the data is assumed to be error-free.

cyclic shift   A shift in which the digits dropped off at one end of a word are returned at the other in a circular fashion. If, for example, a register holds eight digits, 23456789, the result of the cyclic shift two columns to the left would be to change the contents of the register to 45678923.

cylinder   As related to magnetic disks, a vertical column of tracks on a magnetic disk pack; the corresponding tracks on each surface of a disk pack.

cylinder method   The method or concept that data on all tracks above and below the one currently being used are available by merely switching read/write heads. Allows access to large amounts of information with no extra movement of the access device.

cypher   A form of cryptography in which the plaintext is made unintelligible to anyone who intercepts it by a transformation of the information itself, based on a key.

— D —

DA   Abbreviation for **D**IRECT **A**CCESS.

D-A converter   See DIGITAL-TO-ANALOG CONVERTER.

daisy chain   A specific method of propagating signals along a bus that permits the assignment of device priorities based on the electrical position of the device along the bus.

daisy wheel printer   A printer that uses a metal or plastic disk with printed characters along its edge. The disk rotates until the required character is brought before a hammer that strikes it against a ribbon. It is a popular letter-quality printer used with personal computers.

damping   A characteristic built into electrical circuits and mechanical systems to prevent unwanted oscillatory conditions.

dark bulb   A type of cathode ray tube, almost black in appearance when turned off, that gives good contrast to video displays.

darkness   Intensity, especially low intensity or limited brightness.

DASD   Abbreviation for **D**IRECT **A**CCESS **S**TORAGE **D**EVICE.

dash pattern   The sequence of dots or line segments and spaces that make up a dashed line (--------------------).

DAT   Acronym for **D**YNAMIC **A**DDRESS **T**RANSLATION.

data   The formalized representation of facts or concepts suitable for communication, interpretation, or processing by people or by automatic means. The raw material of information; individual pieces of quantitative information, such as dollar sales of carpets, numbers of building permits issued, or units of raw material on hand. Historically, data is a plural noun while datum is singular—a distinction now generally ignored in data processing terminology.

data access   Fetching DATA from a device either sequentially or directly.

data acquisition   The retrieval of data from remote sites initiated by a central computer system; the collection of data from external sensors.

data administration   Performing the functions of specifying, acquiring, providing, and maintaining the data of an organization.

data administrator   See DATABASE ADMINISTRATOR.

data aggregate   Any collection of data items within a record that is given a name and referred to as a whole, such as an array.

data bank   **(1)** A comprehensive collection of libraries of data. **(2)** Loosely, a database.

data base   See DATABASE.

database   Most generally, any clearly identified collection of data, such as a telephone book or the card catalog at a library. In theory, a database should contain all its information in one central store or file, each record in the file containing roughly the same type of information, such as name, address, city, state, zip code, area code, and telephone number. Each of these categories is called a field, while a record consists of a set of fields pertaining to one person or item. The database file is made up of a number of related RECORDS. Some people differentiate between a data base (two words), meaning an underlying collection of data in the real world, and a database (single word), a coherent collection of data entered into a computer system. As applied to data in the computer, it particularly means data organized so that various programs can access and update the information.

database administrator   The person responsible for the creation of the information system database and, once it is established, for maintaining its security and developing procedures for its recovery from disaster.

database analyst   The key person in the analysis, design, and implementation of data structures in a database environment.

database environment   That environment resulting from the integration of users, data, and systems by implementing the database.

database management   The systematic approach to storing, updating, and retrieving of data items, usually in the form of records in a file, by which many users, or even many remote installations, will use common databases.

database management system (DBMS)   A collection of hardware and software that organizes and provides access to a database. The computer program manages data, providing the mechanisms needed to create a computerized database file, to add data to the file, to alter data in the file, to organize data within the file, to search for data in the file, and so forth. Popular database management programs are DBASEIII and PARADOX.

database manager   A program that allows the user to enter, organize, sort, and retrieve information.

database server   An intelligent way of storing database files. The server can sort and manipulate data prior to sending to a node.

database specialist   A person who works with databases.

data bus   A bus system that interconnects the CPU, storage, and all the input/output devices of a computer system for the purpose of exchanging data.

data byte   An eight-bit binary number representing one character of data the computer will use in an arithmetic or logical operation, or store in memory.

data capturing   Gathering or collecting information for computer handling, the first step in job processing; also called DATA COLLECTION.

data cassette   A CASSETTE TAPE that stores data in binary form.

data catalog   An organized listing by full name of all data elements used by an organization.

data center   The department that houses computer systems, related equipment, and data files.

data chaining   The process of linking data items together, with each data item containing the location of the next.

data channel   The communications link between two devices or points.

data clerk   A person who does clerical jobs in a computer installation.

data collection   (1) The gathering of source data to be entered into a data processing system. Also called DATA CAPTURING. (2) The act of bringing data from one or more points to a central point.

data command   A command that consists of a period followed by letters. Used in some older types of word processing programs for embedded commands.

data communications   (1) The movement of encoded information by means of electrical transmission systems. (2) The entire process and science of enabling digital devices, such as computers, to communicate with each other.

data communications equipment   The equipment associated with the transmission of data from one device to another. Examples are MODEMS, REMOTE TERMINALS, and COMMUNICATIONS PROCESSORS.

data communications system   A system consisting of COMPUTERS, TERMINALS, and COMMUNICATIONS LINKS.

data compatibility   The ability of two or more computers to read from and write to each other's data disks or use each other's data files, even if they cannot run the same programs.

data compression   A technique that saves computer storage space by eliminating empty fields, gap redundancies, or unnecessary data to reduce the size or the length of records.

data concentration   (1) The collection of data at an intermediate point from several low- and medium-speed lines for retransmission across high-speed lines. (2) The addition of one item at the end of others to produce one longer data item.

data control section   An organization or group responsible for meeting quality control standards for processing and for collecting input from, and delivering output to, computer users.

data conversion   The process of changing the form of data representation.

data definition   In programming, a statement that gives the size, the type, and often the content of a field or record; that portion of a program that identifies the data to be used in analysis.

data definition language (DDL)   The language used by a DATABASE ADMINISTRATOR to create, store, and manage data in a database environment. Also called data description language.

data dependence   The interdependence of software and data storage.

data description language (DDL)   The language that specifies the manner in which data are to be stored and managed in a database environment by a DATABASE MANAGEMENT SYSTEM. Also called data definition language.

data dictionary   A list of all the files, fields, and variables used in a database management system. A data dictionary helps users remember what items they have to work with and how these have been defined. It is particularly helpful when writing a large number of linked procedures or programs that share a database.

data diddling   The technique whereby data is modified before it goes into a computer file where it is less accessible.

data directory   An ordered collection of data element names and/or identifiers and their attributes that provides the location of the elements.

data directory/dictionary   An ordered collection of data elements that combines the features of a data catalog, data dictionary, and data directory. Describes and locates each DATA ELEMENT.

data division   The third of four main parts of a COBOL program.

data editing   A procedure to check for irregularities in input data. Typical checks are a range check, reasonableness check, and checks to determine whether data is properly alphabetic or numeric, as required.

data element   The combination of one or more data items that forms a unit or piece of information, such as the social security number in an employee/payroll database.

data encryption A coding technique used to secure sensitive data by mixing or jumbling the data according to a predetermined format.

data encryption standard The standardized public key by which senders and receivers can scramble and unscramble their messages.

data entry (1) The process of converting data into a form suitable for entry into a computer system, such as by keying from a terminal onto magnetic disk or tape. (2) The process of entering data directly into a computer system.

data entry device The equipment used to prepare data so the computer can accept it.

data entry operator A person who uses a keyboard device to transcribe data into a form suitable for processing by a computer. Often the member of a computer operations staff who is responsible for keying data into a computer system.

data entry screen A set of requests to the user for data that are displayed on a display screen.

data entry specialist A person responsible for inputting information into the computer for processing.

data export The capacity to transport (write) information from one database in a form that can be used (read) by another program, such as a word processor for form letters and reports, a spreadsheet, or a different database. Opposite of DATA IMPORT.

data field (1) One column or consecutive columns on a coding form or punched card used to record a particular piece of data. (2) Part of a data record.

data field masking Using special characters to offset or divide data fields. For date fields, the slash or hyphen characters are often used to divide the month, day, and year, as in 09/23/95. For telephone numbers, the parentheses and hyphen characters may be needed, as in (999) 999-9999. Similar types of characters may be used for part numbers or in other fields where such offsets improve the readability of character strings. These masks can be inserted by the computer, so that an operator does not have to enter the hyphen or other character manually. Only the numbers 092391 are entered in the above data field example, with the slashes inserted automatically by the computer program. This feature greatly simplifies data entry and ensures standardization. Some programs routinely mask such fields as date and telephone number.

data file   A collection of related data records that have been organized in a specific manner. Also called text file.

data file processing   The updating of data files by adding, changing, or deleting records to reflect the effects of current data.

dataflow   A generic term that pertains to algorithms or machines whose actions are determined by the availability of the data needed for these actions.

dataflow analysis   The study of the movement of data among processing activities.

dataflow diagram   A graphic systems analysis and design tool that enables a systems analyst to represent the flow of data through a system.

data gathering   The task of collecting data from internal and/or external sources.

Data General Corporation (DGC)   A computer manufacturer founded in 1968 by Edson de Castro. In 1969, the company introduced the Nova, an advanced minicomputer. During its early years, the company was successful in marketing its minicomputers in university, scientific, and OEM markets. Over the years, DGC has developed a variety of minicomputer systems.

data import   The ability to use (read) information developed with another program that is particularly important in the use of integrated software, where several programs will use the information gathered or produced by one program.

data independence The status of a database system with storage structure and accessing strategy that can be changed without significantly affecting the application.

data integrity A performance measure based on the rate of undetected errors.

data interchange format (DIF) The standard among software developers that allows data from one program to be accessible to another program.

data item (1) An item of data used to represent a single value. (2) The smallest unit of named data.

data leakage The illegal removal of data from a computer facility.

data librarian The person who maintains custody and control of disks, tapes, and procedures manuals by cataloging and monitoring the use of these data resources.

data link Equipment that permits the transmission of information in data format.

data logging The recording of data about events that occur in time sequence.

data management (1) A general term that collectively describes those functions of a system that provide access to hardware, enforce data storage conventions, and regulate the use of input/output devices. (2) A major function of operating systems that involves organizing, cataloging, locating, retrieving, storing, and maintaining data.

data management system (1) A system that provides the necessary procedures and programs to collect, organize, and maintain the data required by information systems. (2) A system that assigns the responsibility for data input and integrity to establish and maintain the databases within an organization.

data manipulation   The process of using language commands to add, delete, modify, or retrieve data in a file or database.

data manipulation language (DML)   A language that allows a user to interrogate and access the database of a computer system by using English-like statements.

data medium   The material in or on which a specific physical variable may represent data, such as MAGNETIC DISK or CD-ROM.

data model   A formal language for describing data structures and operations on those structures. Usually divided into a data description language and a data manipulating language.

data movement time   The time taken to transfer data to or from a disk once the read/write head is properly positioned on a disk track.

data name   The name of the variable used to indicate a data value, such as *pi* for 3.14159 ....

data origination   The translation of information from its original form into machine-sensible form.

data packet   A means of transmitting serial data in an efficient package that includes an error-checking sequence.

data point   A numeric value for charting purposes. In a simple line chart, time may be plotted across the X-axis and another value against the Y-axis, the intersection being a data point.

data preparation   The process of organizing information and storing it in a form that can be input to the computer.

data preparation device   A device that permits data capture in which the source data is collected and transformed into a medium or form capable of being read into a computer.

Datapro   A research/publishing company that provides in-depth information about computer hardware and software products.

data processing   **(1)** One or more operations performed on data to achieve a desired objective. **(2)** All functions of a computer center.

(3) Operations performed by data processing equipment. **(4)** Operations performed on data to provide useful information to users.

data processing area   The group of computer professionals within an information systems department who are charged with building transaction processing systems.

data processing center   A computer center equipped with devices capable of receiving information, processing it according to human-made instructions, and producing the computed results. Same as information processing center.

data processing curriculum   A course of study, normally offered by a business school or college, that prepares students for entry-level jobs as applications programmers or systems analysts.

data processing cycle   The combined functions of input, processing, and output.

data processing director   The person in charge of developing and/or implementing the overall plan for transaction processing in an organization and for overseeing the activities of programmers, systems analysts, and operations personnel.

data processing management   Management of the data processing function, its people, and its equipment. Since this activity follows the well-recognized principles of planning, control, and operation, its basic prerequisites are the same skills that are needed to manage any other enterprise.

Data Processing Management Association (DPMA)   The largest professional association in the field of computer management. Its purpose is to engage in education and research activities focused on the development of effective programs for the self-improvement of its worldwide membership. The association seeks to encourage high standards of competence, promotes a professional attitude among its members, and sponsors high school clubs and college chapters.

data processing manager   The person who runs the data processing center, usually including the operation of the computer. The biggest part of the manager's job is concerned with developing new systems and keeping them running.

data processing system　The network of data processing hardware, software, people, and procedures capable of accepting information, processing it according to a plan, and producing the desired results.

data processing technology　The science of information handling.

data processor　Any device capable of performing operations on data, such as a desk calculator or a PERSONAL COMPUTER.

data protection　Any measure to safeguard data from undesired occurrences that intentionally or unintentionally lead to destruction, modification, or disclosure of data.

data rate　The rate at which a channel carries data, measured in bauds (bits per second; see BAUD RATE).

data record　A collection of data fields pertaining to a particular subject. Part of a DATA FILE.

data reduction　The process of transforming raw data into useful, condensed, or simplified intelligence. Often adjusting, scaling, smoothing, compacting, editing, and ordering operations are used.

data redundancy　The repetition of data on multiple databases.

data scope　A special display device that monitors a data communications channel and displays the content of the information being transmitted over it.

data security　The protection of data from accidental or malicious destruction, disclosure, or modification.

data set　**(1)** A device that permits transmission of data over communications lines by changing the form of the data at one end so that it can be carried over the lines; another data set at the other end changes the data back to its original form so that it is acceptable to the computer or other machine. See MODEM. **(2)** A collection of related data items, especially a grouping of related records, called a FILE.

data sharing The ability of computer processes or of computer users at several nodes to access data at a single node.

data sink A memory or recording device capable of accepting signals from a data transmission device and storing data for future use.

data source A device capable of originating signals for a DATA TRANSMISSION device.

data storage techniques Methods used by a PROGRAM to store data files.

data stream Serial data transmitted through a channel from a single input/output operation.

data structure The structure of relationships among files in a database and among data items within each file.

data switch box A device that allows users to connect multiple peripherals to one computer or multiple computers to one peripheral.

data tablet A manual INPUT DEVICE for graphic display consoles.

data terminal The point in a computer system or data communications network at which data can be entered or retrieved.

data transfer operations The operations that move data, whether externally through data communications or within main computer storage, by copying from one location to another.

data transfer rate The rate of transfer of data from one place to another, such as from computer main memory to disk or from one computer's memory to that of another.

data transmission The sending of data from one part of a system to another part. See DATA COMMUNICATIONS.

data type The interpretation applied to a string of bits, such as integer, real, or character.

data validation The measures taken to ensure that data fields conform to desired specifications. Fields may be checked for inappropriate characters or for deviation from specified lengths or values. See EDIT.

data value   Any string of symbols that serves as the representative of some item of information.

data word   An ordered set of characters, usually of a preset number, that is stored and transferred by the computer's circuits as a fundamental unit of information.

data word size   The specific length of data word that a particular computer is designed to handle.

datum   A unit of information, such as a COMPUTER WORD.

daughter board   A small circuit board that adds capability to another circuit board (motherboard).

DBA   See DATABASE ADMINISTRATOR.

dBASE™   A relational database management system for IBM-compatible microcomputer systems from Ashton-Tate Corporation. It was the first comprehensive database system for personal computers. Created by Wayne Ratliff to manage a company football pool, it was renamed dBASE II after George Tate and Hal Lashley formed Ashton-Tate Corporation to market it.

dBASE III   A relational database management package that can open (access) more than one file at a time as opposed to a file manager that can open only one file at a time. With its built-in command-processing language, the relational capabilities let the user create complex databases and reports, along with screens that ask questions when input is needed. This enables experienced programmers to set up systems for use by less-experienced users.

dBASE IV   A relational database management system.

DB-9 connector   A plug with either nine pins (male) or nine slots (female).

DB-25 connector   A plug with either 25 pins (male) or 25 slots (female). Most commonly used with an RS-232C interface connection.

DB2 A mainframe-based relational database management system from IBM Corporation.

DBS Abbreviation for **d**irect **b**roadcast **s**atellite.

DC Abbreviation for **(1)** DATA CONVERSION, **(2)** DESIGN CHANGE, **(3)** DIGITAL COMPUTER, **(4)** DIRECT CURRENT, **(5)** DIRECT CYCLE, **(6)** DISPLAY CONSOLE.

DCE Abbreviation for **d**ata **c**ircuit terminating **e**quipment, the name used by the RS-232 standard for modems and other devices that connect terminals or computers to communication lines.

DCTL Abbreviation for **D**irect **C**oupled **T**ransistor **L**ogic.

DDD Abbreviation for DIRECT DISTANCE DIALING, the facility used for making long-distance telephone calls without the assistance of a telephone operator.

DDL The language for declaring data structures in a DATABASE. See DATA DEFINITION LANGUAGE and DATA DESCRIPTION LANGUAGE.

DDP Abbreviation for **d**istributed **d**ata **p**rocessing.

dead halt A halt situation in which the system cannot return to the point at which it halted.

dead letter box In message switching systems, a file capturing undeliverable messages.

deadlock The condition in which each of two programs needs resources held captive by the other, and neither is willing to release the resource it is holding until it gets the one the other is holding.

deallocation The release of a resource by a program when the program no longer needs it. Opposite of ALLOCATION.

debit An accounting term used in double-entry bookkeeping.

deblocking Extracting a logical record from a block or group of logical records.

debounce To prevent spurious closures of a key or switch from being recognized. One method is to introduce time delays that give the switch contacts time to settle down.

debug   To detect, locate, and remove all mistakes in a computer program and any malfunctions in the computing system itself.

debugging aids   The computer routines—such as a tracing routine, snapshot dump, and post-mortem dump—that are helpful in debugging programs.

debugging process   The process of tracking down and correcting execution errors in a program.

DEC   Abbreviation for DIGITAL EQUIPMENT CORPORATION, a large manufacturer of MINICOMPUTER systems.

decatenate   To separate into two or more paths. Contrast with CONCATENATE.

deceleration time   The time required to stop a magnetic tape after reading or recording the last piece of data from a record on that tape.

decentralized computer system   A system in which the computer and some storage devices are in one location, but the devices that access the computer are elsewhere.

decimal   (1) A characteristic or property involving a selection, condition, or choice in which there are ten possibilities. (2) Pertaining to the number system with a radix of 10. (3) A decimal point.

decimal code   A form of notation by which each decimal digit is expressed separately in some other number system.

decimal digit   A numeral in the decimal numeral system. The radix of the decimal system is 10, and the following symbols are used: 0, 1, 2, 3, 4, 5, 6, 7, 8, and 9.

decimal point   The radix point in a mixed decimal numeral, separating the fractional part from the integer part. In the decimal numeral 741.12, the decimal point is between the two ones.

decimal system   A base-10 positional numeration system.

decimal-to-binary conversion The process of converting a numeral written in base 10 to the equivalent numeral written in base 2.

decimal-to-hexadecimal conversion The process of converting a numeral written in base 10 to the equivalent numeral written in base 16.

decimal-to-octal conversion The process of converting a numeral written in base 10 to the equivalent numeral written in base 8.

decision A computer operation of determining whether a certain relationship exists between data storage or registers and of taking alternative courses of action. Determination of future action.

decision block One or more program statements that handle the choice between alternative program sections based on whether a condition is true or false.

decision instruction An instruction that affects the selection of a branch of a program.

decision structure Same as SELECTION STRUCTURE.

decision support graphics BUSINESS GRAPHICS that aid senior business managers in making financial and marketing decisions based on information contained in them.

decision support system (DSS) A system that provides tools and capabilities to managers to enable them to satisfy their own information needs.

decision symbol A diamond-shaped flowcharting symbol used to indicate a choice or a branching in the formation processing path.

decision table A table listing all contingencies to be considered in the description of a problem, with corresponding actions to be taken. Sometimes used instead of flowcharts to describe operations of a program.

decision theory A broad spectrum of concepts and techniques that have been developed both to describe and to rationalize the process of making a choice among several possible alternatives.

decision tree The pictorial representation of the alternatives in any situation.

declaration statement The part of a computer program that defines the nature of other elements of the program or reserves parts of the hardware for special use.

declarative language A programming language that frees the programmer from specifying the exact procedure the computer needs to follow to accomplish a task. Instead, the user informs the program what he or she wants to accomplish.

decluttering Selective erasure of display items.

DECnet A networking architecture that links Digital Equipment Corporation systems, from large minicomputers to workstations, and is based on Ethernet hardware.

decode To translate or determine the meaning of coded information. Reverse of ENCODE.

decoder (1) A device that decodes. (2) A matrix of switching elements that selects one or more output channels according to the combination of input signals present.

decollate To arrange copies of continuous forms in sets and remove the carbon paper from them.

decollator A device that automatically removes carbon interleaves from continuous, fanfold paper.

decrement The amount by which a value or variable is decreased. Contrast with INCREMENT.

decryption The process of taking an encrypted message and reconstructing from it the original meaningful message, or plaintext. Opposite of ENCRYPTION.

DECUS Acronym for the DIGITAL EQUIPMENT COMPUTER (DEC) USERS SOCIETY, a user group whose objective is the exchange and dissemination of ideas and information pertinent to DEC computers.

dedicated Pertaining to programs, machines, or procedures that are designed or reserved for special use.

dedicated chip A chip that performs one task only, such as a memory chip.

dedicated computer A computer whose use is reserved for a particular task. Compare SPECIAL-PURPOSE COMPUTER.

dedicated device A device designed to perform only certain functions that cannot be programmed to perform other functions.

dedicated lines Telephone lines leased for exclusive use by a group or individual for telecommunications. Users pay a set fee for leased lines rather than the per-call or per-minute charges for switched lines.

dedicated system A computer-based device with one primary function, such as word processing. Usually easier to use for its intended task than for any other. General-purpose systems are usually more flexible.

deep In computer graphics, having high color saturation and low color value.

de facto standard A programming language, product, design, or program that has become so widely used and imitated that it has little competition but whose status has not officially been declared by a recognized standard-establishing organization.

default An assumption made by a system or language translator when no specific choice is given by the program or the user; a choice that has been preset. The user can override it or simply accept the setting that the manufacturer or developer has deemed most likely appropriate.

default answer The answer to a prompt that will be accepted if the user presses the Enter key without entering any information.

default drive The disk drive assigned by a system when no drive number is specified by the user.

default format A preset format that is automatically implemented unless the user specifies otherwise.

default settings The settings automatically used by a program unless the user specifies otherwise.

default value A value assumed when no value has been specified.

deferred address An indirect ADDRESS.

deferred entry Entry into a subroutine that occurs as a result of a deferred exit from the program that passed control to it.

deferred exit The passing of control to a subroutine at a time determined by an asynchronous event rather than at a predictable time.

deformation In COMPUTER ANIMATION, changes in the geometry of an object to give the illusion of creating action.

defragmentation A process in which all the files on a hard disk are rewritten so that all parts of each file are written to contiguous sectors.

DEGAS A color paint program for the Atari ST microcomputer developed by programmer Tom Hudson.

degausser A device used to erase information from magnetically recorded media such as a FLOPPY DISK or MAGNETIC TAPE.

degradation A condition in which a system continues to operate but at a reduced level of service. Unavailability of proper equipment maintenance and computer programs not maintained to accommodate current needs are the two most common causes.

deinstall To remove a program or hardware device from active service.

dejagging A computer graphics technique for drawing smooth lines, characters, and polygons.

de jure standard A standard that exists in the marketplace due to its adoption by standard-approving bodies such as the American National Standards Institute (ANSI) and ISO.

delay circuit An electronic circuit that deliberately delays the delivery of a signal for a present interval.

delayed conference A form of teleconferencing in which each participant's comments are stored sequentially as they are entered; the responses to comments may be recorded over a long period of time.

delay line storage A storage device that consists of a delay line and a means for regenerating and reinserting information into that line. Used in early computers.

delete **(1)** To remove or eliminate, as to erase data from a field or to eliminate a record from a file. **(2)** A method of erasing data.

deletion record A new record that will replace or remove an existing record of a master file.

delimit To fix the limits of something, such as to establish maximum and minimum limits of a specific variable.

delimiter A special character, often a comma or space, used to separate variable names or items in a list or to separate one string of characters from another, as in the separation of data items.

delivery The final step in the program development cycle where the program or system is given to the users for execution against actual data.

Dell Computer Corporation A manufacturer of IBM-compatible microcomputers that was founded in 1984 by Michael Dell in Austin, Texas. Dell provides a complete line of microcomputers from laptops to high-end machines.

Deluxe Paint™ A popular paint program for Commodore Amiga and IBM-compatible microcomputers.

demagnetization The process of erasing information stored on magnetic disks or tapes. See DEGAUSSER.

demand paging In virtual storage systems, the transfer of a page from external page storage to real storage at the time it is needed for execution.

demand report A report produced only upon request and used in strategic decision-making to provide responses to unanticipated queries.

demo A demonstration program designed to emulate some of the functions of an application program for advertising and marketing purposes.

democratic team   A software development team structure in which team members share responsibility.

demodulation   In data communications, the process of retrieving an original signal from a modulated carrier wave; used in data sets to make communications signals compatible with computer terminal signals. Counterpart to MODULATION.

demodulator   A device that receives signals transmitted over a communications link and converts them into electrical pulses, or bits, that can serve as inputs to a data processing machine. Contrast with MODULATOR.

demon   (1) In OBJECT-ORIENTED PROGRAMMING, an active object. (2) A section of a computer program or a complete program that waits until an event occurs before running.

demonstration disk   A diskette provided with personal computer software that demonstrates the use of that software.

demount   To remove a magnetic storage medium from a device that reads or writes on it, such as to remove a disk pack from the disk drive.

demultiplexer   A circuit that applies the logic state of a single input to one of several outputs. Contrast with MULTIPLEXER.

dense binary code   A code in which all possible states of the binary pattern are used.

dense list   See SEQUENTIAL LIST.

density   The number of characters that can be stored in a given physical space; measures how close together data are recorded on a magnetic medium, usually in bytes per inch. As recording density increases, the capacity of a storage device increases. See DOUBLE DENSITY.

dependency   A relationship where the execution of one job has to be completed before another can begin.

dependent variable   The output of a model, so called because it depends on the inputs.

depth buffer   See Z-BUFFER.

depth clipping Clipping at the back clipping plane when this plane cuts through the object being displayed.

depth queuing A technique, such as shading, used to enhance the three-dimensional appearance of a two-dimensional object.

deque A **d**ouble-**e**nded **que**ue that allows insertions and deletions at both ends of a list.

DES Abbreviation for **d**ata **e**ncryption **s**tandard, a standard method of coding information into ciphertext.

descender The portion of lowercase letters (g, j, p, q, and y) that extends below the baseline of other characters.

descender line In DESKTOP PUBLISHING, a hypothetical line that connects the bottoms of descender letters.

descending order An order that ranges from highest to lowest in numeric value or alphabetically. Contrast with ASCENDING ORDER.

descriptive art Art that is realistic or representative of actual things.

descriptor A significant word that helps to categorize or index information; sometimes called a KEYWORD.

design (1) A comprehensive scheme, plan, or conception. (2) The process of planning a program or system.

design aids Computer programs or hardware elements intended to assist in implementing a computer system. See DEBUGGING AIDS and PROGRAMMING AIDS.

design automation The use of computers in the design and production of circuit packages, new computers, and other electronic equipment.

design costs The costs associated with systems design, programming, training, conversion, testing, and documentation.

design cycle (1) In a hardware system, the complete cycle of development of equipment, which includes breadboarding, prototyping, testing, and production. (2) In a software system, the complete plan for producing an operational system, which includes problem description, algorithm development, flowcharting, coding, program debugging, and documentation. See PROGRAM DEVELOPMENT CYCLE.

design engineer   A person involved in the design of a hardware product, such as a disk unit or microprocessor chip.

Designer   An illustrative graphics program for IBM-compatible microcomputer systems.

design heuristics   The guidelines that can be followed when dividing a larger problem or program into smaller, more manageable modules.

design language   A programming language whose statements and syntax facilitate its use in design work.

design phase   The process of developing an information system based upon previously established system requirements.

design specifications   Results of an analysis of information needs of a specific system within an organization. Included are specifications for input, processing, and output.

design walkthrough   An overview of a system design by users, programmers, and consultants.

desk accessory (DA)   In a graphical user interface, helpful utilities (such as a calculator, notepad, thesaurus, paint program, or word processor) that can be opened in the middle of any program. Desk accessories are accessed by selecting them from a special pull-down menu. They are conveniences that can be activated when needed and then either put away or moved to a small part of the display screen.

desk checking   Manual checking process in which representative sample data items used for detecting errors in program logic are traced through a program before it is executed on the computer.

DeskPaint/DeskDraw™   An Apple Macintosh paint/draw application in desk accessory form. The application features a full set of paint and draw tools that allow creation or editing of black-and-white, gray scale, and color images, and work with MACPAINT, PICT, and TIFF file formats.

desktop A screen display containing icons that represent programs, files, or resources available to the user.

desktop computer A computer that will fit on the top of a standard-size office desk. Most personal computers and lap computers can be considered desktop computers. A desktop computer is equipped with sufficient internal memory and auxiliary storage to perform business computing tasks.

desktop computer animation The production of computer animation and graphics using a stand-alone microcomputer system, configured with appropriate graphics and video boards, peripherals, and a turnkey animation/graphics software package.

desktop metaphor A view of the computer as a desk equipped with a file cabinet, telephone, wastebasket, scratch pad, and so on.

desktop presentation Presentation of text, video, and graphics on the computer for display to others.

desktop publishing The creation of printed pieces, including words and pictures (such as ads, newsletters, magazines, brochures, and books), almost entirely on a computer. Desktop publishing programs convert normal text into professional-quality documents that can be printed on laser printers or imagesetters. The term was coined by Paul Brainerd, president of Aldus Corporation, the developer of PageMaker.

desktop publishing template An already prepared page layout stored on disk.

desktop video The creation and editing of video images on a computer.

DESQview A program for the IBM PC, IBM PS/2, and compatible computers that runs programs in a windowed, multitasking environment.

destination A device or address that receives data during a data transfer operation.

destructive operation   A process of reading or writing data that erases the data that is read or that was stored previously in the receiving storage location.

destructive read   The process of destroying the information in a location by reading the contents.

destructive replacement   The process of replacing the contents of a computer memory location with a new value, resulting in the loss of the old value.

destructor   In OBJECT-ORIENTED PROGRAMMING, an operation that frees the state of an object and/or destroys the object itself.

detachable keyboard   A keyboard not built into the same case as the video display or desk unit; it connects to the system with a cable and allows greater flexibility in positioning of the keyboard display.

detachable reel tape   Magnetic tape that is wound onto a single reel that in turn is mounted onto a tape unit with an empty take-up reel when data are to be read from or written to the tape.

detail   A small section of a larger file or graphics picture.

detail diagram   A diagram used in HIPO to describe the specific function performed or data items used in a module.

detail drawing   In computer graphics, the drawing of a single part design containing all the dimensions, annotations, and so forth, that are necessary to provide a definition sufficiently complete for manufacturing.

detail file   A file containing relatively transient information, such as records of individual transactions that occurred during a particular period of time. Contrast with MASTER FILE.

detail printing   An operation in which a line of printing occurs for each record read into the computer.

detail report   A printed report in which each line usually corresponds to one input record that has been read.

detection   The passive monitoring of an event for the purpose of discovering a problem.

developer   A person who designs, writes, and tests software. Also called a programmer.

development time   The time used for debugging new programs of hardware.

development tools   Hardware and software aids intended for use in developing programs and/or hardware systems.

device   (1) Any mechanical or electrical device with a specific purpose. (2) Any computer peripheral. (3) Any piece of physical equipment within or attached to a computer.

device cluster   A group of terminals or other devices that share a communications controller.

device code   An eight-bit code for a specific input or output device.

device coordinates   The coordinates in the coordinate system that describe the physical units by which the computer screen is defined.

device dependent   Pertaining to a program or language that must be used with a particular computer or a particular peripheral, such as a printer or modem, in order to function.

device driver   A special section of computer code that translates the general commands from an operating system or user programs into the exact code a specific peripheral device needs. Often, device drivers for a few standard peripherals are built into the operating system, but others must be added in installation. For example, a printer needs a driver. Generally speaking, drivers come with the new hardware or as part of any major software package. Once installed, the user can forget about them.

device flag   A one-bit register that records the current status of a device.

device independence   The ability to command input/output operations without regard to the characteristics of the I/O devices.

device level   A description of the cable, bus, or other connection that goes between peripherals and their controller, or a standard that applies to peripherals. For example, the interface that commonly goes between a hard disk drive and its controller is a device level interface.

device media control language The language used by the database administrator to create the physical description of a database on a disk storage device.

device name **(1)** The label by which a computer system component is identified by the operating system. **(2)** General name for a kind of device.

device number A number assigned to a particular peripheral device, used to identify it in the computer.

DFX A common object format for CAD files from several CAD programs.

DGS Paint A professional PC-based program for doing painting, composition, image retouching, and image processing.

diacritical marks Marks that indicate the phonetic value of a letter in a foreign language.

diagnosis The process of isolating malfunctions in computing equipment and detecting mistakes in programs and systems. See DEBUG.

diagnostic A message sent to the user by a computer system pinpointing errors in syntax or logic; often referred to as an error message.

diagnostic routine A routine designed to locate a malfunction in the central processing unit or a peripheral device.

diagnostics Messages to the user, automatically printed by a computer, that pinpoint improper commands and errors in logic. Sometimes called error messages.

diagram The schematic representation of a sequence of operations or routines. See FLOWCHART.

diagramming package A presentation graphics package that works with shapes to graphically display information in such forms as organizational charts, schedules, office layouts, and flowcharts.

dialect A particular version of a computer language; usually a minor modification of a base language such as BASIC or Pascal, but because of vast differences in modifications it may be significantly different from other dialects of the same language.

dialog A question-and-answer session between a computer system and a human.

dialog base Part of the decision support system that handles the interaction between the user-manager and the computer.

dialog box An interactive message box; a temporary window on the screen that contains a set of choices whenever the executing program needs to collect information from the user.

dial-up In data communications, the use of a dial or push-button telephone to initiate a station-to-station telephone call.

dial-up computer system A COMPUTER SYSTEM that can be reached from a personal telephone.

dial-up line A normal switched telephone line used as a transmission medium for data communications. Contrast with LEASED LINE.

dichotomizing search See BINARY SEARCH.

dictionary program A spelling-check program, often used with word processing systems.

diddle To tamper with data.

die A tiny rectangular piece of a circular wafer of semiconductor silicon, sawed or sliced during the fabrication of integrated circuits. After sawing, leads are bonded to the die and it is mounted in a chip-carrier. When so mounted, also referred to as a CHIP.

dielectric An electrostatic printing process in which an electrical charge is placed on a surface that is nonconductive and therefore holds the charge. Commonly, a coated, dielectric paper is used, and no intermediary is needed. In ionography (Delphax), there is a dielectric drum that accepts a charged image, is toned, and transfers the image to uncoated paper.

DIF Acronym for **D**ata **I**nterchange **F**ormat, a particular standard for data files. It is used by many programs involving forecasting and it allows files created on one software package to be read by another software package—perhaps one produced by an entirely different company. DIF files are not interchangeable between different machines; an Apple DIF file disk cannot be read directly into an IBM machine. While the files are compatible, the disks are formatted differently for different machines.

difference The amount by which one quantity or number is greater or less than another.

Difference Engine A mechanical machine devised by Charles Babbage in the 1800s to perform computations automatically and print their results.

diffuse highlight In computer graphics, object highlights that result when a light source interacts with a nonreflective surface.

diffusion A high-temperature process by which impurity atoms deposited on the surface of a material, such as a silicon wafer, have sufficient thermal energy to penetrate the material, seeking to equalize their densities by displacing the host atoms and altering the electrical properties of the material in desired ways. Normal diffusion temperatures are between 900 and 1,200°C for the most frequently used impurities in silicon.

digit One of the symbols of a numbering system used to designate a quantity. The decimal system has the ten digits, 0 through 9.

digital Pertaining to representation of information by encoding as bits of 1's or 0's that indicate on or off states. Highly important in the technology of computers and data communications. Contrast with ANALOG SIGNAL.

digital audio tape (DAT) A data storage medium.

digital communications The transmission of information by coding it into discrete on/off electronic signals.

digital computer A computer that operates on discrete data. A device that performs arithmetic, logical, and comparative functions upon information represented in digital form and that operates under control of an internal program. Digital means that the computer uses data in the form of discrete numbers, such as binary 1's and 0's. Most computers used today (mainframes, minicomputers, and microcomputers) are digital. Contrast with ANALOG COMPUTER.

digital computer animation A COMPUTER GRAPHICS SYSTEM that generates and animates graphics. The digital signal is understood by the computer as discrete units of data.

digital control The use of digital technology to maintain conditions in operating systems as close as possible to desired values despite changes in the operating environment.

Digital Darkroom™ An image processing program from Silicon Beach Software that acts as a computerized darkroom to compose images. The program uses computer processing techniques to edit and enhance scanned images.

digital data Data represented in discrete, discontinuous form, as contrasted with analog data, which is represented in continuous form.

Digital Equipment Corporation (DEC) A major manufacturer of minicomputer systems, founded in 1957 by Kenneth Olson. DEC pioneered the minicomputer business with its PDP computers in 1959. The popular PDP-8 was introduced in 1965, and the PDP-11 was introduced in 1970. In 1977, DEC announced the VAX series of minicomputer systems and gained a strong foothold in commercial data processing.

digital image (1) An image that has been converted into an array of pixels. (2) A generic term that can apply to all computer graphics images.

digital mapping The digitizing of geographic information for a geographic information system.

digital picture library Based on floppy or hard disks or on optical discs, a system for storing and retrieving graphic images that provides the user with a method of rapid retrieval.

digital plotter   An output device that uses an ink pen (or pens) to draw graphs, line drawings, and other illustrations.

digital recording   A technique for recording information as discrete points onto magnetic recording media.

digital repeater   A unit placed in a data communications path to reconstruct digital pulses, which tend to deteriorate as they travel through long conductors.

digital signal   Two electrical states that communicate a code in binary data (1's and 0's) the computer can understand. Each 1 or 0 is a bit, while eight bits equal a byte, or one character. The digital signal is converted by a modem into an analog signal (modulated) that may be transmitted over phone lines. Incoming analog signals detected by the modem are converted into digital signals (demodulated) the computer can understand.

digital speech   Recorded speech broken into tiny units of sound. Each tiny unit has characteristics—such as pitch, loudness, and timbre—that can be represented by numbers, which become the digital code for speech.

digital-to-analog converter (D-A converter)   A mechanical or electronic device used to convert discrete digital numbers to continuous analog signals. Opposite of ANALOG-TO-DIGITAL CONVERTER.

digital tracer   A special hinged arm that can be used to trace over drawings and graphs and that sends the information to the computer.

digital transmission   The transmission of data as discrete impulses.

digitization   In computer graphics, the assignment of a numerical value to each point of an image, indicating color or gray tone. Photographs can be digitized by an optical scanner and then combined indistinguishably with computer-generated imagery.

digitize   To register a visual image or real object in a format that can be processed by the computer. Digitized data are read into the system with graphics input devices. Digitizing includes scanning an image, tracing a picture on a graphics tablet, and converting camera images into the computer.

digitized image An image put into a computer that can then be manipulated for various purposes.

digitized type Type stored in computer-readable form as a collection of dots or line elements.

digitizer A graphics input device that converts images into digital data that the computer can accept.

digitizing The process of converting graphic representations, such as pictures and drawings, into digital data that can be processed by a computer system.

digitizing camera A camera coupled with a processor used for encoding highly detailed images such as pictures or three-dimensional objects into digital data.

digitizing resolution The fineness of detail that a scanner can distinguish.

digitizing tablet A graphics input device that allows the user to create images. It has a special stylus that can be used to draw or trace images, which are then converted to digital data that can be processed by the computer.

digit place In positional notation, the site where a digit is located in a word representing a numeral. The decimal system has the units place, the tens place, and so on.

dimension The maximum size, or the number and arrangement of the elements, of an ARRAY.

dimmed command A command in a pull-down menu that is grayed-black. A dimmed command means that that choice is not currently available to the user, perhaps because another function needs to be accomplished before that selection can be made.

dimmed icon   A grayed-black icon, which indicates that the object it represents, such as a disk, folder, or document on a disk, has either been opened or ejected from the disk drive.

DIN   Acronym for **D**eutsche **I**ndustrie **N**orm, the German industry standard.

DIN connector   A round connector used on several computers manufactured by Apple Computer, Inc. DIN stands for Deutsche Industrie Norm, a German committee that establishes standards.

dingbats   Small graphic elements used for decorative purposes in a document. Some fonts, such as Zapf Dingbats, are designed to present sets of dingbats.

diode   An electronic device used to permit current flow in one direction and to inhibit it in the opposite direction.

diode transistor logic   See DTL.

DIP   Acronym for **D**ual **I**n-line **P**ackage, a switch found on many computers and peripherals, used to set up or adjust the equipment. The term refers to the switch's plastic housing designed to be attached directly to a circuit board or to an equipment component case.

direct access   The process of storing data in, or getting data from, a storage device in such a manner that surrounding data need not be scanned to locate the desired data. The time required to get desired data from the storage device is independent of the location of the data.

direct access file   A FILE in which each record may be accessed directly, regardless of its relative position on the file.

direct access processing   The same as DIRECT PROCESSING and RANDOM PROCESSING. Contrast with SEQUENTIAL PROCESSING.

direct access storage device (DASD)   A basic type of storage medium that allows information to be accessed by positioning the medium or accessing mechanism directly to the information required, thus permitting direct addressing of data locations.

direct address An address that specifies the storage location of an operand. Contrast with INDIRECT ADDRESS.

direct broadcast satellite (DBS) A satellite that allows the use of inexpensive home reception disks to receive its high-power signals, including software and data.

direct color Same as 24-bit color.

direct-connect modem A modulator/demodulator that plugs directly into a modular telephone jack for use in data transmission.

direct conversion The method of converting from one system to another by ceasing to operate the old system when the new one is implemented.

direct current The flow of electrons in one direction such as supplied by a battery.

direct data entry The entry of data directly into the computer through machine-readable source documents or through the use of on-line terminals.

direct distance dialing See DDD.

directed beam A technique for displaying information on a CRT that directs the beam from point to point on the display screen; the beam traces only the points required to display the desired information.

direct file organization The organization of records so that each is individually accessible.

direct file processing Processing that allows the user to access a record directly by using a record key.

direction The line of movement of some aspect of an image, sometimes known as a vector.

directional light Light emanating from a source that is virtually infinite, such as the sun. Contrast with AMBIENT LIGHT.

direct memory access (DMA) A method by which data can be transferred between peripheral devices and internal memory without intervention by the central processing unit.

directory **(1)** In a partition by software into several distinct files, a listing maintained on a device to locate these files. **(2)** An index file containing the names and locations of all the files contained on a storage medium. **(3)** A major section of a hard disk drive. As many directories as needed can be named and sub-directories can be created within them. As files are created, their names and disk locations are stored in the directory.

direct processing A technique of handling data in random order, without preliminary sorting, and utilizing files on direct access storage devices.

direct organization A method of organizing data on a device so that it can be accessed directly.

directory tree A map of the directories on a disk.

disable **(1)** To remove or inhibit a normal capability. **(2)** To use a command that prevents further operation of a peripheral device. Opposite of ENABLE.

disassembler A program that takes machine-language code and generates the assembler-language code from which the machine language was produced. See ASSEMBLY LANGUAGE.

disaster dump A computer STORAGE DUMP that occurs as a result of a nonrecoverable mistake in a program.

disaster recovery plan A method of restoring data processing operations if those operations are halted by major damage or destruction.

disc A round, flat, circular piece of nonmagnetic, polished metal designed to be read from and written to by optical (laser) technology. Optical discs use the disc spelling. Floppy disks and hard disks are spelled *disk*.

disclaimer A clause associated with many software products that states that the vendor is not responsible for any business losses incurred due to the use of the product.

discrete Pertaining to distinct elements or to representation by means of distinct elements, such as characters or bits.

discrete component An electrical component that contains only one function, as opposed to an integrated circuit.

disk A magnetic device for storing information and programs accessible by a computer. Can be either a rigid platter (HARD DISK) or a sheet of flexible plastic (FLOPPY DISK). Disks have tracks where data is stored.

disk access time The time required to locate a specific track on a disk. Also called seek time. Part of total access time.

disk buffer The area of a computer's memory set aside to hold information not yet written to disk.

disk cache A section of random access memory (RAM) set aside by the operating system to store frequently accessed data and program instructions.

disk cartridge A removable hard disk enclosed in a protective case. Disk cartridges are used by certain types of hard disk drives.

disk controller card A peripheral circuit card that connects disk drives to a computer and controls their operation.

disk commands DOS commands that must be accessed from the DOS disk.

DISKCOMP A DOS and OS/2 command that compares two disks to see if the information they contain is identical.

DISKCOPY A DOS and OS/2 command that copies the entire contents of one disk to another.

disk copying The process of transferring the entire contents of one disk to another.

disk crash The condition of a disk unit that makes it unusable. Usually caused by contact between the read/write head of the disk drive and the surface of the disk.

disk cylinder All tracks on a disk pack that are accessible with a single movement of the access mechanism.

disk directory A CATALOG. This is the computer's own record of where each file or program is stored on the disk. The directory usually takes up a few tracks at the beginning of a disk.

disk doctor A program that enables the user to investigate directly what is stored on a disk. The use of a disk doctor may be the only way of recovering valuable data following a disk crash.

disk drive A device that reads data from a magnetic disk and copies it into the computer, and that writes data from the computer's memory onto a disk so that it can be stored.

disk duplication The process of copying information recorded on one magnetic disk onto another disk.

disk envelope A removable protective paper sleeve used when handling or storing a 5.25-inch diskette. Must be removed before inserting the diskette in a disk drive.

diskette A single magnetic disk on which data is recorded as magnetic spots. Available in both 3.5-inch and 5.25-inch formats.

diskette tray A container used to protect and store diskettes.

disk file A file that resides on a magnetic disk. An organized collection of data stored on a disk.

disk jacket A permanent protective covering for a disk, usually made of plastic. The disk is never removed from the jacket, even when inserted in a disk drive.

disk library A special room that houses a file or disk packs under secure, environmentally controlled conditions, or a storage facility that houses a file of diskettes.

disk memory Storage using rotating disks as its storage element.

disk operating system (DOS) A collection of software stored on disk that controls the operation of the COMPUTER SYSTEM. A computer cannot function unless it has access to its own operating system. Typically, it keeps track of files, saves and retrieves files, allocates storage space, and manages other control functions associated with disk storage.

disk optimizer Equipment that defragments a disk to speed up retrieval.

disk pack A group of removable tiered hard disks mounted on a shaft and treated as a unit. Must be placed on a disk storage unit to be accessed.

disk partition The logical portion of a disk that provides an organization allowing smaller blocks of data to be handled more conveniently.

disk sector A sector corresponding to a block of data storage area between two successive radials on the disk. The cutting of a disk into sectors is analogous to the way a pie would be sliced.

disk unit See MAGNETIC DISK UNIT.

disk unit enclosure A cabinet designed to hold one or more disk drives and a power supply.

dispatch To select the next task and get it ready for processing.

dispatching priority The numbers assigned to tasks and used to determine precedence for use by the central processing unit in a multitask situation.

dispersed data processing See DISTRIBUTED COMPUTING.

dispersed intelligence A network system in which the computing power is scattered or dispersed throughout the COMPUTER NETWORK.

displacement The difference between the base address and the actual machine-language address.

display **(1)** The physical representation of data, as on a screen. **(2)** The lights or indicators on computer consoles. **(3)** The process of creating a visual representation of graphic data on an output device.

display adapter An adapter board that electronically links the computer to a display screen and determines its capabilities, such as degree of resolution, color vs. monochrome, and graphics vs. no graphics.

display background   That part of displayed graphic data that is not part of the image being processed and is not subject to change by the user. Used to highlight the image part of the display, called the DISPLAY FOREGROUND.

display composition   In DESKTOP PUBLISHING, lines of type that are in bold, ornamental, or contrasting typefaces; used to attract attention.

display console   An input/output device consisting of a DISPLAY SCREEN and an input keyboard.

display cycle   The time it takes a visual display screen to be completely refreshed.

display device   A device capable of producing a visual representation of data, such as a GRAPHICS PRINTER, DIGITAL PLOTTER, or VIDEO DISPLAY TERMINAL.

display face   A typeface suitable for titles and headings in a document, distinguished by its ability to stand out from other text on the page.

display font   The font as it appears on the display screen. Ideally, it closely represents the printer font of the same name and size specification.

display foreground   That part of graphic data being displayed on a visual display device that is subject to alteration by the user. Contrast with DISPLAY BACKGROUND.

display frame   One image in an animation sequence.

display highlighting   Ways of emphasizing information on a display screen by using such enhancers as blinking, boldface, high contrast, reverse video, underlining, or different colors.

display image   That portion of a displayed graphics file that is currently visible on the display device.

display list   In computer graphics, a collection of vectors that make up a graphics image; a description of the desired image via a list of primitives and attributes. Display lists provide an intermediate picture storage for quick image redraw.

display list processor   A graphics peripheral board used to speed up the processing of vector graphics information.

display menu   An on-screen series of program options that allows the user to choose the next function or course of action to be executed, such as to print the contents of the visual display or to save a graphic display on a disk.

display PostScript (DPS)   A display language from Adobe Corporation that translates elementary commands in an application program to graphics and text elements on screen. The screen counterpart of the POSTSCRIPT printer language.

display screen   The part of a display unit on which images and text are shown.

display segment   In computer graphics, a collection of graphics primitives that can be manipulated as a single element.

display space   The portion of image space that can be viewed at any one time on the display.

display surface   A medium upon which a visual representation of graphic data is made, such as a visual display screen, printer paper, plotter paper, or film.

display terminal   Any output device capable of producing a visual representation of graphic data.

display tolerance   The measure of accuracy with which graphic data can be output.

display type   Technology of the display, such as CATHODE RAY TUBE (CRT), LIGHT-EMITTING DIODE (LED), and LIQUID CRYSTAL DISPLAY (LCD).

display unit   A device that provides a visual representation of data.

DisplayWrite   A full-featured word processing program for IBM microcomputer systems.

dissolve   In computer graphics, a visual transition between two pictures in which the whole area of the first gradually disappears as it is replaced by the second.

distort To deform, elongate, misshape, twist, or exaggerate.

distortion Any undesired change in the waveform of an electric signal passing through a circuit, including the transmission medium. In the design of any electronic circuit, one important problem is to modify the input signal in the required way without producing distortion beyond an acceptable degree.

distributed computing The concept of performing operations in a computer system whose terminals and central processing unit are separated geographically but are linked together functionally in a communications network. Contrast with CENTRALIZED DATA PROCESSING.

distributed database A database spread throughout the computer systems of a network.

distributed data processing (DDP) system A processing system that uses a mainframe computer for database storage and for large-scale processing, combined with minicomputers or personal computers for local processing.

distributed design An information structure that identifies the existence of independent operating units but recognizes the benefits of central coordination and control.

distributed information processing system A set of interacting computer systems of databases situated in different locations.

distributed network A network configuration in which all node pairs are connected either directly or by redundant paths through intermediate nodes.

distributive sort A sort formed by separating the list into parts and then rearranging the parts in order.

disturbance Any irregular phenomenon that interferes with the interchange of intelligence during transmission of a signal. See NOISE.

dithering The creation of additional colors or shades of gray to create special effects or to make hard edges softer.

dither pattern For a scanner, a pattern of dots used to simulate gray tones or intermediate colors.

division check A multiplication check in which a zero-balancing result is compared against the original dividend.

division/remainder procedure A hashing procedure that uses the remainder from division as a relative address of a record in secondary storage.

DMA Abbreviation for DIRECT MEMORY ACCESS.

DML Abbreviation for DATA MANIPULATION LANGUAGE.

DOA Abbreviation for **d**ead **o**n **a**rrival. Used to describe a product that does not work when received from the manufacturer or supplier.

document (1) Handwritten, typewritten, or printed sheet(s) of paper containing data. (2) Any representation or collection of information or text, whether human-readable or machine-readable.

documentation (1) During systems analysis and subsequent programming, the preparation of documents that describe such things as the system, the programs prepared, and the changes made at later dates. See PROGRAM DEVELOPMENT CYCLE. (2) Internal documentation in the form of comments or remarks.

documentation aids Aids that help automate the documentation process, such as program description write-ups, FLOWCHARTS, HIPO, program runs, and PSEUDOCODE.

documentor A program designed to use data processing methods in the production and maintenance of program flowcharts, text material, and other types of tabular or graphic information.

document compare To mark the differences between an edited version of a document and the original.

document format   In WORD PROCESSING, changing margins, type-style, and so on.

document reader   Any OCR or OMR equipment that reads a limited amount of information.

document retrieval   The process of acquiring data from storage devices and, possibly, manipulating the data and subsequently preparing a report.

document window   A rectangular portion of the screen that displays a separate document or program.

domain   (1) A set of data values from which a relational attribute may draw its values. (2) Any problem area of interest.

domain expert   A human expert who contributes to the development of an EXPERT SYSTEM.

domain knowledge   Knowledge of the application environment.

dongle   A slang term for the I/O device used to protect software. The dongle attaches to the port of a computer and acts as a key.

door swing   The rotation of an image on any screen axis.

dopant   Any substance added in the doping process, such as arsenic or phosphorus. See SEMICONDUCTOR DEVICE.

dope vector   A vector wherein an atom of a linked list describes the contents of the other atoms in the list.

doping   The process of introducing impurity elements into the crystalline structure of pure silicone during semiconductor fabrication. See SEMICONDUCTOR DEVICE.

DOS™   An OPERATING SYSTEM for IBM-compatible microcomputers. DOS is available in both generic MS-DOS and IBM-specific PC DOS versions. DOS is an acronym for **D**ISK **O**PERATING **S**YSTEM.

dot   A small mark. Computers generate dots called PIXELS on visual displays. Printers use dots to form letters and other visual material. The typical dot matrix printer generates 75 dots per inch, in contrast to the laser printer, which produces 300 or more dots per inch.

dot chart A scatter graph, which shows the distribution of quantities as a collection of dots.

dot command A command that consists of a period followed by letters. Used in some older types of word processing programs for embedded commands.

dot density The number of dots per unit of measure in printing; for example, 24 dots per character (dot matrix printers) or 300 dots per inch (laser printers).

dot matrix A technique for representing characters by composing them out of selected dots from within a rectangular matrix of dots.

dot matrix character A character composed from a rectangular matrix of dots.

dot matrix printer A printer that creates text characters and graphs with a series of closely spaced dots. It uses tiny hammers to strike a needle mechanism against the paper at precise moments as the print head moves across the page. Some dot matrix printers produce dot patterns fine enough to approach the print quality of a DAISY WHEEL PRINTER.

dot pitch The resolution of a dot matrix. **(1)** For display screens, it is expressed as the width of an individual dot; for example, a .28 dot pitch refers to a dot that is 28/100 of a millimeter in diameter. The smaller the number, the higher the resolution. **(2)** For printers, it is expressed as the number of dots per linear inch; for example, a desktop laser printer prints at least 300 dpi. The larger the number, the higher the resolution.

dots/mm Abbreviation for dots per millimeter, a unit of measure for the digitizing resolution of scanners and other graphics systems.

dots per inch **(1)** A linear measure of the number of dots a printer can print in an inch. For example, a 300 dpi laser printer can print up to 300 dots for each horizontal or vertical inch on the paper. **(2)** A measure of screen resolution that counts the dots that the device can produce per linear inch.

double buffering   A software or hardware technique to transfer information between the computer and peripheral devices. Information in one buffer is acted on by the computer while information in the other is transferred in or out.

double-click   A method to invoke a command by using the mouse button. The pointer or cursor is placed in the correct position on a display screen and the mouse button is pressed twice in rapid succession. A double-click is used to open a file, disk, or folder.

double density   Having twice the storage capacity of a normal (single-density) disk or tape. In IBM-compatible microcomputers, a double-density 5.25-inch disk has a capacity of 360K bytes, while a double-density 3.5-inch disk has a capacity of 720K bytes.

double-entry bookkeeping   An accounting system in which each transaction recorded changes a credit account and a debit account.

double precision   Pertaining to the use of two computer words to represent a number to gain increased precision.

double quote   Another name for the quote mark (").

double-sided disk   A magnetic disk capable of storing information on both of its surfaces. Contrast with SINGLE-SIDED DISK.

doublestriking   See OVERSTRIKING.

double word   An entity of storage that is two words in length.

doubly linked list   A list in which each atom contains one pointer that relates to the successor atom.

do until   One of the variations of the primitive loop construct of STRUCTURED PROGRAMMING.

do while   A variation of the primitive loop construct of STRUCTURED PROGRAMMING.

Dow Jones Information Service   A computer database containing current information on stock prices and other financial news. It can be accessed by subscribers with microcomputers and modems.

down   A condition that exists when the hardware circuits of a computer are inoperable or there is a failure in the software system. When a computer is down, it is simply not functioning.

down-line processor   A processor at or near the terminal point in a data communications network that facilitates the transmission of data.

downlink   A communications channel from a satellite to an earth station.

download   **(1)** The process of transferring data (files) from a large computer to a smaller one. **(2)** To transfer information to a laser printer from a computer. Opposite of UPLOAD.

downloadable font   A set of characters of the same typeface and size stored on disk and sent (downloaded) to a printer's memory when needed for printing a document.

downtime   The length of time a computer system is inoperative due to a malfunction. Contrast with AVAILABLE TIME and UPTIME.

downward compatible   Pertaining to a computer compatible with a smaller or previous-generation computer.

dpi   Abbreviation for DOTS PER INCH. The density of a printer's output; determines the overall appearance/quality of printed output. LASER PRINTERS offer 300 dpi and up. True typesetting starts at 1,000 dpi. DOT MATRIX PRINTERS, at the low end, range from 72 to 150 dpi.

DPMA   Abbreviation for DATA PROCESSING MANAGEMENT ASSOCIATION.

DPMA certificate   A certificate formerly given by the Data Processing Management Association indicating that a person has attained a certain level of competence in the field of data processing. This Certificate in Data Processing is obtained by passing an examination offered yearly and now administered by the INSTITUTE FOR CERTIFICATION OF COMPUTER PROFESSIONALS.

draft mode   A low-quality printing mode available on some printers.

draft quality   A measure of quality for printed output. Usually refers to the result of top-speed printing and therefore not the most precisely defined or fully filled-in characters. Considered acceptable for working copies but not final work. Contrast with LETTER QUALITY.

drag   The action of moving the mouse while holding the button down; used to move or manipulate objects on a computer's display screen.

dragging   An interactive technique for repositioning an image on a display screen.

drain   One of three connecting terminals of a field effect transistor, the other two being the source and the gate. If the charge carriers are positive, conventional current flows from source to drain.

DRAM   Acronym for **D**ynamic **RAM**, meaning a type of memory chip that keeps its contents only if supplied with regular clock pulses and a chance to periodically refresh the data internally. DRAM is far less expensive than static RAM (which needs no refreshing) and is the type found in most personal computers.

DRAW   A graphics instruction in many versions of the BASIC programming language that is useful for high-resolution graphics.

drawing   The process of creating a graphic image with an OBJECT-ORIENTED drawing program.

drawing program   A program for creating and manipulating object-oriented graphics, as opposed to creating and manipulating pixel images. For example, in a drawing program the user can manipulate an element such as a triangle or a block of text as an independent object simply by selecting the object and moving it.

DrawPerfect   A drawing program for IBM-compatible microcomputers. This charting, drawing, and presentation program provides 256 colors. It creates 2-D bar, pie, and graph charts.

Dr. Halo   A paint program for IBM-compatible microcomputers.

drift A change in the output of an electric circuit that occurs slowly over a period of time.

drill-and-practice program Teaching software that reinforces old lessons.

drive The physical components necessary for writing data to, and reading data from, a diskette or disk. Short name for DISK DRIVE.

drive bay A reserved space in a computer where extra drives may be installed.

drive designator A letter that informs the operating system which disk drive to use.

drive number The naming convention for disk drives. For example, the drives in a two-drive Apple Macintosh system are 0 and 1; in a two-drive IBM-compatible microcomputer system, the drives are A and B.

driver A series of instructions the computer follows to reformat data for transfer to and from a particular peripheral device. Electrical and mechanical requirements differ from one kind of device to another, and software drivers are used to standardize the format of data between them and the computer.

DRO Abbreviation for **d**estructive **r**ead **o**ut. See DESTRUCTIVE READ.

drop (**1**) In a network, the remote terminal location. (**2**) The distance between the top and bottom of a sheet of computer stationery, measured in millimeters or inches.

drop cap An initial letter of a chapter or paragraph enlarged and positioned so that the top of the character is even with the top of the first line and the rest of the character descends into the second and subsequent lines.

drop dead halt A halt from which there is no recovery.

drop-down menu A type of menu that drops from the menu bar when requested and remains open without further action until the user closes it or chooses a menu item. Same as PULL-DOWN MENU.

drop in   A character that appears erroneously—on a display screen, on a printout, or in a file—because the disk drive or tape drive misstored or misread one or more bits.

drop out   **(1)** In data transmission, a momentary loss in signal, usually due to the effect of noise or system malfunction. **(2)** A character that vanishes from a display, printout, or file because the disk drive or tape drive misstored or misread one or more bits.

dropout type   White characters on a black background.

drop shadow   A shadow placed behind an image, slightly offset horizontally and vertically, that creates the illusion that the topmost image has been lifted off the surface of the page.

drum   See MAGNETIC DRUM.

drum plotter   An output device that draws schematics, graphs, pictures, and so forth on paper with automatically controlled pens. The paper is wrapped around a cylindrical drum that turns forward and backward at various speeds under one or more pens that slide to and fro, marking the paper.

drum printer   A printing device that uses a drum embossed with alphanumeric characters. A type of line printer that can print several thousand lines per minute. Each print position has a complete set of characters around the circumference of the drum.

dry plasma etching   A method for developing a mask on a wafer.

dry run   A program-checking technique of examining the logic and coding of a program from an algorithm and written instructions and recording the results of each step of the operation before running the program on the computer.

DSL   Abbreviation for **D**YNAMIC **S**IMULATION **L**ANGUAGE.

DSS   Abbreviation for **D**ecision **S**upport **S**ystem, a general-purpose support package that contains many models which, when combined, can help a user with problem-solving.

DTL Abbreviation for **D**IODE **T**RANSISTOR **L**OGIC, microelectronic logic based on connections between semiconductor diodes and the transistor.

DTP See DESKTOP PUBLISHING.

dual channel controller A controller that enables reading from and writing to a device to occur simultaneously.

dual density (1) Pertaining to tapes or disks on which data is densely recorded. (2) A floppy disk with double-sided recording capability.

dual disk drive A floppy disk system that contains two disk drives, providing an increased storage capacity.

dual in-line package (DIP) A popular type of INTEGRATED CIRCUIT package on which a chip is mounted. Provides a protective casing for the integrated circuit and pin connections for plugging the chip into a circuit board.

dual intensity The ability of a terminal or printer to produce characters in regular as well as highlighted or bold formats.

dual processors (1) Two central processing units within a computer system that can function simultaneously. (2) Computers that use two microprocessors. Dual processors provide faster and more efficient processing. The main objective is to relieve the main processor of the tasks of memory management, graphics displays, and, sometimes, advanced mathematical functions.

dual-sided disk drives Disk drives that use two read/write heads to store and retrieve data on both the top and bottom sides of a disk.

dual Y-axis graph In presentation graphics, a graph that uses two Y-axes when comparing two data series with different measurement scales. Useful when comparing two different data series that must be measured with two different values axes.

dumb terminal A video display terminal with minimal I/O capabilities and no processing capability.

dummy   Pertaining to an artificial argument, instruction, address, or record of data inserted solely to fulfill prescribed conditions.

dummy argument   Variables, used as function arguments, that do not have any values.

dummy instruction   **(1)** An artificial instruction or address inserted in a list to serve a purpose other than its execution as an instruction. **(2)** An instruction in a routine that, in itself, does not perform any functions. Often used to provide a point at which to terminate a program loop.

dummy module   A skeleton of a module with entry and exit, but no actual processing. Particularly useful in top-down testing when subordinate subfunctions are not ready for integration.

dumping   Copying all or part of the contents of a storage unit, usually from the computer's internal storage, into an auxiliary storage unit or onto a printer.

duplex channel   A communications channel that allows simultaneous transmission in both directions.

duplexing   The use of duplicate computers, peripheral equipment, or circuitry so that, in the event of a component failure, an alternate component can enable the system to continue.

duplex printing   Printing a document on both sides of the sheet, so that the verso (left) and recto (right) pages face each other after the document is bound.

duplicate   To copy so that the result remains in the same physical form as the source, such as to make a new diskette with the same information and in the same format as an original diskette. Contrast with COPY.

duplication check   A check requiring that the results of two independent performances of the same operation be identical. May be made concurrently on duplicate equipment or at different times on the same equipment.

duration   The amount of working time it takes to complete a task.

dust cover   A plastic cover used to protect microcomputers, disk units, terminals, printers, and so on from one of their worst enemies.

DVI   Abbreviation for **d**igital **v**ideo **i**nteractive, a term that refers to the use of a compact disk with a drive that allows for full motion video as well as visual, audio, and text information, making it possible for a computer to store and display moving video images.

DVST   Abbreviation for **d**irect **v**iew **s**torage **t**ube, a vector CRT device in which the image is held in a storage grid in the display device.

Dvorak keyboard   A keyboard arrangement designed by August Dvorak. It provides increased speed and comfort and reduces the rate of errors by placing the most frequently used letters in the center for use by the strongest fingers.

DXF   Abbreviation for Drawing Interchange Format, AutoCAD's format for 2-D and 3-D drawings.

dyadic   Pertaining to an operation that uses two operands.

dyadic operation   Any operation on two operands.

dye-polymer recording   An optical disc recording process in which dye embedded in a plastic polymer coating on an optical disc is used to create minute bumps on the surface that can be read by a laser. Dye-polymer bumps can be flattened and re-created, thus making an optical disc rewritable.

dynamic   A term describing operations that are performed on the fly, while the program is running.

dynamic address translation (DAT)   In virtual storage systems, the change of a virtual storage address to a real storage address during execution of an instruction.

dynamic binding   The implementation consequence of inheritance and polymorphism. As an object-oriented program runs, messages are received by objects. Often the method for handling a message is stored high in a class library. The method is located dynamically when it is needed and binding then occurs at the last possible moment.

dynamic dump A dump taken during the execution of a program. See SNAPSHOT DUMP.

dynamic graphics option A technique used in some storage tube products to combine refresh and stored information on the same display. This allows operation in the dynamic mode of the refreshed display while maintaining the advantages of the storage tube.

dynamic RAM (DRAM) The most common type of computer memory; the computer must refresh DRAM at frequent intervals. Contrast with static RAM, which is usually faster and does not require refresh circuitry.

dynamic relocation The movement of part or all of an active (currently operating) program from one region of storage to another. All necessary address references are adjusted to enable proper execution of the program to continue in its new location.

dynamic scheduling Job scheduling determined by the computer on a moment-to-moment basis, depending upon the circumstances.

Dynamic Simulation Language (DSL) A high-level programming language, suited primarily for simulation of engineering and scientific problems of a continuous nature. Because DSL facilitates the solution of ordinary differential equations that frequently are functions of time, it is particularly useful for transient analysis of dynamic systems.

dynamic storage Any memory device that must constantly be recharged or refreshed at frequent intervals to avoid loss of data; very volatile storage.

dynamic storage allocation Automatic storage allocation.

E

e The symbol used to represent the base of the natural logarithms, 2.71828.

E In floating-point numbers, a symbol that stands for exponent; for example, 17E2 means "17 times 10 to the power 2." See E NOTATION.

earth colors Paint colors derived from natural, colored earths, usually browns, reds, and yellows.

early binding In OBJECT-ORIENTED PROGRAMMING, static binding. See BINDING.

EAROM Acronym for ELECTRICALLY ALTERABLE ROM, READ-ONLY MEMORY that can be selectively altered without erasing all stored data, as is done with EPROM devices.

Easy Color Paint An Apple Macintosh graphics program designed for nonprofessionals that emphasizes "simplicity, economy and fun." The user simply picks a color and pattern, chooses a tool, and starts painting.

eavesdropping Passive wiretapping, the interception of messages, usually without detection.

EBAM Acronym for ELECTRON BEAM ADDRESSED MEMORY, an electronic storage device that uses electrical circuits to control a beam that reads from or writes on a metal oxide semiconductor surface.

EBCDIC Acronym for Extended Binary Coded Decimal Interchange Code, an eight-bit code used to represent data in large IBM mainframes. EBCDIC can represent up to 256 distinct characters and is the principal code used in many of the current computers.

ECAD Acronym for ELECTRONIC COMPUTER-AIDED DESIGN.

echo **(1)** In data communications, the return of a transmitted signal to its source, with a delay that indicates the signal is a reflection rather than the original. **(2)** In computer graphics, to provide visual feedback to the designer during graphic input to the system.

echo check   A check on the accuracy of a data transfer operation in which the data received is transmitted back to the source and compared with the original data.

ECHO mode   A mode in DOS and OS/2 that displays a message on-screen as commands are being carried out.

echoplex   In an asynchronous communication, acknowledgment by the receiving station of the receipt of a message by echoing the message back to the transmitting station.

ECL   Abbreviation for EMITTER-COUPLED LOGIC, also called CURRENT MODE LOGIC. It is faster than TTL, but much less popular.

ECOM   Abbreviation for ELECTRONIC COMPUTER-ORIENTED MAIL, a process of sending and receiving messages in digital form over telecommunications facilities.

e-cycle   The part of the machine cycle in which data are located, an instruction is executed, and the results are stored.

edge   (1) In computer graphics, the straight line segment that is the intersection of two planes' faces on a solid, such as an edge of a cube. (2) The connection between two nodes in a graph. See INDEGREE.

edge connector   A row of etched lines on the edge of a printed circuit board that is inserted into a motherboard or an expansion slot.

edge cutter/trimmer   A device for removing the sprocketed margin from continuous-form printer paper.

edge detection   In computer graphics, an image processing technique in which edge pixels are identified by examining their neighboring pixels.

edge enhancement   In computer graphics, an image enhancement technique in which edges are sharpened by increasing the contrast between the lighter and darker pixels on opposite sides of the edge.

edge sharpening   The process of sharpening the edges of a DIGITIZED picture.

edit   (1) To check the correctness of data. (2) To change as necessary the form of data by adding or deleting certain characters. **(3)** Part of a word processing program, page layout program, or graphics program that can edit data for printing, adding special symbols, spacing, deleting nonsignificant zeros, and so on.

editing Making the corrections or changes in a program or in data. See DATA EDITING.

editing run In batch processing, the editing program's checking of the data for ostensible validity—such as testing to ensure that dates and numbers fall within expected ranges, comparing totals with separately entered batch or hash totals, and proving check digits—and identification of any errors for correction and resubmission.

edit line The "status report" line displayed on the screen when certain spreadsheet or word processing programs are in use. Tells the user the present location of the cursor, the amount of memory left, and (in some word processing programs) the name of the file in use. In spreadsheets, it will also show the contents or formula of the cell at the cursor location, and one or two more items of information (depending on which spreadsheet is being used).

edit mode An input mode that allows the editing of previously entered information.

editor A program used to write, enter, and edit programs.

EDP Abbreviation for ELECTRONIC DATA PROCESSING.

EDS Abbreviation for EXCHANGEABLE DISK STORE.

EDSAC Acronym for **E**lectronic **D**elay **S**torage **A**utomatic **C**alculator. EDSAC was the world's first stored program computer and was completed in England in 1949.

EDVAC Acronym for **E**lectronic **D**iscrete **V**ariable **A**utomatic **C**alculator. Completed in 1950, EDVAC was the first stored program computer built in the United States.

EEPROM See ELECTRONICALLY ERASABLE PROGRAMMABLE READ-ONLY MEMORY.

EEROM   A storage device that can be erased electronically and reprogrammed.

effective address   The address derived by performing any specified address modification operations upon a specified address.

effectiveness   The degree to which the output produced achieves the desired purpose.

EFT   Abbreviation for ELECTRONIC FUNDS TRANSFER. An EFT network transfers funds from one account to another with electronic equipment rather than with paper media, such as checks. An increasingly popular method of paying periodic bills.

EGA   Abbreviation for ENHANCED GRAPHICS ADAPTER, a video display adapter introduced by IBM in 1984. The video display standard for IBM-compatible microcomputers featuring 640-by-350-pixel resolution. EGA can display no more than 16 colors at once. It has been superseded by VGA.

egoless programming   The concept of arranging programming tasks so that credit for success or blame for failure must be shared by several programmers rather than just one person. Uses structured walkthroughs and other techniques.

EIA   Abbreviation for ELECTRONICS INDUSTRIES ASSOCIATION, an organization founded in 1924 that is concerned with establishing standards for the electronic industry.

EIA interface   The standard interface between peripherals and microcomputers, and modems and terminals. Another name for RS-232C interface.

Eiffel   An OBJECT-ORIENTED PROGRAMMING LANGUAGE developed by Bertrand Meyer in 1988.

eight-bit chip   A CPU chip that processes data eight bits at a time. Contrast with SIXTEEN-BIT CHIP and THIRTY-TWO-BIT CHIP.

eight-bit color   The color range possible with an eight-bit graphics system. Each pixel in such a system can display one of 256 colors at any given time.

EISA   Abbreviation for **E**xtended **I**ndustry **S**tandard **A**rchitecture, a 32-bit expansion bus for IBM PCs, IBM PS/2s, and compatible computers that is downwardly compatible with existing 16-bit peripherals such as disk drives and display adapters.

elapsed time   The amount of calendar time it takes to complete a computer-related task.

elastic banding   In computer graphics, the movement of a line drawn from a specified point on the screen to another point. The second point can be moved around the screen by using a mouse, and the line length will expand or contract as if the line were made of elastic material. This makes alteration of diagrams much easier than it would be if lines had to be rubbed out and redrawn. Elastic banding is much used in computer-aided design programs. Also called rubber banding.

electrical communications   The science and technology by which information is collected from an originating source, transformed into electric currents or fields, transmitted over electrical networks or through space to another point, and reconverted into a form suitable for interpretation by a receiving entity.

electrical schematic   A diagram of the logical arrangement of hardware in an electrical circuit or system, using conventional symbols. Can be constructed interactively by COMPUTER-AIDED DESIGN.

electric discharge   A printing method where the paper consists of at least three layers: a substrate, a dark-colored layer that is revealed to form the image, and a light-colored surface coating, usually vacuum-coated aluminum. The print head creates the image by emitting sparks that physically remove the surface coating.

electroluminescent display   A type of flat display screen popular for laptop and portable computers.

electromechanical   Pertaining to any system or device for processing data that uses both electrical and mechanical principles.

electron beam   The beam of electrons produced by an electron gun. The electron beam illuminates the phosphors of the monitor to display the pixels on the raster grid in a selected pattern.

electron beam deflection system   A narrow stream of electrons moving in the same direction under the influence of an electric or magnetic field. See GUN and YOKE.

electron gun   The device within a computer CRT that produces an electron beam.

electronic   Pertaining to the flow of electricity through semiconductors, valves, and filters, in contrast with the free flow of current through simple conductors. The essence of computer technology is the selective use and combination of electronic apparatus whereby current can be allowed to flow or can be halted by electronic switches working at a very high speed.

electronically programmable   Pertaining to Programmable ROM or any other digital device in which the data 1's and 0's in binary code can be entered electronically, usually by the user with a piece of equipment called a PROM Programmer.

electronically programmable read-only memory (EPROM)   An EEPROM module capable of having its contents altered when plugged into a peripheral device.

electronic bulletin board   A computer system that maintains a list of messages so that people can call up (with their computer systems) and either post a message or read the messages already there.

electronic computer-aided design (ECAD)   CAD for electronic design.

electronic cottage   The concept of permitting workers to remain at home to perform work, using computer terminals connected to a central office.

electronic data processing (EDP)   Data processing performed largely by electronic equipment, especially computers.

electronic disk   A chip that lets the computer regard part of its memory as a third disk drive. Also called a phantom disk or ram disk.

electronic filing   The means by which computer systems store information electronically on disks or tapes.

electronic funds transfer (EFT)   A cashless method of paying for goods or services. Electronic signals between computers are used to adjust the accounts of the parties involved in a transaction. Commonly used to make periodic payments, such as insurance premiums. Increasingly available as an option for depositing paychecks.

electronic halftoning   To simulate shades of gray by using patterns of black and white dots.

Electronic Industries Association (EIA)   An association of electronic manufacturers and others who set standards, disseminate information, provide industry liaison, and maintain public relations for the industry. EIA was founded in 1924.

electronic journal   A log file summarizing, in chronological sequence, the processing activities performed by a system.

electronic machine   A device that contains electronic components.

electronic magazine   A magazine published in a floppy disk, video disk, or video tape format. A type of electronic publishing.

electronic mail   The process of sending, receiving, storing, and forwarding messages in digital form over telecommunication facilities. Also called E-MAIL.

electronic mailbox   A STORAGE AREA used to hold a recipient's electronic mail.

electronic marketplace   The buying and selling of information through information services and videotex services. Examples of services that can be subscribed to include THE SOURCE, COMPUSERVE, and PRODIGY.

electronic music   Music in which the sounds are produced by electronic means. See COMPUTER MUSIC and SYNTHESIZER.

electronic office   An office that relies on word processing and computer and data communications technologies. See AUTOMATED OFFICE.

electronic pen A pen-like stylus commonly used in conjunction with a CATHODE RAY TUBE for inputting or changing information under program control. Often called LIGHT PEN.

electronic publishing **(1)** Technology encompassing a variety of activities that contain or convey information with a high editorial and value-added content in a form other than print. Includes educational software disks, CD-ROM, online databases, electronic mail videotex, teletext, videotape cassettes, and videodisks. **(2)** The use of a personal computer, special software, and a laser printer to produce very high-quality documents that combine text and graphics. Also called desktop publishing.

electronics The branch of science and technology relating to the conduction and control of electricity flowing through semiconducting materials or through a vacuum or gases.

Electronics Communications Act of 1986 A law that broadens the previous wiretap law to include communications between computers by extending to electronic communications the same constitutional protections afforded telephone conversations.

electronic spreadsheet A computer program that turns a computer terminal into a huge ledger sheet. Allows large columns and rows of numbers to change according to parameters determined by the user. A whole range of numbers can be changed when a single entry is varied, allowing complex projections and numerical forecasts to be performed without tedious manual calculations.

electronic supervision The process of using a computer to monitor the actions of employees.

electronic thesaurus A program that lists synonyms for a given word.

electrophotographic A printing process where light is used to create a latent image on a photoconductive intermediary. The latent image is rendered visible by liquid or powder toner, transferred to a paper, and fixed by heat, cold, pressure, chemical vapors, or a combination of these. Printers using this process often are referred to by the source of light used to create the image—laser, liquid-crystal shutter (LCS), light-emitting diode (LED), and so forth.

electrosensitive paper   Printer paper with a thin coating of conductive material, such as aluminum. The print becomes visible because it darkens where a matrix-type print head allows electric current to flow onto the conductive surface.

electrosensitive printer   A nonimpact printer that uses electricity to form characters on specially treated paper.

electrostatic plotter   An output device that draws graphic data on paper by using static electrical energy. Generally faster than a pen plotter.

electrostatic printer   A high-speed nonimpact printer that forms characters on chemically treated paper.

electrothermal printer   A high-speed printer that uses heated elements to create characters as matrices of small dots on heat-sensitive paper.

element   An item of data within an array, matrix, set, or collection.

elementary diagram   A wiring diagram of an electrical system in which all devices are drawn between vertical lines that represent power sources. Contains logic elements, components, wire nets, and text. Can be constructed interactively on a CAD system.

elite type   A size of type that fits 12 characters into each inch of type. Contrast with PICA.

ellipse   The conic section that is formed when a plane intersects all the elements of a cone but is not perpendicular to the axis.

em   A unit of measure equal to the width of a capital M in a particular font.

E-mail   Electronic mail, a communications service for computer users wherein textual messages are sent to a central computer system, or electronic "mailbox," and later retrieved by the addressee. E-mail usually refers to private messages; BULLETIN BOARD usually refers to public messages.

embedded command   **(1)** One or more codes inserted into a document that do not print, but direct the application program or printer to control printing and change formats. **(2)** Low-level instructions that are inserted within a program written in a high-level language. Embedded code is used to make a program more efficient or to produce a capability not available in the high-level language.

embedded controller A controller that is built either into a peripheral, such as a disk drive, or into the circuitry of the main board of the system unit.

embedded systems Preprogrammed microprocessors built into another device, such as an automobile, a camera, or a copy machine.

embossing The effect of letters being raised from their background.

em dash A dash (—) that is one EM wide.

EMM Acronym for **E**xpanded **M**emory **M**anager, a technique of managing memory.

empty string A string containing no characters. Also called NULL STRING.

EMS Acronym for **E**xpanded **M**emory **S**pecification, a standard form of extra memory that can be used on IBM-compatible microcomputers.

emulate **(1)** To imitate one hardware system with another, by means of an electronic attachment, such that the imitating system accepts the same data, executes the same programs, and achieves the same results as the imitated system. **(2)** To have a program simulate the function of another software or hardware product. Printers often have emulation options so that users can specify a brand name in configuration or setup, even though they don't have that brand.

en One-half the width of an EM.

enable To switch a computer device or facility so that it can operate. Opposite of DISABLE.

encapsulated PostScript (EPS) A file format developed to facilitate the exchange of POSTSCRIPT graphics files between applications. Like all

PostScript files, EPS files are resolution independent and can be printed by a PostScript printer.

encapsulation In OBJECT-ORIENTED PROGRAMMING, the bundling of methods and instance variables within a class or object so that access to the instance variables is permitted only through the object's own methods. The process of hiding all the details of an object that do not contribute to its essential characteristics. Encapsulation is one of the fundamental elements of the object model. The terms *encapsulation* and INFORMATION HIDING are usually interchangeable.

encipher To alter (scramble) data so that it is not readily usable unless the changes are first undone. See ENCRYPTION.

enclosure The housing for any electrical or electronic device.

encode To convert data into a code form acceptable to some piece of computer equipment. Opposite of DECODE.

encoder A device that produces machine-readable output, such as a floppy disk, either from manual keyboard depressions or from data already recorded in some other code.

encryption (1) The process of coding, or encrypting, any data in which a specific code or key is required to restore the original data. (2) The process of encoding communications data.

end-around carry A carry from the most-significant-digit place to the least-significant-digit place.

end-around shift See CIRCULAR SHIFT.

en dash A dash (–) that is one EN wide.

end color One of two colors at either end of a range of colors.

End key A key on the numeric keypad that is often used in WORD PROCESSING packages.

endless loop Endless repetition of a series of instructions with no exit from the loop possible. Same as infinite loop.

end mark A code or signal that indicates termination of a unit of data. See STOP BIT.

endnote A footnote at the end of a document.

end-of-block (EOB) The termination of a block.

end-of-file (EOF) The termination or point of completion of a quantity of data. End-of-file marks are used to indicate this point on magnetic files. See END-OF-TAPE MARKER.

end-of-job (EOJ) A condition that alerts the program that a job is done and starts another action.

end-of-message (EOM) The termination of a message.

end-of-page halt A feature that stops the printer at the end of each completed page of output.

end-of-tape marker A marker on a MAGNETIC TAPE used to indicate the end of the permissible recording area.

end-of-text (EOT) A transmission control character used to indicate to receiving hardware that the previous character was the last character of message text.

end-of-transmission A control character used to indicate that a transmission has been completed.

endpoints In VECTOR GRAPHICS, the points that specify each end of a line segment.

end user A person who buys and uses computer software or who has contact with computers.

end-user development Systems development activities carried out by the end user.

end-user tools Nonprocedural packages that let the average programmer solve problems without having to learn a programming language.

engine The portion of a program that determines how the program manages and manipulates data. Another name for PROCESSOR.

engineering drawing sizes Drawing sizes conforming to the following specifications: A: 8.5 × 11 inches; B: 11 × 17 inches; C: 17 × 22 inches; D: 22 × 34 inches; and E: 34 × 44 inches.

Enhanced Graphics Adapter (EGA) See EGA.

enhanced keyboard A standard keyboard for newer IBM personal computers. It has become the de facto standard for most IBM-compatible microcomputer keyboards.

enhancements Hardware or software improvements, additions, or updates to a computer or software system.

enlargement A proportional copy of an image that is larger than the original.

E notation A system of notation used to express very large and very small numbers. It consists of two parts: a mantissa and an exponent. Also called scientific notation.

ENTER key A special key on some keyboards that means "execute a command." Same as RETURN key on some keyboards. Often used interchangeably with carriage return. See IMMEDIATE-MODE COMMANDS.

entity Any object that has meaning for a particular application. A computer system may be an entity; a job position, a company, or even a technique or concept could be an entity as well.

entrepreneur One who organizes, manages, and assumes the risk of a business or enterprise.

entry In an electronic spreadsheet, the value or information contained within a specific cell.

entry point The point in a module where control is transferred. Each module has only one entry point.

environment In a computing context, a term more likely referring to the mode of operation, such as a network environment, than to physical conditions of temperature, humidity, and so forth. With respect to personal computers, everything surrounding the PC, including peripherals and software.

environment division   The second of four main parts of a COBOL program.

EOB   Abbreviation for END-OF-BLOCK.

EOF   Abbreviation for END-OF-FILE. When all the records in a file have been processed, the computer is said to have encountered an end-of-file condition.

EOJ   Abbreviation for END-OF-JOB.

EOLN   Abbreviation for END-OF-LINE, a flag indicating the end of a line of data. Sometimes abbreviated EOL.

EOM   Abbreviation for END-OF-MESSAGE.

EOT   Abbreviation for END-OF-TRANSMISSION.

EP   Abbreviation for ELECTRONIC PRESENTATION, a process whereby a user creates a presentation using a desktop computer system. The diskette (containing the presentation) is then inserted into an EP player, which can produce an animated video presentation.

EPO   Abbreviation for EMERGENCY POWER OFF, the circuit, and the buttons activating it, that can turn an entire computer off in an emergency. There may be as many as 20 EPO buttons in a large installation.

EPROM   Acronym for ERASABLE PROGRAMMABLE READ-ONLY MEMORY, a special PROM that can be erased under high-intensity ultraviolet light and reprogrammed repeatedly. Compare EAROM. Contrast with ROM.

EPROM programmer   A special machine used to program EPROM chips. Compare PROM PROGRAMMER.

EPS   Acronym for ENCAPSULATED POSTSCRIPT, a directly printable PostScript file; the output of a PostScript compatible printer driver captured in a file instead of being sent to a printer. The typical filename extension for encapsulated PostScript files is EPS.

epsilon   A small quantity of something.

Epson A well-established brand of dot-matrix printers that can print graphics as well as text.

equality The idea expressed by the equal sign, written = . In many programming languages and program designs, the equal sign is also used as a "replacement symbol." Contrast with INEQUALITY.

equalization A process by which the range of gray shades in an image is expanded to make the image more attractive.

equation A mathematical sentence with an equal sign between two arithmetic expressions that name the same number. For example, A + 10 = 6 is an equation from which A is calculated to be −4.

equipment Part of a computer system. See COMPUTER, HARDWARE, and PERIPHERAL EQUIPMENT.

equipment bay A cabinet or case in which electronic equipment is installed.

erasable optical disc An optical disc on which data can be stored, moved, changed, and erased, just as on magnetic media. Erasable drives perform much like large, interchangeable hard disks. They use two lasers rather than one; one laser melts the surface of the media to an amorphous state, effectively erasing any information stored there, and the other laser writes or reads information.

erasable programmable read-only memory See EPROM.

erasable storage A storage medium that can be erased and reused. HARD DISKS, FLOPPY DISKS, and MAGNETIC TAPES are examples of media that can be erased and reused.

erase To permanently remove data from storage.

ergonomics The study of the physical relationships between people and their work environment. Adapting machines to the convenience of operators, with the general aim of maximum efficiency and physical well-being. Numeric keypads on standard keyboards, detachable keyboards, and tilting display screens are tangible results. The word comes from *ergo* (work) and *nomics* (law or management).

EPROM   Acronym for ERASABLE PROGRAMMABLE READ ONLY MEMORY. See EAROM.

error   Any deviation of a computed or a measured quantity from the theoretically correct or true value. Contrast with FAULT, MALFUNCTION, and MISTAKE. See INTERMITTENT ERROR and ROUND-OFF ERROR.

error analysis   The branch of numerical analysis concerned with studying the error aspects of numerical analysis procedures. Includes the study of errors that arise in a computation because of the peculiarities of computer arithmetic.

error checking   (1) Various techniques that test for the valid condition of data. (2) The process by which two telecommunicating computers can verify that the data received was error-free.

error control   Any plan, implemented by software, hardware, or procedures, to detect and/or correct errors introduced into a data communications system.

error-correcting code   (1) A code in which each acceptable expression conforms to specific rules of construction. Nonacceptable expressions are also defined. If certain types of errors occur in an acceptable expression, an equivalent will result and the error can be corrected. (2) A code in which the forbidden pulse combination produced by the gain or loss of a bit will indicate which bit is wrong. Same as SELF-CORRECTING CODE.

error correction   A system that detects and inherently provides correction for errors caused by transmission equipment or facilities.

error-detecting code   (1) A code in which each expression conforms to specific rules of construction. When expressions occur that do not conform to the rules of these constructions, an error is indicated. (2) A code in which errors produce forbidden combinations. A single error-detecting code produces a forbidden combination if a digit gains or loses a single bit; a double error-detecting code produces a forbidden combination if a digit gains or loses either one or two bits, and so on. Also called SELF-CHECKING CODE.

error file A file generated during information processing to retain erroneous information sensed by the computer, often printed as an error report.

error guessing A test data selection technique. The selection criterion is to pick values that seem likely to cause errors.

error handling A program feature that minimizes the possibility of an error occurring if a keyboard operator pushes the wrong key.

error message A printed or displayed statement indicating the computer has detected a mistake or malfunction. See WARNING MESSAGE.

error rate In data communications, a measure of quality of a circuit or equipment; the number of erroneous bits or characters in a sample.

error ratio The ratio of the number of erroneous data units to the total number of data units.

error transmission A change in data resulting from the transmission process. Often a DROP IN or a DROP OUT.

error trapping (1) A mechanism in a software package that prevents a user from entering the incorrect type of data. (2) The ability to recognize an error and respond appropriately.

ESCAPE key A standard control key available on most computer keyboards. Used to take control of the computer away from a program, to escape from a specific program, or to stop a program. Abbreviated ESC.

ESPRIT Acronym for European Strategic Program for Research and Development in Information Technology.

ESDI Abbreviation for ENHANCED SMALL DISK INTERFACE, a version of an industry standard interface that connects hard disks to their controllers. ESDI allows the disk to run faster and more reliably.

Ethernet A form of LOCAL AREA NETWORK (LAN) widely used for interconnecting computers. A relatively fast system, Ethernet is popular in DEC and Unix environments. Operational speeds are around one million characters per second. Ethernet was developed by Xerox Corporation in 1976 and was originally used for linking minicomputers at the Xerox Palo Alto Research Center.

E-time   The portion of the machine cycle when an instruction is actually executed.

ETX   Alternate abbreviation for END-OF-TEXT.

evaluation   The process of determining if a newly created computer system is actually doing what it was designed to do. See SYSTEM FOLLOW-UP.

Evans & Sutherland, Inc.   A manufacturer of graphics workstation equipment and flight simulation visual systems. One of the pioneering companies in computer graphics.

event   Any occurrence or happening. Also called milestone node, it has no time frame associated with it, but typically serves to mark the start or end of activities and to relate activities to each other.

event driven   Referring to multiprogramming, in which programs share resources based on events that take place in the programs.

evocative typeface   A display type design intended to evoke an era or place.

Excel™   A spreadsheet from Microsoft Corporation for the Apple Macintosh and IBM-compatible microcomputer systems. The program provides a wide variety of business graphics and charts and takes full advantage of using laser printers for making presentation materials. It provides a worksheet area of 16,384 rows by 256 columns and contains presentation tools, such as multiple fonts, type sizes, object-oriented graphics, variable row heights, shading, custom number formats, and built-in charts. Excel incorporates some of the features of page layout programs.

exception reporting   A technique for screening large amounts of computerized data to display or print reports containing only specific information, especially items outside normal ranges. Plays a key role in management by exception. An exception report shows only data reflecting unusual circumstances.

exception statement   A control structure that catches errors or unusual occurrences.

exchangeable disk   See DISK PACK.

exchangeable disk store   A type of disk storage, used as a backing storage, in which the disks come in capsules. Each capsule contains several disks; capsules can be replaced during operation of the computer and stored until needed. The exchangeable capsule is often called a DISK PACK.

exchange buffering   A technique using data chaining for eliminating the need to move data in internal storage.

exclusive OR (XOR)   A Boolean operator that gives a truth table value of true if only one of the two variables it connects is true. If both variables it connects are true, then this value is false. Contrast with INCLUSIVE OR.

executable file   A FILE that, when its name is entered, will execute a program.

executable statement   A program statement that gives an instruction or some computational operation to be performed right then, such as an assignment statement. Contrast with NONEXECUTABLE STATEMENT.

execute   (1) To run a program on a computer. (2) To carry out the instructions in an algorithm or program.

execute cycle   The period of time during which a machine instruction is interpreted and the indicated operation is performed on the specified operand.

execution   The operating cycle during which a program is actually being processed, or run.

execution time   The time it takes for a program to run from start to finish.

executive   A master program that controls the execution of other programs.

exerciser   A device that enables users to create and debug programs and hardware interfaces by manual means.

exit   That point in an algorithm or program from which control is transferred elsewhere.

expand   To return compressed data to its original condition.

expandability   The ability to increase the capability of a computer system by adding modules or devices.

expanded memory   Memory added to a computer system.

expanded type   Type that has been increased laterally so that fewer characters are contained per linear inch.

expansion   A means of increasing the capabilities of a computer by adding hardware designed to perform a task that is not built into the basic system.

expansion bus   A collection of wires in a computer that allow for the insertion of an expansion board.

expansion card   A circuit board that plugs into a computer and gives it additional specialized functions (e.g., enhanced graphics, expanded memory, modem).

expansion interface   A circuit board that allows users to add disk drives, additional memory, and other peripherals to a basic computer.

expansion slots   The sockets on the main board of a computer where accessory cards or expansion cards are inserted.

expansion unit   A device, connected to a computer, that contains extra sockets into which additional printed circuit boards can be plugged.

expert system   An interactive computer program that helps users with problems that would otherwise require the assistance of human experts; a program that presents the computer as an expert on a particular topic. Expert systems capture knowledge in rules that can be communicated to others as advice or solutions. The programs often simulate the reasoning process used by human experts in certain well-defined fields.

expert system shell   An expert system building program. The program has the basic structure required to find answers to questions; the questions themselves can be added by the user.

explicit address   A storage address explicitly stated in a source language program.

exploded pie graph   A pie graph in which one or more of the slices has been offset slightly from the others.

exploded view   An illustration of a solid construction showing its parts separately, but in positions that indicate their relationships to the whole.

exponent   (1) A symbol or number written above and to the right of another symbol or number that denotes the number of times the latter is used as a factor. For example, a short way of writing 10×10 is 10^2, where 2 is the exponent and 10 is the base. The exponent tells how many times the base is used as a factor. (2) In floating-point notation, exponents are introduced by E; for example, 77E2 means 77 times 10 to the exponent 2. See E NOTATION.

exponential smoothing   A weighted, moving-average method of forecasting in which past observations are geometrically discounted according to their age, the heaviest weight being assigned to the most recent data. The smoothing is called exponential because data points are weighted in accordance with an exponential function of their age.

exponentiation   A process or function that enables the user to calculate the power of a number. For example, the result of nine to the fifth power may be calculated in a single step without multiplying $9 \times 9 \times 9 \times 9$.

export   To transfer information from one system or program to another. Opposite of IMPORT.

expression   (1) A general term for numerals, numerals with signs of operation, variables, and combinations of these. (2) Any arithmetic formula coded in a programming language.

extended addressing   An addressing mode that can reach any place in memory and requires more than one byte to locate the data in memory.

Extended Binary Coded Decimal Interchange Code   See EBCDIC.

extender board A debugging aid that allows the user to monitor circuit boards more conveniently.

extensible language A concept whereby the user adds new features to a programming language by modifying existing ones.

extension (1) A feature added to a programming language or computer system; a feature beyond what is regularly available in the standard. (2) A reference to a filename that serves to extend or clarify its meaning.

extent A collection of physical records contiguous in auxiliary storage.

extents Lines, rectangles, or solids that separate or surround individual polygons or segments. They are not displayed on the screen, but are devices used by graphics programmers.

external CD-ROM An optical disc equipped with its own case, cables, and power supply.

external commands OPERATING SYSTEM commands that require that the system disk be in the active drive to be implemented.

external data file Data stored separately from the program that processes it.

external disk A DISK UNIT that is not housed within the computer's system unit. Contrast with INTERNAL DISK.

external drive A disk drive that sits in its own case, rather than being mounted in the chassis of the main computer. Often, external drives include their own power supply.

external hard disk A hard disk equipped with its own case, cables, and power supply.

external label An identification label attached to the outside of a file medium holder identifying the file, such as a paper label or sticker attached to the cover containing a magnetic disk or tape.

external modem A MODEM that resides outside the computer but is connected to the computer through the serial port.

external reference   A reference to a symbol defined in another routine.

external report   A report produced by an organization for use outside the company, often on preprinted forms required by government or for distribution to customers.

external sort   The second phase of a multipass sort program, wherein strings of data are continually merged until one string of sequenced data is formed.

external storage   Same as AUXILIARY STORAGE.

external symbol   (1) A control section name, entry point name, or external reference. (2) A symbol contained in the external symbol dictionary.

external symbol dictionary   Control information associated with an object program that identifies the external symbols in the program.

extract   To remove specific information from a computer word as determined by a mask or filter.

extrusion   An interactive modelling technique in which a further dimension can be added to an existing definition; for example, a line can be extruded from a point, a plane from a line, and a solid from a plane.

eye point   The location of the eye in three-dimensional space. Like a camera, the eye is not confined to one location in an area defining a picture; the eye point, or camera, can be repositioned anywhere. In three-dimensional graphics, the user does not simply have a view of an environment from a confined area. Rather, the eye point location can go anywhere in the space. Thus, the images move, but the user's eye point can move dynamically in the space as well.

eyestrain   Eye discomfort sometimes associated with long-term use of a video display terminal.

— F —

f   Frequency.

fabricated language   Same as SYMBOLIC LANGUAGE.

fabrication   The processing of manufacturing materials to desired specifications. See COMPUTER-AIDED MANUFACTURING.

fabric design   An industry with a long history in which computers and graphics are now frequently involved. Where precise repetition of pattern is essential, few artists can operate with the speed and efficiency of a machine. Color combinations can be unlimited when the operation is computerized.

face   (1) In computer graphics or geometry, one side of a solid object, such as a cube. A cube has six faces. (2) In printing and typography, a shortened form of typeface.

FACE   See FIELD ALTERABLE CONTROL ELEMENT.

face list   The list of faces and their vertices that make up the surface shape of a model.

facets   In three-dimensional modeling, polygons that comprise the surface of a computer-generated object. Flat surfaces, usually convex polygons, forming a surface.

facilities   A general term that applies to physical equipment, electrical power, communication lines, and other items used in computer and data communications centers.

facilities management   The use of an independent service organization to operate and manage a data processing installation.

facility   (1) A measure of the ease with which a computer system may be used, a major factor in determining the system's productivity. (2) A channel for electrical transmission between two points.

facing pages   The two pages of a bound document that face each other when the document is open. The even-numbered page (verso) is on the left, and the odd-numbered page (recto) is on the right.

facsimile   The use of computer technology to send digitized text, graphics, and charts from one facsimile machine to another. Abbreviated as fax.

factor analysis   A mathematical technique for studying the interaction of many factors to determine the most significant factors and the degree of significance.

factorial   The product of factors, computed by multiplying all integers from 1 to a specified number. The exclamation point (!) is used to represent a factorial. For example, $4! = 1 \times 2 \times 3 \times 4$; $n! = 1 \times 2 \times 3 \times 4 \ldots (n-1) \times n$.

fail-safe system   A system designed to avoid catastrophe, possibly at the expense of convenience. For example, when a fault is detected in a computer-controlled traffic light system, a fail-safe arrangement might be to set all the traffic lights to red rather than turn them off. Similarly, in a power plant operation, overheating might simply disconnect the power supply.

fail-soft system   A system that continues to process data despite the failure of parts of the system, usually accompanied by a deterioration in performance. Using the two examples described under FAIL-SAFE SYSTEM, the traffic lights might turn to flashing amber rather than red, and the overheat system might maintain battery power for emergency equipment while the main source of power is turned off.

failure prediction   A technique that attempts to determine the failure schedule of specific parts of equipment so that they may be discarded and replaced before failure occurs.

fairness   A condition that holds when every action requested in a system is guaranteed to execute after a finite amount of time.

fair use   A situation in which limited copying of copyrighted material is legal.

fall-back   A backup system brought into use in an emergency situation, especially the reserve database and programs that would be switched on quickly, or even automatically, in the event of a detected fault in a real-time system.

fallout   The failure of electronic components sometimes experienced during the burn-in of a new piece of equipment.

false color   Color that is added to monochrome images by transforming intensity values into color values.

family   (1) In COMPUTER SCIENCE, a compatible series of computers (for example, Apple Macintosh Classic, Macintosh LC, and Macintosh IIsi constitute a family of microcomputers). (2) In DESKTOP PUBLISHING, a family of type (for example, Helvetica, Helvetica Italic, Helvetica Bold, and Helvetica Bold Italic constitute a family of type).

FAMOS   Acronym for **f**loating gate **a**valanche injection **MOS**, a fabrication technology for charge storage devices such as PROMS.

fan   (1) The cooling mechanism built into computer cabinets, laser printers, and other devices to prevent malfunction due to heat buildup. (2) To flip through a stack of laser printer paper to ensure that the pages are loose and will not stick together or jam the printer.

fanfold paper   One long continuous sheet of paper perforated at regular intervals to mark page boundaries and folded fan-style into a stack. Fanfold paper is available with vertical perforations, so that the sprocket hole strip can be removed. The paper can be divided on the perforations, thus enabling it to be separated into sheets.

fan-in   The number of signal inputs to a digital component.

fan-out   (1) The number of TTL unit loads a given TTL device output can supply or drive under the worst-case conditions. (2) The number of programming modules below any given module in a structured program.

farad   A unit of measure of capacitance. A capacitor has a capacitance of 1 farad if it will store a charge of 1 coulomb when a 1-volt potential is applied across it.

fatal error An unexpected failure or other problem that occurs while the program is executing, preventing the computer from continuing to execute the program. If the error is nonfatal, the program will proceed, but incorrectly. An operator's mistake that causes the program to crash, destroying the data stored in RAM, would be a fatal error.

fat bits The selection on a painting and drawing program that enlarges a portion of the screen to allow precise manipulation of individual screen elements. Useful for precision work or font designing.

father file A system of updating records that retains a copy of the original record as well as providing an amended version. When a file-update program is run, the old master file is termed the father file, the updated file is termed the son file, and the file that was used to create the father file is termed the grandfather file. This technique is particularly applicable to files held on magnetic media, such as disk or tape.

fault A condition, such as a broken wire or short circuit, that prevents a component, computer, or peripheral device from performing to its design specifications.

fault tolerant A term describing a continuous operation in the event of failure. Fault-tolerant computer systems contain redundant processors.

fax (1) Facsimile. (2) An equipment configuration that facilitates the transmission of images over a common carrier network. A fax machine sends an image to another fax machine, over standard telephone networks. The process is similar to making a photocopy; however, the reproduction quality of a fax is typically lower.

fax modem A device that attaches to a PERSONAL COMPUTER, giving it the ability to send or receive electronic messages over telephone lines.

FCC Abbreviation for **F**ederal **C**ommunications **C**ommission, an organization of the U.S. Government responsible for regulating interstate communications, communications common carriers, and the broadcast media.

F connector A coaxial connector that uses a screw-on attachment.

FDDI   Abbreviation for **F**iber **D**istributed **D**ata **I**nterface, an evolving standard for 10-Mbps, fiber-optic cable networks.

FE   Abbreviation for FIELD ENGINEER.

feasibility study   A study concerned with the definition of a data processing problem, together with alternative solutions, a recommended course of action, and a working plan for designing and installing the system.

feather   To blend or smooth the edge of a region or shape into a background or other object.

feathering   Adding an even amount of space between each line on a page or column to force vertical justification.

feature   Something special accomplished in a program or hardware device, such as the ability of a paint program to create animation cells, or a word processing program to check the spelling of words.

feature extraction   The selection of dominant characteristics for pattern recognition, enabling a computer-controlled video camera to recognize objects by such features as shapes and edges.

Federal Privacy Act   Federal legislation prohibiting secret personnel files from being kept on individuals by government agencies or contractors. It allows individuals to know what information about them is on file and how it is used within all government agencies and their contractors, and is also known as the Privacy Act of 1974.

feed   (**1**) To supply data or materials to any device. (**2**) A mechanical process whereby lengthy materials—such as MAGNETIC TAPE, LINE PRINTER paper, and PRINTER ribbon—are moved along the required operating position. (**3**) To insert DISKS into a DISK DRIVE.

feedback   (**1**) A means of automatic control in which the actual state of a process is measured and used to obtain a quantity that modifies the input to initiate the activity of the control system. (**2**) In data processing, information arising from a particular stage of processing that affects the processing of subsequent data; for example, the fact that an area of storage is nearly full may either delay the acceptance of more data or divert it to some other storage area. **(3)** Any process whereby output from a sequential task serves to modify subsequent tasks.

feedback circuit A circuit that returns a portion of the output signal of an electronic circuit or control system to the input of the circuit or the system.

female connector A recessed portion of a connecting device into which another part fits. Contrast with MALE CONNECTOR.

femto A prefix indicating one-quadrillionth, or a millionth of a billionth, 10^-.

femtosecond One-quadrillionth of a second. There are as many of them (the number one followed by 15 zeros) in one second as there are seconds in 30 million years. In two seconds, light travels from Earth past the moon; in 12 femtoseconds, it moves only five microns, roughly one-tenth the width of a human hair. Abbreviated fs.

ferrous oxide The substance that coats recording disks and tapes. It can be magnetized, thereby permitting information to be recorded on it magnetically.

FET Acronym for FIELD EFFECT TRANSISTOR. See MOSFET.

fetch To locate and load a quantity of instructions or data from storage.

fetch, decode, and execute process A process in which a computer fetches, decodes, and then executes an instruction.

FF Abbreviation for FORM FEED.

fiber optic cable An advanced form of cabling that uses light to transmit data. This allows for very long distances between nodes.

fiche MICROFICHE, a sheet of photographic film containing multiple microimages. See COM.

field A single piece of information, the smallest unit normally manipulated by a database management system. In a personnel file, the person's name and age would be separate fields. A record is made up of one or more fields.

field alterable control element (FACE)   A chip used in some systems to allow the user to write microprograms.

fieldata code   A U.S. military code used in data processing as a compromise between conflicting manufacturer's codes.

field effect transistor (FET)   A three-terminal semiconductor device that acts as a variable charge storage element. The most commonly used type in microcomputers is the Metallic Oxide Semiconductor (MOS) transistor. See MOSFET.

field emission   The emission of electrons from a metal or semiconductor into a vacuum under the influence of a strong electric field.

field engineer (FE)   The individual responsible for field maintenance of computer hardware and software.

fielding   The arranging for text or numbers to occupy the correct positions on the display screen or on paper.

field name   An identifier given to a field in a DATABASE file.

field of view   In computer graphics, the limits of what a simulated camera can see, usually expressed as a horizontal angle centered at the camera. For simplicity of computation, computer graphicists assume that what a camera sees lies within a pyramid—rather than a cone—with the apex at the camera.

field upgradable   Hardware capable of being enhanced in the field (in one's office or at a local repair center or computer store).

field width   The number of positions set aside for data in a particular field.

FIFO   Acronym for first in-first out, a method of storing and retrieving items from a list, table, or stack, so that the first element stored is the first one retrieved. Same as LILO. Contrast with LIFO.

fifth-generation computers   The next generation of computers. A term describing new forms of computer systems involving artificial intelligence, natural language, and expert systems. Fifth-generation computer systems are expected to appear in the mid-1990s and will represent the next quantum leap in computer technology.

fifth-generation languages Natural languages. These languages use human languages such as English to give people a more natural connection with computers.

figure shift A keyboard key, or the code generated by the key, signifying that the following characters are to be read as figures until a letter shift appears in the message.

file A collection of related records treated as a basic unit of storage.

file allocation table (FAT) A map used by the OPERATING SYSTEM to locate files on a disk.

file attribute A set of characteristics that tells the computer how to treat a file.

file backup Copies of data files that can be used to reactivate (restore) a database that has been damaged or destroyed.

file chaining A function that allows a query application to use data from two database files.

file cleanup The removal of superfluous or obsolete data from a file.

file compression See COMPRESSION.

file control block A RECORD that contains all the information about a file, such as its structure, length, and name.

file conversion The process of changing the file medium or structure.

file definition Information that describes the contents and characteristics of a FILE.

file deletion Removing the FILENAME from the DIRECTORY.

file description A part of a file in which file and field attributes are described.

file directory A DIRECTORY on an input/output medium that provides data such as filename, length, and starting address for each file on the medium.

file extension In DOS, each file has a unique name consisting of two parts: a filename and an extension. The filename can include up to eight characters and the extension can include up to three.

file fragmentation A condition in which there are many scattered areas of storage that are too small to be used productively.

file gap The space at the end of the file (on magnetic media) that signifies to the system where the file terminates.

file handling routine That part of a computer program that reads data from, and writes data to, a file.

file label The external label identifying a file.

file layout The arrangement and structure of data in a file, including the sequence and size of its components.

file level model A model concerned with defining data structures for optimum performance of database application programs or queries.

file librarian The person responsible for the safekeeping of all computer files, such as programs and data on magnetic disks or tapes.

file locking A system that protects shared files by allowing only one user at a time to make changes.

file maintenance The updating of a file to reflect the effects of nonperiodic changes by adding, altering, or deleting data.

file management The creation and maintenance of computer files.

file manager A simple database management program that uses only simple files and indexes. Also called a record manager, it is a little brother to a DATABASE MANAGEMENT SYSTEM.

filename Alphanumeric characters used to identify a particular file.

filename extension A code attached to the filename. It is separated from the filename by a period, and identifies the kind of data in the file.

file organization   The manner in which the applications programmer views the data.

file processing   The periodic updating of master files to reflect the effects of current data, often transaction data contained in detail files such as a monthly inventory run updating the master inventory file.

file processing package   A database management package that can only work with one file at a time to produce various types of reports.

file processing system   A database software system that can only work with one file at a time.

file protection   A technique or device used to prevent accidental erasure of data from a file, such as a gummed tab over the write-protect notch of a 5.25-inch floppy disk.

file-protect ring   A device used to protect data on magnetic tape. Accidental writing on the tape is prevented by removing the ring from the tape reel.

file recovery   A broad term used to describe any method for getting back a file that has been lost or damaged.

file server   The central repository of shared files and applications in a computer network.

file size   The number of records in a file.

filespec   An abbreviation for file specification; in DOS systems, a file's drive letter, pathname, filename, and extension.

file storage   Devices that can hold a reservoir of mass data within the computer system, such as MAGNETIC DISK and TAPE, and CD-ROM units.

file structure   The format of fields within a data record. For example, PART NAME in the first field of a record, PART NUMBER in the second field, PRICE in the third field, and so on, all specify the structure of a file.

file tidying   The removal of superfluous or obsolete data from a file.

file transfer   The movement of a file from one place to another, or from one storage medium to another.

file transfer utility   A utility program that transfers files between different types of hardware, such as between an Apple Macintosh and an IBM PS/2.

file updating   In a FILE, the activity of adding, changing, or deleting data.

filing   The storage of a document either by electronic or optical means or as a hard copy.

fill   **(1)** To place a pattern or color in a defined region. **(2)** A color or pattern occupying a region.

fill algorithm   An algorithm that fills polygons with a color, gray-scale shade, or pattern.

fill character   A character used to occupy an area on a human-readable medium; for example, in a business form, dashes or asterisks used to fill out a field to ensure that nothing is added to the field once the form has been issued.

filled   A term referring to objects in computer images; these, if filled, appear as shaded solids.

filler character   A specific character or bit combination used to fill the remainder of a field after justification.

fillet   The representation of a filled-in or rounded intersection of two lines or curves.

filling   In computer graphics, a software function that allows the interior of a defined area to be filled with a color, shading, or pattern of the operator's choosing.

fill line   In computer graphics, a line that indicates one boundary of an area to be filled.

fill point   In computer graphics, a point that indicates the radial center of an area to be filled.

film recorder   An output device that takes a 35 mm slide picture from a graphics file that has been created using a graphics program. Widely used in producing presentation-quality hard copy, film recorders offer both high resolution (up to 2,000 dots per inch) and a true-color reproduction capability (up to 6 million simultaneous colors). Lines show perfectly smooth edges and colors blend imperceptibly in film recorder images.

FILO   Acronym for **f**irst **i**n-**l**ast **o**ut, a method of storing and retrieving items from a list, table, or stack, so that the first element stored is the last one retrieved. Same as LIFO. Contrast with FIFO.

filter   A software function that modifies an image by altering the gray values of certain pixels. See MASK.

filter command   A DOS and OS/2 command that takes input from one source, changes it, and sends the result to another device or printer.

filtering   An IMAGE-PROCESSING technique that reduces unwanted features or colors in an image.

financial analysis   See SPREADSHEET ANALYSIS.

financial reporting   Internal reports to management and external reports to stockholders and other interested parties on an organization's financial status.

find   Same as SEARCH.

find and replace   See SEARCH AND REPLACE.

finder   A system program that provides the "desktop" metaphor the user encounters when a Macintosh microcomputer is booted up. The finder presents icons (little pictures) depicting applications, documents, file folders, and a garbage can that can be used to discard unwanted files. This highly visual interface program keeps the user from having to type commands directly to the operating system.

fine tune   To make small adjustments in order to get best results.

finite   To have limits, an end, or a last number; not infinite.

finite elements   Discrete mathematical sub-elements of a complex part that are more easily evaluated than the part in its entirety.

finite element method   An approximation technique used to solve field problems in various engineering fields.

fire   To initiate the action specified by a rule when the condition stated by the rule is satisfied.

firmware   Software that has been copied on integrated circuits, usually ROMs. Since it is on ROM, which cannot be altered, it is neither completely soft nor hard, and is therefore referred to as firm.

first draft   A rough draft of a complete document or script.

first generation   The original; not a copy.

first-generation computers   The first commercially available computers, introduced with UNIVAC I in 1951 and terminated with the development of fully transistorized computers in 1959. Characterized by their use of vacuum tubes, they are now museum pieces. Compare SECOND-GENERATION COMPUTERS, THIRD-GENERATION COMPUTERS, FOURTH-GENERATION COMPUTERS, and FIFTH-GENERATION COMPUTERS.

first in-first out   See FIFO.

first-order predicate logic   A form of logic, used in PROLOG, that allows assertions to be made about the variables in a proposition.

fitting   In computer graphics, the calculation of a curve, surface, or line that fits most accurately to a set of data points and design criteria. Compare CURVE FITTING.

fix   A correction of a mistake in a PROGRAM, often a temporary correction or bypass of defective code.

fixed   Pertaining to a field that always exists within a data record.

fixed area   That portion of internal storage that has been assigned to specific programs or data areas.

fixed-head disk unit   A storage device consisting of one or more magnetically coded disks on the surface of which data is stored in the form of magnetic spots arranged in a manner to represent binary data. The data are arranged in circular tracks around the disks and are accessible for reading and writing by read/write heads assigned one per track. Data from a given track are read or written sequentially as the disk rotates under or over the read/write head.

fixed length A specified length for a record or field that cannot be changed.

fixed-length record A record that always contains the same number of characters.

fixed point Pertaining to a number system in which each number is represented by a single set of digits, and the position of the radix point is implied by the manner in which the numbers are used.

fixed-size records File elements, each of which has the same number of words, characters, bytes, bits, fields, and so on.

fixed-spacing Printing of characters at fixed horizontal intervals on a page.

fixed storage Storage whose contents are not alterable by computer instructions, such as READ-ONLY STORAGE.

fixed word length Pertaining to a machine word or operand that always has the same number of bits, bytes, or characters.

flag (1) An indicator used frequently to tell some later part of a program that some condition occurred earlier, such as an overflow or carry. (2) A symbol used to mark a record for special attention. For example, on a listing of a program, all statements that contain errors may be flagged for the attention of the program writer. (3) An indicator of special conditions, such as interrupts.

flashing The blinking on and off of characters on a display screen; used to call attention to something on the screen.

flatbed plotter A digital plotter using plotting heads that move over a flat surface in both vertical and horizontal directions. The size of the bed determines the maximum size sheet of paper that can be drawn. A pair of arms attached to a trolley and controlled by a computer can place the trolley at any part of the paper. A pen attached to the trolley can be raised or lowered to contact the paper. Then, under computer control, this device can draw pictures. If several pens of different colors can be controlled, then pictures can be drawn in color.

flatbed scanner   A scanner with a glass surface upon which material to be scanned is placed. Because the original never moves during the scanning process, flatbeds produce more precise results than sheetfed scanners. The scanner can transform a full-page (8.5-by-11-inch) graphic or page of text into a digitized file.

flat file   Another name for a table in a relational data model.

flat file database   A simple DATABASE MANAGEMENT program that takes or stores information from only one file at a time.

flat pack   A small, low-profile (flat), integrated circuit package that can be spot-welded or soldered to a terminal or a printed circuit board. The pins extend outward rather than pointing down, as on a DIP.

flat panel display terminal   A thin-screened peripheral device, such as a plasma display panel, upon which information can be displayed.

flat screen   A thin panel screen, such as those found on flat panel displays.

flat shading   In computer graphics, a shading method that applies a lighting model to only one point on each polygon face. Each face is rendered in a single color that represents the amount of light interacting with that face. This tends to give the object a faceted appearance, similar to that of a diamond. Uniform shading.

Flavors   An object-oriented extension of LISP, developed at the Massachusetts Institute of Technology.

flexible   See FLOPPY DISK.

flexible disk   A flexible magnetic disk enclosed in a protective container. Same as floppy disk.

flicker   The undesirable, unsteady lighting of a display due to inadequate refresh rate and/or fast persistence. This occurs whenever the refresh speed is not fast enough to compensate for natural luminance delay on the screen. See REFRESHING.

flight computer   A computer resident in a spacecraft, airplane, or missile.

flight simulator   **(1)** The computer-controlled simulator used by airline companies to train pilots on new aircraft. Some simulators are so realistic that they are acceptable to the FAA for use in renewal of pilot licenses. **(2)** On personal computers, software that provides entertainment and practice in instrument reading and navigation.

flip   To reverse an image side to side (to flip horizontally) or top to bottom (to flip vertically).

flip-flop   A device or circuit containing active elements capable of assuming either one of two stable states at a given time. Synonymous with TOGGLE.

flippy-floppy   A single-sided 5.25-inch floppy disk that is recorded on both sides. A second write-protect notch is punched into the disk so that it can be flipped over and inserted upside down.

float   The amount of time following the completion of a task or activity and prior to the start of the next task or activity. Also called SLACK TIME.

floating head   A magnetic head floating on a layer of air away from the recording surface.

floating point   A form of number representation in which quantities are represented by a number called the mantissa, multiplied by a power of the number base.

floating-point arithmetic   A method of calculation that automatically accounts for the location of the radix point.

floating-point constant   A number, usually consisting of two parts, with one part containing the fractional component of the number; the other part is expressed as a power of the number's radix (base). Also called REAL CONSTANT.

floating-point operation   An operation done with FLOATING-POINT ARITHMETIC.

floating-point routine   A set of subroutines that cause a computer to execute floating-point operations with no built-in floating-point hardware.

floppy disk   A type of computer storage medium consisting of a thin flexible disk covered with magnetic oxide held inside a protective sleeve within which it can be rotated. Floppy disks are lightweight, inexpensive, and portable. The first were 8-inch disks (which meant that the whole package was eight inches square), but these earlier disks are now superseded by 5.25- and 3.5-inch versions. The 3.5-inch version is much improved over its predecessors in that it has a hard, rather than flexible, casing and a protective "door" over its access holes, which means that its reliability is likely to be much greater. Storage capacities on disks have increased greatly during development. Early disks offered only about 100 Kbyte on an 8-inch disk; recent drives offer up to 2 Mbyte on a standard 3.5-inch disk. Floppy disks are standard equipment on virtually every PERSONAL COMPUTER.

floppy disk case   A container, usually made of plastic, for storing and protecting floppy disks.

floppy disk controller   A circuit board or chip that controls a floppy disk unit.

floppy disk unit   A peripheral storage device in which data are recorded on magnetizable floppy disks.

FLOPS   Acronym for **fl**oating-point **o**perations **p**er **s**econd, a measure of the speed at which a computer can compute.

floptical   A removable optical disk. The disks and drives have dimensions similar to those of floppy disks, but they hold 20 to 25 Mbytes.

flowchart   A diagram that uses symbols and interconnecting lines to show (1) the logic and sequence of specific program operations (PROGRAM

FLOWCHART), or **(2)** a system of processing to achieve objectives (SYSTEM FLOWCHART).

flowcharter   A computer program that automatically generates flowcharts with a visual display screen, digital plotter, or printer.

flowcharting symbol   The symbol used to represent operations, dataflow, or equipment on a flowchart.

flowchart template   The plastic guide that contains cutouts of the flowchart symbols and is used in the preparation of a flowchart.

flowchart text   The descriptive information associated with FLOWCHART SYMBOLS.

flow diagram   See FLOWCHART.

flowline   On a flowchart, a line representing a connecting path between flowchart symbols.

fluidics   The branch of science and technology concerned with control, information-processing sensing, and actuation functions performed through the use of fluid dynamic phenomena.

flush   **(1)** To empty a portion of storage of its contents. **(2)** Pertaining to type set in alignment with the left (flush left) or right (flush right) edge of the line measure.

flush left   Pertaining to text that is aligned at the left margin but need not be aligned at the right margin.

flush right   Pertaining to text that is aligned at the right margin but need not be aligned at the left margin.

FM   Abbreviation for **f**requency **m**odulation, the process of changing the value represented by a signal by varying the frequency of the signal.

FO   Abbreviation for **f**iber **o**ptic, a connection that uses light pulses traveling in a transparent glass or plastic wire. Fiber optic connections can carry large amounts of data, and they don't pick up electrical noise.

focus The clarity or sharpness of an image. Soft focus generates images that are not precise and clear, producing a dreamlike effect.

focusing Sharpening a blurred image on a display screen.

folder A collection of files. To access a file that has been placed in a folder, the user double-clicks on the folder's icon.

folio A page number.

font A complete assortment or set of all the characters (letters, numbers, punctuation, and symbols) of a particular typeface, all of one size and style (such as 12-pt. Bookman, 18-pt. Helvetica, 36-pt. Cooper Black, 8-pt. Times Roman). Two types of fonts exist: bit-mapped fonts and outline fonts. Each comes in two versions, screen fonts and printer fonts.

font card An expression board that allows certain printers to print additional fonts.

font cartridge A set of bit-mapped or outline fonts for one or more typefaces contained in a module that plugs into a slot in a printer. The fonts are stored in a ROM chip within the cartridge.

font family A set of fonts in several sizes and weights that share the same typeface.

font generator A program that converts an outline font into the precise patterns of dots required for a particular size of font.

font groups Fonts are often divided into three groups: serif, sans serif, and display. Type styles in the serif group have additional strokes (serifs) at the bottom of each letter; type styles in the sans serif group do not. Display (or decorative) type styles, which can be either serif or sans serif, are used to create a dramatic effect in headings, logos, and product names. They are rarely used in long passages of text, since they are typically difficult to read.

font size The size of a character font in points. The size most often used for text is 10 to 12 points. Point size is a vertical measurement; horizontal measurement is not taken into consideration.

font substitution   Substituting an outline font for printing in place of a bit-mapped screen font. In some systems, the laser printer driver substitutes an outline font for a specific bit-mapped screen font.

font weight   The heft and/or slant of a font. Most fonts are available in four weights: Medium (or Roman, Book, or Normal), Italic, Bold, and Bold Italic (or Bold Oblique). Some decorative fonts (e.g., Zapf Chancery Medium Italic) are available in only one weight. A few fonts (e.g., Helvetica) are available in many more weights than the four listed above.

footer   The information printed at the bottom of a page, such as page numbers.

footnote   In a page layout or word processing program, a note positioned at the bottom of the page.

footprint   The surface area occupied by a computer or peripheral. A small computer is said to have a small footprint. A machine with a large footprint may need a desk to itself.

force   To intervene manually in a program and cause the computer to execute a JUMP instruction.

forced page break   A page break inserted by the user.

forecast   The extrapolation of the past into the future. Usually an objective computation involving data, as opposed to a prediction, which is a subjective estimate incorporating the manager's anticipation of changes and new influencing factors.

forecasting   A process that uses currently available information to predict future occurrences.

foreground   An area in computer memory for programs that have a high priority.

foreground processing   The automatic execution of computer programs that have been designed to preempt the use of computing facilities. Contrast with BACKGROUND PROCESSING.

forest   A collection of trees.

form   A template that indicates both items of data and where they are to be placed. Forms assist in the process of collecting and storing data.

formal documentation   For the systems analysis and design process, the data dictionary and list of data elements; for a software package, the user's manual and other written descriptions.

formal language   A combination of syntax and semantics that completely defines a programming language.

formal logic   The study of the structure and form of valid argument without regard to the meaning of the terms of the argument.

format   **(1)** A specific arrangement of data. **(2)** The programming associated with setting up text arrangements for output.

format code   A word processing code that describes how text will be printed or formatted.

format rule   A spreadsheet rule that tells the program how to display a cell's value.

formatted diskette   A DISKETTE on which track and sector control information has been written.

formatted display   A screen DISPLAY in which the attributes or contents of one or more display fields have been defined by the user.

formatting   Preparing a diskette for use so that the operating system can write information on it. Formatting erases any previous information on the diskette.

form feed (FF)   **(1)** The physical transport of continuous paper to the beginning of a new line or page. **(2)** A standard ASCII character that causes a form feed to occur.

form letter program   A program that can be designed to send out "personalized" letters that look like letters produced on a typewriter.

forms control   An operational procedure established by an organization to exercise direction in the utilization of documents used to collect and/or report information.

forms design   The creation of data input forms and source documents.

formula   A rule expressed as an equation; for example, $C = 2\pi r$ is the formula for finding the circumference of a circle.

formula manipulation   Algebraic manipulation of mathematical formulae.

FORTH   A programming language designed for real-time control tasks, as well as business and graphics applications. Developed primarily for use on microcomputer systems by Charles Moore. Capabilities include structured programming, top-down development, and virtual memory.

FORTRAN   Acronym for **for**mula **tran**slator, a widely used high-level programming language for performing mathematical, scientific, and engineering computations. FORTRAN was developed in 1957 by Jim Backus and was the first high-level programming language.

forward   To send information to another destination.

forward chaining   An event-driven method of reasoning that proceeds from known conditions to the desired goal.

forward pointer   A pointer that tells the location of the next item in a DATA STRUCTURE.

FOSDIC   Acronym for **F**ilm **O**ptical **S**ensing **D**evice for **I**nput to **C**omputers, an input device used by the Census Bureau to read completed census questionnaire data into a computer.

four-color printing   Another term for process color, in which the colors cyan, magenta, yellow, and black are used to reproduce all the hues of the spectrum.

fourth-generation computers   Computers that are made up almost entirely of chips with limited amounts of discrete components. Fourth-generation computers are currently being manufactured and sold.

fourth-generation language   A user-oriented language that makes it possible to develop programs with fewer commands than those needed for older procedural languages; a nonprocedural language. Also called 4GL language.

FPLA Abbreviation for **F**ield **P**rogrammable **L**ogic **A**rray, a PLA that can be programmed by the user in the field, whereas an ordinary PLA is programmable only by masking at the semiconductor manufacturer's factory.

FPO Acronym for **f**or **p**osition **o**nly. To be used only as a position indicator and not for final reproduction.

fractal An object (or set of points, curves, or patterns) that exhibits increasing detail with increasing magnification. Deals with curves and surfaces with nonintegral, or fractional, dimension. In COMPUTER GRAPHICS applications, this relates to a technique for attaining a degree of complexity analogous to that in nature from a handful of data points; it is a method of describing real-world surfaces.

fractal geometry A field associated with the modeling of forms exhibiting the properties of fractals that is inextricably linked with computer graphics: computer graphics provides a convenient way of picturing and exploring fractal objects, and fractal geometry is a useful tool for creating computer images. The simple, repeated operations that go into the construction of a fractal are ideally suited to the functioning of a computer, which patiently performs the same set of operations over and over to generate a particular fractal object.

fractal surface A surface exhibiting fractal properties. Fractal surfaces have been used to model natural phenomena such as mountain ranges, seascapes, and clouds.

fragmentation The presence of small increments of unused space spread throughout disk storage; the uneven distribution of data on a disk. Occurs whenever files on a disk are deleted and new files are added.

frame **(1)** A video image produced by one complete scan of the screen of a raster-scan display unit. **(2)** In computer animation, a single picture. **(3)** An area, one recording position long, extending across the width of magnetic tape perpendicular to its movement. **(4)** In computer graphics, an outline or boundary of some type.

frame buffer   In computer graphics, a special area of RAM that holds the contents of a screen display. Sometimes used interchangeably with the term BIT MAP.

frame grabber   A device used to capture a still video image for storage or processing in a computer.

frames per second   In animation, a measurement of the number of individual pictures that are displayed for each second of action.

frame rate   The speed at which screen images are transmitted to, and displayed by, a raster-scan monitor. It is measured in HERTZ and is about 60 times per second (60 Hz) on a monitor in which each pixel on the screen is refreshed.

framework   In OBJECT-ORIENTED PROGRAMMING, a class library that is tuned especially for a particular category of application.

Framework   A suite of programs consisting of a word processor, spreadsheet, database, and graphics generator. The programs are designed to run on IBM-compatible microcomputers.

Freedom of Information Act   Federal legislation that allows ordinary citizens access to data gathered by federal agencies. See FEDERAL PRIVACY ACT.

free form   A type of optical scanning in which the scanning operation is controlled by symbols entered by the input device at the time of data entry.

Freehand™   A professional design/illustration program for the Apple Macintosh computer. Completely integrated, it combines basic shapes and advanced drawing tools, text-handling capability, full-color support, and special effects.

free-form windows   A method of presenting windows on the screen that allows them to overlap one another.

free subprogram   In OBJECT-ORIENTED PROGRAMMING, a procedure or function that serves as a nonprimitive operation upon an object or objects of the same or different classes. A free subprogram is any subprogram that is not a method of an object.

freeware Software provided by a vendor at no charge. Freeware developers often retain all rights to their software, thus preventing users from copying it or distributing it further.

frequency The number of times that sound pressure, electrical intensity, or other quantities specifying a wave vary from their equilibrium value through a complete cycle in unit time. The most common unit of frequency is the HERTZ (Hz); 1 Hz is equal to 1 cycle per second.

frequency counter An electronic device capable of counting the number of cycles in an electrical signal during a preselected time interval.

frequency shift keying (FSK) A method of data transmission in which the state of the bit being transmitted is indicated by an audible tone.

freeze frame The capacity of computers using certain software programs to capture an image and keep it immobile.

friction-feed A paper-feed system that operates by clamping a sheet of paper between two rollers. As the rollers rotate, the paper is drawn into the printing device. Many printers use this method, which is effective for single-sheet feeding.

friend In OBJECT-ORIENTED PROGRAMMING, a method typically involving two or more objects of different classes whose implementation for any one class may reference the private parts of all the corresponding classes that are also friends.

friendliness A measure of how easy to work with a computer or program is. A user-friendly program is one that takes little time to learn and is easy to use.

friendly interface The term applied to a combination of terminal equipment and computer program designed to be easy to operate by casual users of computers.

frob To fiddle with a picking device, such as a joystick or mouse.

front-end computer A dedicated small computer at the front end of a mainframe. May perform communications line assignment, data conversion, error analysis, message handling, and other data communications functions, freeing the mainframe from these tasks.

front-end processor See FRONT-END COMPUTER.

front panel A collection of switches and indicators by which the computer operator may control a mainframe computer system.

frustum of vision The three-dimensional space within which graphics objects are viewed. The space is enclosed by left, right, top, and bottom planes plus near and far clipping planes.

fry To ruin circuitry by subjecting it to excessive heat or current.

fs Abbreviation for FEMTOSECOND.

FSK Abbreviation for FREQUENCY SHIFT KEYING.

full adder A computer circuit capable of adding three binary bits, one of which is a carry from a previous addition.

full color Same as 24-bit color.

full-color monitor See COLOR MONITOR.

full-duplex Pertaining to the simultaneous, independent transmission of data in both directions over a communications link. Contrast with HALF-DUPLEX and SIMPLEX.

full-duplex transmission A type of transmission in which messages may be sent in two directions simultaneously along a data communications path.

full frame The process by which a display image is scaled to use the entire viewing area of a display device.

full-page display A monitor that allows viewing an entire page (an 8.5-by-11 inch vertical page) at actual size, providing greater flexibility and ease in desktop publishing or word processing applications.

full screen   A condition in which the entire face of the video screen is used for display.

full-screen editing   The ability to move the cursor over the entire screen to alter text.

full-text searching   The retrieval of certain information by searching the full text of an article or book stored in a computer's auxiliary storage.

function   (1) A prewritten routine that can be called into a program to provide the commands to do a particular task. (2) A process that generates a value.

functional analysis   A systematic investigation of the functions of a real or planned system.

functional diagram   A diagram that represents the working relationships among the parts of a system.

functional description   A phrase used to identify the requirements of a computer system.

functional design   Specification of the working relationships among the parts of a system in terms of their characteristic actions.

functional information systems   Specialized information systems for the various functions of an organization, such as accounting, marketing, and production.

functional programming   Programming that uses function application as the only control structure.

functional specification   A set of input, processing, output, and storage requirements detailing what a new system should be able to do. Output of the systems analysis function presents a detailed, logical description of a new system.

functional unit   An entity of hardware or software, or both, capable of accomplishing a specified purpose.

function codes   The special codes that help control functions of peripheral devices. "Clear display screen" is an example of a function code.

function keys Specially designed keys that, when pressed, initiate a function on a computer keyboard, word processor, or graphics terminal. Most software assigns function keys (F1, F2, etc.) for common tasks, but not universally. For example, in one word processor, F4 might mean "save file," while in a different word processor, it might mean "increase size of character." These special keys are programmed to execute commonly used commands.

function subprogram A subprogram that returns a single-value result.

fusible link A widely used PROM programming technique. An excessive current is used to destroy a metalized connection in a storage device, creating a 0, for instance, if a conducting element is interpreted as a 1.

futurists People who research the present to make predictions about future conditions.

fuzzy Anything in computing that is indeterminate. Fuzzy action deals in similarities and probabilities and is difficult to program, but it is an essential part of ARTIFICIAL INTELLIGENCE, since humans make considerable use of this type of logic.

fuzzy computer A specially designed computer that uses fuzzy logic. Fuzzy computers are designed for ARTIFICIAL INTELLIGENCE applications.

fuzzy logic A method of handling imprecision or uncertainty that attaches various measures of credibility to propositions. A form of logic used in some EXPERT SYSTEMS and other ARTIFICIAL INTELLIGENCE applications.

G

G   Abbreviation for giga, the prefix for 1 billion.

gain   An increase in signal power or voltage produced by an amplifier in transmitting a signal from one point to another. The amount of gain is usually expressed in decibels above a reference level. Opposite of ATTENUATION.

Gallery Effects   A collection of image-editing filters that may be used to enhance graphics stored in PICT or TIFF formats.

gallium arsenide   Crystalline material used as a superior substitute for SILICON in chip making. It is several times faster than silicon but is far more costly.

game paddle   A hand-held input device used to move the cursor on the screen through the use of a dial. Game paddles are commonly used in video games.

game port   On a MICROCOMPUTER, a port used to connect devices such as JOYSTICKS and PADDLES.

game theory   The branch of mathematics concerned with probability, among other things; the mathematical process of selecting an optimum strategy in the face of an opponent who also has a strategy. The term was first used by John von Neumann in 1928 to describe the strategy of winning at poker.

gamma correction   The intensity of the luminescent phosphor on the raster display when struck by the electron beam is nonlinear; gamma correction is an adjustment to the color map to make up for this inherent nonlinearity, resulting in a truer mix of colors when objects are displayed.

gamut   The total range of colors that can be displayed on a computer display.

Gantt chart   A horizontal bar chart that summarizes a project over time.

It can show the critical path of a project, progress, milestones, start and end dates, and other information.

gap The space between two records (interrecord gap) or two blocks of data (interblock gap) on a MAGNETIC TAPE.

garbage (1) A term often used to describe incorrect answers from a computer program, usually resulting from inaccuracies in data entry or a mistake in a computer program but sometimes from equipment malfunction. (2) Unwanted and meaningless data carried in storage. (3) Incorrect input to a computer.

garbage collection A memory management routine that searches memory for program segments, data, or objects that are no longer active and reclaims the unused space. Loosely, a term for cleaning dead storage locations out of a file.

gas plasma display An output device that works on a principle similar to that of neon signs: a narrow gap filled with neon and argon gas separates two glass plates. An alternating-current voltage applied between closely spaced row-and-column electrodes ionizes the gases between the electrodes, causing them to glow. Once initiated, the glow continues at a reduced voltage.

gate (1) A logic circuit with two or more inputs that control one output. (2) The controlling element of field effect transistors, governing current flow from source to drain.

gateway A hardware/software combination that links systems with different protocols. Used so that one LOCAL AREA NETWORK computer system can communicate and share its data with another local area network computer system.

gating circuit A circuit that operates as a selective switch, allowing conduction only during selected time intervals or when the signal magnitude is within certain limits.

GB Abbreviation for gigabyte, one billion bytes.

G-base An object-oriented LISP-based database.

GCR Abbreviation for **g**ray **c**omponent **r**eplacement, a technique for reducing the amount of cyan, magenta, or yellow not only in a neutral area but also in a colored area and replacing it with an appropriate level of black.

geek Slang for an unsophisticated computer user.

GEM Acronym for **g**raphics **e**nvironment **m**anager, a graphics-based operating environment designed by Digital Research. Used primarily on IBM-compatible and Atari microcomputers.

GEM file format An object file format commonly used by programs that were designed to run under GEM.

Gemstone An object-oriented database.

gender The type of connector being used. Male connectors have pins, and female connectors have receptacles for those pins.

gender changer A connector or cable that has two male or two female connectors wired pin to pin, which, in effect, changes a male connector to which it is connected to female or a female connector to male.

general format The default numeric format in a spreadsheet that displays values with all significant decimal points, but no commas or currency signs.

generality A term pertaining to a computer program whose solution of a problem will serve a variety of users with the same general need.

generalized routine A routine designed to process a large range of specific jobs within a given type of application.

general ledger The record that contains all of a firm's financial transactions.

general-purpose (GP) Being applicable to a wide variety of uses without essential modification. Contrast with SPECIAL-PURPOSE and DEDICATED.

general-purpose computer A computer designed to solve a wide class of problems. The majority of digital computers are of this type. Contrast with SPECIAL-PURPOSE COMPUTER.

general purpose DSS A decision support system that can be used to solve various types of problems; the user develops a model and then manipulates variables to simulate results.

general purpose language A COMPUTER LANGUAGE that is used to solve almost any type of problem.

general register A storage device that holds inputs and outputs of the various functional units of a computing system. Also used for temporary storage of intermediate results.

generate To produce a program by selection of subsets from a set of skeletal codings under the control of parameters; to produce a program by use of a generator.

generation A level of mainframe computer development. The first generation of computers used vacuum tubes; the second generation used transistors; the third generation used early types of integrated circuits; and the fourth generation used large scale integrated circuits. The fifth generation is expected to appear in the mid-1990s and will represent the next quantum leap in computer technology.

generator A software package that contains a number of routines to accomplish specific functions. These routines are capable of accepting input parameters and modifying themselves as the parameters indicate. Used to make the implementation of specific, limited tasks, such as generating a report, very convenient. Typically, the user fills out a set of parameter forms defining the task.

generic Pertaining to an item or device without specific reference to trade names.

generic class In OBJECT-ORIENTED PROGRAMMING, a class that serves as a template for other classes, in which the template may be parameterized by other classes, objects, and/or operations. A generic class must be INITIALIZED before objects can be created. The terms generic class and PARAMETERIZED CLASS are interchangeable.

generic function   In OBJECT-ORIENTED PROGRAMMING, an operation upon an object.

generic operating system   A PERSONAL COMPUTER operating system that runs on many different types of computers.

GEnie   An on-line information service.

geocoding   A method of providing a graphic display of data in relation to a geographic area.

geographic information system (GIS)   A graphics application using a database of specialized information, such as demographic and geographical data.

geographic mapping   An application for graphics systems used for a variety of projects that require meaningful mapping information.

geometric abstraction   The use of geometric shapes—lines, squares, triangles, rectangles, circles, and polygons—to design a composition.

geometric design rules   User-defined design constraints aimed at ensuring a functional, reliable product.

geometric model   See MODEL, GEOMETRIC.

geometric modeling   A complete, geometrically accurate three-dimensional or two-dimensional representation of a shape, part, geographic area, plant, or any part thereof, designed on a graphics system and stored in the database. A mathematical or analytic model of a physical system used to determine the response of that system to a stimulus or load.

geometric object   A two- or three-dimensional shape.

geometric primitive   One of a set of mathematically defined shapes specified for rendering by a graphics system, such as a point, line, triangle, rectangle, or polygon.

geometry   The branch of mathematics that deals with the relationships, properties, and measurements of solids, surfaces, lines, and angles. Considers spatial relationships, the theory of space, and figures in space. In computer graphics, refers to the specific physical arrangement of lines that make up the shape of a specific entity. Geometry is an essential part of COMPUTER GRAPHICS programs.

geosynchronous satellite   A satellite that is positioned at the proper distance from Earth and at the proper relational speed to appear stationary to an observer on Earth. Geosynchronous satellites are necessary for telecommunications over vast distances.

germanium   A chemical element (atomic number 32) used in the manufacture of chips. In its pure state, germanium is an insulator. When small amounts of certain impurities, called dopants, are added, it becomes a semiconductor.

GERT   Acronym for **g**raphical **e**valuation and **r**eview **t**echnique, a procedure for the formulation and evaluation of systems, using a network approach. Compare PERT.

get   To obtain a record from an input file; another name for load. Compare FETCH.

G flops   One billion floating-point operations per second.

ghost   A faint second image that appears close to the primary image on a display or printout.

ghost icon   An outline of an icon or window used to show its current position as it is being dragged to a new location on the desktop.

gibberish   Unnecessary data.

GIF   A graphics format often used for pictures that are transmitted by modem. Especially popular with computer bulletin boards and information services such as COMPUSERVE.

giga   Prefix indicating 1 billion, or 10^9. Abbreviated G. Contrast with NANO.

gigabyte   Specifically, 1,073,741,824, or 2^{30}, bytes. More loosely, one billion bytes, one million kilobytes, or one thousand megabytes. Abbreviated GB. Compare TERABYTE.

gigaflops   One billion floating-point operations per second.

gigahertz A frequency of a billion times per second. Abbreviated GHz.

gigascale integration The process of placing over one billion integrated circuits on one chip.

GIGO Acronym for **g**arbage **i**n-**g**arbage **o**ut, a term used to describe the data into and out of a computer system. If the input data is bad (garbage in), then the output data will also be bad (garbage out).

GIS Abbreviation for **G**eographic **I**nformation **S**ystem.

GKS See GRAPHICAL KERNEL SYSTEM.

glare The reflection from the surface of a display screen.

glare filter A fine mesh screen that is placed over a CRT screen to reduce glare from overhead and ambient light.

glitch A popular term for a temporary or random error, or a problem or malfunction in hardware, such as a malfunction caused by a power surge.

global (1) A general term implying a great breadth of scope, as contrasted with LOCAL. (2) Pertaining to a variable whose name is accessible by a main program and all its subroutines. (3) Any computer operation applied to a broad set of data.

global area A storage area used for communication between two or more main programs.

global backup Copying everything on the hard disk onto floppy disks.

global change (1) In WORD PROCESSING, simultaneous modification or deletion of one or more characters or words wherever they appear in a document. (2) In a SPREADSHEET, a user instruction to change an attitude of all cells.

global character A character used in a searching routine to stand for any character. Allows the operator to search for a character string of a specified length by specifying only some of its characters and using global characters to stand for the others. Also called WILD CARD.

global find and replace   Same as GLOBAL SEARCH AND REPLACE.

global format   The numeric format choice that applies to all cells in a SPREADSHEET program worksheet.

global operation   In WORD PROCESSING, an operation performed throughout an entire file.

global search   In WORD PROCESSING, to find automatically with a single instruction a character or group of characters wherever they appear in a document.

global search and replace   In WORD PROCESSING, the ability to find a string anywhere it appears in a document and to substitute another string for it.

global variable   A variable that has the same value regardless of where or in what program it is used.

glossary   Frequently used phrases stored in a word processing program storage utility that can be inserted into documents as needed.

GMD   Abbreviation for German National Research Center for Computer Science. Its research is particularly strong in the fields of software engineering, parallel computing, communications systems, and expert systems.

gnomon   An object representing direction and dimension that facilitates interpretation of a two-dimensional image of a three-dimensional solid.

go down   To crash. See DOWN.

good enough color   A phrase used for color printing that does not require an exact color match. It is relatively easy to produce with desktop color systems.

Gouraud shading   A sophisticated shading method capable of producing realistic results.

GP   Abbreviation for GENERAL-PURPOSE.

GPPM   Abbreviation for **g**raphics **p**ages **p**er **m**inute.

GPS Abbreviation for **G**eneral **P**roblem **S**olver, the first program for solving general problems that separated solving methods from knowledge.

GPSS Abbreviation for **G**eneral **P**urpose **S**ystems **S**imulation, a problem-oriented language used to develop simulation systems.

grabber **(1)** A device for capturing data, such as a video digitizer. **(2)** A computer program that takes a "snapshot" of the currently displayed screen image by transferring a portion of video memory to a file on disk. **(3)** The fixture on the end of a test equipment lead wire with a spring-actuated hook and claw designed to connect the measuring instrument to a pin of an integrated circuit, socket, transistor, and so forth.

grabber hand In graphics programs, an on-screen image of a hand that the user can position with a mouse to move selected units of graphics or text from place to place on-screen.

graceful degradation The process of undergoing failure in such a way that limited operation can continue. See FAIL-SOFT SYSTEM.

grade Pertaining to the range, or width, of the frequencies available for transmission on a given channel, such as voice-grade.

gradient fill A feature on some graphics programs that adds color or a shade of gray to a region, varying the color or shade smoothly in a defined direction. Sometimes called a graduated fill.

graftal A class of graphics objects sharing some of the properties of FRACTALS in which the rules for generation permit local modification of properties.

grammar The rules prescribing how various elements of a language may be combined. See SYNTAX.

grammatical error An error that results when the rules or syntax of a programming language are not followed. Also called a syntax error.

grandfather file The oldest backup file copy. See FATHER FILE.

granularity The level of modularity of a system. Finer granularity indicates smaller modules and provides greater flexibility.

graph (1) A diagram showing the relationship of two or more variable quantities. A mathematical graph is usually in the form of a curve drawn in a frame of reference formed by the two axes of coordinate geometry. (2) A method of displaying number relationships visually.

graph theory A branch of mathematics that belongs partly to combinatorial analysis and partly to topology.

graphic A symbol produced by a process such as drawing or handwriting.

graphic character Any ASCII character that is represented by a visible symbol and can be printed; includes letters and digits.

graphic data structure A logical arrangement of digital data representing graphic data for graphic display.

graphic digitizer An input device that converts graphic and pictorial data into binary inputs for use in a computer. See DIGITIZER.

graphic display A DISPLAY DEVICE that provides a representation of data in any graphic form.

graphic display mode A mode of operation that allows the computer to print graphics on a display screen.

graphic display program A program designed to display information in graphic or alphanumeric form on a display screen.

graphic display resolution (1) The number of lines and characters per line able to be shown on a video screen. (2) The measure of the detail in which graphics can be drawn.

graphic display terminal A computer terminal that displays information on a screen, usually a cathode ray tube, TV terminal, or video monitor.

graphic file format Any of several formats for storing computer graphics, such as EPS, PICT, and TIFF.

graphic input device Any device, such as a DIGITIZER, that gives the computer the points that make up an image in such a way that the image can be stored, reconstructed, displayed, or manipulated.

graphic language See GRAPHICS LANGUAGE.

graphic limits (1) The boundary of a graphical display screen image in a graphics software program. (2) The plotting area of a graphics device, such as a digital plotter, as defined by its mechanical limits, such as the size of the drum or platen.

graphic output Computer-generated output in the form of visual displays, printouts, or plots.

graphic output device A device used to display or record an image. A display screen is an output device for soft copy; hard-copy output devices produce paper, film, or transparencies of the image.

graphic primitive In computer graphics, a basic element, such as an arc or line, that is used to create diagrams and pictures.

graphic scanner A graphics input device that transforms a picture into an image displayed on-screen.

Graphical Kernel System (GKS) An internationally accepted standard for computer graphics. GKS is an interface that provides computer users with standardized methods of describing, manipulating, storing, and transferring graphical images.

graphical terminal A visual display terminal (VDT) that has a screen to display a drawing as well as textual information.

graphical user interface (GUI) A type of display format that enables the user to choose commands, start programs, and see lists of files and other options by pointing to pictorial representations (icons) and lists of menu items on the screen. Graphical user interfaces are used on the Apple Macintosh microcomputer, by the Microsoft Windows program for IBM-compatible microcomputers, and by other systems.

graphics Any computer-generated pictures produced on a screen, paper, or film. Graphics range from simple line or bar graphs to colorful and detailed images.

graphics accelerator A HARDWARE device dedicated to increasing the speed and performance of graphics. Graphics accelerators calculate pixel values and write them into the frame buffer, freeing the central processing unit for other operations.

graphics adapters CGA-EGA-VGA adapters that must be matched with compatible monitors. Note the alphabetical order—it happens to match their order of age and sophistication. CGA was first; EGA was the new standard for a long while; and VGA is now the popular standard for color presentations. VGA has the highest resolution modes and sharpest text and image quality.

graphics based A term describing the display of text and pictures as graphics images, such as a bit-mapped image.

graphics character A character that can be combined to create simple graphics.

graphics coprocessor A special microprocessor chip, mounted on some video adapters, that can generate graphical images, thereby freeing the computer for other work.

graphics device interface (GDI) A collection of Microsoft Windows routines that allows users to display information without concern for the specific hardware used.

graphics display Any output device that can present an image of graphic data derived from a computer system.

graphics editor A program for editing pictures. Typical operations include drawing, moving, rotating, and enlarging items on the screen.

graphics engine Specialized hardware that performs graphics processing independently of the main central processing unit. Graphics engines are programmed in a graphics language.

graphics file format In a graphics program, the way in which information needed to display the graphic is arranged and stored on disk.

graphics input hardware   The peripherals used to put graphics information in the computer, such as a GRAPHICS TABLET, MOUSE, and LIGHT PEN.

graphics language   A set of instructions that lets a programmer express a graphics image in a high-level language. The language is translated into graphics images by software or specialized hardware.

graphics library   A collection of standard, often-used symbols, components, shapes, or parts stored in the graphics database as templates or building blocks to speed up future design work on the system. Generally an organization of files under a common library name. The graphics library usually includes a defined set of primitives and function calls that enable the programmer to bypass many low-level programming tasks.

graphics mode   Resolution of the image together with the number of colors a particular video system can display. For example, EGA and VGA are considered different graphics modes.

graphics output hardware   PERIPHERALS on which the computer displays graphics, such as a DISPLAY SCREEN, FILM RECORDER, or LASER PRINTER.

graphics package   A program that helps depict ideas through graphs and other types of drawings.

graphics pages per minute (GPPM)   The rate at which a laser printer can print pages with graphics.

graphics preprocessor   An extension of a compiler that permits the syntax of an existing language to be augmented by new graphics commands.

graphics primitive   In computer graphics, a graphical building block, such as a triangle, circle, line, or arc. A graphics primitive is drawn and manipulated as a single unit.

graphics printer   An output device that can produce text, charts, graphics, and artwork.

graphics program   (1) A computer program that assists in the production of computer-generated images. (2) A program that causes the computer to generate graphic images.

graphics resolution A measure of the detail in which graphics can be drawn by output hardware. High-resolution pictures have greater detail than low-resolution pictures. See RESOLUTION.

graphics routine A collection of code in a computer program that draws graphical objects.

graphics screen A screen that displays graphics information.

graphics simulation Graphics simulation is different from ordinary computer simulation, although they may overlap somewhat: while computer simulation may use computer graphics, it is not the primary tool. For example, a simulation of automobiles on a busy highway is a statistical study rather than a visual one, although computer graphics is used to show models of cars on the road. Graphics simulation has come to mean the use of computer graphics to represent any form of dynamic physical phenomenon. As an example, a supercomputer may be used to simulate the collision of galaxies and generate a set of data.

graphics spreadsheet A spreadsheet program that displays the worksheet on-screen, using bit-mapped graphics instead of relying on the computer's built-in character set.

graphics standards Agreed specifications that define the common interfaces between computer graphics systems or subsystems. See INITIAL GRAPHICS EXCHANGE SPECIFICATION and INTERNATIONAL STANDARDS ORGANIZATION.

graphics tablet An input device that converts graphic and pictorial data into binary inputs for use in a computer.

graphics terminal A SMART TERMINAL capable of displaying graphics; usually interprets graphics control codes to render images on the display screen.

graphics utilities Computer programs designed to assist graphics processing in such functions as copying, saving, compressing, and so forth.

Graphics Workshop A color paint program for the Commodore Amiga computer.

gray image   An image composed of the full spectrum of gray shades, ranging from black to white.

gray-map editor   A function found in many imaging programs that allows the user to change the way gray shades are displayed.

gray scale   A strip of standard gray tones, ranging from white to black. **(1)** When used with scanners, it refers to the device's ability to capture more than simply black and white. **(2)** When used with monochromatic displays, variations in brightness level (gray scale) are used to enhance the contrast among various design elements. The larger the gray scale, the better the picture quality. **(3)** Refers to the many levels of gray supported by a scanner or a monitor. Eight and 16 levels were early standards; now the standard is 256 levels.

gray-scale manipulation   An image-enhancement technique in which the appearance of a digital image is improved by adjusting its gray levels.

gray-scale mode   A SCANNER setting for digitizing an image made of grays or intermediate colors by assigning more than one bit of data to each point.

gray value   A number that determines the level of gray in a particular pixel. A pixel that is 80 percent gray is darker than a pixel that is 20 percent gray.

greater than   The relationship of inequality between two values. The symbol is >, with the point toward the smaller number. For example, 9 > 5 means 9 is greater than 5. Commonly used in comparison to determine alternative processing. Contrast with LESS THAN.

greeked text   In desktop publishing, unreadable letters or characters that simulate a typeset line.

green-bar paper   Computer paper with green bands.

grid   **(1)** A network of uniformly spaced points or crosshatched lines displayed on a visual display screen or digitizer and used for exactly locating a position, inputting components to assist in the creation of a design layout, or constructing precise diagrams. For example, coordinate data supplied by digitizers is automatically calculated by the computer from the closest grid point. The grid determines the minimum accuracy with which design entities are described or connected. **(2)** The display of an electronic spreadsheet model composed of columns and rows. **(3)** Horizontal and vertical lines on a chart to aid the viewer in determining the value of a point. **(4)** On a pie chart, an implied set of lines radiating out from the center, representing the degrees of a circle.

grid chart A table that relates input data to its appropriate applications program.

grid constraint An accuracy aid that causes the screen cursor to jump to the nearest grid intersection whenever a point is entered.

gridding A graphic image construction constraint that requires all line endpoints to fall on grid points.

gridsheet Same as GRID, SPREADSHEET, or worksheet.

grounding The process of rendering electrical current harmless to humans and computers.

ground station A station for sending and receiving information via satellite.

group In an object-oriented drawing program, to transfer a collection of objects into one object so that the group can be operated on as a whole.

grouping A feature of drawing and page layout applications in which two or more objects are combined so that they are treated as one object.

group technology A CAD SYSTEM of classifying drawings and parts according to similarities of design and manufacturing. This makes it easier to locate an existing part with specified characteristics and helps to standardize the fabrication of similar parts.

groupware Software designed for use in a network and to serve a group of users who work on a related project.

group work Any indicator signaling the beginning or end of a word or other unit of data.

guest computer   A computer operating under the control of another (host) computer.

GUI   Acronym for GRAPHICAL USER INTERFACE.

gulp   A small group of BYTES.

gun   A group of electrodes constituting the electron beam emitter in a CATHODE RAY TUBE.

gutter   **(1)** The margin at the binding edge of a page. **(2)** The white space between columns in a multiple-column page layout.

GW-BASIC   A version of the BASIC programming language for MS-DOS computers, developed by Microsoft Corporation. GW-BASIC is nearly identical to the BASIC interpreter distributed with IBM microcomputers and is commonly bundled with IBM-compatible microcomputers.

H

h A suffix indicating that a number is in HEXADECIMAL form, as in F2A3**h**.

hacker (**1**) A skilled computer enthusiast who works alone and is obsessed with learning about programming and exploring the capabilities of computer systems. (**2**) A person who gains access to a computer system without authorization.

hacking Using a microcomputer system or terminal to break into the security of a large computer system.

half adder A computer circuit capable of adding two binary bits.

half-duplex Pertaining to a communications path that can carry a message in either direction but only one way at a time.

half-height drive A disk drive that occupies only half the vertical space of earlier disk drives.

halftone A continuous-tone image, such as a photograph, shot through a screen and reproduced as an array of tiny dots. A halftone is a printed reproduction of these tiny dots, which the naked eye sees as various tones of gray shading into one another.

halftone cell A halftone dot created on a laser printer or imagesetter. The cell is created by grouping printer dots into a grid. The more dots present in the grid, the larger the cell appears.

halfword A contiguous sequence of bits, bytes, or characters that comprises half a computer word and is capable of being addressed as a unit.

halting problem A problem for which there is no ALGORITHM.

halt instruction A machine instruction that stops the execution of the program.

hand calculator A hand-held calculator suitable for performing arithmetic operations, including complicated calculations.

hand cursor A hand-held device (often called a puck) for inputting coordinate data that has cross-hairs to identify exact locations and is used with a data tablet.

hand-held computer   A portable, battery-operated computer that can be programmed to perform a wide variety of tasks.

hand-held scanner   An optical scanner that is operated by manually running a scanning head over an image. Small rollers on the bottom of the scanning head serve to guide the hand movement.

handle   (1) In computer graphics, a small square associated with a graphical object that can be used to move or reshape the image. (2) A number that can be used to uniquely identify an object. (3) In programming, a pointer to a pointer; in other words, a variable that contains the address of another variable, which in turn contains the address of yet another variable.

handler   (1) A program with the sole function of controlling a particular input, output, or storage device, a file, or the interrupt facility. (2) In OBJECT-ORIENTED PROGRAMMING, the program instructions (called a script) embedded within an object. The instructions are designed to trap messages that begin within the object.

handshaking   The procedures and standards (protocol) used by two computers or a computer and a peripheral device to establish communication.

hands-on   Pertaining to the process of physically using a computer system.

handwriting recognition   Scanning handwritten material with a computer-controlled visual scanning device to determine information content or to verify a signature.

hanging indent   A paragraphing style with a full-measure first line and indented succeeding lines (called turnover lines).

hang-up   A nonprogrammed stop in a routine. Usually an unforeseen or unwanted halt in a machine run caused by improper coding of a problem, by equipment malfunction, or by the attempted use of a nonexistent or illegal operation code.

hard card A HARD DISK that has been configured onto an add-in board that can be installed in an expansion slot of a personal computer.

hard clip area The limits beyond which lines cannot be drawn on a DIGITAL PLOTTER.

hard contact printing Contact printing in which the mask is pressed against the substrate with appreciable force.

hard copy A printed copy of machine output in readable form, such as a report, listing, graphic image, document, or summary. Contrast with SOFT COPY.

hard disk A fast auxiliary storage device either mounted in its own case or permanently mounted inside a computer. A single hard disk has storage capacity of several million characters or bytes of information. This storage medium makes computers usable in the real world. Contrast with FLOPPY DISK.

hard-disk card The combination of a hard disk and a controller card.

hard error An error caused by a malfunction in the HARDWARE.

hard failure The failure of a piece of equipment; generally requires repair before the unit can be used again.

hard hyphen A hyphen required by spelling and always printed, such as in double-click. Contrast with SOFT HYPHEN.

hard return In WORD PROCESSING, a user-generated movement of the cursor to the beginning of the next line.

hard sector A wedge-shaped storage division on a floppy disk from the time of manufacture. Physically marked by holes punched through the disk to indicate the various sectors. Contrast with SOFT SECTOR.

hard stop An immediate termination of operation or execution.

hardware Physical equipment, such as electronic, magnetic, and mechanical devices. Contrast with SOFTWARE.

hardware configuration The relationships and arrangement of the various pieces of equipment that make up a computer system including the cables and communications paths that connect them.

hardware-dependent   See MACHINE-DEPENDENT.

hardware description languages (HDL)   The languages and notations that facilitate the documentation, design, simulation, and manufacturing of digital computer systems.

hardware key   The means to secure software from illegal copying. The key plugs into a port or expansion slot on a computer and interacts with a program's antipiracy software to allow the program to run only on that machine.

hardware platform   The basic hardware standard on which a computer system is based.

hardware reset   Restart.

hardware resources   CPU time, internal storage space, direct access storage space, and input/output devices, all of which are required to do the work of processing data automatically and efficiently.

hardware specialist   A person who diagnoses, repairs, and maintains the equipment of a computer system.

hardwired   Pertaining to the physical connection of two pieces of electronic equipment by means of a cable.

harness   A group of separate cables bound together.

Harvard Graphics™   A business graphics program for IBM-compatible microcomputer systems from Software Publishing Corporation. It is a versatile and easy-to-use program for producing business-related presentation graphics.

hash   Visual static on the screen.

hashing   **(1)** A key-to-address transformation in which the keys determine the location of the data. **(2)** The process of applying a formula to a record key to yield a number that represents a disk address.

hash totals Totals of the numbers of identifying fields. Used in ERROR CHECKING.

hatching Shading some portion of a drawing with parallel lines in a single direction. Shading in overlapping directions is crosshatching.

Hayes-compatible Describes a modem when it recognizes the commands of a Hayes-manufactured modem.

HDBMS Abbreviation for HIERARCHICAL DATABASE MANAGEMENT SYSTEM.

HDR An abbreviation for HEADER.

head (1) A device that reads, records, or erases data on a storage medium, such as a small electromagnet used to read, write, and erase data on a magnetic disk. (2) A special data item that points to the beginning of a list.

head-cleaning device A material containing a dirt solvent used to clean the read/write head of a floppy disk drive or a tape drive.

head crash The collision of the read/write head with the recording surface of a hard disk, resulting in loss of data. Usually caused by contamination of the disk, such as from a tiny particle of smoke or dust or from a fingerprint.

header (1) The first part of a message, containing all the necessary information for directing the message to its destination(s). (2) The top margin of a page, usually the title of the book, the name of the chapter, the page number, and so on.

header record A record containing constant, common, or identifying information for a group of records that follows.

head gap The clearance between a read/write head and the surface of a rotating diskette or hard disk when the head is at its normal operating position.

heading Words placed above information to identify that information.

head positioning   Placing a read/write head when data is being read or written by a direct-access storage device. Done by moving an ACCESS ARM.

head slot   The opening in a diskette jacket that exposes the disk surface to read/write heads.

head switching   Activating the read/write head that is to read or write data being read or written by a DIRECT-ACCESS STORAGE DEVICE.

head window   The area of a DISKETTE that is in contact with the read/write head.

heap   (1) A collection of storage locations that a program can borrow for computations and then return; free memory currently available to load and run programs. (2) A complete binary tree whose nodes contain search keys arranged in descending order.

heap sort   See TREE SORT.

helical wave guide   A metal tube containing thin glass fibers and wires capable of transmitting thousands of messages over communications lines. See FO.

helmet mounted display   A DISPLAY DEVICE in which the display is attached to a head-tracked helmet worn by the user.

help   (1) A handy function available on many systems, supplying the user with additional information on how the system or program works. (2) On-screen reference material providing assistance with the program.

help balloon   An operating system and application program user help aid that tags a desired object on screen with a comic-book-style "balloon" full of information on how to use that object.

help menu   A menu that describes alternative actions when a user encounters a problem with a system or application.

help panel   Information displayed by a system in response to a help request from a user.

help screen   A screenful of information displayed by a program that has a help facility.

Helvetica   A popular sans serif typeface developed in the 1950s. It is one of the most widely used fonts in the world and is included as a built-in font with many laser printers.

henry   A unit of measure of inductance. One henry is the inductance of a circuit in which an electromotive force of one volt is produced by a current in the circuit that varies at the rate of one ampere per second.

Hercules Graphics Card (HGC)   A monochrome video adapter introduced by Hercules Computer Technology in 1982. HGC provides a monochrome graphics mode for IBM PC graphics with a screen size of 720 × 348 pixels.

hermaphroditic   A term referring to connectors in which each piece has protruding and receptacle parts, rather than one piece configured as male and one as female.

Hertz   Cycles per second; abbreviated Hz. See FREQUENCY.

heterogeneous network   A NETWORK consisting of computers and devices from several manufacturers.

heuristic   A term describing an exploratory method of attacking a problem, in which the solution is obtained by successive evaluations of progress toward the final results. Contrast with ALGORITHM.

heuristic learning   A discovery method of learning from experience. A way computers can learn from their mistakes by eliminating unsuccessful or unproductive options from their operations. See ARTIFICIAL INTELLIGENCE and MACHINE LEARNING.

heuristic method   A method of solving problems that consists of a sequence of trials yielding approximate results, with control of the progression toward an acceptable final result.

heuristic rules   A set of practical rules used by experts to make decisions.

Hewlett-Packard Company (HP)   A major manufacturer of computer equipment, founded in 1939 by William Hewlett and David Packard in a garage behind Packard's California home. HP has introduced several computer series, workstations, and laser printers, as well as many other electronic products.

Hewlett-Packard Graphics Language (HPGL)   A language devised by Hewlett-Packard for storing graphical images.

hex   See HEXADECIMAL.

hexadecimal   Pertaining to a number system with a radix of 16. Digits greater than 9 are represented by the letters A through F. For example, the binary numeral 1110001011010011 can be represented as hexadecimal E2D3.

hexadecimal number   A numeral, usually of more than one digit, representing a sum in which the quantity represented by each digit is based on a radix of 16. The digits used are 0, 1, 2, 3, 4, 5, 6, 7, 8, 9, A, B, C, D, E, and F.

hexadecimal point   The radix point in a mixed hexadecimal numeral, separating the integer part from the fraction part. In the hexadecimal numeral 3F.6A7, the hexadecimal point is between the digits F and 6.

HFS   Abbreviation for HIERARCHICAL FILE SYSTEM.

hidden character   A character that is not normally printed or displayed; for example, in a word processor, an embedded control character.

hidden codes   The hidden text formatting codes embedded in a document by an on-screen formatting program.

hidden file   A file that occupies disk space but does not appear in directory listings; sometimes called invisible file. Files are hidden to prevent their display or change. Users cannot display, erase, or copy hidden files.

hidden line   (1) When displaying a three-dimensional object, any line that would normally be obscured from the viewer's sight by the mass of the object itself, visible as a result of the projection. (2) A line that has been drawn on the screen in background color and will not become visible until the colors are switched. **(3)** A line of a diagram that is invisible.

hidden line removal   The process of deleting line segments from a drawing when they would be obscured if the object were displayed as a solid three-dimensional figure. Many types of computer graphics software and hardware can remove such hidden lines automatically.

hidden object   Distinct graphic entities that would be obscured from view by other entities if they were displayed as solids.

hidden surface   An entire surface or plane that would be obscured from view if the graphics figure were displayed as a three-dimensional solid.

hide   To remove a window and all its associated windows from a desktop.

hierarchical database management system (HDBMS)   A collection of related programs for loading, accessing, and controlling a database in which the data are organized like an inverted tree with a series of nodes connected by branches.

hierarchical data model   A data model in which each element has only one parent or owner.

hierarchical data structures   In a Programmer's Hierarchical Interactive Graphics System, objects are defined in hierarchical relationship to one another. The hierarchical data organization allows structures to inherit the attributes of other structures, enabling the programmer to manipulate objects efficiently.

hierarchical directories   A term used to refer to the organizational method of arranging files either in a DOS tree structure or in the file-and-folder method of Apple Macintosh computers.

hierarchical file system (HFS)   A pyramid-like file system in which each object is linked to those beneath it.

hierarchical local network   A star-shaped local network in which a large central processing unit is at the top of the hierarchy and communications terminals or small CPUs are at the bottom.

hierarchical model   A database model in which each object is of a particular hierarchy in a tree structure.

hierarchical network   A computer network in which processing and control functions are performed at several levels by computers specially designed for the functions performed.

hierarchical structure   In DATABASE MANAGEMENT SYSTEMS, the simplest form of file organization, in which records of various levels are related by owning or belonging to each other.

hierarchy   (1) The order in which arithmetic operations within a formula or statement will be executed. (2) Arrangement into any graded series.

hierarchy chart   A chart that divides the software package into small pieces until a program can be written to implement each piece.

hierarchy plus input-process-output (HIPO)   A design and program documentation method that represents functional structure and data flow in a series of three types of diagrams: visual tables of contents that name the program modules and specify their hierarchical relationships; overview diagrams that describe the input, processing, and output for members of the hierarchy; and detailed diagrams that extend the overview diagrams to include more specific input, processing, and output detail with narrative.

high-density disk   A floppy disk that holds more information than a double-density disk. A 5.25-inch high-density disk holds 1.2 megabytes, and a 3.5-inch high-density disk holds 1.44 megabytes.

high-end   High-priced.

high-level language   Any programming language that allows users to write instructions in a familiar notation rather than in a machine code. Each statement in a high-level language corresponds to several machine-code instructions. Contrast with LOW-LEVEL LANGUAGE.

high-level programming language   See HIGH-LEVEL LANGUAGE.

highlight   (1) In graphics, refers to a user's ability to enhance a graph or drawing by, for example, creating three-dimensional images, superimposing images, "exploding" or pulling out a pie slice, using color, or screening an image. **(2)** See CELL POINTER.

highlighting   **(1)** The process of making a display segment stand out by causing blinking, brightening, or underlining, by reversing the background and the character images, such as dark characters on a light background, or by creating a color combination that draws attention to it. **(2)** In word processing and page design programs, a means of selecting characters that are to be deleted, copied, or otherwise acted upon.

high-order   Pertaining to the digit or digits of a number that have the greatest weight or significance. For example, in the number 7643215, the high-order digit is 7. Contrast with LOW-ORDER.

high-persistence phosphor   A phosphor coating used on some display monitor screens that holds an image much longer than the coating used on standard display screens.

high-resolution   **(1)** Pertaining to the quality and accuracy of detail that can be represented by a graphics display. Resolution quality depends upon the number of basic image-forming units (pixels) within a picture image—the greater the number, the higher the resolution. High-resolution pictures, produced by a large number of pixels, are sharper than low-resolution pictures. In computer graphics displays, an IBM VGA can produce a higher-resolution display (640×480 pixels) than can an IBM CGA (640×200 pixels). **(2)** In printing, a large number of dots per inch (dpi). In general, laser printing is about 300 dpi; typesetters and imagesetters can produce output at 1,000 dpi, 2,000 dpi, or more.

high-resolution graphics (HRG)   A high-quality image on a display screen or printed form.

high-speed printer (HSP)   Any printer capable of printing from 300 to 3,000 lines per minute. See LINE PRINTER.

high storage   The upper address range of a computer. In most machines, it is occupied by the operating system.

high-tech A general term for sophisticated technical innovation; "cutting edge" technology, often involving computers and electronics.

high volatility A high frequency of changes to a file during a given time period. See VOLATILE FILE.

hinting In DESKTOP PUBLISHING, the reduction of the weight of a typeface so that small fonts print without blurring or losing detail on 300-dpi laser printers.

HIPO Acronym for HIERARCHY PLUS INPUT-PROCESS-OUTPUT.

hi-res graphics Abbreviation of high-resolution graphics, a smooth and realistic picture on a display screen produced by a large number of pixels. Contrast with LOW-RES GRAPHICS.

histogram A vertical bar chart often used to graph statistical information. Column widths represent interval ranges; lengths indicate frequencies.

hit The successful comparison of two items of data. Compare MATCH.

holding time In data communications, the length of time a communications channel is in use for each transmission. Includes both message time and operating time.

Hollerith card A punched card consisting of 80 columns, each of which is divided from top to bottom into 12 punching positions. It can hold 80 characters of alphanumeric data.

Hollerith code A particular code used to represent alphanumeric data on punched cards, named after Herman Hollerith, originator of punched-card tabulating. Each card column holds one character, and each decimal digit, letter, and special character is represented by one, two, or three holes punched into designated row positions of the column.

hologram A three-dimensional "photograph" created by holography.

holographic display A three-dimensional display using lasers.

holographic store Storage in the form of a hologram.

holography   A method of storing data by making a multidimensional photograph on a storage medium.

holostore   A system of storing data as a holographic image using light-sensitive crystals that remember light patterns passing through them.

home   The starting position for the cursor on a display screen. Usually in the top left-hand corner.

homebrew   A term describing early microcomputer systems, made by hobbyists, that gave rise to the popularity of the personal computer.

home computer   A PERSONAL COMPUTER designed and priced for use in the home.

homegrown software   Software developed at home rather than in software development businesses. Much PUBLIC-DOMAIN SOFTWARE, FREEWARE, and SHAREWARE is created in the home.

home key   The keyboard function that directs the cursor to its home position, usually the top left portion of the display screen.

home management software   Programs designed for home use to help manage and organize the household, such as check balancing, menu file, and stock portfolio accounting programs.

home record   The first record in a chain of records in the chaining method of file organization.

home row   The row of keys on the keyboard where users rest their fingers between keystrokes.

homunculus   An infinitely recursive model of the brain. Used in studies of ARTIFICIAL INTELLIGENCE.

horizontal   Going from left to right.

horizontal axis   The X-AXIS in a Cartesian coordinate system.

horizontal scrolling   The moving of horizontal blocks of data or text, allowing users to view more data than can fit on the screen at one time.

horizontal software   Programs designed to serve a wide range of users, who must tailor the programs to their own needs. Examples include DATABASE MANAGEMENT SYSTEMS, SPREADSHEETS, and WORD PROCESSORS.

host adapter   A board or circuit that connects a specific computer model to a more general controller.

host computer   (1) A central processing unit that provides the computing power for the remote terminals and peripheral devices connected to it. (2) The computer that is in charge during a telecommunications or local area network session. (3) The central controlling computer in a network of computers.

host language   A programming language in which another language is included or embedded.

hot   As applied to images, very or excessively bright.

hot key   A keystroke selected by the user to call up a special memory resident program.

hot link   A relationship of applications in which changes in one (such as a database management system) are automatically made in another (such as a spreadsheet).

hot site   A fully equipped computer center, ready for use in case of emergency.

hot spot   The position in a mouse pointer that marks the exact display screen location that will be affected by a mouse action such as a button press. The mouse pointer's hot spot is a single pixel in size.

hot zone   On some word processors, a user-defined region beginning at the right margin of a page and extending about seven spaces to the left. If a word ends in the hot zone, the system automatically places the next character entered at the beginning of the next line.

housekeeping   Computer operations that do not directly contribute to the desired results, but are a necessary part of a program, such as initialization, set-up, and clean-up operations. Sometimes called BOOKKEEPING.

housing   A cabinet or other enclosure.

Houston Instrument A major manufacturer of pen plotters, digitizers, and graphic recorders. Many of the early hard-copy graphic images of the late 1960s and 1970s were drawn on plotters made by this company.

HP An abbreviation for Hewlett-Packard Company, a manufacturer of printers, calculators, and computers.

HPC A Hewlett-Packard LaserJet graphics file format.

HPGL Abbreviation for **H**ewlett-**P**ackard **G**raphics **L**anguage, an object file format originally developed to drive plotters and now used to store graphical images.

HSB (Hue, Saturation, Brightness) A type of color system. Hue refers to pure color, or light of a distinct wave length—red, green, violet, and so forth. Saturation refers to the degree that a color is pure or the degree of white it contains. Brightness refers to the color's percentage of black. HSB is used in computer graphics for describing color.

HSP Abbreviation for HIGH-SPEED PRINTER.

HSV (Hue, Saturation, Value) A color model used in some graphics programs that has to be translated into another model for colored printing or for forming screen colors.

hub ring The part of a diskette onto which the disk drive clamps in order to rotate the disk.

hue In the HSB color model, one of the three characteristics used to describe a color. Hue refers to pure color, that is, light of a distinct wavelength—red, green, and so forth.

Huffman tree A tree with minimum values. See MINIMAL TREE and OPTIMAL MERGE TREE.

human engineering The study concerned with designing products that are easier and more comfortable for humans to use. Also called ERGONOMICS.

human/machine interface Any boundary at which people interact with machines.

human-oriented language   A PROGRAMMING LANGUAGE that is considered to be more like a human language than a machine language.

hung   Pertaining to the state in which a system appears to stop processing and does not respond to input from the keyboard.

hybrid computer system   A system that uses both analog and digital equipment, used in process control and robotic systems.

hybrids   Circuits fabricated by interconnecting smaller circuits of different technologies, mounted on a single substrate.

HyperCard   An implementation of a hypertext system for the Apple Macintosh family of computers. A HyperCard document consists of a series of cards collected together in a stack; each card can contain text, graphics, and sound. Items on the cards can be linked in a variety of ways.

hypercube   COMPUTER ARCHITECTURE in which processors are arranged as nodes in multiple dimensions with direct channel communication among neighboring nodes.

hypermedia   A term describing hypertext-based systems that combine text, graphics, sound, and video with traditional data. In a hypertext system, users select a word or phrase and give a command to see related text. In a hypermedia system, such a command reveals related graphics images, sounds, and even snippets of animation or video. HyperCard is an example of a hypermedia application.

hypermedia application   An information processing application that has hypertext and/or multimedia capabilities.

HyperTalk   The programming language used in the HyperCard program to manipulate HyperCard stacks. HyperTalk implements OBJECT-ORIENTED PROGRAMMING principles.

hypertape   A magnetic tape unit that uses a cartridge rather than a reel of tape. The cartridge consists of a reel of tape and the take-up reel.

hypertext   A document retrieval network having full-text files and dynamic indexes for links among documents. The term was coined in 1965 by Ted Nelson to describe documents, as presented by a computer, that express the nonlinear structure of ideas, as opposed to the linear format of books, film, and speech.

hypertext link A connection between one piece of information and another.

hyphenate To separate a word by inserting a hyphen after a syllable to end a line and moving the remainder of the word to the start of the next line.

hyphenation In page layout and word processing programs, an automatic operation that hyphenates words on certain lines to improve word spacing.

hysteresis A tendency for a display element to stay in either the on or off condition once it has been switched. With hysteresis, for example, a sustaining voltage can be applied to a display to keep all lighted pixels glowing without lighting any that are supposed to be off.

HyTime A hypermedia/time-based structuring language for representing hypertext linking, time scheduling, and synchronization.

Hz Abbreviation for Hertz, cycles per second. See FREQUENCY.

——— **I** ———

I-beam pointer In a graphical user interface, a special pointer shaped like a capital "I" that indicates the insertion point of text editing.

IBG Abbreviation for INTERBLOCK GAP.

IBI Abbreviation for Intergovernmental Bureau of Informatics, an organization consisting of members of the United Nations, UNESCO, and U.N. Agencies. Its goal is to promote scientific research, computer education and training, and the exchange of information between developed and developing countries. The main focus of IBI is to promote informatics, particularly in developing countries.

IBM-compatible microcomputer A personal computer that is compatible with the IBM Personal Computer and the PS/2 computer.

IBM draw/paint programs See ARTS & LETTERS GRAPHICS EDITOR, ARTLINE, COLORIX, COREL DRAW, DELUXE PAINT, DESIGNER, DGS PAINT, DR. HALO, LUMENA, PAINTING EFFECTS, PC PAINTBRUSH, PORTFOLIO, RIO-SABLE, TEMPRA, TIPS, and WATER COLOR.

IBM ES/9000 The Enterprise System/9000, a family of mainframes introduced by IBM Corporation in 1990.

IBM PC™ A popular term for personal computers that adhere closely to the appearance and functionality of personal computers in the IBM PC family. Often manufactured abroad, these computers are generally reliable and inexpensive.

IBM PC compatible A term for personal computers that adhere closely to the functionality of personal computers in the IBM PC family. PC compatibles, as opposed to "clones," have never necessarily had to look like standard IBM PC designs, and some manufacturers have insisted on incorporating proprietary, nonstandard features in their compatibles even while maintaining general compatibility with the MS-DOS, Intel-based features of the IBM PC family.

IBM Personal Computer™ A personal computer introduced on August 12, 1981 by IBM corporation that changed history. Based on the Intel 8088 microprocessor, the machine went on to become the most significant technology since the telephone. Although the IBM PC was not the first, it legitimized the machines in the computer market. It has transformed the way millions of people work, spawned new industries, and made computer technology less mysterious. The PC created the home computer movement, allowing people to work out of their living rooms and "commute" by sending reports to the office over the phone. IBM set the stage for clones when it announced the PC by deciding not to block other companies from providing software or accessories for it, reasoning that if the technology were "open," or nonproprietary, the market for the machines would grow faster. But that decision soon led to the creation of clones of the entire computer. Today, every nation from Hong Kong to Hungary has a local industry cranking out inexpensive PC clones. There are three machines in the PC line: IBM PC, IBM PC-XT, and IBM PC-AT.

IBM Personal Computer AT™ A personal computer, based on the Intel 80286 microprocessor, that was introduced by IBM Corporation in 1984. The 80286 chip was "upwardly compatible" with the Intel 8088 in that it could run all the PC software written for the 8088-based PCs that preceded it. It also came standard with a hard disk drive, a feature many users were still not accustomed to having at their disposal.

IBM Personal Computer XT™ A personal computer, based on the Intel 8088 microprocessor, including a hard disk, that was introduced by IBM Corporation in 1983. The XT-type computer occupies a prominent and useful place on desktops throughout the business world.

IBM Personal System/1 (PS/1)™ A home computer introduced by IBM Corporation in 1990. The PS/1 computer uses an Intel 80286 microprocessor and comes in a small, attractive case, with a color VGA display and a 2,400 baud modem built in. The computer contains about everything an ordinary computer user is likely to need.

IBM Personal System/2 (PS/2)™ A series of personal computers introduced by IBM Corporation in 1987. These computers were designed to replace the IBM Personal Computer line: IBM PC, IBM PC-XT, and IBM PC-AT. The PS/2 machines are based on the Intel 8086, 80286, and 80386 microprocessors. The IBM PS/2 runs all or almost all the software developed for the IBM Personal Computer.

IBM System/360™   The family of mainframes that marked the beginning of the third generation of computers. Along with hardware advances, the 360 introduced comprehensive operating systems to users.

IBM 3080   A series of large-scale mainframes introduced by IBM Corporation in 1980.

IBM 3090   A series of large-scale mainframes introduced by IBM Corporation in 1986.

IC   Abbreviation for INTEGRATED CIRCUIT, a complex electronic circuit fabricated on a simple piece of material, usually a silicon chip.

ICCP   Abbreviation for INSTITUTE FOR CERTIFICATION OF COMPUTER PROFESSIONALS.

ICES   Abbreviation for Integrated Civil Engineering System, a system developed to aid civil engineers in solving engineering problems. Consists of several engineering systems and programming languages.

icon   A pictorial representation of a software function; a symbol used on the display screen to represent some feature of the program. For example, in one program, an icon representing a waste-paper basket is selected if the user wants to erase information. Nontechnical users find symbols easier to understand than technical words.

iconic interface   A user interface that displays objects on the screen as tiny pictures that the user can point to and select via a mouse.

ICPEM   Abbreviation for INDEPENDENT COMPUTER PERIPHERAL EQUIPMENT MANUFACTURERS.

I-cycle   The part of a machine cycle in which the control unit fetches an instruction from internal memory and prepares it for subsequent processing.

IDE Abbreviation for **I**ntelligent **D**rive **E**lectronics, a new generation of hard disk drives to compete with ESDI and SCSI interfaces.

idea processor Personal computer application software that allows a user to organize thoughts in outline form and modify, expand, compress, and reorganize topics as required.

identification division The first of four main parts of a COBOL program.

identifier A symbol whose purpose is to identify, indicate, or name a body of data.

identity In OBJECT-ORIENTED PROGRAMMING, the nature of an object that distinguishes it from all other objects.

identity-based database A database in which entities can be referenced by their unique identities.

ideogram In a NATURAL LANGUAGE, a graphic character that represents an object or concept and associated sounds.

ideographic Pertaining to two-byte characters consisting of pictograms, symbolic characters, and other types of symbols.

idle characters The characters used in data communications to synchronize transmission. See SYNCHRONOUS TRANSMISSION.

idle time The time that a computer system is available for use, but is not in actual operation.

IDP Abbreviation for INTEGRATED DATA PROCESSING.

IEEE See INSTITUTE OF ELECTRICAL AND ELECTRONICS ENGINEERS.

IEEE-488 The interface standard mainly used to connect laboratory instruments and other scientific equipment to computers, either for control purposes or to allow the computer to collect data. A type of PARALLEL INTERFACE.

IEEE 696/S-100 The identification of a standard, developed by the Institute of Electrical and Electronic Engineers. Ensures the compatibility of all computing products designed to this standard.

IEEE 802   A set of standards developed by the IEEE to define methods of access and control on LOCAL AREA NETWORKS.

IFAC   Acronym for International Federation of Automatic Control, a multinational organization concerned with advancing the science and technology of control.

IFF   A graphics format designed for the Commodore Amiga and common to almost all Amiga paint, draw, and animation programs.

IFIP   Acronym for INTERNATIONAL FEDERATION FOR INFORMATION PROCESSING, a multinational federation of organizations, each of which represents its individual country in information technology.

if-then-else   One of the three basic building blocks of STRUCTURED PROGRAMMING.

illegal character   A character or combination of bits not accepted by the computer as a valid or known representation.

illuminance   The amount of light falling on a surface area.

illuminate   To increase the brightness or luminosity of graphical output at a display screen.

Illustrator™   A PostScript-based Apple Macintosh drawing program with powerful capabilities. A complete set of tools for drawing, blending, grouping, and transforming objects enables users to create very sophisticated graphics.

image   **(1)** An exact logical duplicate stored in a different medium. If the user displays the contents of memory on a display screen, he or she will see an image of memory. **(2)** In computer graphics, the output form of graphics data, such as a drawn representation of a graphics file.

image analysis   The process of extracting useful information from images, such as estimating types of surface ground cover from satellite photographs.

image area In computer graphics, the portion of a display surface that is available for displaying images.

image averaging The averaging of a small area of an image to reduce picture resolution.

image compression As applied to computer graphics systems and scanners, the encoding of data describing an image in a more compact form to reduce storage requirements or transmission time.

image enhancement Any accentuation of all or part of a graphics image through such techniques as coloring, shading, highlighting, zooming, reverse video, or blinking.

image object An OBJECT that contains image data.

image-oriented backup Any backup system that creates a mirror image of the disk, without regard to the files themselves. With such a system, the entire disk must be restored from the backup medium to allow access to the files.

image processing A method for processing pictorial information by a computer system. Involves inputting graphics information into a computer system, storing it, working with it, and outputting it to an output device.

image reconstruction An imaging technology used in a variety of industries, including medical imaging. Image data are gathered through one of several methods, including CT-scan and magnetic resonance imaging, and are then processed (reconstructed) into viewable two- or three-dimensional images.

image restoration The process of returning an image to its original condition by reversing the effects of degradations.

imagery The art of making images, or pictures, as in drawing or painting, to represent or evoke a particular thing.

image scanner (**1**) An input device that can "read" into digital memory a hard-copy image such as a text page, drawing, or photograph. (**2**) A device, often used in desktop publishing, that allows images to be scanned and converted into a digital form that can be included in a document.

imagesetter A typesetting device that can transfer output of a desktop publishing system directly to paper or film. Imagesetters commonly print at high resolution (from 1,200 dpi to over 3,000 dpi).

imagesetter service bureau A company that specializes in the sale of POSTSCRIPT output, usually at a per-page or per-color charge. Some bureaus specialize in type-only output, others in film.

Image Studio™ A powerful gray-scale painting program for Apple Macintosh computers. The program includes a selection of brush and paint tools.

image synthesis The creation of two- and three-dimensional images from mathematical models with the aid of computers.

image understanding IMAGE PROCESSING and IMAGE SYNTHESIS combined with ARTIFICIAL INTELLIGENCE.

ImageWriter™ A DOT MATRIX printer used with Apple Macintosh and Apple II microcomputers.

imaging The process involved in the capture, storage, display, and printing of graphical two- or three-dimensional images.

imaging model The method of representing output on a display screen. In a graphical user interface, the goal is to use a unified imaging model, so that the text displayed on-screen closely resembles the text printed.

imbedded print codes In WORD PROCESSING, codes placed in a document to print boldface type, underlining, subscripts, italic type, superscripts, and so on.

IMG Commonly, though not always, a bit-mapped GEM file. Used by GEM Paint, Ventura Publisher, and other programs written to run under GEM.

immediate access The ability of a computer to put data in, or remove it from, storage without delay.

immediate access storage   See INTERNAL STORAGE.

immediate address   Pertaining to an instruction whose address part contains the value of an operand rather than its address. It is not an address at all, but rather an operand supplied as part of an instruction.

immediate-mode commands   System and editing commands executed as soon as the carriage control key (ENTER, RETURN) is pressed.

impact dot matrix mechanism   A print head that forms dot matrix characters through IMPACT PRINTING.

impact dot matrix printer   A PRINTER whose print head is an impact dot matrix mechanism.

impact printer   A data printout device that imprints by the momentary pressure of raised type or pins against paper, using ink or ribbon as a color medium. See DAISY WHEEL PRINTER, DOT MATRIX PRINTER, and LINE PRINTER. Contrast with NONIMPACT PRINTER.

impedance   The total opposition (resistance plus reactance) a circuit offers to the flow of alternating current at a given frequency, measured in ohms.

impersonate   In COMPUTER SECURITY, to pose as an authorized user to gain access to a system.

implementation   (1) The process of installing a computer system. Involves choosing the equipment, installing the equipment, training the personnel, and establishing the computing center operating policies. (2) The representation of a programming language on a specific computer system. (3) The act of installing a program.

import   To bring information from one system or program into another. PageMaker, for example, can import MacPaint files created by SuperPaint.

imprinter   Any device used to produce or impress marks or patterns on a surface, such as a printing press or a cash register.

imprinting   The act of using an IMPRINTER.

IMS Abbreviation for **I**nformation **M**anagement **S**ystem, a database management system software package that provides the facilities for storing and retrieving information from hierarchically structured files and databases.

inactive Pertaining to a transaction that has been loaded into the computer's memory but has not yet been executed.

inactive program A nonoperational program.

inactive record Any record that is not currently shown on a display.

inactive station A station currently ineligible for entering or accepting messages.

inactive window Any window not in use.

in-basket An electronic mailbox that contains only received messages.

in-betweens In COMPUTER ANIMATION, the frames coming "in between" the key frames that smooth the movements of cartoon figures being animated.

inches per second (IPS) A measure of the speed of a device, such as a pen plotter.

incidence matrix A two-dimensional array that describes the edges in a graph. Also called connection matrix.

incident light The light falling on an object. The color of an object is perceived as a function of the wavelengths of incident light reflected or absorbed by it.

inclusive OR A Boolean operator that gives a truth table value of true if either or both of the two variables it connects are true; if neither is true, the value is false. Contrast with EXCLUSIVE OR. Compare NOR, NAND, AND, and LOGICAL SUM.

incoming call A call arriving at a data terminal.

incoming message A message transmitted from a STATION to a COMPUTER.

incoming trunk   A trunk coming into a central office.

increment   (1) The amount added to a value or variable. Contrast with DECREMENT. (2) The distance between any two adjacent addressable points on a graphics input/output device.

incremental backup   The copying of only those files that have changed since the last backup operation, rather than all the files on a hard disk.

incremental plotter   A digital plotter that outputs graphic data in discrete movements of the plotting head.

indegree   The number of directed edges that point to a node. Contrast with OUTDEGREE.

indent   To begin or move text a specified number of positions from the left or right edge of a page.

indentation   The white space found at the beginning of a line of text; often denotes the beginning of a paragraph.

Independent Computer Consultants Association (ICCA)   A national network of independent computer consultants, founded in 1976. Through the national organization and local chapters, members exchange ideas and become part of a collective voice in the computer consulting industry.

Independent Computer Peripheral Equipment Manufacturers (ICPEM)   An organization composed of companies that specialize in manufacturing one or more lines of computer equipment.

independent consultant   A person trained in the information processing field who works with businesses and organizations on a temporary basis helping them solve problems. See CONSULTANT.

independent variable   Any input to a model, so called because it can change.

index   (1) A symbol or number used to identify a particular quantity in an ARRAY of similar quantities; for example, X(5) is the fifth item in an array of X's. (2) A table of reference, held in storage in some sequence, that may be accessed to obtain the addresses of other items of data, such as items in a graphics or data file. See INDEX REGISTER.

indexed address   An address modified by the content of an index register prior to or during the execution of a computer instruction.

indexed color   In computer graphics, refers to the indexing in a color lookup table or map of a limited set of colors selected from a much larger palette; the application then accesses them by their index numbers.

indexed sequential access method (ISAM)   A means of organizing data on a direct-access device. A directory or index is created to show where the data records are stored. Any desired data record can be retrieved from the device by consulting the index. The index reveals the approximate location of the record or piece of data on the direct-access device, and the computer searches the area indicated by the index until it locates the desired record or piece of data.

indexer   A program that generates an index for a document.

index hole   A hole punched through a floppy disk that can be read by the electro-optical system in the disk drive to locate accurately the beginning of sector zero on the disk.

indexing   A programming technique whereby an instruction can be modified by a factor called an INDEX.

index register   A register whose contents can be added to or subtracted from an address prior to or during the execution of an instruction.

indicator   Any device that registers a condition in the computer.

indirect addressing   Using an address that specifies a storage location that contains either a direct address or another indirect address. Also called multilevel addressing.

induce   To produce an electrical charge, current, or voltage by induction. A charge on the gate of a field effect transistor induces an equal charge in the channel.

inductance In a circuit, the property that opposes any change in the existing current. The unit of measure is the HENRY.

induction A process by which a body having electric and magnetic properties produces an electrical charge, a voltage, or a magnetic field in an adjacent body, without physical contact.

industrial data collection device An input device that can record the time an employee spends on the job. Can be used to determine wages, costs for jobs being done, and so forth.

industrial robot A reprogrammable, multifunctional manipulator designed to move material, parts, tools, or specialized devices through variable programmed motions for the performance of a variety of tasks. Unlike other forms of automation, robots can be programmed to do a variety of tasks, making them the most versatile of manufacturing tools.

industry standard Parts of a computer hardware or software subsystem that have been standardized and adopted by the industry at large, enabling application developers to write software applications using a standard set of tools.

Industry Standard Architecture (ISA) The industry name and acronym for the architecture and "bus specification" used by most personal computers today. It is based on the 16-bit design specifications of the original IBM PC-AT, although the individual implementation by different manufacturers may deviate in some details to allow for improvements in the original design, features, and performance.

inequality The expression of two values not being equal. A > B and B < A are two ways of expressing the same inequality. A ≠ B expresses an inequality without identifying its order.

infection The presence within a computer system of a VIRUS or TROJAN HORSE.

inference engine The part of an expert system that takes the information from the user, fits it into the rules in the knowledge base, and generates results, which will lead to advice.

inference program In EXPERT SYSTEMS, a program that derives conclusions by making inferences based upon available data.

infinite loop A set of instructions that continuously repeats in a program. A loop with no exit condition; also called endless loop.

infix notation A common arithmetic notation in which operators are embedded within operands. The addition of 5 and 3 would be expressed as 5 + 3. Contrast with PREFIX NOTATION and POST-FIX NOTATION.

informal design review The evaluation of system-designed documentation by selected management, systems analysts, and programmers, prior to the actual coding of program modules, to determine necessary additions, deletions, and modifications to the system design.

informatics A word used more or less synonymously with INFORMATION TECHNOLOGY.

information Meaningful and useful facts that are extracted from data fed into a computer. Processed data; data that is organized, meaningful, and useful.

information banks Large databases that store information pertaining to specific applications.

information bits In TELECOMMUNICATIONS, those bits that are generated by the data source and do not include error-control bits.

information center A department within a business that offers employees computer and software training, help in getting data from other computer systems, and technical assistance. The department is also responsible for computer purchasing decisions.

information center consultant A SYSTEMS ANALYST assigned to an information center who helps end users develop their own systems.

information center director The person in charge of an INFORMATION CENTER.

information explosion The exponential increase in the growth and diversification of all forms of information. Compare INFORMATION REVOLUTION.

information feedback system   A DATA TRANSMISSION SYSTEM that uses an echo check to verify the accuracy of the transmission.

information float   The time between the occurrence of an event and the point at which it is general knowledge.

information format   A format used for information transfer.

information hiding   In OBJECT-ORIENTED PROGRAMMING, a design strategy that aims at maximizing modularity by concealing as much information as possible within the components of a design. The terms *information hiding* and *encapsulation* are usually interchangeable.

information networks   The interconnection, through telecommunications, of a geographically dispersed group of libraries and information centers for the purpose of sharing their total information resources among more people.

information processing   The totality of operations performed by a computer. Involves evaluating, analyzing, and processing data to produce usable information.

information processing center   Same as DATA PROCESSING CENTER.

information processing curriculum   Same as DATA PROCESSING CURRICULUM.

information providers   Large businesses that supply information to a computer network for a fee, such as COMPUSERVE, PRODIGY, and SOURCE (THE).

information reporting system   An INFORMATION SYSTEM whose principal outputs are preformatted, hard-copy reports.

information resource management   A system to manage information as a resource such as labor, capital, and raw material.

information retrieval   (1)   That branch of computer technology concerned with techniques for storing and searching large quantities of data and making selected data available. **(2)** The methods used to recover specific information from stored data.

information revolution The name given to the present era because of the impact of computer technology on society. Sometimes called COMPUTER REVOLUTION.

information science The study of how people create, use, and communicate information in all forms.

information services Broad-based databases that offer a variety of services, ranging from airline reservation information to stock market quotations. See COMPUSERVE, PRODIGY, and SOURCE (THE).

information society A society in which the majority of workers are involved in the transmittal of information.

information specialist A person who works with a PERSONAL COMPUTER to perform such wide-ranging tasks as database management, electronic spreadsheet analysis, and word processing.

information storage and retrieval (ISR) See INFORMATION RETRIEVAL.

information system The collection of people, procedures, and equipment designed, built, operated, and maintained to collect, record, process, store, retrieve, and display information.

information systems department The area in an organization that consists of computer professionals such as analysts, programmers, managers, and operational personnel.

information technology The merging of computing and high-speed communications links carrying data, sound, and video.

information theory The branch of learning concerned with the likelihood of accurate transmission or communication of messages subject to transmission failure, noise, and distortion. See OPERATIONS RESEARCH.

information utility A company from which users can access information via computer.

inherent error A computer error that has incorrect initial values caused by uncertainty in measurements, by outright blunders, or by approximating a value by an insufficient number of digits.

inherit In OBJECT-ORIENTED PROGRAMMING, for one class to acquire the characteristics of another.

inheritance In OBJECT-ORIENTED PROGRAMMING, a mechanism for automatically sharing methods and data types among classes, subclasses, and objects.

inhouse A term describing any activity that takes place on the user's premises.

INIT A UTILITY PROGRAM for Apple Macintosh computers that executes during a system start or restart.

initial In DESKTOP PUBLISHING, an enlarged letter at the beginning of a paragraph or chapter. Initials set down within the copy are DROP CAPS; those raised above the top of the text are stickup caps.

Initial Graphics Exchange Specification (IGES) A standard file format for computer graphics that is particularly suitable for describing models created with computer-aided design programs. IGES offers methods for describing and annotating drawings and engineering diagrams.

initialization The process of formatting a diskette so that it is ready for use. Initialization erases any previous information that happens to be on the diskette.

initialize (1) To preset a variable or counter to proper starting value before commencing a calculation. (2) To format a disk.

ink jet printer A printer that sprays ink from jet nozzles onto the paper. A nozzle emits a continuous stream of ink droplets that are selectively guided either to the paper or to a gutter where they may be recycled for re-use or sent into a discard container. Ink jet printers produce high-quality printouts.

in-line In printing, the direction of successive characters in a line of text.

in-line coding Coding located in the main part of a routine.

in-line processing The processing of data in random order, not subject to preliminary editing or sorting.

in-line recovery Error recovery in which an affected process is resumed from a point preceding the occurrence of the error.

in-line subroutine A subroutine inserted into the main routine as many times as needed.

inner loop A loop contained within another loop. When nesting loops, the inner loop is the one that must run completely before the outer loop can make another run.

input The introduction of data from an external storage medium into a computer's internal storage unit. Contrast with OUTPUT.

input area The area of internal storage reserved for input data. Contrast with OUTPUT AREA.

input block A BLOCK of data received as input.

input crime A COMPUTER CRIME in which the user changes, fabricates, or manipulates data when they are entered into a computer.

input data Data to be processed; often called INPUT. Contrast with OUTPUT DATA.

input data set A DATA SET that contains data to be processed.

input device The unit used to get data from a human user into the central processing unit, such as a disk drive or keyboard. Contrast with OUTPUT DEVICE.

input field In computer graphics, an unprotected field on a display surface in which data can be entered, modified, or erased.

input file A FILE that has been opened in order to allow records to be read.

input job stream   See INPUT STREAM or JOB STREAM.

input media   The material upon which input data are recorded, such as diskettes and magnetic tape. Compare OUTPUT MEDIA and SOURCE MEDIA.

input/output (I/O)   **(1)** Pertaining to the techniques, media, and devices used to achieve human/machine communication. **(2)** Data submitted to, or information received from, a computer.

input message   Any message entered into a system, terminal, or workstation by an end user.

input mode   A mode in which records can be read from the file.

input/output bound   Pertaining to a situation in which the central processing unit is slowed down because of I/O operations, which are usually extremely slow in comparison to the internal processing operations of the CPU. Contrast with PROCESSOR BOUND.

input/output channel   A channel that transmits input data to, or output data from, a computer. See MULTIPLEXER CHANNEL, RS-232C, and SELECTOR CHANNEL.

input/output device   A unit used to get data from the human user into the central processing unit, and to transfer data from the computer's internal storage to some storage or output device. See INPUT DEVICE, OUTPUT DEVICE, and PERIPHERAL EQUIPMENT.

input/output instructions   Directions for the transfer of data between peripheral devices and main storage that enable the central processing unit to control the peripheral devices connected to it.

input/output ports   The sockets on a computer where the peripherals interface. See PERIPHERAL EQUIPMENT.

input/output processor   An auxiliary processor, dedicated to controlling input/output transfers, that frees the central processing unit for non-I/O tasks.

input/output symbol   A parallelogram-shaped flowcharting symbol used to indicate an input operation to a procedure or an output operation from a procedure.

input primitive   In computer graphics, an item of data obtained from an input device such as a keyboard or pick device.

input state   The state occurring on a specified input channel.

input stream   The sequence of control statements and data submitted to the operating system on an input unit especially activated for that purpose by the operator. Same as job stream.

inputting   The process of entering data into a computer system.

inquiry   A request for information.

inquiry processing   The process of selecting a record from a file and immediately displaying its contents.

inquiry station   A device from which any inquiry is made. Can be geographically remote from the computer or at the computer console.

inscribe   In computer graphics, to draw a figure inside another with the maximum number of contact points.

insert   To place data between other previously existing pieces of data.

insertion method   See SIFTING.

insertion point   The position at which text is entered into a document.

insert mode   In WORD PROCESSING, a text input mode in which text is inserted at the current cursor position without overwriting any text already in the document.

installation   **(1)** A program provided with an application program that assists the user in installing it on a hard disk and configuring the program for use. **(2)** A general term for a particular computer system.

installation program A COMPUTER PROGRAM that assists users in installing an application software package.

installation time The time spent installing, testing, and accepting equipment.

installer A program that adds software to a computer system and prepares it for subsequent execution.

install program A program that prepares a software program to run in the computer. It customizes elements of the new program so a specific computer system can use it.

instance In OBJECT-ORIENTED PROGRAMMING, an object that is a member of a class; something a user can do things to. An instance has state, behavior, and identity. The structure and behavior of similar instances are defined in their common class. The terms *instance* and OBJECT are interchangeable.

instance variable In OBJECT-ORIENTED PROGRAMMING, data contained within an object that describe properties that the object possesses. The terms FIELD, *instance variable*, MEMBER OBJECT, and SLOT are interchangeable.

instant feedback An immediate response—to questions, tests, drills, and so forth.

instantiation In OBJECT-ORIENTED PROGRAMMING, the process of filling in the template of a generic or parameterized class to produce a class from which one can create instances.

instant print That feature of some word processing programs that allows the system to be used as a typewriter.

instantiate In OBJECT-ORIENTED PROGRAMMING, to create an object of a specific class.

Institute for Certification of Computer Professionals (ICCP) A non-profit organization established in 1973 to test and certify knowledge and skills of computing personnel. A primary objective is to pool the resources of constituent societies so the full attention of the information processing industry can be focused on the vital tasks of development and recognition of qualified personnel. Administers the CERTIFICATE IN COMPUTER PROGRAMMING (CCP) and the CERTIFICATE IN DATA PROCESSING (CDP).

Institute of Electrical and Electronic Engineers (IEEE)   A professional engineering organization founded in 1963 for the furthering of education, research, and standards in the electronics and electrical fields. IEEE has a strong interest in computer technology. It sponsors many educational opportunities and publications for members.

Institute of Electrical and Electronics Engineers Computer Society (IEEECS)   A computer specialty group within the IEEE; one of the leading professional associations in advancing the theory and practice of computer and information processing technology.

instruction   A group of characters, bytes, or bits that defines an operation to be performed by the computer. Usually made up of an operation code and one or more operands. See MACHINE INSTRUCTION.

instructional computing   The educational process of teaching individuals the various phases of computer science and data processing.

instruction code   Same as OPERATION CODE.

instruction counter   A counter that indicates the location of the next computer instruction to be interpreted. Same as program counter.

instruction cycle   The time required to process an instruction. This includes fetching the instruction from internal storage, interpreting or decoding the instruction, and executing it. Compare INSTRUCTION TIME.

instruction format   The makeup and arrangement of computer instruction.

instruction register   A hardware register that stores an instruction for execution.

instruction set   A set of vendor-supplied codes for a particular computer or family of computers. Synonymous with repertoire.

instruction time   The time it takes for an instruction to be retrieved from internal storage by the control unit and interpreted. Often called I-time. Compare INSTRUCTION CYCLE.

instruction word   A COMPUTER WORD that contains an instruction.

instrument   A document designed as a form, report, questionnaire, or guide to be used in a planned systematic data-gathering procedure for the purpose of providing information to the individual, group, or organization initiating the request.

instrumental input   Data captured by machines and placed directly into the computer.

instrumentation   The application of devices for the measuring, recording, and/or controlling of physical properties and movements.

integer   Any member of the set consisting of the whole numbers and their negatives, for example: $-24, -1, 0, 1, 2, 13, 128$.

integer BASIC   A type of BASIC language that can process whole numbers (integers) only.

integer field   A database field that will contain a number without a decimal.

integer variable   A quantity that can be equal to any integer and can take on different values.

integrate   To put various components together to form a harmonious computer system.

integrated circuit (IC)   An electronic circuit etched on a tiny germanium or silicon chip. Integrated circuits are categorized by the number of elements (transistors, resistors, etc.) they hold. The categories of ICs are SMALL-SCALE INTEGRATION (SSI), MEDIUM-SCALE INTEGRATION (MSI), LARGE-SCALE INTEGRATION (LSI), VERY LARGE-SCALE INTEGRATION (VLSI), SUPER LARGE-SCALE INTEGRATION (SLSI), and ULTRA LARGE-SCALE INTEGRATION (ULSI).

integrated database   A DATABASE that contains all needed information for use by different groups of users.

integrated data processing (IDP)   Data processing in which the coordination of data acquisition with all other stages of data processing is achieved in a coherent system, such as a business data processing system in which data for sales orders and purchasing are combined to accomplish the functions of scheduling, invoicing, and accounting.

integrated injection logic (IIL)   See i^{2}l.

integrated software   An applications software package containing programs to perform more than one function. A package typically includes related word processing, spreadsheet, database, and graphics programs. Since the information from the electronic spreadsheet may be shared with the database manager and the word processor (and vice versa), this software is called integrated.

integration   The combining of diverse elements of hardware and software, often acquired from different vendors, into a unified system.

integrity   (1) The preservation of programs or data for their intended purpose. (2) The adherence to a code of behavior or ethics. (3) The accuracy, completeness, and safety of data.

Intel Corporation   A leading manufacturer of semiconductor devices that was founded in 1968 by Robert Noyce and Gordon Moore in Mountain View, California. In 1971, Intel engineer Marcian E. "Ted" Hoff designed the 4-bit 4004 microprocessor chip. Throughout the years, Intel has developed a wide variety of chips and board-level products.

intelligence   See ARTIFICIAL INTELLIGENCE.

intelligent database   A database with the ability to accept queries written in a language close to that used by humans.

intelligent language   A programming language that can learn from or be changed by the programmer or user.

intelligent terminal   An input/output device in which a number of computer processing characteristics are physically built into, or attached to, the terminal unit. See POINT-OF-SALE TERMINAL and LOCAL INTELLIGENCE. Compare SMART TERMINAL. Contrast with DUMB TERMINAL.

intensity   The amount of light in a graphics display device; the level of brightness emitted by a CATHODE RAY TUBE. On most visual display devices, intensity can be controlled by manipulating a switch.

Intensity Red Green Blue   A type of color encoding used in IBM's color graphics adapters CGA, EGA, and VGA.

interactive   Yielding an immediate response to input. The user is in direct and continual communication with the computer system. Denotes two-way communications between a computer system and its operators. An operator can modify or terminate a program and receive feedback from the system for guidance and verification.

interactive access   See INTERACTIVE INPUT.

interactive graphics   Any graphics system in which the user and the computer are in active communication.

interactive graphics system   A computer graphics system in which workstations are used interactively for computer-aided design, all under full operator control, and possibly also for text-processing, generation of charts and graphs, computer-aided engineering, and generation of 35 mm slides or animation pictures.

interactive input   Input during which the user interacts directly with the computer.

interactive language   A computer language that permits the programmer to converse with the computer, entering instructions, testing them, changing them, etc. Many languages have both interactive and noninteractive versions.

interactive link   The link for interaction between a user and a mainframe computer.

interactive package   A SOFTWARE PACKAGE that allows the user to interact with the computer during data entry and execution.

interactive processing   A type of real-time processing involving a continuing dialogue between user and computer; the user is allowed to modify data and/or instructions. See CONVERSATIONAL MODE and TRANSACTION-oriented PROCESSING.

interactive program   A computer program that permits data to be entered or the flow of the program to be modified during its execution.

interactive query   An operation that allows the immediate retrieval of a specific record or records. Essentially a dialogue in which each user input can elicit a response from the system.

interactive system   A system in which the human user of a device serviced by the computer can communicate directly with the operating program. For human users, this is termed a conversational system.

interactive videodisc   A COMPUTER-ASSISTED INSTRUCTION TECHNOLOGY that uses a computer to provide access to at least two hours of video information stored on a videodisc.

interblock gap (IBG)   The distance on a magnetic tape, or disk, between the end of one block of records and the beginning of the next block of records. Contrast with FILE GAP and INTERRECORD GAP.

interconnection   The physical and electrical connection of equipment furnished by different vendors.

interface   **(1)** The point of meeting between a computer and an external entity, whether an operator, peripheral device, or communications medium. May be physical, involving a connector, or logical, involving software. **(2)** In OBJECT-ORIENTED PROGRAMMING, the outside view of a class, object, or module, which emphasizes its abstraction while hiding its structure and the secrets of its behavior.

interface card   A type of expansion board that permits connection of external devices to computers, such as a disk interface card, serial interface card, or parallel interface card.

interference   Unwanted signals that degrade the quality of wanted signals.

interlace   To assign successive addresses to physically separated storage locations on a magnetic disk in such a way as to reduce the access time.

interleaved memory A method of speeding access to DYNAMIC RANDOM ACCESS MEMORY (DRAM) chips by dividing RAM into two large banks and storing bit pairs in alternate banks; the microprocessor accesses one bank while the other is being refreshed.

interleaving A MULTIPROGRAMMING technique in which parts of one program are inserted into another so that if there are processing delays in one of the programs, parts of the other can be processed.

interlock A protective facility that prevents one device or operation from interfering with another, such as the locking of the switches on the control console to prevent their manual movement while the computer is executing a program.

interlude Preliminary housekeeping.

intermittent error An error that occurs intermittently, but persistently, and is extremely difficult to reproduce or to debug.

internal clock An electronic circuit within the computer system that keeps the time of day.

internal commands OPERATING SYSTEM commands that do not require that the system disk be in the active drive.

internal data representation Data representation in registers, storage, and other devices inside the computer.

internal documentation (1) The insertion of explanatory comments and remarks into source-language programs. Causes no processing by the computer but acquaints present and future programmers with the functions performed by various parts of the program. (2) The documentation used within a business organization.

internal DOS commands The commands that access DOS programs that are loaded into the computer when the system is booted.

internal font A series of typefaces contained within ROM chips built into a printer.

internal hard disk   A HARD DISK designed to fit within a computer's case and to use the computer's power supply.

internal memory   Same as INTERNAL STORAGE.

internal modem   A modem that plugs directly into computer expansion slots inside the computer. Contrast with ACOUSTIC COUPLER and DIRECT-CONNECT MODEM.

internal report   A report produced by an organization for people inside that organization, usually concerning inventory, quality control, payroll, and so on. Contrast with EXTERNAL REPORT.

internal sort   The sequencing of two or more records within the central processing unit; the first phase of a multipass sort program. See EXTERNAL SORT.

internal storage   Addressable storage directly controlled by the central processing unit. Used to store programs while they are being executed and data while they are being processed. Also called immediate access storage, internal memory, main storage, and primary storage. Contrast with AUXILIARY STORAGE.

International Business Machines Corporation   See IBM PERSONAL COMPUTER.

International Federation for Information Processing (IFIP)   A multinational organization representing professional and educational societies actively engaged in the field of information processing. Holds a meeting at a different location in the world every three years.

International Standards Organization (ISO)   An international agency that reviews and approves independently designed products for use within specific industries. ISO is also responsible for developing standards for information exchange.

interoperability   The ability of devices from a variety of vendors to share data and communicate effectively.

interpolation   **(1)** A method of finding values between any two known values. **(2)** In computer graphics, a process often applied to creating curves by joining a series of straight line segments or to defining smoothing curves between specified points. **(3)** The averaging of a number of points to create a new point.

interpretation   The one-by-one translation of high-level language program statements into machine language instructions. When a program is interpreted, each statement is translated and executed before the next statement is processed. Contrast with COMPILATION.

interpreted language   A language implemented by an INTERPRETER.

interpreter   A language translator that converts each source-language statement into machine code and executes it immediately, statement by statement; a program that performs interpretation. Contrast with COMPILER.

interprocess communication   The communication of one process of an OPERATING SYSTEM with another running on the same computer or NETWORK.

interrecord gap   The space between records on magnetic disk and tape. Used to signal that the end of a record has been reached. Contrast with FILE GAP and INTERBLOCK GAP.

interrupt   A signal that, when activated, causes the hardware to transfer program control to some specific location in internal storage, thus breaking the normal flow of the program being executed. After the interrupt has been processed, program control is again returned to the interrupted program.

interrupt driven   A term applied to a computer system that makes extensive use of interrupts.

interruption   Any break in the normal sequence of executing instructions.

intersection   A method of combining two objects into one; the area where the objects overlap remains, creating a new object.

interval timer A mechanism whereby elapsed time can be monitored by a computer system.

interview (1) A fact-gathering method in systems analysis and design. (2) A personal conversation between a job applicant and the person who may offer a job.

intrinsic font A font for which a bit image (an exact pattern) exists that can be used without modification.

inventory control The use of a computer system to monitor an inventory.

inventory management The daily and periodic bookkeeping commonly associated with inventory control and with forecasting needs for items or groups of items.

inverse video A process that shows dark text on a light background display screen. Normally, light text is shown on a dark background. Same as REVERSE VIDEO.

invert To turn over; to reverse. To highlight text or objects by reversing the on-screen display or printout.

inverted file A file organized so that it can be accessed by character rather than by record key.

inverted structure A file structure that permits fast, spontaneous searching for previously unspecified information. Independent lists are maintained in record keys that are accessible according to the values of specified fields.

inverter A circuit in which a binary 1 input produces a binary 0 output, and vice versa.

inverting circuit A circuit for changing direct current to alternating current. Contrast with ADAPTER.

investment analysis A process that determines the best use for available cash.

investment analysis packages Software packages that help a user choose and keep track of the best investments.

invisible backlog A backlog of jobs that have not been submitted to the MIS department for analysis and design.

invisible refresh A scheme that refreshes dynamic memories without disturbing the rest of the system.

invocation The calling up of a SUBROUTINE or PROCEDURE.

I/O Abbreviation for INPUT/OUTPUT.

I/O board A circuit board that controls the input and output of data between the computer and peripheral devices.

I/O bound A term applied to programs that require a large number of input/output operations, resulting in much CPU wait time. Contrast with COMPUTE-BOUND.

I/O channel Part of the input/output system of a computer. Under the control of I/O commands, the channel transfers blocks of data between internal storage and peripheral equipment.

IOCS Abbreviation for **i**nput/**o**utput **c**ontrol **s**ystem.

ion deposition A printing technology that is used in high-speed page printers.

ionographic printer A printer that uses ION DEPOSITION. The image is formed on a dielectric surface and then transferred to plain paper.

I/O port A connection to a central processing unit that provides for data paths between the CPU and peripheral devices, such as display terminals, printers, and disk units.

I/O processor A circuit board or chip used only to handle input/output operations between the computer and peripherals.

IPL-V Abbreviation for **I**nformation **P**rocessing **L**anguage **F**ive, a list processing language primarily used for working with heuristic-type problems.

IRG Abbreviation for INTERRECORD GAP.

IRGB See INTENSITY RED GREEN BLUE.

IRM   Abbreviation for **i**nformation **r**esources **m**anager, the person responsible for operating a company's main computer and monitoring the numerous employees using it.

ISA   See INDUSTRY STANDARD ARCHITECTURE.

ISAM   Acronym for INDEXED SEQUENTIAL ACCESSED METHOD.

ISDN   An acronym for **I**ntegrated **S**ervices **D**igital **N**etwork, an international communications standard for sending data, voice, and video over telephone lines.

ISO   Abbreviation for **I**nternational **S**tandards **O**rganization, an international agency responsible for developing standards for information exchange. Has a function similar to that of ANSI in the United States.

isolation   **(1)** In a computer security system, the compartmentalization of information so that access to it is on a "need to know" basis. **(2)** The state of being separated or set apart from others.

isometric   Describing the two-dimensional representation of a three-dimensional object.

isometric view   In computer graphics, a display method that shows 3-D objects with height and width but without the change in perspective that would be added by depth; in other words, a picture of a three-dimensional object that shows all three dimensions in equal proportions.

ISO 9660   An international format standard for CD-ROM.

ISR   Abbreviation for INFORMATION STORAGE AND RETRIEVAL. See INFORMATION.

issuance   The use of computers to produce transaction processing documents such as paychecks, bills, and customer remainder notices.

italic   A typeface that slants to the right and is commonly used for emphasis.

ITC Avant Garde   A modern SANS SERIF typeface designed by the International Typeface Corporation (ITC) and included as a built-in font with many POSTSCRIPT laser printers.

ITC Bookman   A SERIF typeface design owned by the International Typeface Corporation (ITC) and included as a built-in font with many POSTSCRIPT laser printers.

ITC Zapf Chancery   An italic typeface owned by the International Typeface Corporation (ITC) and included as a built-in font with many POSTSCRIPT laser printers. It was developed by Herman Zapf, a German typeface designer.

item   **(1)** A group of related characters treated as a unit. A RECORD is a group of related items, and a FILE is a group of related records. **(2)** A selection within a MENU.

iterate   To repeat automatically, under program control, the same series of processing steps until a predetermined stop or branch condition is reached. See LOOP and NEWTON-RAPHSON.

iteration control structure   A LOOPING mechanism.

iterative   Repetitive. The term is often used when each succeeding iteration, or repetition, of a procedure comes closer to a desired result.

I-time   The portion of a machine cycle where an instruction is interpreted.

jack   A connecting device to which a wire or wires of a circuit may be attached and that is arranged for the insertion of a plug. Also called socket.

jacket   The plastic cover for a disk. It has holes and slots cut into it to expose the hub and afford the head-of-disk drive access to the disk. 5.25-inch disks use a stiff plastic jacket, with glued or crimped seams. 3.5-inch disks use rigid plastic envelopes, with spring-loaded sliding metal shutters to protect the disk surface from being touched accidentally.

jaggles   In a computer graphics display, the stairstepped or saw-toothed effect of diagonals, circles, and curves.

jargon   The vocabulary peculiar to a group or profession.

JCL   Abbreviation for JOB CONTROL LANGUAGE, the language used to provide control instructions to the computer for IBM mainframe operating systems.

JES   Abbreviation for Job Entry System, a portion of the operating system that accepts and schedules jobs for execution.

jitter   The brief instability of a signal, applied particularly to signals on a video display.

job   A collection of specified tasks constituting a unit of work for a computer, such as a program or group of related programs used as a unit.

job abort   The cancellation of a job because of problems with software, hardware, or data.

job control language (JCL)   The language that defines a job and the resources it requires from the computer system, including constraints on the job, such as time limits. It is more often interpreted than compiled.

job control statement   A statement, written in a job control language, that defines one aspect of a job.

job definition   A series of job control statements that defines a job.

job file   A FILE that exists until the end of the JOB that uses it.

job header   A page in printed output that indicates the beginning of a user job.

job log   A RECORD of jobs submitted to a system over a specified period of time.

job name   The name of a JOB as identified to a system.

job number   The identification number assigned to a job.

job-oriented terminal   A TERMINAL designed for a particular application.

job output file   A DATA SET or DATA FILE consisting of output data produced by a series of jobs.

job priority   The order in which BATCH jobs on a job queue are selected for execution.

job queue   A set of programs and data currently making its way through a computer. In most operating systems, each job is brought into the queue and is processed (given control of the computer) when it is the "oldest" job within its own priority. An exception to this is a job of higher priority that has not yet obtained sufficient resources to be processed.

job scheduler   A person who aids computer operators in the running of a large computer installation.

job stream   Any input to the operating system. May consist of one or more jobs.

job-to-job transition   The process of locating a program and its associated files and preparing the computer for the execution of a particular job.

job turnaround   The elapsed time from when a job is given to the computer system until its printed output reaches the person who submitted the job.

Josephson junction   An ultra-fast microelectronic circuit technology that uses superconductor materials, named after Brian Josephson, who discovered the original theory. Josephson junction circuits are immersed in liquid helium to obtain near-absolute-zero temperatures required for operation.

journal   A chronological record of operations performed in a computer system.

JOVIAL   Acronym for **J**ules' **O**wn **V**ersion of the **I**nternational Algorithmetic **L**anguage, a high-level programming language used in the 1960s and 1970s.

joystick   A lever, pivoted to move in any direction, that controls the movement of a CURSOR on a DISPLAY SCREEN. Similar to a mouse, but used mostly when playing video games.

JPEG   Abbreviation for **J**oint **P**hotographic **E**xperts **G**roup, the International Standards Organization's proposed standard for image compression on the Apple Macintosh microcomputer.

jukebox   A robotically serviced device for storing and retrieving multiple optical discs and servicing on demand one or more optical disc drives.

Julian number   A form of calendar representation within a computer system. The Julian date indicates the year and the number of elapsed days in the year. For example, 92-029 was January 29, 1992, the 29th day of 1992; 92-043 is February 12, 1992, the 43rd day of 1992; and 93-156 is June 5, 1993, the 156th day of 1993.

jump   A departure from the normal sequence of executing instructions in a computer. Synonymous with BRANCH and TRANSFER.

jumper   A CONNECTOR that closes an electrical circuit.

jump line   In DESKTOP PUBLISHING, a notation at the end of a section of a document in any printed medium indicating where the document is continued.

junction   That part of a DIODE or TRANSISTOR where two opposite types of semiconductor material meet.

junk Garbled data received over a communications line. If proper communication is not established with a remote system, random, meaningless characters (junk) may appear on the screen.

justification **(1)** The act of adjusting, arranging, or shifting digits to the left or right to make them fit a prescribed pattern. **(2)** The alignment of text margins on both right and left sides. Justified text is both flush left and flush right. Contrast with RAGGED LEFT and RAGGED RIGHT.

justify To align the characters in a field. For example, to right justify, the last character (the least significant digit) is written in the last or rightmost character position in the field. Alphabetical lists are commonly left justified.

justify to the left In WORD PROCESSING, to align text at the left margin.

justify to the right In WORD PROCESSING, to align text at the right margin.

— K —

K   (**1**) An abbreviation for kilo, or 1,000 in decimal notation. For example, 100K cps means a reading speed of 100,000 characters per second. (**2**) Loosely, when referring to storage capacity, 2^{10}; in decimal notation, 1,024. The expression 8K represents 8,192 ($8 \times 1,024$).

kb   Abbreviation for KILOBYTE.

kc   One thousand characters per second. Used to express the rate of data transfer operations.

kermit   A file transfer protocol used for more error-free modem communications.

kernel   A set of programs in an OPERATING SYSTEM that implement the most primitive of that system's functions; the core of an operating system.

kerning   Adjusting the space between characters to create wider or tighter spacing; the reduction of excess white space between specific letter pairs.

key   (**1**) The control field or fields that identify a record. See PRIMARY KEY. (**2**) The field that determines the position of a record in a sorted sequence. See MAJOR SORT KEY and MINOR SORT KEY. (**3**) A lever on a manually operated machine, such as a typewriter or visual display keyboard. (**4**) To enter data into a system by means of a KEYBOARD.

key abstraction   In OBJECT-ORIENTED PROGRAMMING, a class or object that forms part of the vocabulary of the problem domain.

key assignments   Functions that a computer program assigns to specific keys.

keyboard   An input device used to key programs and data into a computer's storage. Since the keyboard is the most frequently used part of the computer, a good keyboard is an essential part of any computer system intended for business purposes.

keyboarding   The process of entering programs and data into input media or directly into the computer by typing on a keyboard.

keyboard template   A plastic or cardboard card with adhesive that can be pressed onto the keyboard to explain the way a program configures the keyboard.

keyboard-to-disk system   A data entry system in which data can be entered directly onto a disk by typing the data at a keyboard.

keyboard-to-tape system   A data entry system in which data can be entered directly onto a magnetic tape by typing the data at a keyboard.

key bounce   A characteristic of some poorly designed keyboards where a character registers twice for each time the user presses its key.

key disk   A method of software protection that requires the presence of a specific disk in a disk drive before the software will function properly.

key field   A field used to identify a record.

key-in   To enter information by means of a keyboard.

keypad   An input device that uses a set of decimal digit keys (0–9) and two special function keys. Used as a separate device or sometimes located to the right of a standard QWERTY KEYBOARD—one result of ERGONOMICS.

keypunch   A keyboard-operated device used to punch holes in punch cards to represent data to be input to a computer by a CARD READER.

key stations   The terminals used for data input on a multiuser system.

keystroke   The action of pressing a single key or a combination of keys on a keyboard. Speed in many data entry jobs is measured in keystrokes per minute.

key-to-address   See HASHING.

key-to-disk unit   An AUXILIARY DEVICE that uses a keyboard unit to place data directly on magnetic disk.

key-to-tape unit   An auxiliary device that uses a keyboard unit to place data directly on magnetic tape.

keyword **(1)** One of the significant and informative words in a title or document that describe the content of that document. **(2)** The primary element in a programming-language statement, such as LET, PRINT, and INPUT in the BASIC programming language. A keyword is followed by a series of arguments used by it to complete a task. **(3)** A set of letters that has special meaning to a computer program. For example, DIR is a command that directs the operating system to produce a DIRECTORY of a disk.

key-word-in-context See KWIC.

kHz Abbreviation for KILOHERTZ.

kill **(1)** To terminate a process before it reaches its natural conclusion. **(2)** A method of erasing information. **(3)** To stop; frequently, to abort. **(4)** To delete a file.

kilobaud One thousand bits per second. Used to measure data communications speeds.

kilobit One thousand bits.

kilobyte Specifically, 2^{10}, or 1,024, bytes. Commonly thought of as 1,000. Abbreviated K and used as a suffix when describing memory size. Thus, 24K really means a $24 \times 1,024 = 24,576$-byte memory system. Sometimes abbreviated kb.

kilocycle One thousand cycles. Formerly, one thousand cycles per second; now termed KILOHERTZ.

kilohertz One thousand cycles per second. Used to measure data transmission frequencies.

kilomegacycle One billion cycles per second.

kinematic programs In CAD/CAM, visual simulation programs used for solving those design problems that involve moving parts.

kinematics A COMPUTER-AIDED ENGINEERING process for plotting or animating the motion of parts in a machine or a structure under design on the system.

kludge Makeshift. Used to describe a collection of mismatched components that have been assembled into a system.

knots In computer graphics, scalar values that influence a curve shape.

knowledge (1) In ARTIFICIAL INTELLIGENCE, symbolic information used by a domain expert to solve problems. (2) Facts and relationships used to solve problems.

knowledge acquisition In EXPERT SYSTEM programming, the process of acquiring and systematizing knowledge from experts.

knowledge base A database of knowledge about a particular subject. Contains facts, data, beliefs, assumptions, and procedures needed for problem solution.

knowledge crafting The process of building expert systems.

knowledge domain In ARTIFICIAL INTELLIGENCE, an area of problem-solving expertise.

knowledge encoding The process of entering facts, rules, objects, and other knowledge into an EXPERT SYSTEM.

knowledge engineer The individual who develops an expert system. He or she acquires knowledge from human experts and encodes it into an EXPERT SYSTEM.

knowledge engineering An engineering discipline wherein knowledge is integrated into computer systems to solve complex problems normally requiring a high level of human expertise.

knowledge industries The industries that perform data processing and provide information products and services.

knowledge information processor The name used by the Japanese for their proposed fifth-generation computers, which are expected to be totally different from previous generations.

knowledge modeling The procedure by which knowledge engineers organize the data they gain from domain experts.

KnowledgePro   An EXPERT SYSTEM with HYPERTEXT capabilities for personal computers.

knowledge representation   A means of organizing human knowledge into a data structure that can include facts, rules, and common sense.

knowledge system   A large body of knowledge in the form of rules and facts along with an inference mechanism that can be used to solve problems; an EXPERT SYSTEM.

knowledge work   Occupations in which the primary activities involve receiving, processing, and transmitting information.

Koala Pad™   An inexpensive DIGITIZING TABLET for MICROCOMPUTERS.

KWIC   Acronym for **k**ey-**w**ord-**i**n-**c**ontext, a method of indexing information by preselected words or phrases that takes into consideration the context in which the words are used.

label An identifier or name used in a computer program to identify or describe an instruction, statement, message, data value, record, item, or file.

label prefix In a SPREADSHEET PROGRAM, the punctuation mark preceding a cell entry.

lag The relative difference between two events, mechanisms, or states.

LAN Acronym for LOCAL AREA NETWORK, a connection between computers or computerized systems within a building or immediate neighborhood. Employing a LAN enables users to share files and expensive peripherals such as laser printers.

land The available area of a printed circuit board.

landscape An orientation in which data is printed across the wider side of a form.

landscape mode A video display screen whose width is greater than its height, as in a pastoral landscape painting. Contrast with PORTRAIT MODE.

landscape monitor A monitor with a screen shape wider than it is high.

language A set of rules, representations, and conventions used to convey information. A way of passing instructions to the computer other than through direct input of number codes. Programming languages are characterized as low-level or high-level.

language processing The use of computer programs to analyze and understand language.

language processor A program that translates human-written source language programs into a form that can be executed on a computer. There are three general types of language processors: ASSEMBLER, COMPILER, and INTERPRETER.

language statement A statement coded by a user of a computing system that conveys information to a processing program, such as a language translator program, service program, or control program. May signify that an operation be performed, or may simply contain data to be passed to the processing program.

language subset   Part of a language that can be used independently of the rest of the language.

language translator program   A program that transforms statements from one language to another without significantly changing their meaning, such as a COMPILER or ASSEMBLER.

LAN Manager   A LOCAL AREA NETWORK technology developed by Microsoft Corporation. LAN Manager connects computers and allows users to share files and system resources.

laptop computer   A PERSONAL COMPUTER, small and portable enough to be used comfortably in the lap of a person seated in an automobile or an airplane. Laptop computers today feature full-sized keyboards, flat-screen monitors that fold up and down, hard disks, floppy disks, and powerful microprocessors. Also called lap computer.

large-scale integration   The process of placing a large number of integrated circuits on one silicon chip. Today's technology produces chips with 100,000 to 10 million components, known as very large-scale integration. Further refinements should produce ultralarge-scale integration (10 million to 1 billion components) and giga-scale integration (over 1 billion components).

laser   Acronym for **L**ight **A**mplification by **S**imulated **E**mission of **R**adiation, the technology that uses the principle of amplification of electromagnetic waves by simulated emission of radiation and operates in the infrared, visible, or ultraviolet region. A device emitting coherent photon or electromagnetic energy.

laser disk   A form of OPTICAL STORAGE that uses laser technology to read information from a disk.

laser font   Clear, undistorted characters formed by a LASER PRINTER.

LaserJet A series of desktop laser printers from Hewlett-Packard Company. Introduced in 1984, it set the standard for the desktop laser printer market.

laser printer A printer that uses a light beam to transfer images to paper. Laser printers print a full page at a time. A laser is used to "paint" the dots of light onto a photographic drum or belt. The toner is applied to the drum or belt and then transferred onto the paper.

laser storage An auxiliary storage device using laser technology to encode data onto a metallic surface.

LaserWriter A series of desktop laser printers from Apple Computer, Inc.

lasso In many graphics programs, a tool that selects irregularly shaped regions from an image for further processing.

last in-first out See LIFO.

last in-last out See LILO.

late binding In OBJECT-ORIENTED PROGRAMMING, dynamic binding. See BINDING.

latency The rotational delay in reading or writing a record to a direct access auxiliary storage device such as a disk.

launch To start.

layer (1) In computer graphics drawing programs, an overlay on which text or images can be stored. In SuperPaint, for example, a user can create illustrations on two layers: a paint layer for bit-mapped graphics and a draw layer for object-oriented graphics. In some graphics programs the user can draw and paint on many different layers. (2) The third dimension in a 3-D array.

layer discrimination In computer graphics, the process of selectively assigning colors to a layer, or highlighting entities via gray levels, to graphically distinguish among data on different layers displayed on a CRT.

layering A logical concept that associates subgroups of graphic data within a single drawing. Allows a user to view only those parts of a drawing being worked on and reduces the confusion that might result from viewing all parts of a very complex file.

layers User-defined logical subdivisions of data in a graphics database that may be viewed on the CRT individually or overlaid and viewed in groups.

layout (1) In DESKTOP PUBLISHING, the design or process of arranging text and graphics on a page. (2) The arrangement of data items on a data record. (3) The overall design or plan, such as system flowcharts, schematics, diagrams, format for printer output, and makeup of a document (book).

layout sheet Grid paper designed to map the display screen for purposes of program planning. Text and graphics can be sketched in terms of rows and columns or the graphics X–Y coordinates.

LCD Abbreviation for LIQUID CRYSTAL DISPLAY, a way to make letters and numbers appear by reflecting light on a special crystalline substance. Features high visibility in high illumination levels but no visibility in low illumination levels. Because of its thin profile, LCD technology is often used in pocket calculators, hand-held computers, briefcase computers, keyboards, watches, and other devices.

LCD printer Abbreviation for LIQUID CRYSTAL DISPLAY PRINTER, an electro-photographic printer that uses an electrostatically charged drum to transfer toner to a piece of paper. Similar to LASER PRINTERS and LED PRINTERS.

LCS Abbreviation for liquid crystal shutter, a type of optical technology based on using LCD (liquid crystal display) panels to block or pass light through for display or reaction. LCS technology competes with laser beam methods in the design of high-quality page printers.

lead A connection to a CIRCUIT element.

leader (1) In page layout and word processing programs, a row of dots and dashes that provide a path for the eye to follow across the page.

Leaders are sometimes used in tables of contents to lead the reader's eye from the entry to the page number. **(2)** The blank section of tape at the beginning of a reel of magnetic tape.

leading The vertical spacing between lines of type, measured from baseline to baseline. Font styles that have long ascenders and descenders need more leading than fonts that don't. In publishing, the font size and leading is described as a fraction. For example, 10/12 (which is read "10 on 12") indicates 10-point type with two points of leading.

leading edge **(1)** In OPTICAL SCANNING, the edge of the document or page that enters the read position first. **(2)** A buzz word implying technological leadership, as in "the leading edge of technology."

leaf The terminal node of a tree diagram. See ROOT.

learning A procedure in ARTIFICIAL INTELLIGENCE by which an artificial intelligence program improves its performance by gaining knowledge.

learning machine A machine that can monitor its own behavior and employ feedback to modify that behavior.

lease A method of acquiring the use of a computer system. A lease contract requires no financing and is less expensive than renting the system.

leased line A communications line dedicated to one customer. Also called private line.

leasing companies Companies that specialize in leasing computer equipment, which they purchase from a computer manufacturer.

least significant digit (LSD) That digit of a number that has the least weight or significance. In the number 58,371, for example, the least significant digit is 1.

LED Acronym for **l**ight-**e**mitting **d**iode, a commonly used alphanumeric display unit that glows when supplied with a specified voltage.

LED printer Acronym for **l**ight-**e**mitting **d**iode printer, an electrophotographic printer that uses an electrostatically charged drum to transfer toner to a piece of paper. Similar to LASER PRINTER and LCS PRINTER.

left-aligned Pertaining to text that is aligned to the left margin but need not be aligned to the right margin.

left justify See JUSTIFY.

legend (1) The text beneath a graph that explains the colors, shading, or symbols used to label the data points. (2) Any text that describes or explains a graphic.

length The number of characters, bytes, or bits in a computer word. A variable word is made up of several characters, ending with a special end character. A fixed word is composed of the same number of bits, bytes, or characters in each word.

less than The relationship of an inequality between two values. The symbol is <, with the point toward the smaller number; for example, $3 < 8$ means 3 is less than 8. Commonly used in comparison to determine alternative processing. Contrast with GREATER THAN.

LetraStudio™ A graphics program from Letraset USA that has the ability to condense, stretch, slant, scale, rotate, flip-flop, or distort a design in real time.

letter-quality printing The high-quality output produced by some printers. LASER PRINTERS, DAISY-WHEEL PRINTERS, and INK-JET PRINTERS are letter-quality printers. High-end, 24-pin dot matrix printers provide near letter-quality printing.

level The degree of subordination in a hierarchy. A measure of the distance from a node to the root of a tree.

lexicon Any language with definitions for all terms.

LF Abbreviation for LINE FEED.

librarian (1) The person responsible for an organization's library of technical documentation, including manuals used by programmers, operators, and other employees. (2) The person responsible for the safekeeping of all computer files, such as diskettes, disk packs, and magnetic tapes.

library   (**1**) A published collection of programs, routines, and subroutines available to every user of the computer. (**2**) A storage area, usually on hard disk or a diskette, used to store programs. (**3**) A collection of items, such as clip art, intended for inclusion in other programs.

library automation   The application of computers and other technology to library operations and services.

library director   In a library, an area that contains information about each member in the library.

library list   An ordered list of library names used to find an object.

library manager   A program that maintains the programs stored in an operating system.

library program   A PROGRAM in a program library.

library routine   A tested routine maintained in a program library.

license contract   The document that authorizes the purchaser of a software product to run the product on his or her computer.

life cycle   The course of a program or system from its inception with the original idea through development, implementation, and maintenance, until it is either replaced or no longer useful.

licensed application program   A set of licensed computer programs used to perform a particular task.

LIFO   Acronym for **l**ast **i**n-**f**irst **o**ut, the way most microprocessor program stacks operate. The last data or instruction word placed on the stack is the first to be retrieved. Same as FILO. See PUSHDOWN STACK. Contrast with FIFO.

ligature   In typography, two or more characters designed and cast as a distinct unit for aesthetic reasons. Letter combinations such as ae, fi, ff, fl, ffi, ffl, and oe commonly are printed as ligatures. Some outline fonts available for POSTSCRIPT laser printers and imagesetters include ligatures for desktop publishing applications.

light In computer graphics, being closer to white than black. Having a high color value.

light-emitting diode See LED.

lightface In DESKTOP PUBLISHING, an extra-light version of a typeface.

light guide A channel designed for the transmission of light, such as a cable of optical fibers. See FO.

lighting model In computer graphics, a mathematical formula for approximating the physical effect of light striking objects from various sources.

lightness The amount of light or dark present in a particular color.

light pen An electronic device that resembles a pen and can be used to write or sketch on the screen of a CATHODE RAY TUBE to provide input to the computer.

light source In computer graphics, one of several types of light used by a lighting model, such as ambient, directional, positional, and spot.

lightwave system An optical system that transmits light pulses over optical fibers. This system is capable of transmitting over a billion bits per second, which means 16,000 digitized voice conversations can be transmitted simultaneously over one hair-thin optical fiber.

LILO Acronym for last in-last out, a method of storing and retrieving items from a list, table, or stack such that the last item placed on the stack is the last to be retrieved. Same as FIFO. Contrast with FILO.

LIM Acronym for Lotus Intel Microsoft memory, a technique for adding memory to a DOS system.

limit check An input control technique that tests the value of a data field to determine whether values fall within set limits or a given range.

limiting operation That operation in a system that has the smallest capacity or slowest speed. Since the capacity of a total system with no alternative routing can be no greater than the operation with the least capacity, the total system can be effectively scheduled by simply scheduling the limiting operation. See BOUND.

line   (1) In computer graphics, a particular set of points; lines in geometry extended in two directions without end. In mathematics, unless otherwise stated, lines are always thought to be straight. (2) In most PROGRAMMING LANGUAGES, a line begins with an identifying number and contains one or more statements. Sometimes a statement requires more than one line. (3) In DATA COMMUNICATIONS, any type of channel, but especially telephone lines.

linear IC   An analog integrated circuit, as opposed to a digital integrated circuit.

linear language   A LANGUAGE customarily expressed as a linear representation; for example, Pascal is a linear language.

linear list   See SEQUENTIAL LIST.

linear network   A NETWORK in which there are exactly two endpoint nodes, any number of intermediate nodes, and only one path between any two nodes.

linear perspective   In computer graphics, a picture or drawing that gives the illusion of depth. Linear perspective is often shown by parallel lines that recede from the spectator and meet in a point (the vanishing point) on the horizon or at eye-level.

linear programming (LP)   A technique for finding an optimum combination when there may be no single best one.

linear representation   An arrangement of GRAPHICS in one-dimensional space.

linear search   A search that begins with the first element and compares until a matching key is found or the end of the list is reached.

linear structure   (1) In DATABASE MANAGEMENT SYSTEMS, a mode of file organization in which each primary record can own only one secondary

record. The latter functions as an overflow record for the primary record.
(2) The sequential arrangement of data records.

line art   Artwork containing only blacks and whites with no shading. Line art can be reproduced accurately by low- to medium-resolution printers.

line art mode   A SCANNER setting for digitizing an image by characterizing each point either as black or white with no shades of gray.

line-at-a-time printer   Same as LINE PRINTER.

line balancing   A management technique used in production environments wherein tasks are assigned to computer graphics workstations in equal proportions, thus raising efficiency.

line chart   A method of charting business data.

line circuit   A physical circuit path, such as a data communications line.

line concentration   The combining of data from many lines or devices into fewer lines.

linecut   In computer graphics, the reverse of a black-on-white line drawing.

line device   Any of a class of printers that accept one line of text at a time.

line drawing   A drawing in which an object's image is represented by a solid-line outline of the surface.

line editor   A type of software editor that allows the user to make changes in a document on a line-by-line basis.

line feed (LF)   An operation that advances printer paper by one line. See FORM FEED.

line filter   A device used to correct electromagnetic interference that comes in over a power line.

line graph   A graph made by connecting data points with a line. Shows the variations of data over time or the relationships between two numeric variables.

line graphics   Same as COORDINATE GRAPHICS.

line height   The height of one line of type, measured by the number of lines per vertical inch.

line join   The way in which two line segments meet.

line load   Same as CIRCUIT LOAD.

line number   In PROGRAMMING LANGUAGES such as BASIC, a number that begins a line of the source program for purposes of identification; a numerical label.

line of code   A STATEMENT in a PROGRAMMING LANGUAGE usually occupying one line of code.

line plot   A graph with displayed data points and straight lines connecting the points.

line printer   A PRINTER that assembles all characters on a line at one time and prints them out practically simultaneously.

line printer controller   A device that provides character print buffers and automatic control and timing for a specific printer.

line screen frequency   When a continuous tone image is screened, the number of halftone dots per inch making up the screen. Typical line screens are 33, 65, 85, 100, 120, 133, and 150 lines per inch, with 200 to 500 lines per inch for high-quality products.

line segment   The portion of a longer line defined by its two endpoints.

line speed   The maximum rate at which signals may be transmitted over a given channel, usually in bauds, or bits per second.

lines per inch   Abbreviated lpi, the yardstick used to measure halftone resolution.

lines per minute (LPM)   A term usually used to describe the speed of a LINE PRINTER.

line style   In computer graphics, the method of representing a line in a graphics system, such as with dashes, solid lines, or dots.

line surge   A sudden, high-voltage condition. Short surges of high voltage can cause misregistration, false logic, lost data, and even destruction of delicate circuits in computers, data entry terminals, and data communications equipment. These SPIKES can be a result of inductive load switching of transformers and other types of equipment—even from lightning and static. Equipment can be protected from voltage surges by using surge protectors.

line traffic   The number of transmissions and the amount of data sent and received on a telecommunications line.

line turnaround   A change in the direction of transmission from send to receive or from receive to send on a HALF-DUPLEX circuit.

line voltage   The AC voltage that comes out of a standard wall socket.

line width   The actual, physical thickness of a line in a graphics system.

line work   Any noncontinuous tone image, i.e., without shades of gray or other colors. Usually black-and-white line art or diagrams, but can also include EPS art created on a computer that incorporates flat color tints (comic-book coloring).

linguistics   The study of language. Syntax determines what makes a sentence of a natural language, or a program of a programming language, grammatical.

link   (**1**) In DATA COMMUNICATIONS, a physical connection between one location and another whose function is to transmit data, including satellite links. (**2**) In HYPERTEXT systems, connections between one document and another.

linkage   Coding that connects two separately coded routines, such as coding that links a subroutine to the program with which it is to be used.

linkage editor   (**1**) A system program that binds together related object module program segments so that they may be run as a unit. (**2**) The part of an operating system that links the object code with any necessary library routines.

linker A program that links other programs or sections of programs. Combines separate program modules into one executable program.

link/load phase The phase during which prewritten programs may be added to the object module by means of a link/loader.

link register A register of one bit that acts as an extension of the accumulator during rotation or carry operations.

links Data communications channels in a COMPUTER NETWORK.

Linotronic A series of high-quality typesetting machines known as Linotronic laser imagesetters, which can print at resolutions over 1,200 dots per inch (dpi). Imagesetters are commonly used with PostScript desktop publishing systems.

LIPS Acronym for LOGICAL INFERENCES PER SECOND, a measure of the speed of EXPERT SYSTEMS and the PROLOG language.

liquid crystal display (LCD) A flat display used in many portable computers because it is small and requires little power. The display is made of two sheets of polarizing material sandwiched together with a nematic liquid crystal solution between them. Images are produced when electric currents cause the liquid crystals to align so that light cannot shine through.

Lisa A microcomputer introduced in the early 1980s by Apple Computer, Inc. It featured a graphical user interface and a mouse, had its own Apple-generated operating system (the Lisa Operating System), and was designed to perform file management, memory management, event handling, and exception handling. The Lisa was built around the Motorola 68000 microprocessor and was the forerunner of the Apple Macintosh microcomputer.

LISP Acronym for LIST PROCESSING.

list (1) The organization of data, using indexes and pointers to allow for nonsequential retrieval. (2) An ordered set of items. (3) To print every relevant item of input data. (4) A command to print program statements; for example, the LIST command in the BASIC language will cause the system to print a listing of the program. **(5)** An ordered collection of atoms. **(6)** In ARTIFICIAL INTELLIGENCE, a type of knowledge representation.

listing   Generally, any printout produced on a printing device. A source listing is a printout of the source program processed by the compiler; an error listing is a report showing all input data found to be invalid by the processing program.

list price   The manufacturer's suggested retail price of a product. See STREET PRICE.

list processing   A method of processing data in the form of lists. The procedure of going through a list and examining the objects in the list for a purpose, such as finding or deleting a given element, or reordering the elements. A high-level programming language especially suited for text manipulation and analysis.

list processing language   A programming language used for processing nonnumeric data, such as LISP and PROLOG. It provides special commands that work with lists of data.

literal   Another name for constant, a symbol that defines itself. Contrast with VARIABLE.

live data   The actual data to be processed by the computer program.

load   **(1)** To read information into the STORAGE of a COMPUTER. See GET. **(2)** To insert a DISKETTE in a DISK DRIVE.

load-and-go   An operating technique in which the loading and execution phases of a program are performed in one continuous run. See COMPILE-AND-GO.

loader   A service routine designed to read programs into internal storage in preparation for their execution.

load leveling   The balancing of work between processing units, channels, or devices.

load lever   A lever on the front of a floppy disk unit that holds the diskettes in place.

load module   A computer program in a form suitable for immediate execution by the circuitry of a computer.

load point   A spot at the beginning of the recording area of a MAGNETIC TAPE.

load sharing   The technique of using two or more computers to handle excess volume during peak periods. It is desirable to have one computer handle less than peak loads and have the other act as the fallback equipment.

local   **(1)** Pertaining to computer equipment at one's own location. **(2)** Pertaining to items used only in one defined part of a program. Contrast with GLOBAL.

local area network (LAN)   A communications network linking various hardware devices together within a location by means of a continuous cable or an in-house voice-data telephone system.

local change   A change in an electronic spreadsheet that alters an attribute of only a designated group of cells.

local echo   In telecommunications, a process that sends characters typed on the keyboard directly to the screen without waiting for the remote computer to echo the characters.

local intelligence   The processing power and storage capacity built into a terminal so that it does not need to be connected to a computer to perform certain tasks. A dumb terminal has no local intelligence.

local network   A privately run communications network of several machines located within a mile or so of one another.

LocalTalk   The physical connectors and cables manufactured by Apple Computer, Inc. for use in AppleTalk networks.

location   A place in a computer's memory where information is to be stored.

locator device A GRAPHIC INPUT DEVICE, such as a mouse or tablet, that is used to specify coordinate data.

lock (1) To permit exclusive use of a computer resource. (2) To protect a disk or tape file from being changed or erased.

lockbuster package A SOFTWARE PACKAGE that circumvents the copy protection devices on a disk.

lock code A sequence of letters and/or numbers provided by the operators of a time-sharing system to prevent unauthorized tampering with a user's program. Serves as a secret password in that the computer will refuse any changes to the program unless the user supplies the correct lock code.

locked-up keyboard A situation in which the computer does not respond to key presses.

locking a disk Ensuring that the contents of a disk are preserved from being written over by other data from a computer. A disk is locked when it has been WRITE PROTECTED.

lockout (1) The suppression of an interrupt. (2) A programming technique used in a multiprocessing environment to prevent access to critical data by both CPUs at the same time.

lock-up A situation in which no further action may occur.

lofting An interactive graphics technique in which the third dimension is obtained from a two-dimensional representation, as in elevating the contours of a topographic map.

log (1) A record of the operations of data processing equipment, listing each job or run, the time it required, operator actions, and other pertinent data. (2) Abbreviation for LOGARITHM, often denoting the base 10 logarithm. Several programming languages use LOG to mean the natural logarithm.

logarithm An exponent of the power to which a fixed number is to be raised to produce a given number. The fixed number is called the base and is usually 10 or e. In the example $2^3 = 8$, 3 is the logarithm of 8 to the base 2; this means that 2 must be raised to the third power to produce 8.

logarithmic graph In presentation graphics, a graph displayed with a y-axis incremented exponentially in powers of 10. On an ordinary y-axis, the 10 is followed by 20, 30, 40, 50, and so on. On a logarithmic scale, however, 10 is followed by 100, 1,000, 10,000, 100,000, and so on.

logged drive The disk drive to which the operating system goes when looking for files to retrieve or save. Also called CURRENT DRIVE and DEFAULT DRIVE.

logger A unit that records events and physical conditions, usually with respect to time.

logging The recording of data about specific events.

logging-in The process of establishing communication with, and verifying authority to use, the computer during conversational programming.

logging-off The process of terminating communication between the computer and the user.

logic (1) A science dealing with the formal principles of reasoning and thought. (2) The basic principles and application of truth tables and the interconnection among logical elements required for arithmetic computation in an automatic data processing system.

logical comparison The examination of two strings to discover whether they are identical.

logical constant A constant with a value of true or false.

logical data design A design showing relationships among data; the way the data are viewed by applications programs or individual users.

logical decision A decision as to which of two possible courses of action is to be followed, based upon some comparison of values.

logical design A specification of the working relationships among the parts of a system in terms of symbolic logic and without primary regard for hardware implementation.

logical error   A programming mistake that causes the wrong processing to take place even though the program is syntactically correct.

logical expression   An expression that contains logical operators and operands and that can be reduced to a value that is true or false.

logical file   A collection of one or more logical records.

logical format   The way that files are arranged on a disk and the way a directory or other pointers show what goes where. Sometimes two computers use the same physical format but different logical ones. In such a case, although the units won't be able to deal with other disks directly, they will be able to do so with a special transfer program.

logical graphic function/logical operations   A computer-aided design capability that applies Boolean operations (AND, OR, NOT) to areas of graphic entities. This provides the user with interactive tools to create new figures from existing ones or to expand a design, such as a rules checking program, in integrated circuit design.

logical instruction   An instruction that executes an operation defined in symbolic logic, such as AND, OR, or NOR.

logical multiply   An AND operator. Compare LOGICAL PRODUCT.

logical network   A subnetwork of machines set up to function as a whole and separate network.

logical operations   Computer operations that are logical in nature, such as logical decisions. Contrast with ARITHMETIC OPERATIONS and DATA TRANSFER OPERATIONS, which involve no decision.

logical product   The AND function of several terms. The product is 1 only when all of the terms are 1; otherwise it is 0.

logical record   A complete unit of information that contains all fields describing something. In an inventory file containing 2,000 different product items, there are 2,000 logical records, one for each item. Contrast with PHYSICAL RECORD.

logical representation A knowledge representation consisting of a collection of logical formulas.

logical schema A standard way of organizing information into accessible parts.

logical sum The inclusive OR function of several terms. The sum is 1 when any or all of the terms are 1; it is 0 only when all are 0.

logical unit number A number assigned to a physical peripheral device.

logical value A value that may be either true or false, depending on the result of a particular logical decision.

logic bomb A program modification that causes damage when triggered by some condition such as a date, or the presence or absence of data such as a name.

logic card A circuit board containing components and wiring that perform one or more logic functions or operations.

logic circuits A series of flip-flops and gates that directs electrical impulses to and from the appropriate portions of a computer system.

logic diagram A diagram that represents a logical design, and sometimes, the hardware implementation.

logic element A device that performs a logic function.

logic error An omission or incorrect or misplaced statement in a program.

logic gates Components in electrical digital circuitry. See GATE.

logic operator Any of the Boolean operations, such as AND, OR, NAND, EXCLUSIVE OR, and NOR.

logic programming A type of programming based on logic that is relatively independent of the underlying structure of the machine on which it is operating.

logic seeking The ability of a printer that works bidirectionally to seek out the shortest printing path.

logic structure   A structure that controls the sequence in which computer program instructions are executed. The three structures are SEQUENCE, SELECTION, and LOOP.

logic symbol   A symbol used to graphically represent a logic element.

logic theorist   An early information processing program able to prove theorems.

logic theory   The science that deals with logical operations, which are the basis of computer operations.

log in   To sign in on a computer. Same as LOG ON.

LOGO   A high-level programming language that assumes the user has access to some type of graphics terminal. Designed for students and easily employed by those in the younger age groups, LOGO has wide-ranging application in graphic reports of business and industry. It is highly interactive, permitting users to learn quickly how to draw geometric patterns and pictures on the screen.

log on   The action by which a user begins a terminal session. Same as LOG IN.

log off   To terminate connection with the computer. Same as LOG OUT.

log out   (1) To stop using the computer. (2) The process of signing off the system. Same as LOG OFF.

long card   In a MICROCOMPUTER, a full-length printed circuit card that plugs into an expansion slot.

look-alike   (1) A program that imitates another program so closely that users of the original program can use the look-alike program without learning any new operating instructions. (2) Any product that copies another. Often when a vendor produces a successful product, its competitors offer look-alikes.

look-up   See TABLE LOOK-UP.

loop   A sequence of instructions in a program that can be executed repetitively until certain specified conditions are satisfied.

loop body   The part of the loop that achieves its primary purpose.

loop code   The repetition of a sequence of instructions by using a program loop.

loop construct   In PROGRAMMING LANGUAGES, a construct that specifies an iteration in the execution sequence, such as FOR/NEXT in BASIC and FOR/END in Pascal.

loop control   The parts of a loop that modify the loop control variables and determine whether to execute the loop body or exit from the loop.

loop counter   A COUNTER used to stop execution of a loop when a specified value is reached.

loophole   Any mistake or omission in software or hardware that allows the system's access controls to be circumvented.

looping   Executing the same instruction or series of instructions over and over again.

looping program   A program whose main action is a loop. Most programs are of this variety.

looping statement   A STATEMENT that runs any number of times, depending on the value of a specified EXPRESSION.

loop initialization   The parts of a LOOP that set its starting values.

loop network   A NETWORK configuration in which there is a single path between all nodes that is a closed circuit.

loop structure   One of three primary structures of a structured program. Provides for repetitive execution of a function until a condition is reached. See SEQUENCE STRUCTURE and SELECTION STRUCTURE.

loop technology   A method of connecting communicating machines together in a COMPUTER NETWORK.

loop termination decision   A decision that determines when a program loop ends.

Lotus 1-2-3™   A SPREADSHEET developed by Lotus Development Corporation. Introduced in 1982, it was the first integrated program developed for the IBM Personal Computer. Lotus 1-2-3 was the first program to include graphics and database management along with spreadsheet capabilities.

low activity   The condition when a small proportion of the total records are processed during an updating run. See ACTIVITY RATIO.

lowercase   Noncapitalized alphabetic letters. Contrast with UPPERCASE.

low-level formatting   The most basic formatting done on the hard disk to prepare it for partitioning and high-level formatting. This is often done by the manufacturer, which locks out bad sectors at this time.

lower-level management   First-time supervisors who make the operating decisions to ensure that specific jobs are done.

low-level language   A machine-dependent programming language translated by an assembler into instructions and data formats for a given machine. Same as assembly language. Contrast with HIGH-LEVEL LANGUAGE.

low-order   Pertaining to the digit or digits of a number that have the least weight or significance. In the number 7643215, the low-order digit is 5. Contrast with HIGH-ORDER.

low-res graphics   Abbreviation of **low-res**olution graphics, a blocky and jagged picture on a display screen produced by a small number of pixels. Contrast with HI-RES GRAPHICS.

low-resolution   Pertaining to the quality and accuracy of detail that can be represented by a graphics display. Resolution quality depends upon the number of basic image-forming units (pixels) within a picture image—the greater the number, the higher the resolution. Low-resolution pictures, produced by a small number of pixels, are not as sharp and clear as high-resolution pictures.

LP   Abbreviation for LINEAR PROGRAMMING and LINE PRINTER.

LPM   Abbreviation for LINES PER MINUTE.

LSC   Abbreviation for LEAST SIGNIFICANT CHARACTER. See LEAST SIGNIFICANT DIGIT.

LSD   Abbreviation for LEAST SIGNIFICANT DIGIT.

LSI   Abbreviation for LARGE SCALE INTEGRATION.

luggable   A term describing a computer that weighs less than 30 pounds and can be carried in one unit.

Lukasiewicz notation   See POLISH NOTATION.

Lumena™   A professional draw/paint graphics program designed for use by visual communications professionals who design sophisticated images for output to print, film, and video. It runs on IBM-compatible microcomputer systems.

luminance   **(1)** A measure of the amount of light radiated by a given source, such as a computer display screen. **(2)** Those portions of a composite video signal controlling brightness.

luminance decay   A reduction in screen brightness on a VISUAL DISPLAY TERMINAL that inevitably occurs over time.

luminosity   Same as LUMINANCE.

— M —

M Abbreviation for mega, meaning one million. Also used to represent 1,048,576. Often used to label the capability of storage devices, such as hard disks, diskettes, and RAM.

Mac™ A nickname for the Apple Macintosh computer.

MAC Acronym for **M**essage **A**uthentication **C**ode, a cryptographic check sum for a message. Unlike a digital signature, a MAC requires knowledge of a secret key for verification.

MacBinary A file transfer protocol that allows Apple Macintosh computer files to be stored in non-Macintosh computers without losing graphics, icons, and other information.

MacDraw™ A fast, flexible, and precise drawing program for the Apple Macintosh computer. Nine drawing tools are provided, which have become drawing program standards: line, text, selection, rectangle, rounded rectangle, oval, arc, polygon, and freehand drawing.

MacDraw file format The object file format used by the MacDraw drawing program and other programs.

MacDraw Pro An advanced version of the MacDraw drawing program with features to aid specific needs, such as desktop publishing.

machine address Same as ABSOLUTE ADDRESS.

machine-aided graphics for illustration and composition (MAGIC) An interactive program for preparation, editing, and storage of graphic designs and technical documentation for computers using the UNIX operating system.

machine code An operation code that a machine is designed to recognize.

machine cycle The time period it takes for a computer to perform a given number of internal operations.

machine-dependent Pertaining to a language or program that works on only one particular type of computer. Synonymous with hardware-dependent. Contrast with MACHINE-INDEPENDENT.

machine error The deviation from correctness in data resulting from an equipment failure.

machine-independent (1) Pertaining to a language or program developed in terms of the problem rather than in terms of the characteristics of the computer system. (2) Pertaining to the ability to run a program on computers made by different manufacturers or on various machines made by the same manufacturer. Contrast with MACHINE-DEPENDENT.

machine instruction An instruction that a computer can directly recognize and execute.

machine instruction set Same as COMPUTER INSTRUCTION SET.

machine intelligence See ARTIFICIAL INTELLIGENCE.

machine language The basic language of a computer. Programs written in machine language require no further interpretation by a computer. Contrast with SOURCE LANGUAGE.

machine learning (1) A heuristic process whereby a device improves its performance based on past actions. (2) A field of ARTIFICIAL INTELLIGENCE that attempts to build programs that learn from experience.

machine operator See COMPUTER OPERATOR.

machine-oriented language A PROGRAMMING LANGUAGE that is more like a machine language than a human language.

machine-readable information Information recorded on any medium in such a way that it can be sensed or read by a machine. Also called machine-sensible.

machine run See RUN.

machine-sensible See MACHINE-READABLE INFORMATION.

machine vision The process by which a computer perceives or recognizes objects in the external world.

Macintosh™   A series of popular microcomputers from Apple Computer, Inc., introduced in 1984. It uses the Motorola 68000 family of microprocessors and a proprietary operating system that simulates a user's desktop on screen. This standard user interface, combined with its built-in QuickDraw graphics language, has provided a visual, easy-to-use microcomputer. The Macintosh uses a mouse as a primary input device, in addition to a keyboard. Since the introduction of the Macintosh, Apple Computer, Inc. continues to offer progressively faster and more powerful models.

Macintosh Classic™   Introduced in 1990, the computer that replaced the Macintosh Plus and the SE. The Classic runs up to 25 percent faster than the Macintosh Plus. It uses a Motorola 68000 processor, a 1.4 MB floppy disk unit, and an optional 40 MB internal hard disk unit. The Classic is the lowest-priced Macintosh system offered to date.

Macintosh Classic II™   A 1991 upgrade to the Macintosh Classic. The Classic II uses a Motorola 68030 microprocessor running at 16 MHz, which doubles the performance of the Classic.

Macintosh control panel   A DESK ACCESSORY that allows a user to set many of the system parameters.

Macintosh draw programs   See CANVAS, COLORSTUDIO, DESKPAINT/DESKDRAW, FREEHAND, ILLUSTRATOR, MACDRAW, and PHOTOSHOP.

Macintosh 128K   The original Macintosh, introduced in 1984. A revolutionary system due to its ease of use, it had a 68000 microprocessor running at 8MHz, 128K of memory, and a built-in 400K disk drive.

Macintosh 512K   An upgrade to the Macintosh 128K; a system with 512K of main memory.

Macintosh 512Ke   A 1986 upgrade to the Macintosh 128K and 512K systems. The upgrade included new ROMs and an 800K double-sided disk drive.

Macintosh LC™   A low-priced color-capable modular Macintosh system. The LC is powered by a Motorola 68020 microprocessor running at 16

MHz. It is up to 100 percent faster than the SE and Classic systems. The LC includes a two-megabyte ROM memory, a 1.4 MB floppy disk unit, and an internal 40-megabyte hard disk unit. The Macintosh LC was introduced in 1990.

Macintosh paint programs   See DESKPAINT/DESKDRAW, EASY COLOR PAINT, MACPAINT, OASIS, PIXELPAINT, STUDIO/1, STUDIO/8, STUDIO/32, SUPERPAINT, ULTRAPAINT, and VIDEOPAINT.

Macintosh Plus™   A computer with 128K ROMs, an internal 800K disk drive, and one megabyte of memory that quickly became the standard for a minimum configuration. Many programs for the Macintosh require a minimum one-megabyte memory. This computer also introduced the now-standard SCSI (Small Computer System Interface) port, which allows the easy addition of one or more hard disks and other peripherals. Apple Computer, Inc. introduced the Macintosh Plus in 1986.

Macintosh Portable   A portable computer powered by a Motorola 68000 microprocessor running at 16 MHz. When the original Macintosh was introduced, many people liked it because it was "portable," but in reality, it was luggable if you did not have to carry it very far. Since then, the Macintosh has been evolving into larger, heavier, harder-to-move systems. In 1989, Apple Computer, Inc. released a portable Macintosh. This battery-operated computer used a liquid crystal display of 640 by 400 pixels and a standard 4 MB RAM memory.

Macintosh PowerBooks™   Three notebook Macintoshes, called the Macintosh PowerBook 100, 140, and 170, introduced in 1991. These notebook computers have a built-in hard disk, built-in floppy drives (140 and 170), and an optional internal fax/data modem.

Macintosh Quadra 700/900™   High-performance Macintoshes, introduced in 1991, that use Motorola 68040 microprocessors.

Macintosh SE™   A System Expansion computer. This system offers a single expansion slot for adding a card to attach a peripheral. Introduced in 1987, the SE was very similar to the Macintosh Plus in performance.

Macintosh SE/30™   A high-performance Macintosh that uses the powerful

Motorola 68030 microprocessor, has a disk drive that is capable of storing 1.4 megabytes, and has a math coprocessor. The SE/30 was introduced in 1989.

Macintosh II ™   The first serious Macintosh for professional production; introduced in 1987. The Macintosh II was the first of the "modular" Macintoshes. The system unit does not contain a monitor, allowing each user to choose a monitor that will perform best in that user's environment. The Macintosh II was the first Macintosh to support color and multiple video screens. It has stereo sound and six expansion slots. It was powered by the Motorola 68020 microprocessor running at 16 MHz and had a math coprocessor. The Macintosh II had a one-megabyte RAM and a built-in hard disk drive.

Macintosh IIci ™   A faster version of the Macintosh IIcx, with a processor that operates about 1.5 times faster (a Motorola 68030 running at 25 MHz). The Macintosh IIci has a standard 5 MB RAM memory. The IIci was introduced in 1989. It contains fewer parts than earlier Macintoshes due to its use of 13 special Apple-designed VLSI chips.

Macintosh IIcx ™   Introduced in 1989, a Macintosh II upgrade that used a Motorola 68030 microprocessor running at 16 MHz. The IIcx is a compact version of the Macintosh IIx.

Macintosh IIfx ™   A Macintosh computer designed for intensive graphics, CAD, and numeric calculations. The IIfx uses a Motorola 68030 microprocessor running at 40 MHz, or 1.6 times faster than the IIci's 25 MHz speed. The IIfx has two additional processors (each with the power of an Apple II microcomputer) to handle the flow of information inside the computer. The IIfx uses a standard 4 MB RAM memory. Available as an option is a 160 MB internal hard disk unit. The Macintosh IIfx was introduced in 1990.

Macintosh IIsi ™   A computer that uses a Motorola 68030 microprocessor running at 20 MHz and runs about five times faster than the Macintosh Classic. Introduced in 1990, the IIsi uses a standard 3 MB RAM memory, a 1.4 MB floppy disk unit, and a 40 MB internal hard disk unit.

Macintosh IIx ™   A Macintosh II update that used a Motorola 68030 microprocessor, a 68882 math coprocessor, and a standard 4 MB RAM memory. The Macintosh IIx was introduced in 1988.

Macintosh user interface   The method of operating an Apple Macintosh microcomputer, originally developed by Xerox Corporation and introduced in 1981 on the Xerox Star workstation. It uses a graphics screen that places objects on a two-dimensional desktop. Programs, files, folders, and disks are represented by small pictures (icons) that look like the objects they represent. A mouse is used to select, activate, or delete an object represented on the desktop. The Macintosh user interface style has been adapted to many non-Macintosh products, including Windows, GEM, and Presentation Manager.

MacPaint™   A full-featured paint program for the Apple Macintosh microcomputer from Claris Corporation. Originally developed by Bill Atkinson at Apple Computer, Inc., the program was bundled with every Macintosh microcomputer until Claris Corp. was formed in 1987. Claris produces a more advanced version of the program.

MacPaint file format   A bit-map graphics format used by MacPaint and some other Apple Macintosh paint programs. MacPaint files are limited to a resolution of 72 dpi, the same as the screen on the original Macintosh computers.

macro   A single, symbolic programming language statement that, when translated, results in a series of machine-language statements.

macro assembler   An assembler that allows the user to create and define new computer instructions (called macro instructions).

macro facility   A spreadsheet facility that enables programs to be embedded in a worksheet.

macro instruction   (1) SOURCE-LANGUAGE instruction equivalent to a specified number of machine-language instructions. (2) MACHINE-LANGUAGE instruction composed of several micro instructions.

MacroMind Director An animation program for Apple Macintosh computers.

macroprogramming Programming with macro instructions, such as writing control programs for a microprocessor. Contrast with MICROPROGRAMMING.

MacWrite™ A full-featured word processing program for the Apple Macintosh microcomputer from Claris Corporation. It was originally developed by Apple Computer, Inc. and bundled with every Apple Macintosh microcomputer until Claris Corporation was formed in 1987. Claris enhanced MacWrite by adding many new word processing features.

mag Abbreviation for **mag**netic.

magazette A magazine recorded on a DISKETTE.

MAGIC See MACHINE-AIDED GRAPHICS FOR ILLUSTRATION AND COMPOSITION.

magnetic Of, producing, caused by, or operated by magnetism.

magnetic bubble memory A memory that uses magnetic "bubbles" that move. The bubbles are locally magnetized areas that can move about in a magnetic material, such as a plate of orthoferrite. It is possible to control the reading in and out of this bubble within the magnetic material.

magnetic characters A set of characters—used for checks, insurance billings, utility bills, invoices, and so forth—that permit special character-reading devices (MICR readers) to be employed to read the characters automatically. See MAGNETIC INK CHARACTER RECOGNITION.

magnetic core storage A system of storage in which data is represented in binary form by means of the directional flow of magnetic fields in tiny, doughnut-shaped arrays of magnetic cores. Retains stored data in the event of a power loss; used in older computers.

magnetic disk A magnetic device for storing information accessible by a computer; can be either a rigid platter (HARD DISK) or a sheet of flexible plastic (FLOPPY DISK).

magnetic disk unit   A peripheral storage device in which data are recorded on a magnetizable disk surface.

magnetic drum   A peripheral storage device consisting of a cylinder with a magnetizable surface on which data are recorded. Used in older computer systems.

magnetic head   A device used for reading and writing information on devices such as magnetic tapes or disks.

magnetic ink   An ink that contains particles of a magnetic substance whose presence can be detected by magnetic sensors.

magnetic ink character recognition (MICR)   Recognition by machines of characters printed with a special magnetic ink. Used primarily in the banking, credit card, and public utilities industries.

magnetic media   The generic name for floppy disks, tapes, and any other devices that store data in the form of magnetic impulses.

magnetic printing   A process wherein a magnetic write head is used to create a latent image on a drum or belt, which is then toned, usually with a dry toner. The toned image is transferred to the paper and fixed with either heat or pressure.

magnetic resonance   A phenomenon in which a movement of a particle or system of particles is coupled resonantly to an external magnetic field.

magnetic storage   Any system that utilizes the magnetic properties of materials to store data on such devices and media as disks and tapes.

magnetic stripe   A strip of magnetic material on which data, usually identification information, can be recorded and from which the data can be read.

magnetic tape   Plastic tape having a magnetic surface for storing data in a code of magnetized spots. Information may be represented on tape using an eight-bit coding structure. Information is written on the tape and retrieved from the tape by a tape drive. Tapes are available in reels of 600, 1,200, 2,400 and 3,600 feet, which allows up to 270 MB to be stored.

magnetic tape cartridge   Magnetic tape contained in a cartridge. The cartridge consists of a reel of tape and the take-up reel. It is similar to a cassette but of slightly different design.

magnetic tape cassette   A magnetic tape storage device consisting of .25-inch magnetic tape housed in a plastic container.

magnetic tape code   A system of coding used to record magnetized patterns on magnetic tape. The magnetized patterns represent alphanumeric data.

magnetic tape density   The number of characters that can be recorded on one inch (2.54 cm) of magnetic tape.

magnetic tape drive   A device that moves tape past a head. Synonymous with magnetic tape transport.

magnetic tape reel   A reel used to preserve the physical characteristics of magnetic tape.

magnetic tape transport   Same as MAGNETIC TAPE DRIVE.

magnetic tape unit   A device containing a magnetic tape drive together with reading and writing heads and associated controls.

magneto-optic disc   An ERASABLE STORAGE disk, similar to a CD-ROM disc. Uses a recording method that combines laser and magnetic technologies to create high-density erasable storage discs. Magneto-optic (MO) drives are immune from disc head crash damage since nothing physically touches the media. They provide greater storage capacity than magnetic media, and offer more flexibility of use, since the media is removable from the drive.

magnify   In computer graphics, to increase by a common factor the dimensions of a display image.

magnitude   (**1**) The absolute value of a number. (**2**) The size of anything.

magstripe   The small stripe of magnetic material found on the back of most major cards and computerized transit fare cards. Contains information such as account number and card holder's name, or points of entry and exit and amount of paid fare remaining.

magtape   MAGNETIC TAPE.

mailbox   A disk storage area assigned to a network user for receipt of electronic mail messages.

mailing list program   A program that maintains names, addresses, and related data, and produces mailing labels.

mail-merging   The process of automatically printing form letters with names and addresses from a mailing list file. A mail-merge program merges address information from one file with textual information from another.

mainframe   A large, expensive computer generally used for information processing in large businesses, colleges, and organizations. Originally, the phrase referred to the extensive array of large rack-and-panel cabinets that held thousands of vacuum tubes in early computers. A mainframe can occupy an entire room and have a very large data-handling capacity. Far more costly than microcomputers or minicomputers, mainframes are the largest, fastest, and most expensive class of computers. SUPERCOMPUTERS are the largest, fastest, and most expensive of the mainframes. Before MINICOMPUTERS became popular in 1965, all computers were mainframes.

main-line program   That section of a program that controls the order of execution of other modules in the program.

main memory   Same as INTERNAL STORAGE.

main storage   Addressable storage directly controlled by the central processing unit. Used to store programs while they are being executed and data while they are being processed. Same as internal storage and primary storage. Contrast with AUXILIARY STORAGE.

maintainability   A characteristic associated with the isolation and repair of a failure.

maintenance   Any activity intended to eliminate faults or to keep hardware or programs in satisfactory working condition, including tests, measurements, replacements, adjustments, and repairs.

maintenance programmer   An individual who works with programs that have already been implemented into an information system, making changes as needed from time to time. See SOFTWARE MAINTENANCE.

maintenance routine   A routine designed to help a CUSTOMER ENGINEER carry out routine preventive maintenance on a computer system.

major sort key   A field containing data (such as a last name) by which most data items can be distinguished and sorted. When duplications occur in this field, a minor sort key (such as a first name) may supply the necessary distinction.

male connectors   Connectors that have pins or protruding parts rather than sockets or receptacles. Contrast with FEMALE CONNECTORS.

malfunction   A failure in the operation of the central processing unit or peripheral device. The effect of a fault. Contrast with ERROR and MISTAKE. See CRASH.

Maltron keyboard   A keyboard layout that allows potentially much faster speeds and is easier to learn than the traditional QWERTY keyboard layout. The keyboard is designed so that the keys used most frequently are positioned beneath the strongest digits.

MAN   See METROPOLITAN AREA NETWORK.

management graphics   Charts, graphs, and other visual representations of the operational or strategic aspects of a business, intended to aid management in assimilating and presenting business data.

management information system (MIS)   Any information system designed to supply organizational managers with the necessary information needed to plan, organize, staff, direct, and control the operations of the organization.

management report A report designed to help managers and decision makers perform their jobs.

management science The mathematical or quantitative study of the management of a business's resources, usually with the aid of a computer.

management support system (MSS) A subsystem of the MANAGEMENT INFORMATION SYSTEM that provides reports to managers on a scheduled or demand basis.

management system A system for the management of an organization through planning, organizing, and controlling functions.

manager The person responsible for guiding the operations of a computer center, programming group, software development group, service organization, and so on.

manipulating The act of working on data to put it into a form that has greater meaning to the user.

mantissa That part of a floating-point number that specifies the significant digits of the number. In 0.64321×10^3, .64321 is the mantissa. See CHARACTERISTIC.

manual input Data entered manually by the computer user to modify, continue, or resume processing of a computer program.

manual operation The processing of data in a system by direct manual techniques.

manufacturer's software The operating system or set of programming aids that the computer manufacturer supplies or makes available with a computer. See SYSTEMS PROGRAMS.

many-to-many relationship In a network data model, a relationship that allows a data element to have multiple parents.

map   A list that indicates the area of storage occupied by various elements of a program and its data. Also called STORAGE MAP.

MAP   Acronym for **M**anufacturing **A**utomation **P**rotocol, a communications protocol introduced by General Motors Corporation in 1982. The goal of MAP is to provide common standards for the interconnection of computers and programmable machine tools used in factory automation.

map generalization   An automatic mapping process for reducing the amount of graphic and nongraphic information displayed on a map. Often used in the creation of composite maps from a series of large-scale maps. The process may employ line filtering, symbol revision, reclassification, and other generalizing techniques.

MAPPER   Acronym for **MA**intaining, **P**reparing and **P**rocessing **E**xecutive **R**eports, a fourth-generation language from Unisys Corporation that runs on Unisys mainframes.

mapping   The transformation from one set to another; a correspondence. For example, the process by which a graphic system translates graphic data from one coordinate system into a form useful on another coordinate system. See SYMBOLIC TABLE.

margin   The number of spaces between the right or left edge of a page (or window) and the beginning of text.

marginal checking   A preventive maintenance procedure in which the unit under test is varied from its normal value in an effort to detect and locate components that are operating in a marginal condition.

margin indent   In WORD PROCESSING, the temporary displacement of one or more lines with respect to the original margin.

mark   Any sign or symbol used to signify or indicate an event in time or space.

marker   In computer graphics, a glyph with a specified appearance that is used to identify a particular location.

Mark 1 Completed in 1944 by Harold Aiken of Harvard University, the first large-scale electromechanical computer.

mark sense To mark a position on a paper card with an electrically conductive pencil for later conversion to machine interpretation.

mark sensing The ability to mark cards or pages with a pencil to be read directly into the computer via a mark sense reader, a very useful technique for acquiring data by hand and for avoiding the time lag and potential inaccuracy of keypunching. See OPTICAL MARK READER.

marquee A rectangular area surrounded by dotted lines, used to select objects or selected portions of an image in a drawing/painting program.

maser Acronym for **m**icrowave **a**mplification by the **s**timulated **e**mission of **r**adiation, a device capable of amplifying or generating radio frequency radiation.

mask **(1)** A patterned plate used to shield sections of the silicon chip surface during the manufacture of integrated circuits. **(2)** A machine word containing a pattern of bits, bytes, or characters used to extract or select parts of other machine words by controlling an instruction that retains or eliminates selected bits, bytes, or characters.

mask design The final phase of integrated circuit design in which the circuit design is realized through multiple masks corresponding to multiple layers on the integrated circuit.

masked diffusion A process that uses a mask to selectively impregnate a semiconductor material with impurities.

massage To process data.

mass properties The physically related properties of an object, such as volume, weight, inertia, and center of gravity.

mass storage device Any device used to supply relatively inexpensive storage for large amounts of data.

mass storage file A collection of RECORDS assigned to a MASS STORAGE DEVICE.

master An original document, tape, or film.

master clock A device that controls the basic timing pulses of a computer.

master data A set of data that is altered infrequently and supplies basic data for processing operations.

master disk A DISK that must be used to operate a software package.

master file A file containing relatively permanent information used as a source of reference and generally updated periodically. Contrast with DETAIL FILE.

master file maintenance The process of updating, changing, or modifying master files.

master key In COMPUTER SECURITY, the top-level key in a hierarchy of key-encrypting keys.

master/slave computer system A COMPUTER SYSTEM consisting of a master computer connected to one or more slave computers. The master computer provides the scheduling function and jobs to the slave computer(s).

match To check for identity between two or more items of data. Compare HIT.

matching A data processing operation in which two files are checked to determine whether there is a corresponding item or group of items in each file.

math coprocessor A special chip added to a computer to handle advanced mathematic functions, thereby freeing up the processing power of the main CPU.

mathematical check A programmed check that uses mathematical relationships.

mathematical expression An expression representing a numeric value.

mathematical functions A set of mathematical routines available in most programming languages. Usually supplied as part of the language.

mathematical logic The use of mathematical symbols to represent language and its processes. These symbols are manipulated in accordance with mathematical rules to determine whether or not a statement or a series of statements is true or false. See LOGIC.

mathematical model A group of mathematical expressions that represents a process, a system, or the operation of a device. See SIMULATION.

mathematical programming In OPERATIONS RESEARCH, a procedure for locating the maximum or minimum of a function subject to constraints.

mathematical symbols The symbols used in formulas, equations, and flowcharts.

mathematics The study of the relationships among objects or quantities, organized so that certain facts can be proved or derived from others by using logic.

matrix An orderly array of symbols by rows and columns. The symbols comprising the matrix are called elements or entries of the matrix. Subscripts are customarily used to indicate the row and column positions of an element in any matrix. Matrices provide a way in which complicated mathematical statements can be expressed simply. Computers are often used in work with matrices.

matrix printer A character printer that uses a matrix of dots to form an image of the character being printed. See DOT MATRIX PRINTER.

matrix storage Storage whose elements are arranged so that access to any location requires use of two or more coordinates.

mature system Any system that is fully operational and performing all the functions it was designed to accomplish.

maximize In a WINDOWS program, enlarging a window to its largest possible size, the size of the screen.

MB Abbreviation for **m**ega**b**yte, one million bytes.

MBPS Abbreviation for one **m**illion **b**its **p**er **s**econd.

MCAD Abbreviation for MECHANICAL COMPUTER-AIDED DESIGN. CAD for mechanical design.

MCGA Abbreviation for multi-color graphics array, a type of display adapter for IBM PS/2 compatible computers.

MDA Abbreviation for monochrome display adapter, a video adapter that provided text on IBM Personal Computers. MDA cards were often replaced with adapter cards, which provided both text and graphics. MDA was superseded by VGA.

MDT Abbreviation for MEAN DOWN TIME.

mean access time An average ACCESS TIME resulting from normal operation of a device.

mean down time (MDT) The expectation of the down time.

mean repair time Mean time to recovery.

means/ends analysis A method of reasoning that looks backward and forward from the initial point to the goal in an attempt to reduce differences.

mean time between failures (MTBF) The average length of time a system or component is expected to work without failure.

mean time to failure (MTTF) The average length of time a system or component works without fault.

mean time to recovery See MEAN TIME TO REPAIR.

mean time to repair (MTTR) The average time expected to be required to detect and correct a FAULT in a COMPUTER SYSTEM.

mechanical calculating machine A COMPUTER that works by means of gears and levers rather than electric power.

Mechanical Computer-Aided Design (MCAD) CAD for mechanical design.

mechanical mouse A mouse that uses a rubber ball that makes contact with several wheels inside the unit. Contrast with OPTICAL MOUSE.

mechanicals Graphic art materials in camera-ready form.

mechanism In OBJECT-ORIENTED PROGRAMMING, a structure whereby objects work together to provide some behavior that satisfies a requirement of the problem.

mechanization The use of machines to simplify or replace work previously accomplished by human workers. Compare AUTOMATION.

media The plural form of MEDIUM. See SOURCE MEDIA, INPUT MEDIA, and OUTPUT MEDIA.

media compatibility The ability of two or more different style units to use the same type of disks as blank disks, whether or not each can read data recorded by the other.

media eraser A device designed to demagnetize magnetic tapes and diskettes. See DEGAUSSER.

media interchangeability The extent to which disks recorded on one machine can play back on another with the same type of drive.

media specialist The person responsible for cataloging and maintaining storage media such as CD-ROMS, diskettes, disk packs, magnetic tapes, and other related materials.

medical imaging A field that employs various image-generation techniques, such as computerized axial tomography (CAT), magnetic resonance imaging (MRI), and X-ray, to collect image samples from a patient's internal tissue for analysis. Computers have revolutionized medicine: computer imaging techniques have led to new insights in anatomy and physiology, and are an excellent means of representing three-dimensional medical data for clinical inspection.

medium Any physical substance upon which data are recorded, such as FLOPPY DISK, MAGNETIC DISK, MAGNETIC TAPE, and PAPER.

medium-scale integration (MSI) A class of integrated circuits having a density between those of LARGE-SCALE INTEGRATION and SMALL-SCALE INTEGRATION.

mega A prefix indicating one million, or 10^6. Abbreviated M. Contrast with MICRO, one-millionth.

MEGA A personal computer series from Atari Corporation that is compatible with the Atari ST series of microcomputers.

megabit Loosely, one million bits or one thousand kilobits. Actually, 1,048,576 bits, or 1,024 kilobits.

megabyte (MB) Specifically, 2^{20}, or 1,048,576 bytes; 1,024 kilobytes. Roughly, one million bytes or one thousand kilobytes.

megacycle One million cycles per second.

megaflop One million floating-point operations per second. Also called Mflops.

megahertz (MHz) A unit of electrical frequency equal to one million cycles per second, a measure of transmission frequency. Megahertz is used to measure a CPU's clock rate.

megapel display In computer graphics, a display system that handles a million or more pixels. A resolution of 1,000 lines by 1,000 dots per line requires a million pixels for a full-screen image.

member object In OBJECT-ORIENTED PROGRAMMING, a repository for part of the state of an object; collectively, the member objects of an object constitute its structure. The terms FIELD, INSTANCE VARIABLE, *member object*, and SLOT are interchangeable.

membrane keyboard A keyboard constructed of two thin plastic sheets (called membranes) that are coated with a circuit made of electrically conductive ink. The keyboard is sensitive to touch. It is an economical, flat type used in several early microcomputers. Today, such keyboards are used primarily on printers.

memory Storage facilities of the computer, capable of storing vast amounts of data.

memory allocation See STORAGE ALLOCATION.

memory board An expansion board that adds RAM to the computer system, making it possible to store and use additional information.

memory card A plastic card or key on which information is stored either magnetically or optically.

memory cartridge A plug-in module containing RAM chips that can be used to store programs or data.

memory cells Storage locations in a computer's memory.

memory chip A semiconductor device used to store information in the form of electrical charges. There are two types of memory chips: ROM holds information permanently, while RAM holds it temporarily.

memory cycle The amount of time required to move one byte or word of information into or out of memory.

memory dump A printout showing the contents of memory.

memory management The technique of efficiently controlling and allocating memory resources.

memory map A diagram that shows how memory is used. For example, in a display unit there is a memory map of the screen display, with one memory location corresponding to each pixel on the display.

memory partitioning See STORAGE PARTITIONING.

memory protection The process of keeping a program from straying into other programs and vice versa.

memory sniffing The continuous testing of storage during processing.

menu A list of command options available to the user of a computer software program; an on-screen list of command choices.

menu-driven software Computer programs that make extensive use of menus. Software of this type is designed so that it may be used easily by people with minimal computer experience. Menus are used to select tasks to be performed.

menu item Any choice in a MENU.

merge   To combine items into one sequenced file without changing the order of the items. Same as COLLATE.

merge-print program   A program that lets the user produce personalized form letters.

MESFET   Acronym for **Me**tal **S**emiconductor **F**ield **E**ffect **T**ransistor, the main active device used in gallium arsenide integrated circuits to provide current gain and inversion.

mesh   A set of branches forming a closed path in a network.

mesh network   A network in which nodes are connected to several other nodes (possibly each node is connected to every other) allowing a variety of paths for transmissions of messages. Contrast with RING NETWORK. See NETWORK TOPOLOGIES.

message   (1) A group of characters having meaning as a whole and always handled as a group. (2) In OBJECT-ORIENTED PROGRAMMING, a request sent to an object to change its state or return a value, or an operation that one object performs upon another.

message format   Rules for the placement of such portions of a message as message heading, address text, and end of message.

message header   The leading part of a message that contains information concerning the message, such as the source or destination code, priority, and type of message.

message-passing   In OBJECT-ORIENTED PROGRAMMING, a mechanism that allows objects to send messages among themselves.

message queuing   In a DATA COMMUNICATIONS SYSTEM, a technique for controlling the handling of messages, allowing them to be accepted by a computer and stored until they have been processed or routed to another destination.

message retrieval   The capability to retrieve a message sometime after it has entered an information system.

message switching   A switching technique of receiving a message, storing it until the proper outgoing circuit and station are available, and then retransmitting it toward its destination. Computers are often used to perform the switching function.

message switching center   A center in which messages are routed according to information contained within the messages themselves.

messaging system   A system that manages electronic messaging.

metacharacter   In programming language systems, characters having some controlling role in respect to the other characters with which they are associated.

metaclass   In OBJECT-ORIENTED PROGRAMMING, the class of a class; a class whose instances are themselves classes.

metacompiler   A compiler for a language used primarily for written compilers, usually syntax-oriented compilers. A special-purpose metacompiler language is not very useful for writing general programs.

metalanguage   The language used to describe a language.

metallic oxide semiconductor (MOS)   (1) A field effect transistor in which the gate electrode is isolated from the channel by an oxide film. See MOSFET. **(2)** A capacitor in which semiconductor material forms one plate, aluminum forms the other plate, and an oxide forms the dielectric. See COMPLEMENTARY MOS.

meta-metalanguage   The language used to describe a metalanguage.

metamorphosis   In computer graphics, the change, over a varying period of time, from an object of one shape to an object of another shape.

metaphor   In software development, the use of words or pictures to suggest a resemblance. For example, the Apple Macintosh computer uses a desktop metaphor with its icons for paper, files, folders, wastebaskets, and so on.

meter (m)   1.0936 yards, 3.2808 feet, and 39.3696 inches.

method   In OBJECT-ORIENTED PROGRAMMING, the function or procedure that implements the response when a message is sent to an object. Methods determine how an object will respond to a message that it receives.

methodology A procedure or collection of techniques used to analyze information in an orderly manner. A set of standardized procedures, including technical methods, management techniques, and documentation, that provides the framework to accomplish a particular function.

metric system Système International d'Unités, or SI, the modern version of the metric system currently in use worldwide. It is based on seven base units: meter, kilogram, second, ampere, Kelvin (degrees Celsius), candela, and mole.

metropolitan area network (MAN) A computer network that serves customers in the same city or region and can be accessed by mobile (cellular) telephone.

MFLOP One million floating-point operations per second. Used as a rough measure of a computer's processing speed.

MFT Abbreviation for **m**ultiprogramming with a **f**ixed number of **t**asks, the tasks being programs.

MHz Abbreviation for **m**ega**h**ertz, a million cycles per second.

MICR Abbreviation for MAGNETIC INK CHARACTER RECOGNITION.

MICR inscriber A device that adds magnetic characters to a document.

micro **(1)** One-millionth, used as a prefix; for example, a microsecond is one-millionth of a second. **(2)** Computerese for "quite small," as in *microcomputer*. From the Greek letter mu, meaning "very small." Contrast with MEGA.

MicroChannelBus The bus design used in the high-end IBM PS/2 computers. This design allows for more than one processor in a single computer and better handshaking between expansion cards.

microchart A chart showing the ultimate details of a program's or system's design.

microchip A popular nickname for the INTEGRATED CIRCUIT CHIP.

microcircuit A miniaturized electronic circuit like those etched on the silicon and germanium wafers characteristic of processors and other products of the semiconductor industry. A microcircuit is made up interconnected transistors, resistors, and other components.

microcode Permanent basic subcommands, built into the computer, that are executed directly by the machine's electronic circuits. Generally, in a special read-only storage unit, these commands define the instruction set of a microprogrammable computer.

microcomputer The smallest and least expensive class of computer; any small computer based on a microprocessor. Also called PERSONAL COMPUTER.

microcomputer chip A microcomputer on a chip. Differs from a MICRO-PROCESSOR in that it not only contains the CPU but also includes, on the same piece of silicon, a RAM, a ROM, and input/output circuitry.

microcomputer system A system that includes a MICROCOMPUTER, peripherals, operating system, and applications programs.

microdisk A 3.5-inch diskette.

microelectronics The field that deals with techniques for producing miniature circuits, such as integrated circuits, thin-film techniques, and solid logic modules.

microfiche A sheet of microfilm, about 4 inches by 6 inches (10 cm by 15 cm), upon which the images of computer output may be recorded. Up to 270 pages of output may be recorded on one sheet of fiche.

microfilm Photographic film used for recording graphic information in a reduced size.

microfilmer A device for COMPUTER OUTPUT MICROFILMING.

microfloppy disk A 3.5-inch floppy disk, which in recent years has become the disk of choice. A 3.5-inch disk holds more data and is much easier to store, transport, and handle than its 5.25-inch counterpart. The microfloppy disk was developed by Sony.

microform   Any medium that contains miniaturized images, such as MICROFICHE and MICROFILM.

microfreeze   A machine state in which a CENTRAL PROCESSOR is stopped.

Micrografx Designer   A graphic arts and technical illustration program for IBM-compatible microcomputers.

micrographics   A generic name for the MICROFILM, MICROFICHE, and computer output of the microfilm processing industry.

micro image   An image too small to be read without magnification.

micro instructions   Low-level instructions used to obtain a macro instruction in a machine language or in a source language available to the computer user. See MICROPROGRAMMING.

microjustification   In some word processing programs, the ability to add small slivers of blank space between words and between letters within words. The result is easier to read than ordinary justified copy, where the computer merely adjusts space between words. See MICROSPACING.

micrologic   The use of a permanent stored program to interpret instructions in a microprogram.

micro manager   The person responsible for managing the acquisition, modification, and maintenance of an organization's microcomputer systems.

micrometer   One-millionth of a meter.

microminiature chip   An LSI or VLSI chip used for computer storage (MEMORY CHIP) or control (microprocessor chip).

microminiaturization   A term implying very small size, one step smaller than miniaturization.

micron   One-millionth of a meter, or approximately 1/25,000 of an inch.

The tiny elements that make up a transistor on a chip are measured in microns. See ANGSTROM.

microprocessor The complex chip that is the CENTRAL PROCESSING UNIT (CPU) of the computer. The job of the microprocessor is to control what goes on inside the computer. All processing that a computer does takes place there.

microprogram A sequence of microinstructions, mainly used to implement machine instructions.

microprogrammable computer Any computer whose instruction set is not fixed but can be tailored to individual needs by the programming of ROMS or other memory devices. Consequently, whether the computer is a MAINFRAME, MINICOMPUTER, or MICROCOMPUTER, theoretically it can be microprogrammed.

microprogramming A method of operating the control part of a computer in which each instruction is broken into several small steps (microsteps) that form part of a microprogram. Some systems allow users to microprogram, and thus determine the instruction sets of their own machines.

MicroPROLOG A reduced version of the PROLOG programming language, designed for use on microcomputer systems.

MicroRIM Database software developed for microcomputers. MicroRIM can be used to create, update, and select data from files, and sort and print reports.

microsecond One-millionth of a second, abbreviated μs or μsec.

Microsoft BASIC™ One of the most popular versions of the BASIC programming language, developed by Microsoft Corporation. Also called MBASIC. A version for the IBM PC is called PC BASIC.

Microsoft Corporation A leading software company founded in 1975 by William H. Gates and Paul G. Allen. The company's first product was Microsoft BASIC for the Altair 8800 microcomputer. Later products include MS-DOS, Microsoft Windows, Microsoft Word, Microsoft Works, and GW-BASIC, as well as many other software systems. Microsoft's position as the supplier of the major software to the world's largest computer base (IBM-compatible microcomputers) gives it considerable influence over the future of the computer industry.

Microsoft Excel   See EXCEL.

Microsoft Windows™   A graphics-based operating environment for IBM-compatible microcomputers from Microsoft Corporation. It runs in conjunction with DOS. Some of the graphical user interface features include pull-down menus, multiple typefaces, desk accessories, and the ability to move text and graphics from one program to another via a clipboard.

Microsoft Word™   A full-featured word processing program for IBM-compatible microcomputers and Apple Macintosh computers from Microsoft Corporation. It has a spelling checker, hyphenation, style sheets, a glossary, mail merge, automatic text wrap, and a column design feature.

Microsoft Works™   An integrated application program that includes a spreadsheet, database, and word processor. It provides desktop publishing with drawing and word processing documents. The drawing tools and linked columns of the desktop publishing section let users create professional-style layouts.

microspacing   A feature of some printers that allows them to move extremely small distances. Used to do MICROJUSTIFICATION and SHADOW PRINTING.

micro-to-mainframe   Refers to connecting a MICROCOMPUTER to a MAINFRAME network.

microwave   An electromagnetic wave that has a wavelength in the centimeter range. Microwaves occupy a region in the electromagnetic spectrum bounded by radio waves on the side of longer wavelengths and by infrared waves on the side of shorter wavelengths. Used in DATA COMMUNICATIONS.

microwave hop   A microwave radio channel between two dish antennas aimed at each other.

microwave relays Towers that allow voice and data transmission over line-of-sight distances using microwaves.

microwave transmission Line-of-sight transmission of data signals through the atmosphere from relay station to relay station.

MICR reader An input device that reads documents imprinted with MAGNETIC INK characters.

MIDI Acronym for MUSICAL INSTRUMENT DIGITAL INTERFACE.

migration **(1)** The movement of computer users from one hardware platform to another. **(2)** The process of moving data from one computer system to another without converting it.

milestone An essential activity or step in a project that helps measure its progress.

milk disk A disk used to gather data from a small computer with a view to processing the data in a larger computer later.

milli One-thousandth, used as a prefix; a millisecond is a thousandth of a second.

millimicrosecond Same as NANOSECOND, one-billionth of a second.

millisecond One-thousandth of a second; abbreviated ms or msec.

mind tool An alternate name for a COMPUTER.

mini Short for MINICOMPUTER.

miniaturization The process of making an object smaller in physical size without decreasing its efficiency.

minicomputer A class of computers with capabilities and price between microcomputers and mainframes.

minifloppy A 5.25-inch diskette, introduced by Shugart in 1978.

minimal tree A tree whose terminal nodes are ordered to make it operate at optimum.

minimax A technique for minimizing the maximal error of a process.

minimize   To remove from the screen all windows associated with an application and replace them with an icon that represents that application.

minor sort key   A data field that provides a secondary source of distinctions by which to sort records. Used only when duplications occur in the major sort key.

minuend   In subtraction, the number or quantity from which another number or quantity is subtracted.

MIPS   Acronym for one **m**illion **i**nstructions **p**er **s**econd, a measure of the processing speed of a computer. Used to describe the average number of machine-language instructions a large computer performs in one second.

mirroring   The display or creation of graphic data that portrays an image in exactly the reverse of its original orientation. Many computer graphics systems will automatically create a mirror image of a graphic entity on the display screen by flipping the entity or drawing on its x- or y-axis.

MIS   Abbreviation for MANAGEMENT INFORMATION SYSTEM.

mistake   A human failing, such as faulty arithmetic, use of incorrect computer instructions, incorrect data entry, or use of incorrect formulas in a computer program, that produces an unintended result.

miter   In computer graphics, the treatment of thick lines at a corner intersection in such a way that each line is beveled to make the join.

mixed number   Any number having both a fractional part and an integer part, such as 63.71, 18.006, and 2,948.413.

mixed-type expression   An arithmetic expression that contains both integer and real arithmetic primaries.

mixing   In computer graphics, the result of the intersection of two or more colors.

ML   Abbreviation for **M**anipulator **L**anguage, an IBM Corporation programming language for controlling robots.

MMU   Abbreviation for **M**emory **M**anagement **U**nit, a specialized coprocessor that takes care of the mapping of logical memory (as seen by programs) to physical memory (the actual memory provided on the system). That procedure lets software act as if it had more memory to work with than the system actually provides (the missing part is simulated by a hard disk) and lets multiple programs running simultaneously share memory more easily.

mnemonic (1) Pertaining to any technique used to aid human memory. (2) A word or name that is easy to remember and identify.

mnemonic code An easy-to-remember assembly-language code; for example, a code that uses an abbreviation such as MPY for "multiply."

mnemonic language A programming language based on easily remembered symbols that can be assembled into machine language by the computer.

MNP Abbreviation for **M**icrocom **N**etworking **P**rotocol, a communications protocol used by many high-speed modems.

mode (1) An operational state to which a system has been switched. (2) One form of a number, name, or expression. (3) The most common or frequent value in a group of values.

model (1) The representation of certain key features of an object or system to be studied. Scientific models often make use of complex formulas and involve substantial use of mathematics. If a computer is used to solve the equations and carry out the necessary calculations, the process is called a computer simulation. Modeling and simulation are essential tools in every area of science, business, economics, and a number of other fields. (2) A type of database, each type representing a particular way of organizing data. The three database models are HIERARCHICAL, NETWORK, and RELATIONAL.

model base In a DECISION SUPPORT SYSTEM, a collection of models that are used and solved as needed to arrive at a solution.

model-based expert system A system that uses a model-based representation of the underlying structure or behavior of the entity involved. A model-based system is based on deep knowledge rather than surface knowledge. Model-based expert systems are more capable of handling unexpected situations than heuristic-based systems, which are based more on surface knowledge.

model coordinates   The coordinate system used for describing a single object.

model driven   In ARTIFICIAL INTELLIGENCE, pertaining to a method of inference that uses a model of a problem area in an expert system.

model, geometric   A complete, geometrically accurate 3-D or 2-D representation of a shape, a part, or a geographic area, designed on a computer graphics system and stored in the database.

modeling   (1) The process of accurately describing or representing certain parts of a system; using mathematics to describe a situation or a physical object. (2) The simulation of a condition or activity by performing a set of equations on a set of data. (3) The method of creating an object in COMPUTER GRAPHICS through computational descriptions of the object's polygonal makeup, surface shape, and attributes.

modem   Acronym for **mo**dulator/**dem**odulator, a device that translates digital pulses from a computer into analog signals for telephone transmission, and analog signals from the telephone into digital pulses the computer can understand. Provides communication capabilities between pieces of computer equipment over common telephone facilities.

modification   An addition or change to, or a deletion of, stored data.

modifier   In OBJECT-ORIENTED PROGRAMMING, an operation that alters the state of an object.

modify   (1) To alter a portion of an instruction so that its interpretation and execution will be other than normal. (2) To alter a program according to a defined parameter.

Modula-2   A high-level programming language similar to PASCAL. It supports separate compilation of modules, whereas Pascal does not. Modula-2 is very popular as a teaching language at colleges and universities.

Modula-3 A Digital Equipment Corporation/Olivetti collaboration to extend the Modula-2 programming language.

modular architecture A design consisting of self-contained components that can be connected together.

modular coding A programming technique in which the logical parts of a program are divided into a series of individual modules or routines so that each routine may be programmed independently. See TOP-DOWN PROGRAMMING.

modular constraint In computer graphics, a limitation on the placement of images such that some or all points of an image are forced to lie on the intersections of an invisible grid.

modularity The concept of designing computers in a building-block format to promote efficient and economical upgrading of equipment.

modular programming Programming that produces relatively small, easily interchanged computer routines that meet standardized interface requirements. Modularity is accomplished by breaking the program into limited segments that perform complete functions and are therefore understandable in themselves. This greatly facilitates development and verification of complex programs and systems. See MODULE and STRUCTURED PROGRAMMING.

modulation In data communications, the process by which some characteristic of a high-frequency carrier signal is varied in accordance with another, lower-frequency "information" signal. Used in data sets to make computer terminal signals compatible with communications facilities.

modulation depth The difference in brightness between black and white in a CRT display.

modulation transfer function (MTF) The curve that expresses the luminance contrast between black and white lines on a display screen as the number of lines increases.

modulator A device that receives electrical pulses, or bits, from a data processing machine and converts them into signals suitable for transmission over a communications link. Contrast with DEMODULATOR.

module   (1) One logical part of a program. In modular programming, a major program may be broken down into a number of logically self-contained modules. These modules may be written (and possibly tested separately) by a number of programmers. The modules can then be put together to form the complete program. (2) An interchangeable plug-in item containing components. (3) A set of logically related statements that perform a specific function.

module diagram   Part of the notation of OBJECT-ORIENTED DESIGN, used to show the allocation of classes and objects to modules in the physical design of a system.

modulo   A mathematical function that yields the remainder of division. For example, 25 modulo 4 equals 1. This is derived by dividing 25 by 4, which leaves a remainder of 1; this is the modulo value of the operation.

moire pattern   (1) An interference pattern created when two regular dot patterns are asymmetrically superimposed. (2) An undesirable grid pattern that may occur when a bit-mapped graphic with gray fill patterns is reduced or enlarged. (3) In scanning, an objectionable pattern caused by the interference of halftone screens. Often produced when a halftone is rescanned and a second screen is applied on top of the first.

molecular modeling   A sophisticated chemical engineering application using computer graphics to simulate chemical reactions in molecules.

monadic   Pertaining to an operation that uses only one operand. Contrast with NILADIC.

monadic Boolean operator   A Boolean operator with only one operand, such as the NOT operator.

monitor   (1) The device on which images generated by a computer's video adapter are displayed. (2) A control program or supervisor.

monochrome   The term applied to a monitor that displays a single color (white, amber, or green) image on a contrasting (black) background, producing a sharp, clear display that is easy to read.

monochrome adapter   A video adapter capable of producing one foreground color.

monochrome display   A video display capable of displaying only one color.

monolithic   (1) Pertaining to a single silicon substrate upon which an integrated circuit is constructed. (2) Complete and all in one piece. For example, a linkage editor combines several fragmentary program modules into a single monolithic program.

monolithic integrated circuit   A circuit formed in a single piece of substrate material (as opposed to a hybrid circuit) in which individual (physically separate) circuit components are electrically interconnected to form the final circuit.

monolithic storage   Storage made up of monolithic integrated circuits.

monolithic technology   A TECHNOLOGY in which all electronic components of a circuit, such as transistors, capacitors, and diodes, are integrated into one chip.

monospace   A typeface in which the width of all characters is the same, producing output that looks like typed characters. Courier is an example of a monospace typeface.

Monte Carlo method   A trial-and-error method of repeated calculations to discover the best solution to a problem. Often used when a great number of variables are present with interrelationships so extremely complex as to eliminate straightforward analytical handling.

more than   See GREATER THAN.

morphemics   Rules describing how words are changed to form variations such as plurals or verb conjugations.

MOS   Abbreviation for **M**ETALLIC **O**XIDE **S**EMICONDUCTOR.

MOSFET   Acronym for **m**etallic **o**xide **s**emiconductor **f**ield **e**ffect **t**ransistor, a semiconductor characterized by an extremely high input impedance, a fairly high active impedance, and low switching speeds.

MOS/LSI   See METALLIC OXIDE SEMICONDUCTOR and LARGE-SCALE INTEGRATION.

most significant digit (MSD)   That digit of a number that has the greatest weight or significance. In the number 58,371, the most significant digit is 5. See HIGH-ORDER and JUSTIFY.

motherboard   An interconnecting assembly into which printed circuit cards, boards, or modules are connected; the main circuit board of a microcomputer. Also called SYSTEM BOARD and BACKPLANE.

motion graphics   See ANIMATION.

Motorola, Inc.   A leading manufacturer of semiconductor devices. Although the company produces many consumer electronics products, it is best known in the computer business as the manufacturer of the 68000 family of microprocessors.

Motorola™ 88000   A family of 32-bit RISC microprocessors introduced by Motorola, Inc. in 1988.

Motorola™ 68000 family   The family of microprocessors developed by Motorola, Inc. MC 68000, a 16-bit processor developed in 1979; MC 68010, a 16-bit processor developed in 1983; MC 68020, a 32-bit processor developed in 1984; MC 68030, a 32-bit processor developed in 1987; and MC 68040, a 32-bit processor announced in 1987. The MC 68000 family of microprocessors is used in several popular microcomputers, including the Apple Macintosh, Commodore Amiga, and Atari ST.

mouse   A hand-operated pointing device that senses movements as it is moved across a flat surface and conveys this information to the computer. The mouse also has one or more buttons that can be pressed to signal the computer. Its main advantage is that it can move a cursor around on the display screen, even diagonally, with great precision.

mouse button   The switch on top of the MOUSE that transmits commands to the computer. See CLICK and DOUBLE-CLICK.

mouse pad A surface to be used with a MOUSE. As the user moves the mouse across the mouse pad, the cursor moves across the screen in the same direction.

mouse pointer The on-screen ICON or CURSOR, the movement of which is controlled by the MOUSE.

mouse scaling The distance the cursor moves relative to the movement of the mouse.

movable-head disk unit A storage device or system consisting of magnetically coated disks, on the surface of which data are stored in the form of magnetic spots arranged in a manner to represent binary data. The data are arranged in circular tracks around the disks and are accessible to reading and writing heads on arms that can be moved mechanically to the desired tracks on the disks. Data from a given track are read or written sequentially as the disk rotates. Contrast with FIXED-HEAD DISK UNIT.

move (1) To transfer (copy) data from one location of storage to another location. (2) In computer graphics, to change the current position on a graphics coordinate system.

movement In computer graphics, a sense of activity or change in position. It is created in drawings by use of character shapes, lines, color, and lighting.

moving average A method of averaging out the roughness of random variation in a data series. Uses only the most recent historical data in the series. The method gets its name from the way it slides along the data series, averaging each data point with its immediate predecessors. The average may disclose trends that would otherwise be obscured by the minor fluctuations along a line.

MPU Abbreviation for **M**icro**P**rocessing **U**nit. See MICROPROCESSOR.

MPX Abbreviation for **M**ULTI**P**LEXER.

ms Abbreviation of millisecond. Also msec.

MSD   Abbreviation for MOST SIGNIFICANT DIGIT.

MS-DOS™   Acronym for **M**icrosoft-**D**isk **O**perating **S**ystem, the standard operating system for IBM-compatible microcomputers. MS-DOS was created by Microsoft Corporation and released in 1981. MS-DOS oversees such operations as disk input and output, video support, keyboard control, and many internal functions related to program execution and file maintenance.

MSI   Abbreviation for MEDIUM-SCALE INTEGRATION.

MSSG   Abbreviation for MESSAGE.

MS-Windows   See WINDOWS.

MTBF   Abbreviation for **m**ean **t**ime **b**etween **f**ailures, the average length of time a system or component is expected to work without failure.

MTTF   Abbreviation for **m**ean **t**ime **t**o **f**ailure, the average length of time in which the system, or a component of the system, works without fault.

MTTR   Abbreviation for **m**ean **t**ime **t**o **r**epair, the average time expected to be required to detect and correct a fault in a computer system.

mu   Name of the Greek letter μ, the symbol used to denote the prefix *micro*. For example, μs means "microsecond."

μC   Abbreviation for MICROCOMPUTER (μ is the Greek letter *mu*).

MUG   Acronym for **M**UMPS **U**sers **G**roup (see MUMPS).

multiaccess computer   A computer system in which computational and data resources are made available simultaneously to a number of users who access the system through terminal devices, normally on an interactive or conversational basis. It may consist of only a single central processor connected directly to a number of terminals (star network), or it may consist of a number of processing systems that are distributed and interconnected with one another (ring network) as well as with other terminals.

multiaddress   Pertaining to an instruction format containing more than one address part.

multi-bit Any scan that uses more than one BIT to store information about a PIXEL.

multicast The transmission of the same data to a selected group of destinations.

multicomputer system A computer system consisting of two or more CENTRAL PROCESSING UNITS.

multidimensional language A LANGUAGE whose expressions, such as decision tables and flowcharts, are assembled in more than one dimension.

multidrop line A communications system configuration that uses a single channel or line to service several terminals.

multifile sorting The automatic sequencing of more than one file, based upon separate parameters for each file, without operator intervention.

multifrequency monitor A video monitor that can accept signals at more than one frequency range and support different video standards.

multifunction board A device that plugs into computers, giving the system more than one new capability, such as a clock/calendar, memory expansion board, or parallel/serial interface.

multifunction optical drive An optical drive that has both WORM and erasable capabilities and can read or write. A multifunction drive in conjunction with a CD-ROM drive, it will provide enormous capabilities and storage facilities.

multifunction peripheral A device that combines the functions of several input/output devices.

multijob operation The concurrent execution of job steps from two or more jobs. Compare MULTIPROGRAMMING.

multilaunching The opening of an APPLICATION PROGRAM by two or more users in a LOCAL AREA NETWORK.

multilayer A type of printed circuit board that has several circuit layers connected by electroplated holes.

multilevel addressing See INDIRECT ADDRESSING.

multilevel sort The determination by two or more DATA FIELDS of the order in which DATA is displayed in a DATABASE program.

multilinked list A list with each atom having at least two pointers.

MultiMate A WORD PROCESSING program.

multimedia Multiple types of media, such as film, videotape, computer disks, sound recordings, photographs, paper, and slides.

multipass The process of running through the same data more than once to accomplish a task too complicated to be completed in one pass.

multipass sort A sort program designed to sort more data than can be contained within the internal memory of a central computer. Intermediate storage, for example, on disk or tape, is required.

Multiplan A SPREADSHEET program with data-management features, produced by Microsoft Corporation.

multiple-access network A flexible system by which every station can have access to a network at all times; provisions are made for times when two computers decide to transmit at the same time.

multiple-address instruction An instruction consisting of an operation code and two or more addresses.

multiple-address message A message to be delivered to more than one destination.

multiple connector A connector to indicate the merging of several lines of flow into one line, or the dispersal of one line of flow into several lines.

multiple inheritance In OBJECT-ORIENTED PROGRAMMING, the ability of subclasses to inherit instance variables and methods from more than one class.

multiple-job processing Controlling the performance of more than one data processing job at a time.

multiple-pass printing A technique used on some dot matrix printers to obtain higher-quality characters. The print head makes one pass; the paper is moved slightly and another pass is made. The end product is a printed character that is easier to read.

multiple regression A statistical technique for predicting the value of a "dependent variable" that is assumed to be dependent upon one or more explanatory or "independent variables."

multiple user system A computer system designed to allow more than one user on the system at a time. See NETWORK.

multiplex To interleave or simultaneously transmit two or more messages over a single channel or other communications facility.

multiplexer (MPX) A device that allows several communications lines to share one computer data channel. Also abbreviated MUX.

multiplexer channel A special type of input/output channel that can transmit data between a computer and a number of simultaneously operating peripheral devices.

multiplexing Transmitting multiple messages simultaneously over one channel in a LOCAL AREA NETWORK.

multiplexor Alternate spelling of MULTIPLEXER.

multiplication time The time required to perform a multiplication. For a binary number, it will equal the total of all the addition times and all the shift time involved in the multiplication.

multiplier In multiplication, the number by which the multiplicand is multiplied.

multipoint line A line configuration in which several terminals are connected on the same line to one computer.

multiprecision arithmetic A form of arithmetic in which two or more computer words are used to represent each number.

multiprocessing The simultaneous execution of two or more sequences of instructions by multiple central processing units under common control.

multiprocessor   A COMPUTER NETWORK consisting of two or more central processors under a common control.

multiprogramming   Running two or more programs concurrently in the same computer. Each program is allotted its own place in memory and its own peripherals, but all share the central processing unit. It is made economical by the fact that peripherals are slower than the CPU, so most programs spend most of their time waiting for input or output to finish. While one program is waiting, another can use the CPU.

multireel sorting   The automatic sequencing of a file having more than one input tape, without operator intervention.

multiscanning/multisync monitor   A color monitor that automatically adjusts to the frequency of the video display board to which it is connected.

multistar network   A DATA COMMUNICATIONS network in which several host computers are connected, and each host computer has its own STAR NETWORK of smaller computers.

multitasking   The ability to execute more than one program at the same time on the same computer. The computer performs this by rapidly switching its attention between the various tasks or programs.

multithreading   Pertaining to concurrent operation of more than one path of execution within a computer.

multiuser   A term describing a computer system that allows several users to share the computer's processor, memory, and mass storage simultaneously.

multiviewports   A screen display that shows two or more viewing screens that are adjacent but independent.

multivolume file   A file so large that it requires more than one diskette, replaceable hard-disk cartridge, disk pack, or magnetic tape to hold it.

μP   Abbreviation for MICROPROCESSOR (μ is the Greek letter *mu*).

μs   Abbreviation for MICROSECOND, one-millionth of a second (μ is the Greek letter *mu*). Same as μsec.

Musical Instrument Digital Interface (MIDI) A standard communications protocol for the exchange of information between computers and sound-producing equipment, such as synthesizers.

musical language A method by which musical notation may be represented in code suitable for computer input.

musicomp A compositional programming language that provides techniques for generating original musical scores as well as for synthesizing music.

music synthesizer A device that can be linked to a computer for recording or playing music.

MUX Acronym for MULTIPLEXER.

MUMPS Acronym for **M**assachusetts General Hospital **U**tility **M**ulti-**P**rogramming **S**ystem, a high-level programming language designed specifically for handling medical records. The language is heavy on data management and text manipulation features.

MVT Acronym for **m**ultiprogramming with a **v**ariable number of **t**asks, the tasks being programs. (Also jokingly called multiprogramming with a vast amount of trouble.)

mylar™ DuPont's trademark for polyester film, often used as a base for magnetically coated or perforated information media, such as magnetic tape.

— N —

naive user   A person who wants to do something with a computer but does not have the experience needed to program it.

NAK   An international transmission control code returned by a receiving terminal to signify that a frame of information has been received but is incorrect. Contrast with ACK.

name   An alphanumeric term that identifies a program, a control statement, data areas, or a cataloged procedure.

name clashing   In OBJECT-ORIENTED PROGRAMMING, a conflict that can occur in multiple inheritance, when the same method or instance variable is inherited from multiple classes.

NAND   A logical operator having the property that if P is a statement, Q is a statement, ... then the NAND of P, Q, ... is true if at least one statement is false and false if all statements are true. Combination of NOT-AND. Compare AND, OR, NOR, and XOR.

nano   Prefix meaning one-billionth. Contrast with GIGA.

nanoacre   One-billionth of an acre, used figuratively to describe the area of an integrated circuit.

nanocomputer   A computer capable of processing data in billionths of a second.

nanosecond   One-billionth of a second; one-thousand-millionth of a second; abbreviated ns. Same as millimicrosecond. Light travels approximately one foot per nanosecond, electricity slightly less. The most powerful computers now being manufactured can carry out an instruction in less than a nanosecond. That is, such a machine can execute more than one billion instructions in one second!

narrowband   A term describing a data communications system that handles low volumes of data at a low range of frequencies.

NASA   Acronym for **N**ational **A**eronautics and **S**pace **A**dministration.

National Computer Graphics Association (NCGA) A nonprofit organization dedicated to developing, promoting, and improving computer graphics applications in business, government, science, and the arts. NCGA brings together users and producers of computer graphics technology in a common, independent forum to share experience and knowledge.

National Crime Information Center (NCIC) An FBI computerized network of data related to crimes that have occurred throughout the United States. The network is used by law enforcement agencies throughout the United States and Canada.

national data bank A DATA BANK that would contain detailed information on everyone in the United States, a concept that has been proposed but never implemented.

National Educational Computing Conference (NECC) An annual meeting of educators interested in the use of computers in education.

National Software Testing Laboratory (NSTL) A software testing group, created to assist personal computer product manufacturers with real-world testing of software to aid in comparisons with other, similar products and to discover areas where improvements in product performance may be made.

native compiler A compiler that produces code usable only for a particular computer.

native file format The format to which a program defaults when sorting data on a disk.

native language A computer language peculiar to the machines of one manufacturer. See MACHINE LANGUAGE.

native mode (1) A computer that is running a program in its native machine language. (2) A computer that is running in its highest-performance state, such as the Intel 80386 microprocessor running in 32k-bit protected mode.

natural intelligence Intelligence derived from neural networks. The term was coined to emphasize the difference between ARTIFICIAL INTELLI-GENCE and that derived from NEURAL NETWORKS.

natural language (1) The fifth generation of programming languages. These languages use human languages such as English, German, and French to give people a more natural connection with computers. (2) Ordinary human language; unlike precisely defined computer languages, it is often ambiguous and is thus interpreted differently by different hearers.

natural language processing The study of strategies for computer programs to recognize and understand language in spoken and written form.

NBS Abbreviation for **N**ational **B**ureau of **S**tandards. Now called the National Institute of Standards and Technology. See NIST.

NCGA Abbreviation for NATIONAL COMPUTER GRAPHICS ASSOCIATION.

N-channel MOS (NMOS) A circuit that uses current made up of negative changes; at least twice the speed but lower density than PMOS.

NCIC Abbreviation for the FBI's computerized NATIONAL CRIME INFORMATION CENTER, the heart of a large law enforcement network.

NCR Corporation A major manufacturer of computer equipment. Throughout the years, NCR has continued to develop integrated point-of-sale and financial computer systems.

NCR paper Multiple-copy computer paper that produces copies without using carbon paper.

NCSN Abbreviation for **N**ational **C**omputer **S**ervices **N**etwork, an organization formed to provide a voice for large and small third-party maintenance companies.

NDBMS Abbreviation for NETWORK DATABASE MANAGEMENT SYSTEM.

NDC See NORMALIZED DEVICE COORDINATES.

NDRO Abbreviation for **n**on**d**estructive **r**ead**o**ut. See NONDESTRUCTIVE READ.

near letter quality Printing produced by dot matrix printers with 24-pin printheads.

NECC Abbreviation for the NATIONAL EDUCATIONAL COMPUTING CONFERENCE.

negate To perform the logical operator NOT.

negative true logic A system of logic in which a high voltage represents the bit value of zero and a low voltage represents the bit value 1.

neighborhood operator A procedure applied to a PIXEL that incorporates information about those pixels that surround and touch it.

NEO A neochrome bitmap graphics format used by many programs for the Atari ST computer.

NEO chrome A color paint program for the Atari ST microcomputer, developed by Dave Staugas, an engineer at Atari Corporation.

nerd A computer amateur. Also called geek.

nest The result of one program structure being placed inside another structure of the same type. For example, a loop can be contained in another loop.

nested block A program block inside another program block.

nested loop A loop that is contained within another loop.

nested subroutine A subroutine reached by a subroutine calling statement (such as GOSUB in the BASIC language) in another subroutine.

nesting Embedding program segments of blocks of data within other program segments or blocks of data. Algebraic nesting involves grouping expressions within parentheses; for example, $(W * X * (A-B))$.

NetWare A LOCAL AREA NETWORK operating system developed for IBM personal computers and Apple Macintosh computers.

network (1) The result of two or more computers being connected to allow them to share the same software and information. Used primarily in businesses and schools. (**2**) A system of interconnected computer systems and terminals. (**3**) The structure of relationships among a project's activities, tasks, and events. (**4**) A means of organizing data in artificial intelligence systems. A type of knowledge representation in ARTIFICIAL INTELLIGENCE.

network administrator   The person responsible for maintaining LOCAL AREA NETWORKS and assisting users.

network analysis   A listing of the components of a project network, with their start/end dates and float and dependency parameters.

network architecture   (**1**) The hardware, software, and cable standards for a LOCAL AREA NETWORK. (**2**) The logical structure and operating principles of a computer network.

network chart   A chart that depicts time estimates and activity relationships.

network database   A database that is similar to a hierarchical database, except that each child node may have more than one parent node.

network database management system (NDBMS)   A collection of related programs for loading, accessing, and controlling a database. Data records are linked by a complex system of pointers that must be updated frequently.

network gateway   A connection by which a local area network (LAN) may be linked to other LANs or to larger networks.

networking   (**1**) A technique for distributing data processing functions through communications facilities. (**2**) The design of networks.

network interface card   An adapter that enables a user to hook a network cable directly to a microcomputer.

network management   Software that controls LOCAL AREA NETWORK access and network resources.

network manager A PROGRAM that is used to monitor, manage, and diagnose the problems of a network.

network operating system A control program that resides in a file server within a LOCAL AREA NETWORK. It handles the requests for data from all the users on the network.

network protocol The rules and signals that networked computers use to communicate.

network server A computer that allows users in a LOCAL AREA NETWORK to share data and program files.

network theory The systematizing and generalizing of the relationships among the elements of an electrical network.

network topologies Physical arrangements of nodes and interconnecting communication links in networks based on application requirements and geographical distribution of users. Patterns include STAR NETWORK, RING NETWORK, multidrop network, TREE NETWORK, and MESH NETWORK. In practice, most networks are made up of some combination of these topologies.

network version An APPLICATION PROGRAM revised to function in a NETWORK environment.

network weaving In COMPUTER SECURITY, a penetration technique in which different communication networks are used to gain access to a system without detection.

neural-net computing Hardware or software systems that organize memory as in human brain cells.

neural network (1) A computer simulation of the brain. (2) Self-organizing systems of simple interconnected processing units that possess a learning rule and are capable of learning.

New Century Schoolbook An easily read typeface developed for textbooks and magazines. New Century Schoolbook often is offered as a built-in font in POSTSCRIPT laser printers.

new media Information delivery systems that combine media such as text, graphics, voice, and video, using a microcomputer as the controlling framework.

newspaper columns A page format in which two or more columns of text are printed vertically on the page so that the text flows down one column and continues at the top of the next.

Newton A pocket-sized, pen-based computer introduced by Apple Computer, Inc. in 1992. Newton combines electronic calendar, card index, note-taking, and telecommunications functions.

Newton-Raphson An interactive procedure used for solving equations. See ITERATE.

NewWave An operating environment that provides an object-management shell facility allowing data from various different applications to be merged together to create a compound document.

NeXT Computer A UNIX-based computer system introduced in 1988 by NeXT, Inc. It includes a 68030 microprocessor, high-resolution (1,120 × 832) graphics, and a 256 MB erasable optical disc. NeXT, Inc. was founded in 1985 by Steven Jobs, co-founder and former chairman of Apple Computer, Inc.

NFS Abbreviation for **N**etwork **F**ile **S**ystem, a portable file server system (able to be moved from system to system) used mostly in UNIX workstation environments.

nibble Half a byte, or four adjacent bits. Sometimes spelled *nybble*.

NIC Acronym for **n**etwork **i**nterface **c**ard.

NiCad battery pack Abbreviation for **n**ickel **cad**mium battery pack, used for many portable computers.

niladic Pertaining to an operation for which no operands are specified. Contrast with MONADIC.

nil pointer A pointer used to denote the end of a linked list.

nine's complement A numeral used to represent the negative of a given value. Obtained by subtracting each digit from a numeral containing all nines; for example, 567 is the nine's complement of 432 and is obtained by subtracting 432 from 999.

ninety-six column card A punched card used with card-handling equipment. It contains 18 rows and 36 columns, and three characters can be punched in each column.

NIST Acronym for National Institute of Standards and Technology. Formerly known as the National Institute of Standards, its primary function is to promote maximum use of science and technology in U.S. industry. Another function of NIST is to help define and promote standards for computer equipment and techniques.

nixie tube A vacuum tube used to display legible numbers.

NLP Abbreviation for natural language processing, a discipline that attempts to develop systems that can communicate with humans using the natural language of the user.

NMOS Abbreviation for N-CHANNEL MOS.

nodal point The central point on the axis of movement.

node (1) Any terminal, computer, or peripheral in a computer network. (2) A point in a tree structure where two or more branches come together. (3) The connecting point on a component, printed circuit board, or logic element where electrical connections can be made. (4) In computer graphics, an endpoint of a graphical element.

noise (1) Loosely, any disturbance tending to interfere with the normal operation of a device or system, including interference attributable to equipment components, natural disturbance, or manual interference. (2) Spurious signals that can introduce errors. (3) Any unwanted signal.

noise immunity A device's ability to accept valid signals while rejecting unwanted signals.

noise pollution   Noise, especially office noise, that distracts and cuts into productive work time, such as noise from printers and copy machines.

nonconductor   A substance through which electricity cannot pass. Contrast with SEMICONDUCTOR.

nondestructive fetch   A process in which data can be retrieved from any memory cell but not destroyed.

nondestructive read   A read operation that does not alter the information content of the storage media.

nondisplay   A field attribute that prevents display of data.

nondocument   A FILE that is not a WORD PROCESSING document.

nonerasable storage   A storage device whose information cannot be erased during the course of computation, such as certain nondestructible readout magnetic memories.

nonexecutable statement   A program statement that sets up a program but does not call for any specific action on the part of the program in which it appears. Contrast with EXECUTABLE STATEMENT.

nongraphic character   A character that, when set for a printer or display unit, does not produce a printable character image, such as carriage control and upper case.

nonimpact printer   A printer that uses electricity, heat, laser technology, or photographic techniques to print output; one that prints without striking the paper.

noninterlaced   A term describing a display monitor that does not use interlacing techniques to improve resolution.

nonlinear programming   The area of applied mathematics concerned with finding the values of the variables that give the smallest or largest value of a specified function in the class of all variables satisfying prescribed conditions. Contrast with LINEAR PROGRAMMING.

nonnumeric programming   Programming that deals with symbols rather than numbers. Usually refers to the manipulation of symbolic objects, such as words, rather than the performance of numerical calculations.

nonoverlap processing   A technique whereby reading, writing, and internal processing occur only in a serial manner. Contrast with OVERLAP PROCESSING.

nonprint   Pertaining to an impulse that inhibits line printing under machine control.

nonprocedural language   Language that states what task is to be accomplished but does not state the steps needed to accomplish it; for example, where the computer language for interacting with a database specifies what the user wants to know rather than the steps needed to produce the information, which are worked out by the computer. See QUERY LANGUAGE.

nonreflective ink   Any color of ink recognizable to an optical character reader; also called read ink.

nonsequential computer   A computer that must be directed to the location of each instruction.

nonswappable storage   The STORAGE containing PROGRAMS or data that must remain in storage.

nonswitched line   A communications link permanently installed between two points.

nonvolatile storage   A storage medium that retains its data in the absence of power. Contrast with VOLATILE STORAGE.

no-op (NOP)   Abbreviation of **no-op**eration, as in NO-OPERATION INSTRUCTION.

no-operation instruction   A computer instruction whose only effect is to advance the instruction counter. Accomplishes nothing more than to advance itself to the next instruction in normal sequence.

NOP   Acronym for **no-op**eration. See NO-OPERATION INSTRUCTION.

NOR   A Boolean operator that gives a truth table value of true only when both of the variables connected by the logical operator are false. Compare AND, OR, and XOR.

normal   **(1)** At right angles to another line segment, object, or plane. **(2)** The vector that is perpendicular to a surface at a specific point.

normal direction flow   A flow direction from left to right or top to bottom on a FLOWCHART.

normalize   **(1)** To adjust the exponent and fraction of a floating-point quantity so that the fraction is within a prescribed range. **(2)** To break down data into record groups for efficient processing in a relational database system.

normalized device coordinates (NDC)   The COORDINATE SYSTEM between the user's world coordinates and the graphics system's physical device coordinates in the viewing pipeline.

Norton Utilities   A package of utility programs for IBM-compatible microcomputers, including a benchmark program that measures a computer's throughput, an undelete program that restores files accidently deleted from the disk, management utilities for directories and subdirectories, and data security programs. Developed by Peter Norton Computing, Inc., these programs are designed to make computing easier and are useful for floppy and hard disk users.

NOT   A logic operator having the property that if P is a statement, then the NOT of P is true if P is false and false if P is true.

notation   See POLISH NOTATION and POSITIONAL NOTATION.

notebook computer   A small, self-contained, portable computer that will fit in an attaché case. It usually weighs less than five pounds.

NOT gate   A circuit equivalent to the logical operation of negation.

Novell   A networking protocol very popular in IBM-oriented corporate environments.

NRZ   Abbreviation for **n**on**r**eturn to **z**ero, one of several methods for coding digital information on magnetic tape.

ns Abbreviation for nanosecond, one-billionth of a second.

NSTL See NATIONAL SOFTWARE TESTING LABORATORY.

NTSC Abbreviation for National Television Standards Committee, which sets the standards for the transmission of U.S. television.

NuBus A high-speed Apple Macintosh II expansion bus.

nucleus That portion of the control program that must always be present in internal storage.

null Pertaining to a negligible value or a lack of information, as contrasted with a zero or a blank that conveys information, such as a numerical value and a space between words; empty.

null cycle The time required to cycle through an entire program without introducing new data.

null modem A small connection box for hooking up two computers, each of which expects to be linked up through a modem. In addition to crossing the main data wires so that one computer's output is the other's input, it connects the proper hardware control lines to simulate the signals that a modem would provide when a complete connection had been made.

null modem cable A serial cable that connects two computers directly, without the need for a modem.

null string A string with no characters. Also called EMPTY STRING.

number (**1**) A symbol or symbols representing a value in a specific numeral system. (**2**) Loosely, a numeral.

number base See RADIX.

number crunching (**1**) The rapid processing of large quantities of numbers. Number crunching can be repetitive, mathematically complex, or both, and involves considerable internal processing. Parallel processing and the use of math coprocessors greatly enhance the ability of computers to perform these tasks. (**2**) A computer-based calculation performed by electronic spreadsheets.

number representation   The representation of numbers by agreed sets of symbols according to agreed rules.

number system   An agreed-upon set of symbols and rules for number representation. Loosely, a numeral system.

numeral   A conventional symbol representing a number; for example, 6, VI, and 110 are different numerals that represent the same number in different numeral systems.

numeralization   The representation of alphabetic data through the use of digits.

numeral system   A method of representing numbers. In computing, several numeral systems in addition to the common decimal system are of particular interest: the binary, hexadecimal, and octal systems. In each system, the value of a numeral is the value of the digits multiplied by the numeral system radix, raised to a power indicated by the position of the digits in the numeral. See POSITIONAL NOTATION.

numeric   Pertaining to numerals or to representation by means of numerals. Compare ALPHANUMERIC.

numerical analysis   The branch of mathematics concerned with the study and development of effective procedures for computing answers to problems.

numerical control   A method of controlling machine tools through servomechanisms and control circuitry so that the motions of the tools will respond to digital coded instructions on tape or to direct commands from a computer.

numerical indicator tube   Any electron tube capable of visually displaying numerical figures.

numeric character   Same as DIGIT.

numeric coding   Coding that uses only digits to represent data and instructions.

numeric constant   Data using integers or real numbers. See CONSTANT.

numeric coprocessor   A microprocessor support chip that performs mathematical computations in conjunction with the main microprocessor of a system. It works in tandem with another CENTRAL PROCESSING UNIT to increase the computing power of a system.

numeric coprocessor socket   A socket on a motherboard into which a numeric coprocessor chip can be inserted.

numeric data   DATA that consists entirely of numbers.

numeric field   A field that contains numbers used for calculations.

numeric keypad   See KEYPAD.

numeric representation   A discrete representation of data by numerals.

numeric variable   The name of a numeric data item whose value is assigned or changed during program processing.

num lock key   A TOGGLE KEY that locks the numeric keypad into the numbers mode, disabling cursor movement keys.

NURB   An acronym for **n**on**u**niform **r**ational **b**-spline, a complex curve that can be represented by a series of piecewise curve segments. This process is done with a sequence of knots, which are values that join the separate splines in a curve, each knot interval representing one curve segment. NURBS have high precision and flexibility due to the use of the knot sequence. Their relative spacing has an impact on the curve shape, and because the knots can be nonuniformly spaced, the user can exert extra control over the shape of the curve. A relatively small amount of memory is required to represent NURBS, making them an efficient curve-defining method.

nybbler package   A lockbuster package that circumvents copy protection by copying a program one bit at a time.

OA Abbreviation for **O**FFICE **A**UTOMATION.

oasis A multiuser operating system used on several microcomputer systems.

Oasis An Apple Macintosh graphics program designed specifically to take advantage of input from a pressure-sensitive digitizing tablet. It offers 18 brushes with pressure control, including its ArtistBrush, which allows virtually any traditional or fine art medium to be replicated, including oil paint, water color, gouache, chalks, ink, pastels, magic marker, finger paint, and charcoal.

obey The process whereby a computer carries out an operation as specified by one or more of the instructions forming the program currently being executed.

object (1) In computer graphics, a distinct entity. For example, a star might be an object in a graphics program. (2) A shorthand term for OBJECT CODE. (3) In OBJECT-ORIENTED PROGRAMMING, a variable comprising both routines and data that is treated as a discrete entity.

object-based programming A method of programming in which programs are organized as cooperative collections of objects, each of which represents an instance of some type, and whose types are all members of a hierarchy of types united via other than inheritance relationships.

object code Executable machine-language commands; the code, generated by a compiler or an assembler, that was translated from the source code of a program.

object computer A computer used for the execution of an object program.

object description The attributes that describe an object.

object diagram Part of the notation of OBJECT-ORIENTED DESIGN, used to show the existence of objects and their relationships in the logical design of a system.

object file A file containing object code, usually the output of a compiler or an assembler.

object file graphic formats See CDR, MACDRAW, CEM, DFX, EPS, GEM, HPGL, HPC, PIC, PICT, SLD, WMF, and WPG. Contrast with BITMAP FILE FORMATS.

object identity In OBJECT-ORIENTED PROGRAMMING, something about an object that remains invariant across all possible modifications of its state. Can be used to point to the object.

Objective-C An object-oriented programming language formed by adding Smalltalk-inspired constructs to the C language.

object language The output of a translation process. Usually, object language and machine language are the same. Synonymous with TARGET LANGUAGE. Contrast with SOURCE LANGUAGE.

object language programming Programming in a machine language executable on a particular computer.

object library An area on a direct access storage device used to store object programs and routines.

object model In OBJECT-ORIENTED PROGRAMMING, the collection of principles that form the foundation of object-oriented design; a software engineering paradigm emphasizing the principles of abstraction, encapsulation, modularity, hierarchy, typing, concurrency, and persistence.

object module The machine-language version of a program.

object name The name of an OBJECT.

object orientation In OBJECT-ORIENTED PROGRAMMING, a level of computer abstraction beyond that of procedures and data. Object orientation involves thinking about the world as a set of entities or objects that are related to and communicate with one another.

object-oriented analysis In OBJECT-ORIENTED PROGRAMMING, analysis of a system's requirements in terms of real-world objects.

object-oriented database In OBJECT-ORIENTED PROGRAMMING, a database that allows data to be stored as objects.

object-oriented decomposition In OBJECT-ORIENTED PROGRAMMING, the process of breaking a system into parts, each of which represents some class or object from the problem domain.

object-oriented design In OBJECT-ORIENTED PROGRAMMING, translating the logical structure of a system into a physical structure composed of software objects. A type of software design that adds greater emphasis to the design and abstraction of data structures than does top-down design.

object-oriented graphics Computer graphics that are based on the use of "construction elements" such as curves, lines, and squares, describing an image mathematically as a set of instructions for creating the objects in the image. Object-oriented graphics enable the user to manipulate objects as entire units. Because objects are described mathematically, object-oriented graphics can also be rotated, magnified, and layered relatively easily. Object-oriented graphics can usually be displayed or printed at the full resolution of the monitor or output device, offering more precision than bit-mapped images.

object-oriented interface A graphical interface that uses icons and a mouse, such as the Apple Macintosh Finder, Microsoft Windows on IBM-compatible microcomputers, or GEM environment on Atari ST and IBM-compatible microcomputers.

object-oriented language A computer language that supports objects, classes, subclasses, methods, messages, and inheritance. Secondary features may include multiple inheritance, dynamic binding, and polymorphism.

object-oriented programming (OOP) A programming technology that is generally more flexible and adaptable than standard programming. Object-oriented programming allows the user to create procedures about objects whose exact type is not known until run time.

object owner A user who creates an OBJECT or an owner to whom the ownership of an object has been reassigned.

object program The instructions that come out of the compiler or assembler, ready to run on the computer. Also called object code and target program. Contrast with SOURCE PROGRAM.

object rights   The authority that controls what a system user can do to an object.

object space   **(1)** The space in which a GRAPHICS OBJECT is defined. **(2)** The COORDINATE SYSTEM in which a graphics object is defined.

object structure   In OBJECT-ORIENTED PROGRAMMING, a set of graphs whose vertices represent objects and whose arcs represent relationships among those objects. An object diagram may represent all or part of the object structure of a system.

object table   A helpful tool for organizing objects in an object-oriented program. It consists of a listing of the objects, their methods, and the use to which they will be put.

object time   The time during which an OBJECT PROGRAM is executed.

object user   A USER who has been authorized to perform certain functions on an OBJECT.

oblique   A style of text created by slanting a roman font to simulate italics when a true italic font doesn't exist on the computer or printer.

oblique axis   An axis that is placed at an angle to the margins of a page.

occlusion   In computer graphics, the result of an object or a portion of an object surface being drawn behind another solid object or opaque surface; an occluded object is one that is hidden from view.

OCR   Abbreviation for OPTICAL CHARACTER RECOGNITION.

OCR-A   A standard typeface for optical characters.

octal   Pertaining to a number system with a radix of 8. Octal numerals are frequently used to represent binary numerals, with each octal digit representing a group of three binary digits (bits); for example, the binary numeral 111000010001101 can be represented as octal 70215.

octal numeral   A numeral of one or more digits expressing a sum in which the quantity represented by each figure is based on a radix of 8. The digits used in octal numerals are 0, 1, 2, 3, 4, 5, 6, and 7.

octet A BYTE composed of eight bits.

odd header In WORD PROCESSING, a header appearing only on odd-numbered pages.

odd parity A type of error-checking protocol for asynchronous communications using an odd number of set bits.

OEM Abbreviation for **o**riginal **e**quipment **m**anufacturer, a company or organization that purchases computers and peripheral equipment for use as components in products and equipment that they subsequently sell to their customers.

office automation (OA) Application of computers and communications technology to improve the productivity of clerical and managerial office workers. Involves the integration of all information functions in the office, including word processing, electronic mail, graphics, desktop publishing, and data processing. The backbone of office automation is a LOCAL AREA NETWORK, which serves as a pathway between all users and computers.

office automation area The group of computer professionals within the information systems department that is charged with managing office-related computer activities within the organization.

office computer Usually, a microcomputer system for use in an office environment. Likely to include disk units, a printer, and software developed for specific office functions. A LOCAL AREA NETWORK is often used to connect users and computers.

office information system A system that can include a variety of data entry terminals, word processors, graphics terminals, printers, and computer systems.

office of the future An office that makes extensive use of computers, data communications, and other electronic technologies. In such an office, numerous clerical, secretarial, and communications tasks are done automatically.

offline   Pertaining to equipment, devices, or persons not in direct communication with the central processing unit of a computer. Contrast with ONLINE.

offline storage   Storage not under control of the central processing unit.

offload   **(1)** To transfer jobs from one computer system to another that is more lightly loaded. **(2)** To output data to a peripheral device.

offpage connector   A pentagonal symbol used on a flowchart to link a line of flow on one page with its continuation on a different page.

off-screen formatting   In WORD PROCESSING, when formatting commands are embedded in the text but are not visible on the screen.

offset   The difference between the value or condition desired and that actually attained.

offset printing   A widely used printing process in which a page is reproduced photographically on a metal or paper plate attached to a revolving cylinder. Ink is transferred from the plate to a rubber blanket from which it is transferred to paper.

off-the-shelf   Pertaining to any standard, mass-produced hardware or software product readily available from the vendor.

omnifont   The ability of an OCR program to recognize most fonts without the need to learn them.

OMR   Abbreviation for OPTICAL MARK, a direct-entry method that senses the presence or absence of a mark, such as a pencil mark.

on-board computer   A computer resident in another device; for example, a computer aboard a spacecraft.

on-board regulation   An arrangement in which each board in a system contains its own voltage regulator.

on-demand report   A report providing information in response to an unscheduled demand from a user.

one-address computer   A computer that employs only one address in its instruction format.

one-address instruction   An instruction consisting of an operation and exactly one address. In special cases, the instruction code of a single-address computer may include both zero and multiaddress instructions. Most present-day computers are of the one-address-instruction type.

one-alternative decision   In PROGRAMMING, a decision that results in only one action; for example, if a condition is true, action is taken by the program, but if it is false, no special action is taken.

one-chip computer   A complete microcomputer that is implemented on a single chip.

one-dimensional array   An array consisting of a single row or column of elements.

one-for-one   (1) A phrase often associated with an assembler in which one source-language statement is converted to one machine-language instruction. (2) The most commonly used type of correspondence.

one-level memory   Memory in which all stored items are accessed by a uniform mechanism.

one-pass compiler   A language processor that passes through a source-language program one time and produces an object module.

one-point perspective   Describing the perspective in a drawing having a single vanishing point.

one's complement   A numeral used to represent the negative of a given value. A one's complement of a binary numeral is obtained by alternating the configuration of each bit in the numeral. For example, 01100101 is the one's complement of the binary numeral 10011010.

one-to-many relationship   In a NETWORK or HIERARCHICAL data model, a relationship that allows a parent to have many children but each child to have only one parent.

one-to-one relationship   In a NETWORK or HIERARCHICAL data model, a relationship that allows only one-to-one links between data elements.

onion diagram   A graphical representation of a system that is made up of concentric circles. The innermost circle is the core upon which all outer layers are dependent.

online   Pertaining to equipment, devices, and persons that are in direct communication with the central processing unit of a computer; equipment physically connected to the computer. Contrast with OFFLINE.

online backup   To copy all or part of a file while it is being created so that it can be recreated in the event that it is lost or damaged.

online batch processing   The sharing of COMPUTER RESOURCES between one or more REAL-TIME programs and a BATCH PROGRAM.

online database   A database that can be directly accessed by a user from a terminal, usually a visual display device.

online fault-tolerant system   A computer system designed to function correctly in the presence of hardware failures.

online information   INFORMATION stored in a COMPUTER SYSTEM that can be displayed, used, and modified in an interactive manner without any need to obtain hard copy.

online problem solving   A teleprocessing application in which a number of users at remote terminals can concurrently use a computing system in solving problems online. Often, in this type of application, a dialogue or conversation is carried on between a user at a remote terminal and a program within the central computer system.

online storage   Storage under control of the central processing unit.

online system   A system in which the input data enters the computer directly from the point of origin or in which output data is transmitted directly to where it is used.

on-screen help Operating assistance for applications that appear directly on the monitor, saving users the bother of looking them up in a manual.

on-screen pasteup A layout on a COMPUTER MONITOR.

on-the-fly encryption The encryption of data just before it is written to the disk and decrypted after it has been read from the disk. Software for on-the-fly encryption can be simple to use, as it is often transparent to the user.

OODB Abbreviation for OBJECT-ORIENTED DATABASE.

OOP Abbreviation for OBJECT-ORIENTED PROGRAMMING.

OOPL Abbreviation for OBJECT-ORIENTED PROGRAMMING LANGUAGE.

OOPS Abbreviation for OBJECT-ORIENTED PROGRAMMING SYSTEM.

OOSD Abbreviation for OBJECT-ORIENTED STRUCTURAL DESIGN.

op Abbreviation for OPERATION.

opacity The ease with which light passes through a sheet of paper, making it appear more or less translucent.

OPAL Acronym for **O**perational **P**erformance **A**nalysis **L**anguage, a data definition and manipulation language provided with the object-oriented database Gemstone.

op-code See OPERATION CODE.

open The process required to begin work with a file or document.

open architecture (1) A computer or operating system design for which detailed specifications are published by the manufacturer, allowing others to produce compatible hardware and software. (2) A personal computer design that allows additional circuit boards to be inserted in expansion slots inside the computer to support add-ons; an architecture that allows integration with other languages, conventional software programs, and graphics user interfaces.

open bus system An expansion bus that accepts various adapters.

open-ended Capable of accepting the addition of new programs, instructions, subroutines, modifications, terms, or classifications without disturbing the original system.

open file A file that can be accessed for reading, writing, or possibly both. Contrast with CLOSED FILE.

open prepress interface Developed by the Aldus Corporation, a system for automating the placement of color photographs, usually when sending desktop files to a high-end system.

open shop The operation of a computer facility in which most productive problem programming is performed by each problem originator rather than by a group of programming specialists. Contrast with CLOSED SHOP.

open subroutine A subroutine inserted into a routine at each place it is used. Contrast with CLOSED SUBROUTINE.

open system A vendor-independent system that is designed to interconnect with a variety of products that are commonly available.

operand The data unit or equipment item that is operated upon. Usually identified by an address in an instruction. For example, in "ADD 100 TO 400," 100 and 400 are operands. See OPERATION CODE.

operating environment (1) The environment in which programs are executed; for example, an IBM PS/2 computer for DOS or WINDOWS, or an Apple Macintosh computer for SYSTEM 7. (2) A PROGRAM that overlays the OPERATING SYSTEM to allow a menu-driven operating system, multitasking, or the use of windows.

operating ratio See AVAILABILITY.

operating system (OS) The master set of programs that manage the computer. Among other things, an operating system controls input and output to and from the keyboard, screen, disks, and other peripheral devices; loads and begins the execution of other programs; manages the storage of data on disks; and provides scheduling and accounting services.

operating system shell   Software that translates instructions entered by a personal computer user into commands to the operating system.

Operating System/2™   See os/2.

operation   (1) Any defined action. (2) An action specified by a single computer instruction or high-level-language statement. Abbreviated *op*.

operational management   The supervisors or leaders responsible for operating details and the employees who perform them.

operation center   The physical area containing the human and equipment resources needed to process data through a computer and produce the desired output.

operation code   An instruction code used to specify the operations a computer is to perform; for example, in "ADD 100 TO 400," ADD is the operation code. See OPERAND.

operations analysis   Same as OPERATIONS RESEARCH.

operations personnel   Those responsible for controlling the equipment in a computer center. Operations personnel power up systems, load programs, run programs, report equipment malfunctions, and so on.

operations research   The mathematical science devoted to carrying out complicated operations with the maximum possible efficiency. Includes such scientific techniques as linear programming, probability theory, information theory, game theory, the Monte Carlo method, and queuing theory.

operator   (1) In the description of a process, that which indicates the action to be performed on operands. See ARITHMETIC OPERATOR. (2) A person who operates a machine. See COMPUTER OPERATOR.

opm   Abbreviation for **o**perations **p**er **m**inute.

optical character   A character from a special set of characters that can be read by an OPTICAL CHARACTER READER.

optical character reader   An input device that accepts a printed document as input, identifying characters by their shape. See OPTICAL CHARACTER RECOGNITION.

optical character recognition (OCR)   Information processing technology that converts human-readable data in a special OCR font into another medium for computer input; the process by which text on paper is scanned and converted into text files in a computer. Light reflected from characters is recognized by OCR equipment.

optical communications   The transmission of data, pictures, speech, or other information by light. An information-carrying light-wave signal originates in a transmitter, passes through an optical channel, and enters a receiver, which reconstructs the original information. OPTICAL FIBERS and lasers make up a technology that offers maximum transmitting capacity using devices that occupy little physical space.

optical computer   A type of computer, still largely experimental, that uses laser beams instead of wires to process information and works far faster than traditionally wired computers.

optical disc   A large-capacity storage device. Several types of optical discs are available: CD-ROM (compact disc, read-only memory), WORM (write once, read many), and ERASABLE OPTICAL DISC DRIVES that let users write data as well as read it. Erasable optical discs are impervious to magnetic fields and can hold data for many years. This storage technology uses a laser beam to store large amounts of data at relatively low cost.

optical drive   A drive mechanism that rotates an OPTICAL DISC.

optical fiber   A thread of highly transparent glass that is pulsed very rapidly to carry a stream of binary signals. As well as carrying a high volume of data, optical fibers are immune to the electrical interference that can plague conventional cables. The use of optical fibers is rapidly becoming standard in computer communications.

optical laser disc   See OPTICAL DISC.

optical mark reader   A input device that reads graphite marks on cards or pages.

optical mark recognition (OMR)   Information processing technology that converts data into another medium for computer input by the presence of a mark in a given position, each position having a value known to the computer that may or may not be understandable to humans.

optical media   Storage devices that function through principles of light. For example, optical discs, which belong to this category, use light to store and retrieve information.

optical memory   A STORAGE DEVICE that uses optical techniques.

optical mouse   A mouse that uses reflected light to determine position and movement. Contrast with MECHANICAL MOUSE.

optical page reader   An input device that accepts a page of printed matter.

optical printer   See ELECTROSTATIC PRINTER.

optical reader   See OPTICAL CHARACTER READER and OPTICAL MARK READER.

optical reader wand   A device that reads BAR CODES and enters appropriate information into a computer.

optical recognition system   A system that converts optical characters, optical marks, BAR CODES, and handwritten characters into electrical signals to be sent to the computer.

optical reflective disc   An optical videodisc that is read by means of the reflection of a laser beam from the shiny surface on the disc.

optical ROM   A form of READ-ONLY MEMORY that uses an OPTICAL DISC for storage.

optical scanner   A scanner that uses light for examining patterns. See OPTICAL CHARACTER READER.

optical scanning   Any input method by which information is converted for machine processing by evaluating the relative reflectance of that information to the background on which it appears.

optical wave guide A structure capable of guiding optical power. See OPTICAL FIBER.

optimal merge tree Tree representation of the order in which strings are to be merged so that a minimum number of move operations occurs.

optimization In its most general meaning, the efforts and processes of making a decision, a design, or a system as nearly perfect, effective, or functional as possible. The attempt to seek the best possible solution for a given problem.

optimize To write a program or design a system in such a way as to improve performance.

optimizing compiler A compiler that attempts to correct inefficiencies in a program's logic to improve execution times, main storage requirements, and so forth.

optimum The best and most desirable in view of established criteria.

optimum programming Programming to maximize efficiency with respect to some criterion, such as least storage usage, least usage of peripheral equipment, or least computing time.

optimum tree search A tree search whose object is to find the best of many alternatives.

option key A modifier key on some keyboards; a special control key. When held down, it gives a different interpretation to characters next typed.

optoelectronic integrated circuit (OEIC) A computer CHIP that uses light instead of electrons and wire to transmit information. Its high-speed optical connections use less power and can be packed on a circuit board more densely than the copper wires and traces that carry signals from chips.

opto electronics The technology concerned with the integration of optics and electronics.

optomechanical mouse A type of mouse in which motion is translated into directional signals through a combination of optical and mechanical means.

OR   See INCLUSIVE OR.

ORACLE   A PROGRAM that enables an Apple Macintosh and IBM personal computer or compatible users to access data from large corporate databases.

OR circuit   See OR GATE.

order   **(1)** The arrangement of items according to any specified set of rules. **(2)** A command found in most electronic spreadsheet programs that permits the user to determine the order of calculation.

order processing   A business accounting software module that a retail or wholesale operation uses to ensure that customers' orders are filled in a timely manner.

ordinal number   A number that identifies the sequence of an item; for example, file #21. Compare CARDINAL NUMBER.

ordinate   The Y-axis of a graph or chart. Contrast with ABSCISSA.

organizational control   Personnel administrative procedures implemented to protect an information system from infiltration, tampering, or sabotage.

organization chart   A diagram showing the organization of a business (how responsibilities are divided within the business). Pictorial representation of the organizational hierarchy, showing the formal relationships among employees.

OR gate   A computer circuit containing two switches whose output is a binary 1 if either or both of the inputs are binary. Implements the OR operator. Contrast with AND GATE.

origin   In coding, the absolute memory address of the first location of a program or program segment.

original data   Data to be processed; also called raw data.

original equipment manufacturer (OEM)   A manufacturer who buys equipment from other suppliers and integrates it into a single system for resale.

originate/answer   A term describing a modem that can both originate and answer messages. Most telecomputing services are in ANSWER MODE, so the user must be in ORIGINATE MODE.

originate mode   In full-duplex data communications, one of two audio frequencies that a computer uses to send information.

originator   The user who creates, addresses, and usually sends a message.

OROM   Short for OPTICAL READ-ONLY MEMORY, optical discs in which data is permanently embedded during manufacturing.

OR operator   A logical operator having the property that if P is a statement and Q is a statement, then OR of P + Q is true if, and only if, at least one statement is true and false if all statements are false.

orphan   (1) The first line of a paragraph sitting alone at the bottom of a page of text. Considered undesirable in all forms of printing. (2) A personal computer that has been discontinued and is no longer supported by its manufacturer.

orthographic   A type of layout, drawing, or map in which the projecting lines are perpendicular to the plane of the drawing or map.

OS   Abbreviation for OPERATING SYSTEM, a group of programs that control a computer and make it possible for users to enter and run their own programs. Some examples of OS are MS-DOS, OS/2, SYSTEM 7, and UNIX.

oscillating sort   An external tape sort that capitalizes on a tape drive's ability to read forward and backward.

oscilloscope   An electronic instrument that produces a luminous plot on a fluorescent screen, showing the relationship of two or more variables. Used by computer maintenance technicians.

OSI   Acronym for OPEN SYSTEMS INTERCONNECTION, a networking standard for interconnecting disparate computer systems strongly supported by DEC.

OS/2™   A microcomputer OPERATING SYSTEM from Microsoft Corporation and IBM Corporation that allows multitasking by a single user. Several important OS/2 subsystems include Presentation Manager, which provides a graphical user interface, and LAN Manager, which provides networking facilities. Introduced in 1987, OS/2 is designed for use on microcomputers based on Intel 80 x 86 processors: 80286, 80386, and 80486.

outdegree   The number of directed edges leaving a node. Contrast with INDEGREE.

outdent   In WORD PROCESSING, a line of text that extends farther to the left than other lines in the same paragraph. Opposite of INDENTATION.

outline drawing   A drawing consisting of an outline shape or a repeated sequence of outline shapes.

outline font   A font that is made up of basic outlines for each character; a printer or screen font in which a mathematical formula generates each character, producing a graceful and undistorted outline of the character, which the printer then fills in at its maximum resolution. Outline fonts are available as built-in fonts in many POSTSCRIPT laser printers and as downloadable fonts provided on disk.

outline utility   In WORD PROCESSING, a feature of some programs that assists users in organizing a document by creating an outline.

out-of-line   A term describing statements in a computer program that are not in the main line of the program, such as closed subroutines.

output   **(1)** Data transferred from a computer's internal storage unit to some storage or output device. **(2)** The final result of data that have been processed by the computer. Contrast with INPUT.

output area   The area of main storage reserved for output data. Contrast with INPUT AREA.

output buffer   A buffer used to transfer data to an external device.

output channel   A channel that connects peripheral units and the central processing unit, and through which data may be transmitted for output.

output crime   The theft of processed information for resale, extortion, or a criminal's personal use.

output data   Data to be delivered from a device or program, usually after some processing. Synonymous with OUTPUT. Contrast with INPUT DATA.

output device   A unit used for taking out data values from a computer and presenting them in the desired form to the user, such as a printer or display screen.

output line   A line of text produced by an OUTPUT DEVICE.

output media   A physical substance upon which output information is recorded, such as paper, magnetic disk, or magnetic tape. Compare INPUT MEDIA and SOURCE MEDIA.

output primitive   Simple graphical objects provided by a graphics library for use in the construction of more complex objects.

output program   A utility program that organizes the output process of a computer.

output stream   The sequence of data to be transmitted to an output device.

outputting   The process of producing useful information output.

overflow   In an arithmetic operation, the generation of a quantity beyond the capacity of the register or storage location that is to receive the result.

overflow error   An ERROR that occurs when the computer's predefined range of values is exceeded.

overhead   (1) A collective term for the factors that cause the performance of a program or device to be lower than it would be in the ideal case. (2) The nonproductive effort that takes place when the operating system and programs are performing administrative tasks rather than productive work.

overhead scanner   A DIGITAL SCANNER that resembles a photographic en-
larger. The original is placed on a table or bed beneath the sensor head,
which is suspended about a foot over the copy. No internal light source
is required, as ambient illumination in the room provides the sensor with
enough light. A pivoting mechanism inside the sensor head directs the
scanner's "eye" at each line of the original in turn.

overlaid window   On a monitor screen, a window, appearing on top of
the other windows, in which the current task is shown.

overlap   To do something at the same time that something else is being
done; for example, to perform an input operation while instructions are
being executed by the central processing unit. This approach permits the
computer to work on several programs at once. See MULTIPROGRAMMING.

overlapping   A condition in which windows on a screen display are on top
of one another, or overlap each other's borders.

overlap processing   The simultaneous execution of input, processing,
and output activities by a computer system. Contrast with NONOVERLAP
PROCESSING.

overlay   **(1)** In DESKTOP PUBLISHING, a sheet laid on top of another to specify
spot colors for printing. **(2)** In PROGRAMMING, a portion of a program
that is called into memory as needed, overlaying the previous redundant
section of the program. Overlays allow for writing of programs that are
much bigger than those that could fit into memory all at once.

overprint   The process of printing more than once at the same position in
order to emphasize or improve the type. For example, to print an element
of one color over one of another color.

override   To force a preexisting value to change in a program by super-
seding it.

overrun   The condition that occurs when data is transferred to or from a
nonbuffered control unit with a synchronous medium and the activity
initiated by the program exceeds the channel capacity.

overscan The loss of text at the end of a line if a computer and monitor are not matched properly.

overstriking The ability of a hard-copy printer to strike a character more than once to produce special effects: boldface characters, a character with a line through it, etc.

overwrite To place data in a location and destroy or mutilate the data previously contained in that location.

—— P ——

PABX Abbreviation for PRIVATE AUTOMATED BRANCH EXCHANGE.

pack To store several short units of data in a single storage cell in such a way that the individual units can later be recovered; for example, two four-bit BCD digits in one eight-bit storage location. Opposite of UNPACK.

package A program or collection of programs to be used by more than one business organization.

packaged file A FILE in compressed format.

packaged software Software that is packaged and sold in stores and by mail order. The prepared package consists of the program on diskette(s), an operating manual, and possibly other documentation.

packaged system A fully integrated computer system that includes both hardware and software.

packet A block of data for data transmission. Contains control information—such as routing, address, and error control—as well as data.

packing The process of storing two numbers in a single storage byte.

packing density The number of useful storage cells per unit of area or length, such as the number of characters per inch.

pad **(1)** The area of plated copper on a printed circuit board that provides a contact for soldering component leads, a means of copper-path transition from one side of the printed circuit board to the other, and contact for test probes. **(2)** To fill a data field with blanks.

pad character A buffer character used to fill a blank.

padding A technique used to fill out a fixed-length block of information with dummy characters, items, words, or records.

paddle A hand-held INPUT DEVICE used to move the cursor on the display screen through the use of a dial. Paddles are commonly used in computer games.

page (1) That area of a computer memory large enough to store a complete image or several lines of text. (2) A leaf in a book.

page break (1) In WORD PROCESSING, the location where one page ends and another begins. (2) A special code placed in a document to mark the end of a page.

page composition The addition of type to a layout.

page composition program A program for designing and producing professional-looking documents; also called desktop publishing program.

page description language (PDL) A PROGRAMMING LANGUAGE with specialized instructions for describing how to print a whole page. If an application generates output in a page description language, the output can be printed on any printer that supports it.

page description software A type of software that is used in desktop publishing to create on-screen pages of documents by combining text and graphics.

page design The process of specifying the boundaries of text or graphics on a page. Includes choosing margins, page length, headings, and footers.

page frame A location in the rear storage of the computer that can store one page.

page-in The process of swapping programs or data from disk storage to the computer's main storage.

page layout In publishing, the process of arranging text and graphics on a page.

page layout program In DESKTOP PUBLISHING, an application program that assembles text and graphics from a variety of files with which the user can determine the precise placement, scaling, sizing, and cropping of material in accordance with the page design represented on-screen. Popular page layout programs include PAGEMAKER, QUARK XPRESS, and VENTURA PUBLISHER.

PageMaker   A DESKTOP PUBLISHING program for IBM-compatible and Apple Macintosh microcomputers, introduced in 1985 by Aldus Corporation. This program set the standard for desktop publishing, a term coined by Paul Brainerd, president of Aldus.

page makeup program   A program for designing and producing professional-looking documents. Also called DESKTOP PUBLISHING program.

page makeup software   Programs used to compose page layouts in a DESKTOP PUBLISHING system.

page orientation   The way type or graphics are printed on a page, either landscape (horizontally) or portrait (vertically).

page-out   The process of swapping programs or data from the computer's main storage to disk storage.

page preview   A mode found on many page layout and word processing programs that shows a full-page view of how a page will look when printed out, including added elements such as headers, footers, and margins.

page printer   A printer in which an entire page of characters is composed and determined within the device prior to printing. The most common example is a LASER PRINTER.

page reader   A piece of optical scanning equipment that scans many lines of information, with the scanning pattern being determined by program control and/or control symbols intermixed with input data.

page recognition   A program that recognizes the content of a printed page that has been scanned into the computer.

pages   **(1)** The equal-size blocks into which a program is divided for storage. **(2)** The amount of text or graphic material displayed on a screen at one time.

page scan   The electromechanical process of scanning a page of paper to create a bit image of the page.

page skip A control character that causes a printer to skip the rest of the current page and move to the top of the next page.

page swapping The exchange of pages between main storage and auxiliary storage.

pagination (1) The electronic manipulation of graphics and blocks of type for the purpose of setting up an entire page. (2) The breakup of a printed report into units that correspond to pages. (3) The process of numbering or ordering pages.

paging (1) The process of keeping program pages on disk and calling them into memory as needed. (2) A technique for moving programs back and forth from real (internal) storage to virtual (auxiliary) storage.

paging rate In virtual storage systems, the average number of page-ins and page-outs per unit of time.

paint In computer graphics, the process of creating a graphic image (painting) on the display screen using a paint program and a mouse or graphics tablet.

paintbrush In computer paint programs, a tool used to sketch or paint brushstrokes of varying width and, in some cases, calligraphic or shadowing effects.

paintbrush software A program that generates drawings or illustrations.

paint file format A bit-mapped graphics file format found in paint programs such as DELUXE PAINT, MACPAINT, PC PAINTBRUSH, and SUPERPAINT.

painting (1) The process of displaying graphic data on a visual display screen. (2) In a paint program, filling a selected area with a solid color or pattern. (3) Displaying the trail of movements of a graphical input device.

Painting Effects An image editing/paint program for IBM-compatible microcomputer systems operating in MS-DOS. The program imports video or scanned images and can create different variations of the scanned or captured image.

paint packages   Graphics packages that are used to develop artistic creations on a computer system.

paint program   A program for creating and manipulating pixel images, as opposed to creating and manipulating object-oriented graphics. A paint program, because it treats a drawing as a group of dots (pixels), is particularly appropriate for freehand drawing. Paint programs create RASTER graphics images.

Palatino   A SERIF typeface included as a built-in font with many POSTSCRIPT laser printers.

palette   (1) The set of available colors or patterns in a computer graphics system. (2) In a paint program, a collection of drawing tools such as patterns, colors, different line widths, and brush shapes, from which the user can choose.

palmtop   A sublaptop portable computer weighing as little as one pound.

PAM   Acronym for **p**ulse **a**mplitude **m**odulation, in which the modulation wave is caused to amplitude-modulate a pulse carrier.

pan   (1) In computer graphics, to move (while viewing) to a different part of an image. (2) To move the cursor across a spreadsheet.

pane   The term for each of the windows that results from splitting a single window.

panel   See CONTROL PANEL.

panning   The movement of displayed graphic data across a visual display screen; moving a graphic image inside a frame to see its various sections.

Pantone Matching System (PMS)   Specific ink color specifications widely used in printing and color graphics. An extensive catalog of Pantone colors is available that describes about 500 colors, each assigned a unique PMS number. The Pantone color-selection system is supported by a variety of high-end illustration programs.

paper feed   A method by which paper is pulled through a printer. See FRICTION-FEED and TRACTOR-FEED MECHANISM.

paperless engineering The use of computer-aided design and drafting (CADD) systems to design products and buildings without the use of paper materials.

paper tape A continuous strip of paper in which holes are punched to record numerical and alphanumerical information for computer processing. Paper tape is used in older computer systems, and has been replaced by newer and more efficient storage methods.

paradigm The fundamental concept that underlies a possible complex structure; the central kernel within a concept. New paradigms result in new concepts. A popular buzzword among computer designers; the original Greek word meant merely an example or pattern.

Paradox A relational database management system for IBM-compatible microcomputers.

paragraph A set of one or more COBOL sentences making up a logical processing entity and preceded by a paragraph header or name.

paragraph assembly A process in which a document is assembled on a word processor from paragraphs stored on disks.

paragraph indention A function of a word processing package that allows an entire paragraph to be indented.

paragraph key In WORD PROCESSING, a control used to process text one paragraph at a time.

parallel (1) Handling all the elements of a word or message simultaneously. Contrast with SERIAL. (2) In computer graphics, a term that describes lines or planes in a graphics file that are an equal distance apart at every corresponding point.

parallel access The process of obtaining information from, or placing information into, storage where the time required for such access is dependent on the simultaneous transfer of all elements of a word from a given storage location. Also called direct access. Contrast with SERIAL ACCESS.

parallel adder   Adder that performs its operations by bringing in all digits simultaneously from each of the quantities involved. Contrast with SERIAL ADDER.

parallel circuit   An electric circuit in which the elements, branches, or components are connected between two points, with the two ends of each component connected to each other.

parallel computers   Computers that have multiple processors and are able to perform many mathematical operations and decisions at the same time. Unlike conventional supercomputers, which work on problems sequentially, massively parallel processing computers harness the computing power of hundreds or more microprocessors to tackle different parts of a problem at once.

parallel conversion   The process of changing to a new data processing system that involves running both the old and new systems simultaneously for a period of time. Also called parallel run. Contrast with DIRECT CONVERSION. Compare PHASED CONVERSION.

parallel device   A device that can perform two or more concurrent activities.

parallel form   The processing of data 8, 16, or 32 bits at a time.

parallel input/output   Data transmission in which each bit has its own wire. All the bits are transmitted simultaneously, as opposed to being sent one at a time (serially). Contrast with SERIAL INPUT/OUTPUT.

parallel interface   An equipment boundary where information is transferred simultaneously over a set of paths. Contrast with SERIAL INTERFACE.

parallel operation   The performance of several actions, usually of a similar nature, simultaneously, through the provision of individual, similar, or identical devices for each such action. Contrast with SERIAL OPERATION.

parallel port   The portion of a computer through which a parallel device (such as a printer) can communicate with the computer.

parallel printer A printer that receives information from the computer one character (letter, number, etc.) at a time through eight wires. Additional wires are used to exchange control signals. A parallel printer is designed to be connected to the computer's parallel port.

parallel processing (1) The technique by which all levels of a process are carried out simultaneously. Contrast with SERIAL PROCESSING. (2) A method of processing that can run only on a type of computer containing two or more processors running simultaneously. (3) A procedure that consists of the breaking down of a problem into separate components so that the computer program and the computer can work on each component simultaneously.

parallel processor A computer that is capable of performing multiple operations at the same time.

parallel projection The process of projecting an image from the three-dimensional view volume onto the two-dimensional graphics display with parallel projectors. Objects at any distance from the eye point maintain their apparent size under parallel projection.

parallel run The process of running a new system or program parallel with the old system to ensure a smooth transition and error-free conversion. Same as parallel conversion.

parallel storage device An AUXILIARY STORAGE DEVICE on which an entire byte or word is encoded in one operation.

parallel transmission In DATA COMMUNICATIONS, a method of data transfer in which all bits of a character are set simultaneously. Contrast with SERIAL TRANSMISSION.

parameter (1) Any arbitrary constant, especially one characteristic or even definitive of a given system. (2) A variable in an algebraic expression that temporarily assumes the properties of a constant. For example, in $y = mx + b$, m and b are parameters if either is treated as a constant in a family of lines.

parameterized class In OBJECT-ORIENTED PROGRAMMING, a class that serves as a template for other classes, in which the template may be parameterized by other classes, objects, and/or operations.

parametric Pertaining to the technique by which a line, curve, or surface is defined by equations based on some independent variable. Used often in COMPUTER-AIDED DESIGN systems.

parasitic virus A type of computer VIRUS that attaches itself to another program and is activated when that program is executed. A parasitic virus can either append itself to the end of a program (in which case the program functionality is normally preserved) or overwrite a part of the program (in which case the program functionality is destroyed).

PARC Acronym for **P**alo **A**lto **R**esearch **C**enter, an advanced research and development arm of Xerox Corporation, which developed many of the underlying techniques for SMALLTALK and GRAPHICAL USER INTERFACES.

parent A file whose contents are required, and in some cases are the only sources of information available, to create new records. See CHILD.

parent/child relationship The passing of information from one generation to the next. Older information (parent) is necessary to create new information (child).

parent directory The DIRECTORY above the directory currently in use.

parentheses A grouping symbol ( ). In arithmetic calculations, operations in parentheses are treated as entities with the highest priority.

parent node A node one level above the node being considered in a hierarchical database or network.

parity The characteristic of being odd or even.

parity bit The extra bit added to a byte, character, or word to ensure that there is always either an even number or odd number of bits, according to the logic of the system. If through a hardware failure a bit should be lost in transmission, its loss can be detected by checking the parity.

parity checking Automatic error detection by using checking bits along with the data bits. See PARITY BIT.

parity error An ERROR detected in a PARITY CHECK.

park To position a hard drive's read/write head so that the drive is not damaged while being transported.

Parkinson's Law The rule that a task expands to fill the time available for its completion.

parse To break input into smaller pieces so that a program can act upon the information.

parser A program or subroutine that analyzes and understands statements.

parsing (1) The process of separating statements into syntactic units. (2) Analyzing a character string and breaking it down into a group of more easily processed components.

particle systems A method of graphically producing the appearance of amorphous substances, such as smoke, fire, and clouds.

partitioning (1) Subdividing a computer storage area into smaller units allocated to specific jobs or tasks. (2) Breaking up a problem into subtasks.

parts explosion A drawing of all the pieces composing an assembly that illustrates the relation of the pieces to one another.

parts list A collection of the quantities, names, and numbers of all parts used to produce a manufactured item. Most CAD/CAM systems maintain and update such lists automatically during the course of a design and manufacturing process.

parts programmer A programmer who translates the physical explanation for machining a part into a series of mathematical steps and then codes computer instructions for those steps. See APT and NUMERICAL CONTROL.

party-line A large number of devices connected to a single line originating in the central processing unit.

Pascal A high-level structured programming language that has gained wide acceptance as a tool for both applications programming and system development. Pascal was developed in the early 1970s by Niklaus Wirth and was named after the French mathematician Blaise Pascal (1623–1662). The language provides a flexible set of control structures and data types to permit orderly, top-down program design and development. Pascal is used extensively in the educational field for teaching programming principles and practices. See TURBO PASCAL.

Pascaline A mechanical calculating machine developed by Blaise Pascal in the 1600s.

pass **(1)** A complete input, processing, and output cycle in the execution of a computer program. **(2)** The scanning of source code by a compiler or assembler.

passive device A device that passes signals without altering them.

passive graphics A computer graphics operation that transpires automatically and without operator intervention.

password A special word, code, or symbol that must be presented to the computer system to gain access to its resources. Used for identification and security purposes.

paste To place information previously cut from a document into a new position. With some computer systems, areas of text or graphics may be cut from a document, saved, and later pasted into another document. See CUT AND PASTE.

pasteboard In DESKTOP PUBLISHING, the work area displayed on a screen upon which art and text will be placed.

patch **(1)** A section of coding inserted into a program to alter it or correct a mistake. **(2)** A temporary electrical connection. **(3)** In computer graphics, a piece of curvilinear surface, typically with three or four sides. These are attached together at their edges with at least first-order continuity to form complex 3-D surfaces. **(4)** To modify a computer system by adding post-installation enhancements.

patching **(1)** A makeshift technique for modifying a program or correcting programming errors by changing the object code of the program, usually to avoid recompiling or reassembling the program. **(2)** Making temporary patches to hardware.

patent   The legal protection granted by the Patent Office for exclusive use of an original idea or invention.

path   **(1)** A route from one point to another. **(2)** In computer graphics, an accumulation of line segments or curves, to be filled or overwritten with text. **(3)** The hierarchy of files through which control passes to find a particular file.

PATH   A DOS and OS/2 command that tells the OPERATING SYSTEM which directories to search.

path name   The name that identifies a file and the path DOS and OS/2 operating systems must take to locate it.

pattern fill   A graphics technique that involves creating a pattern by drawing a pattern element and placing it into temporary storage, so that it can later be accessed and used for filling a bounded area.

pattern generation   Transforming CAD integrated circuit design information into a simpler format (rectangles only or trapezoids only) suitable for use by a photo- or electron-beam machine in producing a reticle.

pattern matching   The search for similarities between symbolic expressions; i.e., matching a pattern with images or templates in a database.

pattern recognition   **(1)** The recognition of forms, shapes, or configurations by automatic means. A subfield of ARTIFICIAL INTELLIGENCE. **(2)** The use of a computer to identify patterns. **(3)** The use of statistical techniques and templates to process and classify patterns of data.

pause   To temporarily stop.

payroll   A list of employees and the amount each is paid by an organization.

PBX   Abbreviation for **p**rivate **b**ranch e**x**change, a switching station that an organization acquires for its own use.

PC PERSONAL COMPUTER, POCKET COMPUTER, PRINTED CIRCUIT and PROGRAM COUNTER. The most common use of PC is in reference to IBM Corporation's Personal Computer line. For example, *PC-compatible* refers to a computer that can run the same programs as IBM PC or IBM PS/2 microcomputers.

PCB Abbreviation for PRINTED CIRCUIT BOARD, the plastic board into which a computer's various electronic components are soldered. These are linked by thin interconnecting wires printed on its surface.

PC compatibility The compatibility of a microcomputer with the popular IBM Personal Computer and IBM PS/2. Many levels of compatibility are possible.

PC-DOS™ Acronym for **P**ersonal **C**omputer–**D**isk **O**perating **S**ystem, IBM Corporation's trade name for its version of MS-DOS, an operating system developed and licensed by Microsoft Corporation for computers that use Intel Corporation microprocessors. There is effectively no difference between PC-DOS and MS-DOS.

P-channel MOS (PMOS) Relatively old metallic oxide semiconductor technology for large-scale integration devices. See PMOS. Contrast with N-CHANNEL MOS.

PCL Abbreviation for **p**rinter **c**ontrol **l**anguage, a page description language recognized by Hewlett-Packard laser printers.

PCM Abbreviation for PLUG-COMPATIBLE MANUFACTURER, a business that makes computer equipment that can be plugged into existing computer systems without requiring additional hardware or software interfaces.

p-code A method of translating a source code to an intermediate code, called p-code, by means of a compiler, and then using a special p-code interpreter on a host machine to obtain an executable object code. Several versions of PASCAL use p-code.

PC Paint A popular painting program for microcomputers, developed by Mouse Systems Corporation.

PC Paintbrush™ A popular paint program for IBM-compatible micro-computers. Virtually every paint program for IBM-compatible micro-computers is in some way a subset of Paintbrush. The industry standard PCX graphic format is a product of Paintbrush.

PC Tools A SOFTWARE PACKAGE of file and disk management utility programs for Apple Macintosh computers and IBM personal computers and compatibles.

PCX A bit-mapped graphics file format, originally developed for the PC PAINTBRUSH paint program and now used by many other programs.

PDL Abbreviation for PAGE DESCRIPTION LANGUAGE, a standardized coding system that presents all the elements on a page, i.e., type, images and graphics, using the same descriptive metaphors. Common PDLs are POSTSCRIPT, Apple Computer's QUICKDRAW, and Hewlett-Packard's HPGL. PostScript has become the default standard for most desktop systems and PostScript interpreters are designed to convert the others to PostScript.

PDM Abbreviation for **p**ulse **d**uration **m**odulation, pulse time modulation in which the duration of a pulse is varied. Contrast with PAM and PPM.

PEEK A computer-language instruction that allows the programmer to look at (peek at) any location in a computer's programmable memory. See POKE.

peer-to-peer architecture A LOCAL AREA NETWORK with no file server, in which each workstation has equal capabilities and access to the public files of all other workstations.

pel The picture element. See PIXEL.

pencil tool A freehand drawing tool found in all popular paint programs.

pen plotter See PLOTTER and DRUM PLOTTER. Contrast with ELECTROSTATIC PLOTTER.

perform To execute instructions in a computer.

performance A major factor in determining the total productivity of a system. Largely determined by a combination of availability, throughput, and response time.

performance, graphic   The degree to which visual graphics achieves its specified result(s). Useful measurement criteria include display screen resolution, picture element resolution, display writing speed, internal intelligence, working area, accuracy, and precision.

performance monitor   A program that keeps track of service levels being delivered by a computer system.

perfory   The detachable perforated strips on the two sides of fanfold computer paper.

perfs   Perforations in paper to facilitate removing pin-feed edges and tearing continuous paper into separate pages.

periodic report   A report that provides information to users on a regular basis, such as weekly, monthly, or yearly.

peripheral equipment   Input/output units and auxiliary storage units of a computer system, attached by cables to the central processing unit. Used to get data in and data out, and to act as a reservoir for large amounts of data that cannot be held in the central processing unit at one time. The LASER PRINTER, HARD DISK, and OPTICAL SCANNER are examples of peripherals.

peripheral equipment operator   An operator who assists the main operator by mounting and demounting disk packs and tapes, labeling outputs, and operating the various input/output devices as directed.

peripheral slots   Empty slots built into the housing of some computers so that printed circuit cards can be added to increase capabilities without hardware modification; motherboard sockets into which circuit boards can be plugged.

permanent storage   Same as STORAGE.

persistence   (1) In computer graphics, the rate of decay of luminance of a CRT display after the stimulus is removed. In essence, the "staying power" of a lighted phosphor to dim more slowly. (2) In OBJECT-ORIENTED

PROGRAMMING, the permanence of an object, particularly relevant in the context of object-oriented databases, which maintain a distinction between objects created only for the duration of execution and those intended for permanent storage. Persistence is one of the fundamental elements of the object model. **(3)** In ARTIFICIAL INTELLIGENCE, the length of time data are kept during a program run.

personal budgeting package   A group of computer programs that includes checkbook accounting and home budget planning.

personal computer   The smallest and least expensive class of computer, designed for use by one user at a time. Abbreviated PC. Also called microcomputer.

personal computing   The use of a personal computer by individuals for applications such as entertainment, home management, education, word processing, and family business.

personal identification number (PIN)   The security number that computer systems sometimes require before a user can access the system or before a point-of-sale terminal user can enter or receive information. Commonly used with AUTOMATIC TELLER MACHINES.

personal information manager (PIM)   A computer program that helps a user organize personal information, with features such as appointment calendars and notebooks.

personalized form letter   A computer-generated form letter produced by a word processing system or a merge-print program.

perspective view   In computer graphics, a display method by which an illusion of depth is achieved on a two-dimensional surface and by which the space depicted is organized from one point of view.

PERT   Acronym for **p**rogram **e**valuation and **r**eview **t**echnique, a management technique for control of large-scale, long-term projects involving analysis of the time frame required for each step in a process and the relationships of the completion of each step to activity in succeeding steps. See CRITICAL PATH METHOD. Compare GERT.

PERT chart   A diagram representing the interdependencies of work elements against time, typically shown graphically as circles and connecting lines.

Pet computer   A low-cost, versatile computer from Commodore Business Machines, Inc., introduced in 1977. The Pet 4032 was designed for personal, educational, and scientific applications. It was one of the earliest personal computers, weighed 46 pounds, and featured 32K bytes of RAM and 18K bytes of ROM.

petri nets   A popular and useful model for the representation of systems with concurrency or parallelism.

PFS: First Choice   A program that combines five powerful business productivity tools. It is an integrated software program that includes word processing, a database manager, a spreadsheet program, a business graphics program, and an electronics communications program.

PFS: First Publisher   An entry-level desktop publishing program for people who want to create newsletters, memos, flyers, and reports. PFS: First Publisher directly reads files from most popular word processing programs and supports a wide variety of printers.

PGA   Abbreviation for PROFESSIONAL GRAPHICS ADAPTER, a type of display adapter for IBM-compatible microcomputers.

phantom disk   A chip that lets the computer regard part of its memory as another disk drive.

phased conversion   A method of system implementation in which the old information system is gradually replaced by the new one. Compare PARALLEL CONVERSION. Contrast with DIRECT CONVERSION.

PHIGS   Acronym for **P**rogrammer's **H**ierarchical **I**nteractive **G**raphics **S**ystem, an international standard three-dimensional graphics library consisting of a graphical tool for application programmers. PHIGS is designed for easy portability to many graphics systems.

phonemes   The distinct sounds that make up human speech (speech utterances such as *lk*, *cb*, and *sb*); the smallest components of speech. The basic sounds of human speech.

phonemics   Rules describing variations in pronunciation that occur when spoken words are run together.

phonetic system   A system that uses data based on voice information (phonemes) to produce sounds that emulate speech.

Phong shading   In computer graphics, a sophisticated smooth shading algorithm originated by Phong Bui-tuong and best known for its ability to render precise, realistic specular highlights. Phong shading achieves excellent realism by calculating the amount of light on the object at tiny points across the entire surface. Each pixel representing the image is given its own color based on the lighting model applied at that point.

phonology   The analysis of sounds that are synthesized to produce speech.

phosphor   A rare earth material used to coat the inside face of cathode ray tubes; it holds the light generated by a monitor's electron guns. Each dot on the screen is actually a phosphor that glows for a given length of time. The dots are used to create an image.

phosphor burn-in   What occurs when the same image is left on the screen for extended periods of time, burning itself in so that the image can be seen even when the monitor is turned off.

photocomposition   The application of electronic processing to the preparation of print. Involves the specification and setting of type, and its production by a photographic process. In DESKTOP PUBLISHING, the use of laser printers and imagesetters to accomplish the same ends.

photoelectric devices   Devices that give an electrical signal in response to visible, infrared, or ultraviolet radiation.

photolithographic process   The procedure used to print the mask pattern of integrated circuits on a silicon wafer.

PhotoMac   A Macintosh graphics program from Avalon Development that is designed for manipulating and color separating scanned images. The program features many powerful separation controls. Like all color separation programs, PhotoMac produces four separate versions of a page.

photomask A procedure similar to the production of a photographic negative used to imprint an electronic circuit on a microchip.

photonic chip A chip that uses light instead of electricity for transmitting information.

photonic integrated circuit A system that uses light as well as electrons to process information.

photonics The science of building machine circuits that use light instead of electricity.

Photon Paint A paint program intended for Macintosh II computer systems equipped with a color card.

photo-optic memory Memory that uses an optical medium for storage. For example, a laser might be used to record on photographic film. See OPTICAL DISC.

photo-pattern generation The production of an integrated circuit mask by exposing a pattern of overlapping or adjacent rectangular areas.

photo plotter An output device that generates high-precision artwork masters photographically for printed circuit board design and integrated circuit masks.

photorealism The process of creating images that are as close to photographic quality as possible. In computer graphics, photorealism requires powerful computers and highly sophisticated software and is heavily mathematical.

photoresist The process, used in etching semiconductor devices, of selectively removing the oxidized surface of a silicon wafer by masking the part that is to be retained.

Photoshop™ A powerful and versatile 24-bit image processing program for the Apple Macintosh computer that can be used as a paint, pre-press, color correction, and darkroom system. Designers can work with scanned photos, slides, or electronic artwork, or create original graphics using a full range of filters, painting, drawing, and selection tools.

phototypesetter   A computer-controlled device that converts text into professional-quality type. A printer similar to a laser printer, but capable of resolutions over 2,000 dpi. See IMAGESETTER.

physical design   The design by which data is kept on storage devices and how it is accessed.

physical format   The general pattern of magnetic pulses and tracks on a disk or other medium, ignoring what those pulses mean when translated into digital 1's and 0's. Two computers using the same physical format can read each other's disks, but if their logical formats are not the same, they may not be able to make sense of the information.

physical record   A collection of LOGICAL RECORDS. Also called block.

physical schema   The description of how data are physically stored on a disk.

physical security   Guards, badges, locks, alarm systems, and other measures to control access to the equipment in a computer center.

pi   The ratio of the circumference of any circle to its diameter, approximately equal to 3.14159265358979 ....

PIC   Acronym for **pic**ture file format, a graphics file format used by some spreadsheet and graphing programs for IBM-compatible microcomputers.

pica   **(1)** A unit of measure used in typography. A pica is one-sixth of an inch, or equivalent to 12 points. **(2)** A character font that has a print density of 10 characters per inch.

picking   A feature of a graphics library that enables an application user to select primitives and objects with a pointing device.

picking device   An input device, such as a light pen, mouse, or joystick, used to enter data on a display screen.

pico   Prefix meaning one-trillionth.

picocomputer   A computer capable of processing data in trillionths of a second.

picosecond   One-trillionth of a second; one-thousandth of a nanosecond; abbreviated psec.

PICT   Acronym for **pict**ure file format, a black-and-white object/bit-mapped format used by many programs for the Apple Macintosh line of microcomputers and by some programs for IBM-compatible microcomputers.

PICT2   Acronym for **pict**ure file format **2**, a graphics file format used in many programs for the Apple Macintosh line of microcomputers that can support both black-and-white and color images.

pictorial   That having to do with the art of painting and drawing.

picture   In computer graphics, the display image of an area on a document.

picture graph   A bar graph that uses symbols instead of bars.

picture processing   (**1**) In computer graphics, a method for processing pictorial information by a computer system. Involves inputting graphic information into a computer system, storing it, working with it, and outputting it to an output device. (**2**) In ARTIFICIAL INTELLIGENCE, the transformation of an input image into a second image, which has important properties that will help in better understanding the scene.

Picture Publisher™   A graphics program that allows working with scanned images. The user can adjust contrast, brightness, gray map, and other parameters and edit the image on a pixel-by-pixel basis.

pie chart   A type of graphical representation of information; a charting technique used to represent portions of a whole.

piezoelectric   The property of some crystals that undergo mechanical stress when subjected to voltages, or that produce a voltage when subjected to mechanical stress.

piggyback board   A small printed circuit board mounted on a larger circuit board to add additional features to the larger circuit board.

piggyback file   A file capable of having records added at the end, without having to be entirely recopied.

PIL   Acronym for **P**ublishing **I**nterchange **L**anguage, an Apple Macintosh file format that lets applications exchange page-description information.

PILOT   A textually based computer language originally designed as an author language for computer-assisted instruction. Also used for teaching computer programming to beginners.

pilot system   The act of trying a new computer system in one area only, rather than on a wider range of activities.

PIM   Acronym for PERSONAL INFORMATION MANAGER.

pin   The point on a component, printed circuit board, or logic element where electrical connections can be made.

PIN   Acronym for PERSONAL IDENTIFICATION NUMBER.

pin compatible   A term describing chips and devices that perform identical functions and can be substituted for one another. The devices use the same pins for the same input/output signals.

pin-feed   A paper-feed system that relies on a pin-studded roller to draw paper, punched with matching sprocket holes, into a printer. See TRAC-TOR-FEED MECHANISM. Contrast with FRICTION-FEED.

pingpong   To alternate two or more storage devices so that processing can take place on a virtually endless set of files.

pins   The small metal connectors on a DIP that fit into sockets on a printed circuit board.

pipeline processing   **(1)** The overlapping operating cycle function used to increase the speed of computers. Involves decomposing a computer instruction into parts so it can be executed simultaneously. **(2)** The connection of processors so that the output of one processor becomes the input of another.

piracy   Either theft, as in the appropriation of a computer design or program, or unauthorized distribution and use of a computer program.

pitch   The density of characters on a printed line, usually expressed in terms of characters per inch; for example, 10 pitch means that 10 characters are printed in every inch.

pixel   Abbreviation for picture element, a picture cell; a single dot on the computer display screen. The visual display screen is divided into rows and columns of tiny dots, squares, or cells, each of which is a pixel, the smallest unit on the display screen grid that can be stored, displayed, or addressed.

pixel graphics   A technique for representing a picture image as a matrix of dots.

pixel image   The representation of a color graphic in a computer's memory.

pixel operations   (1) Arithmetic and logical operations performed for image modification on pixel data, which is stored as numbers that are converted into color or other information. (2) The process of modifying a pixel value for a specific purpose.

PixelPaint Professional™   A popular Apple Macintosh paint program.

pixmap   The array of values in the frame buffer for a given picture.

PLA   Abbreviation for PROGRAMMABLE LOGIC ARRAY, an alternative to ROM that uses a standard logic network programmed to perform a specific function. Implemented in either MOS or bipolar circuits. See FPLA.

plaintext   The opposite of CIPHERTEXT. It comprises text or data in normally readable rather than encrypted form.

planar   (1) In computer graphics, a term applied to objects lying within a plane. (2) In the fabrication of chips, a processing method used to create silicon-based transistors.

planar board   The motherboard of an IBM PS/2 personal computer.

plane   Any flat or level surface.

plane figures   Any set of points in a plane. Some common plane figures are angles, triangles, rectangles, and circles.

PLANIT   Acronym for **P**rogramming **Lan**guage for **I**nteractive **T**eaching, a language designed for use with computer-assisted instruction systems.

plansheet   Same as SPREADSHEET or worksheet.

plasma display panel   A type of VDT utilizing trapped neon/argon gas. The image is created by turning on points in a matrix (energized grid of wires) comprising the display surface. The high-resolution image is steady, long-lasting, bright, and flicker-free; selective erasing is possible.

plasticity   The degree of flexibility available in ARTIFICIAL INTELLIGENCE programs.

plate   A thin, flexible sheet of metal, paper, or plastic used in offset printing. It contains a photographic reproduction of the page being printed.

platen   A backing, commonly cylindrical, against which printing mechanisms strike to produce an impression, such as the roller in a printer against which the keys strike.

platform   (**1**) The COMPUTER HARDWARE in a COMPUTER SYSTEM. (**2**) A SOFTWARE library. (**3**) The basic hardware or software standard on which a computer system is based.

platform independence   The ability of a LOCAL AREA NETWORK to link computers with different platforms, such as Apple Macintosh and IBM personal computers.

PLATO   Acronym for **P**rogrammed **L**ogic for **A**utomatic **T**eaching **O**perations, a computer-based instructional system developed by Donald Bitzer and marketed by Control Data Corporation. PLATO typically runs on large computer systems and combines graphics and text with touch-screen display terminals to provide course instruction in many different disciplines.

platonic objects Figures constructed from regular polygons, such as tetrahedrons, cubes, octahedrons, icosahedrons, and dodecahedrons.

platter That part of a hard disk drive that actually stores the information; a round, flat, metallic plate covered on both surfaces with a brown magnetic substance. See HARD DISK.

PLB Acronym for **P**icture **L**evel **B**enchmark, a graphics system perform-ance indicator that measures frames per second, or the length of time it takes to draw a picture on the display screen. The PLB is intended to provide a consistent method of measuring graphics performance.

PL/C A version of the PL/I programming language designed to be used in an educational environment.

PL/I A high-level, general-purpose language designed to process both scientific and business applications. Contains many of the best features of FORTRAN, COBOL, ALGOL, and other languages, as well as a number of facilities not available in previous languages.

PL/M A high-level programming language used to program microcom-puters, developed by Intel Corporation, that can fully command a micro-computer to produce efficient run-time object code.

plot To diagram, draw, or map with a plotter; to create an image by drawing a series of lines.

plotter An output device that draws images with ink pens. A plotter draws images as a series of point-to-point lines.

plotting a curve Locating points from coordinates and connecting these points with a curve that approximates or resembles the actual curve that pictures the relationship existing between variables.

PLT Abbreviation for plotter, a peripheral device for providing output of graphs and technical drawings.

plug The connector on a cable that goes to a jack on a part of the system.

plug compatible Any peripheral device that requires no interface modi-fication to be linked directly to another manufacturer's computer system.

plug compatible manufacturer (PCM)   A business that makes computer equipment that can be plugged into existing computer systems without requiring additional hardware or software interfaces.

PMOS   Acronym for P-CHANNEL MOS, the oldest type of MOS circuit, in which the electrical current consists of a flow of positive charges. Contrast with N-CHANNEL MOS.

PMS   Abbreviation for PANTONE MATCHING SYSTEM.

PN   Abbreviation for POLISH NOTATION.

poaching   Accessing files or program listings in search of information to which the user is not entitled.

pocket computer   A portable, battery-operated, hand-held computer that can be programmed in BASIC to perform a wide number of applications. Able to process small amounts of data under the control of complex stored programs. Pocket computers can be plugged into personal computers for data transfer.

point   (1) A typographic measurement equaling approximately ¹⁄₇₂ inch. Abbreviated pt. (2) The smallest unit of graphic information, representing a single location on a coordinate system.

point and click   To position the cursor over an object displayed on the screen (point) and press the mouse or pointing device to select it (click).

pointer   (1) An indicator on a screen that shows where the next user-computer interaction will be. Also called cursor. (2) An address or other indication of one storage location as held in another storage location. Used in a network database to point to related records in the same or different files. (3) A device such as a mouse or tablet stylus that moves the cursor on the screen. (4) The additional connections in a network database between parent nodes and child nodes. (5) A variable that holds the address of another memory object.

pointer tool   A tool used in layout and drawing programs to select objects or an entire block of text. It is usually represented by an on-screen arrow.

point identification   The complete description of a graphics point, including its coordinate location and any special processing functions implied by it.

pointillism   A painting procedure in which dots or spots of color are used to create colors and values by optical mixing. In a computer graphics system, the paintbrush tool, found in most paint programs, can be used to produce the pointillism type of art form.

pointing device   An INPUT DEVICE, such as a MOUSE or GRAPHICS TABLET, used to move the CURSOR on the DISPLAY SCREEN.

point-of-sale terminal (POS)   A device used in retail establishments to record sales information in a form that can be input directly into a computer. This intelligent terminal is used to capture data in retail stores, often with the capability of verifying the creditworthiness of the customer.

point set curve   A curve defined by a series of short lines drawn between points.

point size   The vertical measurement of type, roughly equivalent to the distance between the highest ascender and lowest descender, plus a small bit of breathing room on top and bottom.

point-to-point line   A communications system configuration consisting of a direct line between the host computer and a remote terminal. Either leased lines or switched lines may be used. Contrast with MULTIDROP LINE.

Poisson theory   The mathematical method for estimating the number of lines needed to handle a given amount of data communications traffic.

POKE   A computer-language instruction used to place a value (poke) into any location in the computer's programmable memory. See PEEK.

Pol   Abbreviation for PROCEDURE-ORIENTED LANGUAGE or PROBLEM-ORIENTED LANGUAGE.

polar   Pertaining to a situation in which binary 1 is represented by current flow in one direction and binary 0 by current flow in the opposite direction. Contrast with POSITIVE TRUE LOGIC.

polar coordinates A graphic system for specifying the location of a point by reference to an angle and a distance from a fixed point. Contrast with CARTESIAN COORDINATE SYSTEM.

polarizing filter An accessory for terminal screens to reduce glare.

Polish notation (PN) The logical notation for a series of arithmetic operations in which no grouping symbol is used. A form of a prefix notation developed by Polish logician Jan Lukasiewicz in 1929. Contrast with REVERSE POLISH NOTATION.

polling A communications control method used by some computer/terminal systems in which a host station asks many devices attached to a common transmission medium in turn whether they have information to send. Contrast with ADDRESSING.

polygon A multisided object.

polygon mesh A portion of a MESH model surface constructed from polygons.

polyline In computer graphics, a line consisting of multiple connected segments.

polymorphic tweening An animation technique that, based on information about its starting and ending shapes, creates the necessary "in-between" steps to change one object into another.

polymorphism (1) In OBJECT-ORIENTED PROGRAMMING, the ability of the same message to be interpreted differently when received by different objects. (2) The state of having many shapes. (3) The ability of a variable to be set equal to a variety of structures.

polyphase sort An external tape sort used for six or fewer tapes.

pooler A device for consolidating and/or converting key entry data into a form acceptable to the main computer.

pop To pull or retrieve data from the top of a program pushdown stack. The stack pointer is decremented to address the last word pushed on the stack. The contents of this location are moved to one of the accumulators or to another register. Also called PULL. Contrast with PUSH.

pop erase   A method for erasing graphic entities that clears parts of the screen in a single action, so that all dots appear to turn off simultaneously.

pop instruction   The computer instruction that executes the POP operation.

popping   In PROGRAMMING, removing data from a stack.

populate   To fill the sockets of a circuit board. A fully populated circuit board is one that contains all the devices it can hold.

populated board   A circuit board that contains all its electronic components. Contrast with UNPOPULATED BOARD.

pop-up menu   A menu that appears on-screen anywhere other than in the standard menu bar location.

port   That portion of a computer through which a peripheral device may communicate; a plug-in/socket on the back of the computer for connecting cables for peripherals.

portability   The ease with which a program can be moved from one computer environment to another. Many programs written in high-level languages may be used on different machines and are therefore portable.

portable computer   A self-contained computer that can be easily carried and moved. Compared to desktop models, it has limited expansion slots and disk capacity.

portable program   SOFTWARE that can be used on compatible computer systems.

Portfolio   A professional illustrative graphics program for IBM-compatible microcomputers. Aside from an enhanced list of the usual drawing tools, Portfolio has a raster- and vector-based system, a full-featured text editor with scalable fonts and spelling checker, a feature to import files directly from word processors, an autotrace feature, and templates of 2-D and 3-D charts and graphs.

port protection device   A black box between a computer system and incoming telephone lines that protects the system from unauthorized access.

portrait   An orientation in which the data is printed across the narrow side of the form.

portrait mode   A video monitor display screen whose height is greater than its width, similar to a portrait painting. Contrast with LANDSCAPE MODE.

portrait monitor   A monitor with a screen shape higher than it is wide. A popular type of monitor in desktop publishing systems.

POS   Abbreviation for POINT-OF-SALE TERMINAL.

positional notation   A method for expressing a quantity by using two or more figures wherein the successive right-to-left figures are to be interpreted as coefficients of ascending integer powers of the radix. For example, in the decimal numeral 634, which has a radix of 10, the value is $4 \times 10^0 + 3 \times 10^1 + 6 \times 10^2$.

position stat   A copy of a halftone that can be placed on a mechanical to illustrate positioning and cropping of the image.

positive true logic   A logic system in which a lower voltage represents a bit value of 0 and a higher voltage represents a bit value of 1. Contrast with POLAR.

possibility theory   The theory on which FUZZY LOGIC is based.

POS systems   Systems, currently used by department stores and supermarkets, in which the cash register is actually a special-purpose computer terminal that can monitor and record transactions directly in the store's data files for inventory control, check on credit card validity, and perform other data handling functions. See POINT-OF-SALE TERMINAL.

post   To enter a unit of information on a record.

post edit   To edit output data from a previous computation.

posterization   A photographic effect in which the number of tones and colors in an image is reduced to achieve a poster-like effect. The same effect can be achieved in computer graphics by reassigning color values, substituting one color scale for another.

posterize   In computer graphics, to make an image starker by rounding tonal or color values to a smaller number of possible values.

postfix notation   An arithmetic notation system wherein the operator follows the operands. For example, the addition of 5 and 3 would be expressed as 53 + . REVERSE POLISH NOTATION is a form of postfix notation.

post-implementation review   The evaluation of a system after it has been in use for several months. Compare SYSTEM FOLLOW-UP.

post mortem   The analysis of an operation after its completion.

post-mortem dump   A storage dump taken at the end of the execution of a program. Contrast with SNAPSHOT DUMP.

PostScript   A proprietary language developed by Adobe Corporation to tell a printer what to print on a particular page. PostScript's chief benefit is its device independence, which means that the same file can be printed on printers of varying resolutions.

PostScript font   A font defined in terms of the POSTSCRIPT page-description language rules and intended to be printed on a PostScript-compatible printer.

PostScript laser printer   A laser printer that includes the processing circuitry needed to decode and interpret printing instructions phrased in POSTSCRIPT, a page-description language widely used in DESKTOP PUBLISHING. The printer converts the PostScript instructions (sent by the computer) into the dots that make up the printed image.

PostScript Level 2   An updated version of the PostScript language that adds support for color, forms handling, data compression, and many other features.

post-test loop   A PROGRAM LOOP in which the loop termination decision comes after the body of the loop.

posture   The slant of the characters in a font.

potentiometer A device used to develop electrical output signals proportional to mechanical movement.

power The symbolic representation of the number of times a number is multiplied by itself. The process is called exponentiation. 4 to the power of 3 means $4 \times 4 \times 4$ and is written 4^3.

power amplifying circuit An electronic circuit that converts an input AC voltage into an output DC voltage. Compare POWER SUPPLY.

power down **(1)** To turn off a computer or peripheral device. **(2)** The steps a computer may take to preserve the state of the processor and to prevent damage to it or to connected peripherals when the power fails or is shut off. Contrast with POWER UP.

power fail/restart The facility that enables a computer to return to normal operation after a power failure.

powerful As a description of hardware, faster, larger, and able to accomplish more work than comparable machines. Software is considered powerful if it is efficient and provides a wide range of options.

power line filter A device that plugs into a power source and a computer system to smooth out voltage fluctuations that could damage the system.

power manager A device that controls the power going to several other devices in a computer system.

power on To turn the power switch to the ON position or otherwise supply electric current to a device. Also called POWER UP.

PowerPoint A presentation graphics software program.

power supply A device that provides power to electronic equipment such as computers and peripherals. Power supplies are rated by wattage; the higher the wattage, the stronger the power supply.

power surge A sudden, brief increase in the flow of current that can cause problems in the proper operation of computer equipment.

power up   (1) To turn on a computer or peripheral device. (2) The steps taken by a computer processor when the power is turned on or restored after a power failure. The processor and peripherals are INITIALIZED so that program execution may be started. Contrast with POWER DOWN.

power user   A computer user who has gone beyond the beginning and intermediate stages of computer use to exploit the advanced features of application programs.

pph   Abbreviation for **p**ages **p**er **h**our.

ppm   (1) Abbreviation for **p**ulse **p**osition **m**odulation, in which the value of each instantaneous sample of the wave modulates the position in time of a pulse. (2) Abbreviation for **p**ages **p**er **m**inute, a measure of output for printing devices, i.e., the number of printed pages output per minute.

pragmatics   (1) The investigation of the relationship between symbols and the users of those symbols. (2) The field of linguistics that copes with the ambiguities found in language. (3) The part of NATURAL LANGUAGE PROCESSING that attempts to ascertain the intent of the dialogue and give a reasonable reply.

precedence   Rules that state which operators should be executed first in an expression.

precision   The degree of exactness with which a quantity is stated. A calculation may have more precision that accuracy; for example, the true value of π is accurate only to about five places.

precompiler   A computer program that processes the source code of another computer program immediately before that program is to be compiled.

predefined function   A standard mathematical procedure available to the user for inclusion in a program.

predefined process   (1) A process identified only by name and defined elsewhere. (2) A CLOSED SUBROUTINE.

predefined process symbol   A rectangular flowcharting symbol used to represent a subroutine.

predicate   Another name for keyword in certain programming languages, such as PROLOG and STRUCTURED QUERY LANGUAGE.

prediction expert system   A type of EXPERT SYSTEM whose conclusion is the prediction of a future event.

predictive reports   Business reports used for tactical and strategic decision making.

pre-edit   See EDIT.

prefix notation   A method of forming mathematical expressions in which each operator precedes its operands. For example, the expression "x plus y multiplied by z" would be represented by + xy × z, and the addition of 5 and 3 would be expressed as + 53. POLISH NOTATION is a form of prefix notation.

p-register   The program-counter register in which the location of the current instruction is kept.

preliminary study   The first phase of the systems file cycle. It involves defining the problem, suggesting alternative systems, and preparing a short report.

preprinted forms   Forms that can contain computer-produced output but that enter a computer system with headings and identifying information already imprinted. Commonly used in producing external reports.

preprocessed display   A DISPLAY on which processing is done before being shown.

preprocessing   (1) The steps that may be used on an image between the capturing of the image and any analysis. Typically, preprocessing might include contrast enhancement, averaging, and so on. (2) Processing for a display that occurs before the display is shown.

preprocessor   A program that performs some preliminary processing, such as conversion, formatting, condensing, or other functions on input data prior to further processing.

prescriptive language   A computer language that relies on the programmer to provide explicit procedures to compute an answer. PASCAL and C are prescriptive languages. Also called procedural languages.

presentation graphics   High-quality, professional-looking business graphics used in proposals, business presentations, manuals, and other business-related documents; an easy-to-understand display of numerical information. Presentation graphics are visually appealing and easily understood by an audience.

presentation graphics package   A productivity software package used to prepare bar charts, line charts, pie charts, and so forth.

presentation graphics program   An application program designed to create and enhance charts and graphs so that they are visually appealing and easily understood by an audience.

Presentation Manager   The graphical user interface provided in OS/2, jointly developed by Microsoft Corporation and IBM Corporation. Running on the OS-2 operating system, Presentation Manager brings to IBM-compatible microcomputers many of the graphical user interface features associated with the Apple Macintosh computer—pull-down menus, multiple on-screen windows, desktop accessories, and multiple on-screen typefaces.

preset   To establish an initial condition, such as control values of a loop or initial values in index registers. See INITIALIZE.

press   To push down and hold the button on a mouse. See CLICK.

pressure-sensitive keyboard   A keyboard constructed of two thin plastic sheets coated with a circuit made of electrically conductive ink. An economical, flat keyboard used in several older, low-priced microcomputers.

pressure-sensitive pen   The stylus used with a DIGITIZER. Contains a pressure transducer that detects and transmits writing pressure as Z-axis data.

PRESTEL   A commercial videotex service in Great Britain.

pretest loop   A PROGRAM LOOP in which the termination decision comes before the body of the loop.

preventive maintenance   Maintenance done on a scheduled basis to prevent major problems. Involves cleaning and adjusting the equipment as well as testing it under both normal and marginal conditions. Contrast with CORRECTIVE MAINTENANCE.

preview   In WORD PROCESSING, to display a formatted document on the screen to see exactly what the printed page will look like.

primary cluster   A buildup of table entries around a single table location.

primary colors   A set of colors from which all others can be derived, but which cannot be produced from each other. The additive primaries (light) are blue, green, and red. The subtractive primaries (colorant) are cyan, magenta, and yellow. The physiological primaries are the pairs red/green, yellow/blue, and black/white.

primary key   A unique field for a record, used to sort records for processing or to locate a particular record within a file.

primary storage   The electronic circuitry that temporarily holds data and program instruction needed by the CPU. Also called memory, primary memory, main storage, internal storage, and main memory.

Prime Computer, Inc.   A company founded in 1972 for the purpose of manufacturing minicomputers. In 1973, Prime announced their first minicomputer, the 200 system. Over the next two decades, they introduced several minicomputers, many developed using innovative technology.

primer   An elementary instruction manual.

prime shift   A work shift that coincides with the normal business hours of an organization, as opposed to a swing shift or graveyard shift.

priming read   The first READ statement in a program.

primitive   (1)   One of the basic building blocks of a language; in the English language, individual words are primitives. In this vein, keywords in BASIC or Pascal may be considered as primitives. **(2)** In computer graphics, the most basic graphic entities available, such as points, line segments, and characters. Primitives are the elements from which large graphic designs are created. **(3)** The basic or fundamental unit, often the lowest level of a machine instruction or the lowest unit of language translation.

primitive element   A graphics element such as a line segment or point that can be readily called up and extrapolated or combined with other primitive elements to form more complex objects or images.

print   An impression produced on a graphics printer or plotter.

print buffer   Extra RAM in the printer or an add-on board that allows the user to send a print job to the printer all at once, thereby freeing the computer for other work.

print chart   A form used to describe the format of an output report from a printer. Also called printer spacing chart, printer design form, and print layout sheet.

print control character   The control character for operations on a line printer such as carriage return, page ejection, or line spacing.

print density   The number of printed characters per unit of measurement, such as the number of characters on a page.

printed circuit (PC)   An electronic circuit that is printed, vacuum deposited, or electroplated onto a flat insulating sheet.

printed circuit board   A flat board that holds chips and other electronic components. Each chip contains hundreds of thousands of elementary components. The back side of the board is "printed" with electrically conductive pathways between the chips and components.

print element   That part of an impact printer that actually puts the image on paper.

print engine   Part of a LASER PRINTER. The mechanism that uses a laser to create an electrostatic image of a page and fuses that image to a sheet of paper.

printer An output device that produces hard-copy output.

printer control language The language used to control printers.

printer driver A DEVICE DRIVER used to control a printer.

printer engine That part of a page printer such as a laser printer that actually performs the printing.

printer font A font available for printing. There are three types of printer fonts: BUILT-IN FONTS, CARTRIDGE FONTS, and DOWNLOADABLE FONTS.

printer format The format of printing paper divided into print zones. Only one VALUE can be printed in each zone.

printer resolution The number of dots a laser printer can print on a linear inch. For example, most laser printers image at 300 dpi, while high-end imagesetters print at resolutions of 1,270, 2,250, and higher.

printer server A device in a LOCAL AREA NETWORK that shares a printer among all users connected to the network. Using a technique called print spooling, the printer server receives files to be printed from network computers, stores the files on disk, and places them in a queue based on the order received. The printer server then parcels out the files, one at a time, to the printer.

printer spacing chart A chart used to determine and show a report format.

printer stand A wood or metal stand designed to support a printer.

print file A FILE that is created for the purpose of printing data.

print head See PRINT ELEMENT.

printing orientation See LANDSCAPE or PORTRAIT.

print layout sheet A chart used for establishing margin and spacing requirements for a printed report. See PRINT CHART.

printout   One form of computer system output, printed on a page by a printer. See HARD COPY.

print quality   The quality of a printout produced on a printer. See DRAFT QUALITY and LETTER QUALITY.

print server   A microcomputer dedicated to managing one or more printers in a LOCAL AREA NETWORK.

Print Shop   A simple graphics package that performs several useful printing services easily and well. It prints standard and customized signs, greeting cards, posters, and letterheads, as well as multipage banners on fanfold paper with a wide selection of fonts, icons, borders, and graphics. Developed by Broderbund Software.

print speed   The number of characters printed per unit of time.

print spooling   Routing jobs to be printed to a buffer that releases them when the printer is ready to print, allowing users to continue to work on the computer while printing takes place.

print wheel   A single element providing the character set at one printing position of a wheel printer. See DAISY WHEEL PRINTER.

print zone   In BASIC programming, a fixed-length area on an output device within which data are aligned in columns.

priority   (1) The level of importance attached to a job in the computer. (2) A measure of the relative importance of goals that is used to decide which goals will be attempted first.

priority interrupt   Any interrupt given preference over other interrupts within the system.

priority processing   Processing of a sequence of jobs on the basis of assigned priorities. See JOB QUEUE.

privacy   Those personal aspects a person chooses to shield from public scrutiny. The right of individuals to select the time and circumstances where information about them is to be made public.

Privacy Act of 1974   An act passed by the U.S. Congress to regulate the storage of data in federal-agency databases and to give individuals the right to see their records, correct errors, and remove data that should not be on the file.

privacy lock A facility used to prevent an operation from proceeding unless the matching privacy key is presented.

privacy protection study commission A federal commission established to study the impact of public and private organizations' data banks and make recommendations regarding their use.

private In OBJECT-ORIENTED PROGRAMMING, a declaration that forms part of the interface of a class, object, or module; what is declared as private is not visible to any other classes, objects, or modules.

private automatic branch exchange (PABX) A private automatic telephone switching system that provides telephone communications within a business or factory and controls the transmission of calls to and from the public telephone network.

private line A communications line dedicated to one customer. Also called LEASED LINE.

privately leased line A communications line intended for the use of a single customer. See LEASED LINE.

privileged instruction A computer instruction not available for use in ordinary programs written by users; its use is restricted to the routines of the operating system.

probability theory A measure of the likelihood of occurrence of a chance event. Used to predict the behavior of a group. See OPERATIONS RESEARCH.

problem analysis The use of a plan to solve a problem; the first step in the program development cycle.

problem definition **(1)** The formulation of the logic used to define a problem. **(2)** A description of the task to be performed.

problem description In INFORMATION PROCESSING, the statement of a problem. May include a description of the method of solution, the solution itself, the transformation of data, and the relationship of procedures, data, constraints, and environment.

problem-oriented language (POL)   A programming language designed for the convenient expression of a given class of problems.

problem program   A program executed when the central processing unit is in the "problem state"; any program that does not contain privileged instructions.

problem scenario   A problem and a proposed solution.

problem solving   The solving of a problem by a computer. It need not be described by an exact mathematical equation, but it does need a certain set of rules that the computer can follow. If the solution to a problem depends upon intuition or guessing, or if the problem is badly defined, the computer cannot be used to solve it; a computer cannot perform tasks properly unless problems are specified correctly in every detail. The instructions must also list in complete detail each step of the solution.

procedural knowledge   Knowledge that specifies how to solve a given problem rather than describing or specifying the problem.

procedural modeling   Time-saving methods for constructing computer models in which the object geometry is not defined directly but is represented as a procedure; for example, a staircase is created with three input variables: height, width, and stair type.

procedure   (1) The course of action taken for the solution of a problem. (2) The portion of a high-level language program that performs a specific task necessary for the program. (3) An alternate name for a computer program.

procedure division   The fourth of four main parts of a COBOL program.

procedure-oriented language (POL)   Any high-level, machine-independent programming language designed for the conventional expression of procedures used in the solution of a wide class of problems. Contrast with ASSEMBLY LANGUAGE, MACHINE LANGUAGE, and PROBLEM-ORIENTED LANGUAGE.

process (1) The systematic sequence of operations to produce a specified result. (2) To transform raw data into useful information. (3) An element in a data flow diagram that represents actions taken on data: comparing, checking, authorizing, filing, and so forth.

process architecture In OBJECT-ORIENTED PROGRAMMING, the hierarchy of processes that form the physical structure of a system.

process bound A term describing a computer system limited by the speed of the processor.

process box In FLOWCHARTING, a rectangular box that indicates an action to be taken.

process control Use of the computer to control industrial processes such as oil refining and steel production.

process-control computer A digital computer used in a process-control system. Generally limited in instruction capacity, word length, and accuracy. Designed for continuous operation in non-air-conditioned facilities.

process conversion Changing the method of running the computer system.

process diagram Part of the notation of OBJECT-ORIENTED DESIGN, used to show the allocation of processes to processors in the physical design of a system. A process diagram may represent all or part of the process architecture of a system.

processing Computer manipulation of data in solving a problem.

processing block One or more program statements that handle input, output, and calculation functions.

processing rights The determination of which people have access to what kinds of data in databases.

processing symbol A rectangular flowcharting symbol used to indicate any processing operation, such as calculating, initializing a counter, or moving data.

processing unit A functional unit that consists of one or more processors and their internal storages.

processor (1) The CENTRAL PROCESSING UNIT of a computer. (2) A COMPILER is sometimes referred to as a language processor.

processor bound Pertaining to system performance that is slowed by the time it takes the central processing unit to perform the actual processing or computations. Same as compute-bound. See LIMITING OPERATION. Contrast with I/O BOUND.

PROCOMM PLUS An online telecommunications program for IBM personal computers and compatibles.

Prodigy An online information service that offers business, shopping, news, and information services. Prodigy is a partnership of IBM Corporation and Sears. Innovative features of Prodigy include the use of a bit-mapped graphical user interface and unlimited use of the system for a flat fee.

ProDOS Acronym for **Pro**fessional **D**isk **O**perating **S**ystem, a system for the Apple II microcomputer designed to support both mass and floppy disk storage devices.

production run The execution of a debugged program that routinely accomplishes its purpose. For example, running a payroll program to produce weekly paychecks is a production run.

productivity Measures of the work performed by a software/hardware system. Largely depends on a combination of the system's facility and performance.

Professional Graphics Adapter (PGA) A video adapter introduced by IBM Corporation and used primarily for COMPUTER-AIDED DESIGN applications.

Professional Write A full-featured WORD PROCESSING program designed for executive users.

program A series of instructions that will cause a computer to process data.

It may be in a high-level source form, which requires intermediate processing before the computer can execute it, or it may be in an object form directly executable by the computer.

program chaining   The process of linking programs or program sections together. Allows a program that is larger than internal memory to be executed through sequential loading and execution of successive sections or modules of that program.

program coding   The process of writing instructions in a PROGRAMMING LANGUAGE.

program control   A term descriptive of a system in which a computer is used to direct the operation.

program counter   A counter that indicates the location of the next program instruction to be executed by the computer. Same as instruction counter.

program design tool   A tool, such as a structure chart or pseudocode, that helps the programmer or systems analyst decide how a program is to work.

program development cycle   The steps involved in the solution of a problem with a computer: problem analysis, algorithm development, coding, program testing, documentation, and delivery. See DESIGN CYCLE.

program file   A file containing computer programs.

program flowchart   A diagram composed of symbols, directional lines, and information about how the computer will be used to solve a problem. See FLOWCHART. Contrast with SYSTEM FLOWCHART.

program generator   See GENERATOR.

program ID   Program identification.

program inspection   A formal technique in which software requirements, design, or code are examined by a person or group other than the author to detect flaws.

program language   See PROGRAMMING LANGUAGE.

program library A collection of available computer programs and routines, or portions of programs. Contents of the library are stored for re-use.

program listing See LISTING.

programmable automation The manufacturing uses of robots and numerically controlled tools.

programmable calculator A calculatorlike device with certain computerlike features.

programmable communications interface An interface board used for communications control.

programmable function key A keyboard key whose function changes with each program within the computer.

programmable logic array (PLA) A device that provides the sum of a partial product with outputs for a given set of inputs. See FPLA and PLA.

programmable memory Content-changeable memory, where most computer programs and data are stored. Usually RAM or PROM. Contrast with ROM. See STORAGE.

programmable read-only memory (PROM) Memory that can be programmed by electrical pulses. Once programmed, it is read-only. A special machine (called a PROM PROGRAMMER) is used to write in the new program on blank PROM chips.

program maintenance The process of keeping programs up to date by correcting errors, making changes as requirements change, and altering the programs to take advantage of equipment changes.

programmed check A check consisting of tests inserted into the programmed statement of a problem and performed by the use of computer instructions.

programmed label A label record at the beginning of the file. To make the identification of disk and tape files more reliable, most programs include a built-in routine that creates one. Contrast with EXTERNAL LABEL.

programmed learning An early version of CAI, which used feedback to tell the user if he or she was correct; it could individualize instruction to a limited extent.

programmer (1) The person whose job is to design, write, and test software. (2) A device used to write machine code to a PROM chip.

programmer/analyst The person whose major tasks involve combining system analysis and design functions with programming activities.

programmer board A board that allows a user to program PROM or EPROM memories for use in his or her computer system. See PROM PROGRAMMER.

programming (1) The process of translating a problem from its physical environment to a language that a computer can understand and obey. (2) Planning the procedure for solving a problem. This may involve, among other things, the analysis of the problem, coding of the problem, establishing input/output formats, establishing testing and checkout procedures, allocation of storage, preparation of documentation, and supervision of running of the program on a computer.

programming aids Computer programs that aid computer users, such as compilers, debugging packages, linkage editors, and mathematical subroutines.

programming environment Facilities that aid in the development of programs. The tools may be libraries of subroutines, editors, debuggers, and so forth.

programming language A set of statements that control the operations of a computer; a means for computer users to provide a series of instructions for a computer to follow. There are four types of programming languages: MACHINE LANGUAGE, ASSEMBLY LANGUAGE, HIGH-LEVEL LANGUAGE, and FOURTH-GENERATION LANGUAGE.

programming librarian One of three nucleus members of the chief programmer team. The programming librarian maintains and operates the development support library. Duties include code creation, submission of computer runs, and filing and logging of all outputs.

programming linguistics Three interconnected concepts of syntax, semantics, and pragmatics that can be used to describe languages for communication between any two systems, whether mechanical, electrical, or human.

programming team   A group of individuals assigned to a programming project. See CHIEF PROGRAMMER TEAM.

program overlay   A program module that is moved from auxiliary storage into computer memory when it is needed for processing.

program specifications   A document that identifies the data requirements of a system, the files required, the input/output specifications, and the processing details.

program stack   The area of computer memory set aside for temporary storage of data and instructions, particularly during an interrupt. See POP, PUSH, PUSHDOWN LIST, PUSHDOWN STACK, and STACK.

program stop   A stop instruction built into a program that will automatically stop the computer under certain conditions, upon reaching the end of the processing or upon completing the solution of a problem.

program storage   A portion of internal storage reserved for the storage of programs, routines, and subroutines. In many systems, protection devices are used to prevent inadvertent alteration of the contents.

program switch   The point in a programming routine at which two courses of action are possible, the correct one being determined by a condition prevailing elsewhere in the program or by a physical disposition of the system.

program testing   Executing a program with test data to ascertain that it functions as expected. See TESTING.

progress reporting   The input of actual time, resource utilization, and task/activity completions.

project control   The phase of a project management cycle that compares actual performance with the planned schedule and implements corrective measures to avoid project completion delays.

projecting   Producing a two-dimensional graphics display of a three-dimensional scene.

projection   The extension of past trends into the future. Computer-supplied information can be invaluable in this business management technique.

project library   A database of projects, tasks, and activities that can be modified and applied when planning new projects.

project management program   A program that keeps track of all the separate parts of a project.

project manager   The person responsible for the enforcement of a project's goals. Sometimes called a project team leader.

project plan   The phase of a project management cycle that involves the development and organization of the work plan.

project schedule   The phase of a project management cycle that details the start and completion times for each task and activity.

PROLOG   Acronym for **Pro**gramming in **Log**ic, a logic-based programming language. PROLOG is widely used in programming applications such as EXPERT SYSTEMS and ARTIFICIAL INTELLIGENCE software.

PROM   Acronym for **P**rogrammable **R**ead-**O**nly **M**emory, a permanent memory chip that is programmed by the customer rather than the chip manufacturer. Contrast with ROM, which is programmed at the time of manufacture.

PROM programmer   A device used to program PROMs and reprogram EPROMS by electrical pulses. Sometimes called PROM burner. See PROGRAMMER BOARD.

prompt   A character or message provided by the computer to indicate that it is ready to accept keyboard input. Usually an on-screen question or instruction that tells the user which data to enter or what action to take, as, for example, "Enter name:".

proof   (**1**) A trial copy of a page or publication used to check accuracy. (**2**) Short for proofread, meaning to check for mistakes.

proofing program Same as DICTIONARY PROGRAM or SPELLING CHECKER.

proofreader's marks In DESKTOP PUBLISHING, a standard set of notations for indicating errors or corrections on a proof.

propagated error An error or mistake occurring in one operation and affecting data required for subsequent operations so that the error or mistake is spread through much of the processed data.

propagation delay The time delay in a satellite communications system.

proportion The relation, or ratio, of one part to another and of each part to the whole with regard to size, height, width, length, or depth.

proportional font A set of characters in a particular style and size in which a variable amount of horizontal space is allotted to each letter and number of special character. In a proportional font, the letter *l*, for example, is allowed less space than the letter *w*.

proportional spacing The respective proportioning of a printed character's horizontal space and its width. Since this book is typeset in proportional spacing, the *w* in the word *write* consumes more space than the *i*. Standard typewriter style, in contrast, allots equal space to all characters.

proposition A statement in logic that can be true or false.

proprietary operating system A personal computer operating system that runs on only one type of computer.

proprietary software A program owned by an individual or business because it is either copyrighted or not yet released to the public. This software cannot be legally used or copied without permission. Contrast with PUBLIC DOMAIN SOFTWARE. See SOFTWARE PIRACY.

prosodics Rules for interpreting variations in stress and intonation in speech.

protect To prevent unauthorized access to programs or a computer system; to shield against harm. Often means WRITE-PROTECTING a disk.

protected cell A spreadsheet cell that cannot be edited, deleted, or moved.

protected mode   In IBM-compatible microcomputers using Intel 80×86 microprocessors, an operating mode in which programs running simultaneously cannot invade each other's memory space or directly access input/output devices, thus preventing system failures during multitasking operations.

protected storage   Storage locations reserved for special purposes in which data cannot be stored without undergoing a screening procedure to establish suitability for storage therein.

protocol   A software method that allows programs on separate machines to communicate. Protocols define signal type, how the signals are received, and the physical arrangement of the network. In OBJECT-ORIENTED PROGRAMMING, the set of messages to which an object can respond.

prototype   A limited working system or subset of a system (hardware or software) that is developed to test design concepts. The initial version of a system.

prototyping   A systems development alternative whereby a small model, or prototype, of the system is built before a full-scale systems development effort is undertaken.

proving   Testing a machine to demonstrate that it is free from faults, usually after corrective maintenance.

PS/1   A home computer from IBM Corporation introduced in 1990. The PS/1 computer uses an Intel 80286 microprocessor.

PS/2   A series of personal computers from IBM Corporation introduced in 1987. This second generation of IBM personal computers superseded its original personal computer series. The PS/2 introduced three major changes: VGA graphics, Micro Channel bus, and 3.5-inch floppy disks.

psec   Abbreviation for PICOSECOND; one-trillionth of a second.

pseudocode   An intermediate form of writing program instructions; instructions that approach the computer programming language but are written in an English-like language instead of a true programming language so that programming logic can be checked more easily.

pseudocomputer A software interpreter program written in the native machine language of a conventional microprocessor.

pseudolanguage Language not directly understandable by a computer used to write computer programs. Before a pseudoprogram can be used, it must be translated into a language that the computer understands (machine language). Same as SYMBOLIC LANGUAGE.

pseudo-operation An operation that is not part of the computer's operation repertoire as realized by hardware; hence, an extension of the set of machine operations.

pseudorandom number A number generated by a computer in a deterministic manner. Pseudorandum numbers have been subjected to many statistical tests of randomness and, for most practical purposes, can be used as random numbers.

p-system A microcomputer operating system with a principal advantage: programs written for it will work on a wide variety of machines. Translates P-CODE into the machine language appropriate to a specific computer. See UCSD P-SYSTEM.

publication language A well-defined form of a programming language suitable for use in publications. A language such as this is necessary because some languages use special characters that are not available in common type fonts.

publication window In DESKTOP PUBLISHING, a display screen consisting of a pasteboard, icons, a scroll bar, a ruler, and a toolbox.

public domain software Software not protected by copyright laws and therefore free for all to reproduce and trade without fear of legal prosecution; any computer program donated to the public by its creator. Public domain software may be duplicated by others at will.

public key A cryptographic key that can be used to encrypt but is not capable of decryption. See SECRET KEY.

public network A communications service open to anyone, usually on a fee basis.

publishing cycle In DESKTOP PUBLISHING, the movement of a document from creation to final printing.

Publish It! A full-featured desktop publishing program that allows for the designing, layout, production, and printing of professional-looking documents. Publish It! runs on IBM-compatible microcomputers.

puck A hand-held, manually controlled graphics input device used to pinpoint coordinates on a digitizing tablet. A transparent window containing cross hairs allows coordinate data to be digitized into the system from a drawing placed on the digitizing tablet surface.

pull See POP.

pull-down menu A second-level menu, or list of commands, that appears from the top of the screen when a command needs to be given and then disappears when the selection has been made. A pull-down menu is usually used as an extension to a menu bar. To select an option on a pull-down menu, users press and hold down the mouse button while dragging the mouse pointer down the menu until the desired option is highlighted.

pull instruction An instruction that pulls or retrieves data from the top of the program PUSH-DOWN STACK. Same as POP instruction.

pull-out quote In DESKTOP PUBLISHING, a quotation extracted from the copy of text and printed in larger type in the column.

pulse An abrupt change in voltage, either positive or negative, that conveys information to a circuit.

pulse modulation The use of a series of pulses that are modulated or characterized to convey information. Types of pulse modulation include amplitude (PAM), position (PPM), and duration (PDM) systems.

punched card A cardboard card used in data processing operations, in which tiny rectangular holes at (possibly) hundreds of individual locations denote numerical values and alphanumeric codes. Punched cards were used extensively in early computer systems, but have been replaced by interactive display terminals and floppy disks.

purchasing   The buying of raw materials and services.

pure procedure   A procedure that never modifies any part of itself during execution.

purge   To erase a file from memory or from a disk; to clean up.

push   To put data into the top location of a program stack. The stack pointer is automatically incremented to point to the next location, which becomes the top of the stack. Also called put. Contrast with POP.

pushdown list   A list written from the bottom up, with each new entry placed at the top of the list. The item to be processed first is the one on the top of the list. See LIFO.

pushdown stack   A set of memory locations or registers in a computer that implement a PUSHDOWN LIST.

pushing   In programming, to add data to a stack.

push instruction   A computer instruction that implements a push operation.

push-pop stack   A register that receives information from the program counter and stores the address locations of instructions on a last-in-first-out basis. Two operations are involved in stack processing: pushing describes the filling of the stack from registers; popping involves emptying the stack for transfer to registers.

pushup list   A list of items in which each item is entered at the end of the list and the other items maintain their relative positions in the list. See FIFO.

put   See PUSH.

Q & A A combination word processing and database program for IBM personal computers and compatible computers.

QIC Acronym for **q**uarter **i**nch **c**artridge, a cartridge tape used as a backup storage medium for personal computers.

quad Abbreviation for QUADRILATERAL.

quad-density A term used to specify the data storage density of a computer disk system. Quad-density systems can store up to four times the data that can be stored on single-density disks. Double-sided, double-density disks are quad-density disks.

quadratic quotient search A hashing algorithm that uses a quadratic offset when probing subsequent table locations.

quadrilateral A closed polygon with four vertices and thus four sides.

quadrilateral mesh A surface defined by four-sided polygons, each attached to other quadrilaterals.

quality control A technique for evaluating the quality of a product being processed by checking it against a predetermined standard and taking the proper corrective action if the quality falls below that standard.

quality engineering The establishment and execution of tests to measure product quality and adherence to acceptance criteria.

quantify To assign numeric values to nonnumeric objects.

quantity Any positive or negative real number in the mathematical sense.

quantization In IMAGE PROCESSING, a process in which each pixel in an image is assigned one of a finite set of gray levels.

quantum The smallest unit of measure employed in a system.

Quark Xpress™ A page layout program for the Apple Macintosh computer from Quark, Inc. It is noted for its precise typographic control and sophisticated graphics capabilities.

quasi language   See PSEUDOLANGUAGE.

Quattro   A spreadsheet for IBM-compatible microcomputers from Borland International, Inc. The program provides advanced graphics and presentation capabilities.

query   To ask for information; to make a request for information from a database system.

query by example   To ask for information from a database system by defining the qualifications for selected records on a sample record, rather than by describing a procedure for finding the information.

query language   A user's language for retrieving data from a database management system. A query is typically issued in the form of a sentence or near-English command.

query response   A message sent to a computer terminal in answer to a specific request from the operator.

question-answer   The process of interacting with the computer. The computer asks the user a question, and the user provides the answer.

queue   A group of items waiting to be acted upon by the computer, such as messages to be transmitted in a data communications system. The arrangement of items determines the processing priority. See JOB QUEUE.

queued access method   Any access method that automatically synchronizes the transfer of data between the program using the access method and the input/output devices, thereby eliminating delays for I/O operations.

queuing theory   A form of probability theory useful in studying delays or lineups at servicing points; a research technique concerned with the correct sequential orders of moving units. May include sequence assignments for bits of information or whole messages. See OPERATIONS RESEARCH.

quibinary code   A binary-coded decimal code used to represent decimal numbers in which each decimal digit is represented by seven binary digits.

QuickBASIC   A variation of the BASIC programming language published by Microsoft Corporation. QuickBASIC is a compiler that recognizes modern control structures and enables programmers to omit line numbers. The compiler allows users to create structured programs, complete with indentations. QuickBASIC programs execute much faster than their interpreted counterparts.

QuickC   A variation of the C programming language published by Microsoft Corporation.

quick disconnect   A type of electrical connector that allows rapid locking and unlocking of the mating connector halves.

QuickDraw   A graphics language system built into the ROM of the Apple Macintosh computer. Application programs call on QuickDraw for on-screen displays. QuickDraw consists of a series of primitive shapes, lines, and fill patterns that can be mathematically modified. When printing to PostScript printers, QuickDraw must be translated during the printing process by a program called a PostScript interpreter.

Quicken   An accounting/checkbook management program for IBM-compatible and Apple Macintosh microcomputers.

QuickPascal   A variation of the PASCAL programming language published by Microsoft Corporation.

quit   To exit the current program.

QWERTY keyboard   The keyboard arrangement standard on most keyboards found on typewriters, word processors, and computers.

R   Abbreviation for register, request, and reset.

race condition   The indeterminate state that results when two computer instructions are operating concurrently and it is not possible to know which one will finish first.

rack   The metal frame or chassis on which panels of electrical, electronic, or other equipment such as amplifiers and power supply units may be mounted.

radial fill   A varying color or tint that changes smoothly from one color or brightness to another, usually moving from the center of an object out toward the edges.

radial symmetry   A characteristic of some computer-generated objects. A radially symmetrical object is generated around a central axis, much like an object is shaped on a lathe. Many 3-D programs allow the user to set the number of segments the object should have.

radian   The central angle subtended in a circle by an arc whose length is equal to the radius of the circle. Trigonometric functions in many high-level programming languages work on radians rather than degrees.

radiation   An alternate name for the stream of electrons that generates the picture on a video display terminal.

radio buttons   In a GRAPHICAL USER INTERFACE, the round option buttons that appear in dialog boxes. Only one radio button can be selected within a group of radio buttons.

Radio Shack   A manufacturer and distributor of electronic equipment, including microcomputer systems sold under the name of TRS-80 or Tandy. A division of the Tandy Corporation, Radio Shack developed one of the first personal computer systems, the TRS-80 Model 1, in 1977.

radiosity   A technique that calculates the lighting in a complex diffuse lighting environment, based on the geometry of the scene.

radix The base number in a number system, such as 2 in the binary system or 10 in the decimal system. Synonymous with BASE.

radix complement See COMPLEMENT.

radix point In a number system, the character (a dot) or implied character that separates the integral part of a numeral from the fractional part. See BINARY POINT, DECIMAL POINT, HEXADECIMAL POINT, and OCTAL NUMBER.

radix sorting Same as DIGITAL SORTING.

rag The irregularity along the left or right ends of the lines on a printed page. See RAGGED LEFT MARGIN and RAGGED RIGHT MARGIN.

ragged left margin A term applied to text printed with a straight right margin and an uneven left margin. Also called flush right.

ragged right margin A term applied to text printed with a straight left margin and an uneven right margin. Also called flush left.

raised flooring Elevated flooring used in computer rooms so that connecting cables can be laid directly between equipment units.

RALU Acronym for **r**egister, **a**rithmetic, and **l**ogic **u**nit, a major part of a microprocessor where arithmetic and logic operations are performed.

RAM Acronym for **r**andom **a**ccess **m**emory, a memory into which the user can enter information and instructions (write) and from which the user can call up data (read). It is the working memory of the computer into which applications programs can be loaded from outside and then executed.

RAM card A printed circuit board containing RAM chips. By plugging such a board into some computers, their internal storage can be expanded.

RAM cache A section of random access memory (RAM) set aside to serve as a buffer between the central processing unit and the disk drives.

RAM chip A semiconductor storage device. RAM chips can be either static or dynamic memory.

RAM disk   A chip that lets the computer regard part of its memory as a third disk drive. Also called phantom disk.

RAM-resident program   A PROGRAM that, once run, remains resident in RAM and can be called up during the operation of another program.

random access   The process of obtaining data from, or placing data into, a storage location in which access is independent of the order of storage. Another name for direct access. Contrast with SEQUENTIAL ACCESS.

random access memory (RAM)   Memory whose contents can be read or written on directly without regard to any other memory location. See RAM.

random files   Files not organized in any sequence. Data are retrieved based on the address of the record on the direct access device.

randomizing   The process of applying a formula to a key to yield a number that represents a disk address. Also called hashing.

random logic design   The designing of a system by using discrete logic circuits.

random number   A patternless sequence of digits; an unpredictable number, produced by chance, that satisfies one or more of the tests for randomness. See PSEUDORANDOM NUMBER.

random-number generator   A computer program or type of hardware designed to produce a PSEUDORANDOM NUMBER or series of pseudorandom numbers according to specified limitations.

random processing   The processing of data randomly; same as direct access processing. Contrast with SEQUENTIAL PROCESSING.

random scan   A term used for describing display devices that allow the drawing of vectors between specified endpoints.

range   The span of values that an element may assume.

range check   A check applied to a numeric element to verify that it falls within a particular range, such as the months of the year being in the range of 01 to 12. See DATA EDITING.

range format   The numeric format choice that applies to a specific range of cells in a SPREADSHEET program worksheet.

range name   A name given to a specific range of cells in a SPREADSHEET program worksheet.

rank   (**1**) To arrange in an ascending or descending series according to importance. (**2**) A measure of the relative position in a group, series, array, or classification.

raster   In computer graphics, a predetermined pattern of lines that provides uniform coverage of a display space.

raster display   A video display that sweeps a beam through a fixed pattern, building up an image with a matrix of points. See RASTER GRAPHICS.

raster fill   The process used by a graphics camera to fill in the spaces between the raster lines of a video screen to give the screen picture a more finished appearance.

raster graphics   The manner of storing and displaying data as horizontal rows of uniform grid or picture cells (pixels). Raster scan devices recreate or refresh a display screen 30 to 60 times a second to provide clear images for viewing. RASTER DISPLAY devices are generally faster and less expensive than vector tubes.

raster grid   On a display device, the grid of addressable coordinates on the display surface.

raster image   A display image formed by a pattern of pixels in a rectangular array.

raster image file format (RIFF)   A file format for paint-style graphics.

raster image processor   A device that converts a vector image into a RASTER IMAGE prior to printing on an output device that requires raster technology.

rasterization   The conversion of vector graphics to equivalent images composed of pixel patterns (bit-mapped images).

raster pattern   A series of picture elements arranged in scan lines to form an image.

raster plotter   A PLOTTER that generates a display image on a display surface using a line-by-line scanning technique.

raster scan   The generation of an image on a display screen made by refreshing the display area line by line.

raster unit   In computer graphics, the distance between adjacent picture elements.

rat's nest   The feature on printed circuit design systems that allows users to view all the computer-determined interconnections between components. This makes it easier to determine whether further component placement improvement is necessary to optimize signal routing.

raw data   Data that have not been processed. Such data may or may not be on machine-readable media. Also called ORIGINAL DATA.

ray tracing   In computer graphics, a method of adding a degree of realism to an image through the use of reflections, refractions, and shadows; a sophisticated and complex approach to producing high-quality computer graphics. Ray tracing is a very process-intensive operation.

RDBMS   Abbreviation for RELATIONAL DATABASE MANAGEMENT SYSTEM.

read   To get information from any input or file storage medium, such as to read a floppy diskette by sensing the patterns of magnetism. Contrast with WRITE.

reader   Any device capable of transcribing data from an input medium.

read head   A magnetic head designed to read data from a medium. Contrast with WRITE HEAD. Compare READ/WRITE HEAD.

reading wand   A device that senses marks and codes optically, such as a device that reads price tags in a point-of-sale terminal.

read ink   See NONREFLECTIVE INK.

read-only memory (ROM)   A special type of computer memory, permanently programmed with one group of frequently used instructions. It does not lose its program when the computer's power is turned off, but the program cannot be changed by the user. In many microcomputers, the BASIC language intrepreter and operating systems are contained in ROM. See EPROM, FIRMWARE, PROM, and SOLID STATE cartridge.

read-only storage   See READ-ONLY MEMORY.

readout   The manner in which a computer represents processed information, such as by visual display, printer, and digital plotter.

read/write   The ability to view and modify or delete data on a storage medium.

read/write head   A small electromagnet used to read, write, or erase data on a magnetic storage device, such as a disk or tape. See READ HEAD and WRITE HEAD.

real address   Same as ABSOLUTE ADDRESS.

real constant   Any number that contains a decimal point, such as 26.4 or −349.0. Also called floating-point constant.

real field   A database field destined to contain a number having a decimal.

real number   Any rational or irrational number.

real storage   In a virtual storage system, internal rather than external storage.

real-time   A term describing online computer processing systems that receive and process data quickly enough to produce output to control, direct, or affect the outcome of an ongoing activity or process. For example, in an airline reservation system, a customer-booking inquiry is entered into the computer to see whether space is available. If a seat is booked, the file of available seats is updated immediately, thus giving an up-to-date record of seats reserved and seats available. See TRANSACTION PROCESSING.

real-time clock   A piece of hardware that interrupts the processor at fixed time intervals to synchronize the operations of a computer with events occurring in the outside world, often involving human/computer interaction.

real-time conference A form of TELECONFERENCING in which all participants are logged on to the system at the same time.

real-time control The control of a process by REAL-TIME PROCESSING.

real-time expert system An EXPERT SYSTEM with input data from an ongoing, constantly varying process.

real-time image generation Performance of the computations necessary to update an image being completed within the REFRESH RATE so that the sequence appears correctly to the viewer. One example is flight simulation, in which thousands of computations must be performed to present an animated image, all within the rate of 30 to 60 cycles per second at which the frames change.

real-time input Input data received by a DATA PROCESSING SYSTEM within time limits that are determined by the requirements of some other system or at instants that are so determined.

real-time operation See REAL-TIME PROCESSING.

real-time output Output data removed from a system at a time of need by another system.

real-time processing The manipulation of data that are required or generated by a process while it is in operation.

real-time systems Computer systems in which the computer is required to perform its tasks within the time constraints of a process or simultaneously with the system it is assisting. Usually, the computer must operate faster than the system assisted so as to be ready to intervene appropriately.

reasonableness check A technique whereby tests are made on processed data to indicate whether a gross error exists. Programming instructions determine whether the data lies within preset upper and lower limits and initiate an action if the data are not reasonable. See DATA EDITING.

reboot To stop and boot the operating system again; to restart. Usually occurs by human intervention as the result of a problem. Rebooting a system is similar to resetting a home appliance.

recalculating   The process of automatically recomputing values in electronic spreadsheets.

receive   To capture messages transmitted by a sender.

receive only (RO)   The designation used to indicate the read-only capabilities of terminals and other equipment lacking keyboards. See RO TERMINAL.

receiver   The recipient of messages dispatched by a sender.

recompile   To compile a program again, usually after debugging or because the program needs to be run on a different type of computer.

reconstruction   Restoration of the database system to a previous state after data have been tampered with or destroyed.

record   A collection of related items of data treated as a unit; the description of an item in a database. Each item is represented by a record that consists of one or more fields. Everyday examples of a record include an entry in a dictionary and a listing in a phone book.

recording density   The number of useful storage cells per unit of length or area; for example, the number of characters per inch on a magnetic tape or the number of bits per inch on a single track of a disk. Also called PACKING DENSITY.

record layout   The arrangement and structure of data elements in a record, including the size and sequence of its components.

record length   The measure of the size of a record, usually specified in units such as words, bytes, or characters.

record locking   The protection of shared database records by allowing only one user at a time to make changes. Used in LOCAL AREA NETWORKS.

record manager   An alternate term for FILE MANAGER.

record number   The number automatically assigned to each new record as it is created. Serves as a reference number and may be transparent to the user.

record-oriented   A term describing a database management program that displays records in response to queries.

records management   Custodial care concerned with the creation, retention, and scheduled destruction of an organization's paper and film documents.

recover   (1) To continue program execution after a failure. **(2)** To overcome a problem.

recoverable error   An error condition that can be sensed and corrected, thereby allowing continued operation of a program.

rectangular coordinate system   A system in which every point in a plane is given an address in the form of a pair of numbers, called the coordinates of the point. Same as Cartesian coordinate system.

rectifier   An electrical device that changes alternating current into direct current. Compare POWER SUPPLY.

recto   The right-hand (odd-numbered) page in a two-sided printing of a book or document.

recurring costs   Budgeted items that are not one-time expenditures, such as personnel, supplies, equipment rental, and overhead costs associated with a computer system.

recursion   A set of operations or program statements in which one of the operations or statements is specified in terms of the entire set; continued repetition of the same operation(s).

recursive   Pertaining to a process that is inherently repetitive. The result of each repetition is usually dependent upon the result of the previous repetition. An object is said to be recursive if it partially consists of or is defined in terms of itself.

recursive procedure   Procedure A that, while being executed, either calls itself or calls another procedure B, which in turn calls procedure A.

recursive subroutine A subroutine capable of calling itself, or a subroutine that invokes another subroutine, which in turn invokes the original subroutine.

red-green-blue monitor A high-resolution color display unit. See RGB MONITOR.

redlining A WORD PROCESSING facility that provides the electronic equivalent of the editor's red pen.

reduced instruction set computer (RISC) A MICROPROCESSOR that has only a relatively small set of instructions. RISC design is based on the premise that most of the instructions a computer decodes and executes are simple; thus RISC architecture limits the number of instructions that are built into the microprocessor but optimizes each so that it can be carried out very rapidly.

reduction The process of saving computer storage by eliminating empty fields or unnecessary data to reduce the length of records.

redundancy **(1)** The duplication of a feature to prevent system failure in the event of the feature's malfunction. **(2)** The repetition of information among various files, sometimes necessary but often undesirable.

redundancy check A check based on the transfer of more bits or characters than the minimum number required to express the message itself, the added bits or characters having been inserted systematically for checking purposes. See PARITY BIT and PARITY CHECKING.

redundant code A binary-coded decimal value with an added check bit.

redundant information A message expressed in such a manner that the essence of the information occurs in several ways.

reentrant Pertaining to a routine that can be used by two or more independent programs at the same time.

reentrant code Assembly-generated machine-language programs that may be shared simultaneously by any number of users.

reentrant subroutine   In a MULTIPROGRAMMING system, a subroutine with only one copy residing in internal storage, shared by several programs.

reference edge   See ALIGNING EDGE.

reflect   To make a mirror image of an object around a specified point or line.

reflectance   In OPTICAL SCANNING, a relative value assigned to a character or color of ink when compared with the background.

reflectance ink   In OPTICAL SCANNING, ink that has a reflective level that very nearly approximates the acceptable paper reflectance level for a particular optical character reader.

reformat   To change the representation of data from one format to another.

reformatting command   In WORD PROCESSING, a command that realigns a paragraph's margins after editing.

refresh circuitry   Electronic circuitry necessary to restore (1) the information displayed on a visual display screen, and (2) the data stored in DYNAMIC RAM, which steadily lose their charge.

refresh display cycle   The time between successive raster scans or passes through the vectors to be displayed on a vector device. The phosphors on the face of a CRT are excited and glow as the result of each pass of the electron beam in each refresh cycle. The refresh rate usually occurs at a level fast enough to eliminate the flicker from the brightening and fading of the phosphors each time they are struck. Typically, the image must be regenerated at a rate of $\frac{1}{30}$ or $\frac{1}{60}$ of a second.

refreshing   The process of constantly reactivating or restoring information that decays or fades away when left idle. Phosphor on a CRT screen needs to be constantly reactivated by an electron beam to remain illuminated. Typically, the image must be regenerated at a rate of 30 to 60 hertz to avoid flicker. Likewise, cells in dynamic memory elements must be repeatedly accessed to avoid losing their contents. See DYNAMIC RAM and RASTER SCAN.

refresh memory   The area of computer memory that holds values indicating whether a particular dot of a graphics RASTER is on or off. May also contain information on brightness and color.

refresh rate   The rate at which the graphic image on a CRT is redrawn in a refresh display; the time needed for one refresh of the displayed image.

regenerate   To renew some quantity; to write back information in storage devices that has been read in a destructive manner.

regeneration   The production of a new screen image after a change in scale, position, or elements.

region   In multiprogramming with a variable number of tasks, a term often used to mean the internal storage space allocated.

region fill   In computer graphics, the technique of filling a defined region on the screen with a selected pattern, color, or other attribute.

register (R)   A high-speed device used in a CENTRAL PROCESSING UNIT for temporary storage of small amounts of data or intermittent results during processing. See GENERAL REGISTER.

registration   Accurate positioning relative to a reference.

regression analysis   (1) A technique in model-building used to define a dependent variable in terms of a set of independent variables. (2) The construction of a "line of best fit" to best illustrate the pattern of a set of data points.

regression testing   Tests performed on a previously verified program whenever it is extended or corrected.

relation   (1) Equality, inequality, or any property that can be said to hold (or not hold) for two objects in a specified order. (2) In a RELATIONAL DATABASE model, a table, the basic form of information storage. (3) In a network/hierarchical database model, a named association among sets of entities.

relational database management system (RDBMS)   A DATABASE organization scheme that treats files as tables of data in which rows represent fixed-length records and columns represent fields. Multiple keys can be used for retrieving data stored within the database. A database in which some data items in one type of record refer to records of a different type. Relational databases give the user the flexibility to link (join, or create a relationship between) information stored in many disk files. This allows users to interchange and cross-reference information between two different types of records, such as comparing the information in a group of invoices to the information in an inventory. Most people do not need relational databases: to merely keep track of a mailing list doesn't require a relational database, nor is such a database needed to keep a simple inventory. However, those who want to print out a mailing list of people who ordered products from their inventory need a relational database. Relational databases are more powerful, more complex, more difficult to use, and more expensive than other database systems.

relational data structure   A data structure in which data are represented in tables, which may be interrelated by the user.

relational expression   An expression that contains one or more relational operations.

relational language   In a DATABASE MANAGEMENT SYSTEM, a language for accessing, querying, and modifying a relational database.

relational model   A database model that organizes data logically in tables.

relational operator   A symbol used to compare two values; specifies a condition that may be either true or false, such as = (equal to), < (less than), and > (greater than).

relational structure   A form of database organization in which all data items are contained in one file and are linked together by a trail of logical pointers. Relationships among these data items can be altered at will, and the information can be obtained by interactive query or batch processing.

relative address   The address to which a base address must be added to form the absolute address of a particular storage location.

relative cell reference In SPREADSHEET processing, a reference to a location in the worksheet that is interpreted with respect to the formula's current cell location.

relative coding Coding that uses machine instructions with relative addresses.

relative coordinates (1) Coordinates relative to a coordinate system whose origin is set at the initial position of a point selected on an object. (2) One of the coordinates that identify the position of an addressable point with respect to another addressable point.

relative copy A copy of a spreadsheet formula that is entered into another cell; the original formula structure is retained, but the formula copy matches the new cell location.

relative data set A DATA SET in which each record is assigned a record number according to its relative position within the data set storage space.

relative movement Movement of an object on the screen to a new position in terms of the last position rather than from 0.0. For example, the command "Move 4, 8" would move a marked point four units to the right and eight units up from the last recorded point.

relative vector In computer graphics, a vector with endpoints designated in relative coordinates.

relay A magnetically operated switch used in pre-electronic computers.

release number The number that identifies a specific version of a program. A program labeled 3.5, for example, is the sixth release of Version 3 of the program (the first was Version 3.0).

release version That version of a program currently available for purchase.

reliability The measure of the ability of a program, system, or individual hardware device to function without failure.

relocatable addresses Addresses used in a program that can be positioned at almost any place in internal storage.

relocatable program   A program existing in a form that permits it to be loaded and executed in any available region of a computer's internal storage.

relocate   To move a program or part of a program coded so that it may be executed anywhere in computer storage.

remarks   The verbal messages inserted into a source language program that do not cause any computer processing steps but are helpful notes for future users who may attempt to understand or alter the program. Used as internal documentation. See COMMENTS.

remote   Physically distant from a local computer, such as a terminal or printer.

remote access   Communication with a computer facility by a station (or stations) distant from the computer.

remote batch processing   Processing data in batches at a remote location by using a small computer system. See BATCH PROCESSING.

remote computing services   Services offered to customers by computer service centers, such as batch processing, interactive problem solving, and consulting.

remote job entry (RJE)   The use of computer programs to submit processing jobs from remote terminals.

remote processing   The processing of computer programs through an input/output device remotely connected to a computer system. See RE-MOTE BATCH PROCESSING.

remote sensing   A method of gathering image data remotely, such as by satellite or aerial photography.

remote site   An outpost in a distributed computer network.

remote station   See REMOTE TERMINAL.

remote terminal   A device for communicating with a computer from sites that are physically separated from the computer, often distant enough so that communications facilities such as telephone lines are used rather than direct cables. See TERMINAL.

removable media Diskettes, hard disk cartridges, or optical disc cartridges that can be removed from the device that reads data from them or writes data to them.

renderer A program or function that produces the corresponding images of a geometric model or description of a scene.

rendering In computer graphics, a three-dimensional image that incorporates the simulation of lighting effects such as reflections and shadows.

reorder point The lowest amount of stock that can be on hand before ordering more of an item; an essential parameter in inventory control.

repagination The process in which a page layout or word processing program adjusts a multipage document as it is revised to ensure uniform page length and appearance.

repaint The redrawing of an image on a visual display device to reflect updated graphic or textual data. A feature on many graphics systems that automatically redraws a design displayed on the visual display screen.

repeat counter A program counter that records the number of times an event takes place in a program for later comparison.

repeater A device used to extend the reach of cables in a LOCAL AREA NETWORK.

repeating decimal number A nonterminating decimal number, such as .3333333 ... or .31282828 ....

repeat key A keyboard key that can be held down so that it repeatedly makes contact without the need for additional pressing.

repertoire A complete set of instructions that belongs to a specific computer or family of computers. Also called instruction set.

repetition block A block of program statements that handles the repetition of one or more actions.

repetition instruction   An instruction that causes one or more instructions to be executed an indicated number of times.

replace   In WORD PROCESSING, a command that enables the user to search for a word and replace it with another one.

replace mode   In WORD PROCESSING, a mode in which current symbols are replaced by new symbols.

repligraphics   In COMPUTER-AIDED DESIGN AND DRAFTING (CADD), a concept for obtaining multiple copies of plots.

report   The grouping of related facts so as to be easily understood by the reader; usually associated with output data. A common means of presenting information to users. Most reports are on-screen display or printed listings showing selected information extracted from a database.

report file   A file generated during data processing, usually used to print out or display desired output.

report generation   The manipulation and organization of data to create an on-screen or hard-copy document from all or part of a database file.

report generator   A program that is used to create a report.

reporting by exception   See EXCEPTION REPORTING.

report writer   A utility program that generates standard and custom reports from information stored in data files.

reproduce   To copy information on a similar medium, such as to obtain a duplicate diskette from a specific diskette.

reprogramming   Changing a program written for one computer so that it will run on another.

reprographics   The duplication of printed materials using high-speed duplicators and offset printing presses. The technology includes reproduction and duplication processes for documents, written materials, pictures, drawings, and films, as well as methods of their mass reproduction, such as photocopying, offset printing, microfilming, and offset duplicating.

request for bid (RFB)   After specifications regarding hardware or software are developed and made available to vendors, the submission of a bid by vendors that describes the hardware or software and tells the price and conditions under which it can be purchased or leased.

request for proposal (RFP)   A document sent to hardware/software vendors requesting them to propose equipment and software to meet system specifications.

request for quotation (RFQ)   A document sent to hardware/software vendors requesting them to quote prices for equipment and/or software that meets system requirements.

requirements list   A formal written statement that specifies what software must do or how it must be structured.

rerun   To repeat all or part of a program on a computer, usually because of a correction, a false start, or an interrupt.

rescale   (1)   The process of changing characters of one point size to another point size. **(2)** The process of reducing or enlarging a graphics image.

reserve accumulator   An auxiliary storage register allied to the main accumulator in a central processing unit. See ACCUMULATOR.

reserved words   Certain words that, because they are reserved by operating systems, language translators, and so on for their own use, cannot be used in an applications program. See KEYWORD.

reset (R)   (1)   To return computer components to a specified static state. **(2)** To place a binary cell into the zero state.

reset key   The key on a keyboard that normally is used to restart the computer.

reside   To be recorded in. For example, a program may reside on a disk or in memory.

resident commands   DISK OPERATING SYSTEM commands that reside in internal memory when the computer is in use.

resident font   The built-in FONT in a printer.

resident program   A program that occupies a dedicated area of a computer's main memory (ROM or RAM) during the operating session. Contrast with TRANSIENT PROGRAM.

residual value   The value of a piece of equipment at the end of a lease term.

resilient   A term describing a system capable of continuing execution despite failure.

resist   A chemical that is used to build up each layer of a chip.

resistor   The component of an electrical circuit that produces heat while offering opposition, or resistance, to the flow of electric current.

resizing   The process of scaling a graphics file or entity according to predetermined parameters.

resolution   A term used to describe the amount of information that a video display can reproduce. A pixel is the smallest unit on the display screen grid that can be stored, displayed, or addressed. The resolution of a picture is expressed by the number of pixels in the display. A high-resolution picture looks smooth and realistic; it is produced by a large number of pixels. A low-resolution picture is blocky and jagged; it is produced by a small number of pixels. Low-resolution pictures represent surfaces with ragged edges, while high resolution produces a finely defined image. A picture with 640×480 pixels is much sharper than a picture with 512×342 pixels.

resolution, plotter   A measure of the quality of a plotted image. The number of addressable points on a digital plotter determines the resolution; the more points, the higher the resolution.

resource   Any component of a computer configuration. Memory, printers, visual displays, disk storage units, software, materials, and operating personnel are all considered resources.

resource allocation   The sharing of computer resources among competing tasks or activities.

resource file   Programs or data, stored on disk or tape, for use by applications programs.

resource leveling   The scheduling of activities with float time to optimize the use of resources, thereby avoiding large fluctuations in resource requirements.

resource sharing   The sharing of one central processor, as well as several peripheral devices, by several users.

response position   In OPTICAL SCANNING, the area designated for marking information on an optical mark recognition form.

response time   The time it takes the computer system to react to a given input; the interval between an event and the system's response to it.

restart   To resume execution of a program; to REBOOT.

results   The product of computer processing.

reticle   The photographic plate used to create an integrated circuit mask.

retrieval   The recovery of data stored in a computer system.

retrieving   The process of making stored information available when needed.

retrofit   To update or add to an existing system to improve it.

return   A set of instructions at the end of a subroutine that permits control to return to the proper point in the main program.

RETURN key   The key on a computer keyboard used to make the display cursor or a printer carriage move to the beginning of the next line. Its function is similar to that of the ENTER key on other keyboards.

reusable   That attribute of a routine that permits the same copy of the routine to be used by two or more tasks.

reusable code   Program segments that can be reused several times in constructing application programs.

reverse Polish notation   A form of postfix notation in which the operands are entered before the operators. The expression $z = a(b + c)$ is represented in reverse Polish notation as $bc + a \times z =$, where this expression is read from left to right. Contrast with POLISH NOTATION.

reverse print   Having white type or graphics on a black background (or some variation on that theme) instead of the usual black type or graphics on a white background.

reverse video   A term used to indicate, in some video terminals, the ability to display dark characters on a light background; the inverse of the normal foreground and background colors on a video screen. For example, the reverse video of light characters on a dark background would be dark characters on a light screen background. Commonly used to highlight text or special items on the screen.

review   An evaluation of a new system's performance.

rewind   To return a MAGNETIC TAPE to its starting position.

rewrite   To erase and reset.

RF   Abbreviation for **r**adio **f**requency, the general term for a broad spectrum of electromagnetic radiation ranging in frequency from 10,000 to 40 billion cycles per second. RF radiation has been used primarily for the purpose of communication.

RFI   Abbreviation for **r**adio **f**requency **i**nterference, disrupting electrical interference on the radio frequency spectrum.

RF modulator   A device that lets a microcomputer use any ordinary television set for output.

RFP   Abbreviation for **R**EQUEST **F**OR **P**ROPOSAL.

RFQ   Abbreviation for **R**EQUEST **F**OR **Q**UOTATION.

RGB (Red, Green, Blue)   The most common color model; the way color is created on computer monitors. Red, green, and blue are called the additive primaries because they create white light when combined and any two produce the subtractive primaries: cyan, magenta, and yellow.

RGB monitor   A display screen that requires separate red, green, and blue video signals from the video source. RGB monitor is synonymous in IBM-compatible microcomputer computing with the Color Graphics Adapter (CGA) standard.

RIB   Acronym for **R**enderMan **I**nterface **B**ytestream, an Apple Macintosh file format for 3-D images rendered in Pixar's RenderMan.

ribbon cable   A type of flat cable made of individual insulated wires joined side by side. It is inexpensive to manufacture, easy to put connectors on with automated equipment, and physically flexible. Commonly used to connect disk drives or printers to a computer.

ribbon cartridge   The plastic holder that contains a printer ribbon.

RIFF   Acronym for **r**aster **i**mage **f**ile **f**ormat, a graphics file format used to store gray-scale images. Used most often in Letraset's ImageStudio and Ready, Set, Go software packages.

right-aligned   A term describing text that is aligned to the right margin but need not be aligned to the left.

right justify   See JUSTIFY.

RightWriter   A PROGRAM that checks grammar and punctuation.

rigid disk   Same as HARD DISK.

ring   A cyclic arrangement of data elements. See CIRCULAR LIST.

ring network   A computer network in which each computer is connected to other computers, forming a continuous loop, or circle. Usually employed when the computers are geographically close. Contrast with STAR NETWORK.

Rio-Sable   A true-color object-oriented draw and image processing program. It allows users to compose scenes that combine video capture, TV-quality electronic color images, or high-resolution scanned images with vector-based text and geometric shapes.

RIP   Abbreviation for **r**aster **i**mage **p**rocessor, the part of a printing system that translates from the input data in the form provided by the computer to the actual dots or lines sent to the marking device.

ripple sort   See BUBBLE SORT.

RISC   Acronym for REDUCED INSTRUCTION SET COMPUTER, a computer system designed to minimize the number of different underlying operations that the microprocessor does in hardware in order to optimize the execution speed. Such systems depend on the software for functions that formerly were handled by the microprocessor.

risk analysis   The analysis of a system's assets and vulnerabilities in an attempt to establish the expected loss when a given disaster occurs.

river   In DESKTOP PUBLISHING, the presence of irregular white space between words that accidently line up vertically or diagonally.

RJE   Abbreviation for REMOTE JOB ENTRY.

RO   Abbreviation for RECEIVE ONLY.

roam   To move a display window around on a visual display screen.

robo stick   An input device used to manipulate the cursor and to create graphics.

robot   A computer-controlled device that can physically manipulate its surroundings. It is equipped with sensing instruments for detecting input, signals, or environmental conditions, a calculating mechanism for making decisions, and a guidance mechanism for providing control. Often robots speak, respond to verbal instructions, move about, and pick up objects.

robotic control language   A computer language specifically designed to control a robot. It differs from other computer languages in that it controls the movements of robots.

robotics   The science of robot design and use; the branch of engineering devoted to the creation and training of robots. ROBOTS are computer-controlled devices capable of performing many of the tasks performed by humans.

robustness   The quality that enables a software program or set of programs to handle, or at least avoid disaster in the face of, unexpected circumstances, such as when given improper data.

roll   In computer graphics, to scroll in an upward or downward direction.

rollback   A system that will restart the running program after a system failure. Snapshots of data and programs are stored at periodic intervals, and the system rolls back to restart at the last recorded snapshot.

roll out   To record the contents of INTERNAL STORAGE in AUXILIARY STORAGE.

rollover   A buffer that can store typed characters and commands when they are entered faster than the computer system can process them.

roll paper   Printer paper in continuous form on a spool. Contrast with FANFOLD PAPER.

ROM   Acronym for READ-ONLY MEMORY, generally a solid-state storage chip programmed at the time of its manufacture that cannot be reprogrammed by the computer user. Also called firmware, since this implies software that is permanent or firmly in place on a chip. Contrast with PROM and EPROM.

Roman   In typography, a medium-weight typeface in which all letters are upright.

ROM BIOS   Acronym for Read-Only Memory, Basic Input/Output System. A special chip used to provide instructions to the computer when the computer is turned on.

ROM cartridge   A plug-in module that contains software permanently stored in ROM; a method of entering data and/or programs into a computer. The module can contain one or more printer fonts, programs, games, or other information.

ROM simulator   A general-purpose device used to replace ROMS or PROMS in a system during program checkout. Because it offers real-time in-circuit simulation, it can be used in the engineering prototype or reproduction model to find and correct program errors or in the production model to add new features.

root   The top element or node in a tree diagram, from which branches extend eventually to LEAF nodes.

root directory   Under DOS, the first, top-level directory.

roping   An aliasing effect in a graphics image in which a line or thin polygon appears to vary in width, color, or brightness according to a repeating pattern that suggests the braiding of a rope.

rotating memory   A magnetic information storage device in the form of a round platter that is spun like a phonograph record. See MAGNETIC DISK.

rotation   In computer graphics, the turning of a computer-modeled object relative to an origin point on a coordinate system. In three-dimensional graphics, an object can be rotated in space, usually around the axis, to provide different views. See TRANSFORMATION.

rotational delay   The time it takes for a record contained on one of the sectors of a disk to rotate under the read/write head.

rote learning   A type of learning in which all knowledge is explicitly provided by an external source, as by programmers in conventional computer programming.

rough draft   In DESKTOP PUBLISHING, the preliminary page layouts done by the designer using pencil sketches to represent page design ideas; a roughly drawn sketch of a finished document.

round   See ROUND OFF.

rounding   The process of dropping the least significant digit or digits of a numeral, and adjusting the remaining numeral to be as close as possible to the original number.

rounding error   An error due to ROUNDING.

round off   To truncate the rightmost digit of a number, and to increase by one the remaining rightmost digit if the truncated digit is greater than or equal to half of the number base.

round-off error   The error resulting from rounding off a quantity by deleting the less significant digits and applying the appropriate rule of correction to the part retained; for example, 0.2751 can be rounded to 0.275 with a round-off error of 0.0001, or rounded to 0.28 with a round-off error of 0.0049. Contrast with TRUNCATION ERROR.

round robin   A scheduling method that engages each device and process at its turn in a fixed cycle.

router   A device that connects networks of the same type, allowing equipment on one LAN to communicate with devices on another. Also called a bridge.

routine   A short set of program code that performs a specific task. Typically used in reference to assembly language programs. Sometimes used as a synonym for program.

routing   Assignment of a path for the delivery of a message.

row   **(1)** Horizontal members of one line of an array. **(2)** The vertical divisions of an electronic spreadsheet. Together with columns, rows serve to form the spreadsheet matrix. Contrast with COLUMN.

row-wise recalculation   The recalculation of cells in a spreadsheet row by row, one after the other.

RPG   Abbreviation for **R**eport **P**rogram **G**enerator, a popular business-oriented programming language, highly structured and relatively easy to learn. Allows users to program many business operations as well as to generate reports.

RPROM   Acronym for **r**eprogrammable **PROM**. See EPROM.

RS   Abbreviation for **R**ecommended **S**tandards, developed by the Electronic Industries Association.

RS-422/423   A standard sanctioned by the Electronic Industries Association for connecting serial devices such as modems to Apple Macintosh computers.

RS-232C   The standard for serial interfaces (serial refers to the eight bits of each character successively sent down one wire) used by most computers, modems, and printers; a 25-pin physical interface.

RTF   Abbreviation for **r**ich-**t**ext **f**ormat, a de facto document-formatting standard developed by Microsoft Corporation for exchanging information between program applications running within its Windows environment.

rubber banding   In computer graphics, changing the shape of an object made up of connected lines by "grabbing" a point on an anchored line and "pulling" it to the new location.

rubber stamp   The ability to duplicate an electronically drawn object on other parts of the display screen as many times as desired through use of a single, simple command.

ruggedized computer   A computer designed to be used in special environments, such as aboard a space vehicle, on a ship, in a missile, in a submarine, in a tank, or in farm equipment.

rule   (**1**) A statement about the relationships of various facts or data. (**2**) A thin line printed above, below, or to the side of an element, either to set that element off from the remainder of the page or to improve the look of the page. (**3**) In EXPERT SYSTEMS, a statement that can be used to verify premises and to enable a conclusion to be drawn.

rule-based expert system   An EXPERT SYSTEM based on a set of rules that a human expert would follow in diagnosing a problem.

ruler   An on-screen ruler, marked off in inches or other units of measure, used to show line widths, paragraph indents, center of page, tab settings, and so forth.

ruler line   In WORD PROCESSING, the line at the top or bottom of a document that defines the margins and tab stops.

rules-based deduction   The technique of obtaining conclusions in which knowledge is represented as a set of simple rules that guide the dialogue between the system and the user.

run   A single or continuous execution of a program by a computer on a given set of data. See EXECUTE.

runaround   In WORD PROCESSING, type with measures adjusted to fit around an illustration or another design element on the page.

run manual   A manual or book documenting the processing system, program logic, controls, program changes, and operating instructions associated with a computer run.

running foot   A line of text at the bottom margin of a page; usually a page number or footnote. Also called footer.

running head   A line of text at the top margin of a page; usually the title of the book, the name of the chapter, the page number, and so on. Also called HEADER.

run time   The time during which data are fetched by the control unit and actual processing is performed in the arithmetic-logic unit. Also called execution time. Contrast with COMPILATION TIME.

run-time error   An ERROR that occurs while a program is running, as opposed to a compile-time error, which occurs while a program is being compiled.

RWOD   Abbreviation for **r**ewritable **o**ptical **d**isc; generally erasable and reusable, like a magnetic disk.

SAGE Acronym for **S**emi-**A**utomatic **G**round **E**nvironment, a U.S. Air Force command and control system developed in the mid-1950s. It was one of the first computer systems to use computer graphics.

salami technique The theft of small amounts (slices) of assets from a large number of sources; an embezzlement technique that gets its name from taking a "slice" at a time, such as a few cents from many bank accounts.

sales representative A person who sells computers and related equipment and software. Most representatives work for computer manufacturers, service organizations, or computer stores.

SAM Acronym for **s**equential **a**ccess **m**ethod, a method for storing and retrieving data on a disk file.

sample data A set of hypothetical data used to see if a flowchart is logical and if a program works. See TEST DATA.

sampling Collecting a subset of data relevant to a system.

sampling rate The frequency at which sampling occurs.

sampling ratio When electronically scanning art or photographs, the number of pixels recorded from the original image over the final line screen during printing. The scanner may record at 300 dpi, but the finished piece is printed at 150 dpi, a ratio of 2:1. The desired ratio of desktop scans is 1.5:1 to 2:1; that is, 1.5 or 2 pixels are scanned for every halftone dot printed.

sans serif Letters of typefaces without serifs— the ornate, widened bases and tops seen on certain characters of some type fonts. *Sans* means "without" in French. Sans serif fonts have very clean lines and are typically considered friendly, casual, and familiar.

sapphire One material used as a substrate for some types of integrated circuit chips.

satellite An earth-orbiting device capable of relaying communications signals over long distances; a radio receiving/transmitting station in geosynchronous orbit 25,000 miles (35,965 kilometers) above Earth and broadcasting with a geographically focused beam.

satellite computer (1) An additional computer, usually smaller, that supports a larger computer system. An economy of processing can be effected if the satellite computer handles lower-level functions such as remote terminal coordination, data validity checking, code conversion, and input/output functions. (2) Any offline auxiliary computer.

satellite imaging Computer-enhanced images taken from orbiting satellites that scientists use to gather data and study the Earth. Satellite-imaging systems are capable of acquiring imagery that has a wider dynamic range than that of the human eye or photographic film. This imagery can be processed and manipulated into data that can be analyzed and studied by scientists for a wide variety of uses and applications.

satellite links The transmission of voice and data over great distances using satellites.

saturate To reach maximum capacity, beyond which nothing else can be absorbed or retained. For example, a diskette is saturated when all of its tracks are full of data.

saturation In the HSB color model, one of the three characteristics used to describe a color. Saturation refers to the degree that a color is pure or the degree of white it contains. A highly saturated color is one that contains little white; a less saturated color looks washed out.

save To store information somewhere other than in the computer's internal memory, such as on a tape or disk, so that it can be used again.

SBC Acronym for **s**mall-**b**usiness **c**omputer and SINGLE-BOARD COMPUTER.

scalable font Characters that can be scaled to any size via a page-description language. By contrast, bit-mapped fonts must be loaded for every size, using up storage space. Scalable fonts provide more flexibility than bit-mapped fonts by eliminating the need to store a variety of different font sizes in the computer's memory.

scalar value   An integer declared as such in a programming language and possessing a value within a fixed range. Contrast with VECTOR.

scale   (**1**) To adjust the magnitude of a quantity so as to fit it into the available storage location. (**2**) To change the size of a graphics file by a specified quantity to make it fit a specified boundary. (**3**) The quantity by which graphic data are multiplied or divided to fit size limitations.

scale factor   One or more factors used to multiply or divide quantities occurring in a problem and to convert them into a desired range, such as the range from +1 to −1.

scaling   (**1**) The process of changing one bit-map density into a bit-map of another density. Scaling usually involves enlarging or contracting an image. (**2**) The process of changing the size of an image. For example, scaling by a factor of three multiplies all dimensions of an image by 3.

scan   (**1**) To examine point by point in logical sequence. (**2**) An algorithmic procedure for visiting or listing each node of a data structure. (**3**) The operation required to produce an image on a visual display screen. (**4**) In optical technologies, to view a printed form a line at a time in order to convert images into bit-mapped representations.

scan area   That area of a form or document that contains information to be scanned by an OPTICAL CHARACTER READER.

scan head   An optical sensing device in an optical scanner or facsimile machine that is moved across the image to be scanned.

scan line   A horizontal line on a RASTER DISPLAY screen.

scanned image   A bit-mapped, or TIFF, image generated by an optical scanner.

scanner   An optical reading device that can recognize text, drawings, and photographs and convert them into electronic representation of the images. Scanners can be differentiated by whether they process color or are limited to shades of gray. Scanner resolution is determined by the amount of information available from the scanning sensor for a given area. Common resolutions in desktop scanners are 200 to 600 dots per inch. More powerful systems can scan up to 8,000 lines per inch or more.

scanner channel A device that polls individual channels to see if they have data ready to be transmitted. See POLLING.

scanning area The dimensions of the largest original image that can be captured by a particular scanner.

scan path In optical scanning, a predetermined area within the clear area where data to be read must be located. The position of the scan path and the amount of data that can be read will generally depend upon the machine involved.

scan rate The number of times a CRT screen is REFRESHED in a given time period.

scatter diagram An analytical graphic in which data items are plotted as points on X–Y coordinate axes.

scatter read/gather write *Scatter read* refers to placing information from an input record into nonadjacent storage areas. *Gather write* refers to placing information from nonadjacent storage areas into a single physical record.

SCDP Abbreviation for **S**OCIETY OF **C**ERTIFIED **D**ATA **P**ROCESSORS.

scenario An imagined sequence of events that determine key system inputs to and the parameters of a decision-making model. For each scenario, a user can then run the model on a computer, observing how system variables interact over time.

scene matching A PATTERN-RECOGNITION technique that involves recognizing a portion of a scene when other images of the same scene have been taken at different times and under different viewing conditions.

schedule A list of events in the order they should occur.

scheduled report   A report produced at regular intervals to provide routine information to users.

scheduled maintenance   Maintenance of a computer system at fixed intervals to maintain its reliability.

scheduler   A program that schedules jobs for processing.

scheduling   (1) The task of determining what the succession of programs should be in a multiprogramming computer center. **(2)** Allocating a nonsharable resource, such as CPU time or an I/O device, to a particular task for a period of time.

schema   A structure for organizing knowledge relative to context or expectations; the definition of an entire database.

schematic symbols   The symbols used in schematic diagrams.

scientific applications   Tasks that are traditionally numerically oriented and often require advanced engineering, mathematical, or scientific capabilities. They seldom require the extensive file-handling capabilities of business applications.

scientific computer   A computer that is capable of high-speed mathematical processing or "number crunching." See SUPERCOMPUTER.

scientific notation   Notation in which numbers are written as a "significant digits" part, or mantissa, times an appropriate power of 10, or exponent.

scientific programming language   A programming language that is designed to handle mathematical formulas and matrices, such as BASIC, FORTRAN, PASCAL, C, or MODULA-2.

scientific visualization   A term describing technology that enables scientists to store vast amounts of mathematical data, generate graphical models that represent that data, and visually analyze the results, usually through interactive software programs. Scientific visualization is a multidisciplinary methodology that employs the largely independent but converging fields of computer graphics, image processing, computer vision, signal processing, and computer-aided design. Its specific goal is to act as a catalyst between scientific computation and scientific insight. Scientific visualization came into being to meet the ever-increasing need to deal with highly active, very dense data sources, including, for example, satellite data and data from supercomputer computations.

scissoring Automatic erasing of all portions of a design on the visual display device that lie outside user-specified boundaries.

SCM Abbreviation for **S**ociety for **C**omputer **M**edicine, an organization that brings together physicians and computer scientists, emphasizing the use of automation for medical applications.

scope (1) The range of control of a software program. (2) An OSCILLO-SCOPE.

SCR Abbreviation for **S**ILICON-**C**ONTROLLED **R**ECTIFIER, a semiconductor device useful in controlling large amounts of DC current or voltage.

scrambling Similar to encryption, in which data or transmissions are "scrambled" so that they can only be retrieved by authorized users.

scrapbook A storage location for frequently used text and pictures. The stored images can be inserted into new documents as required.

scratch To delete data from memory.

scratch file A temporary file created during the processing of substantial files of data by copying all or part of a data set to an auxiliary storage device.

scratchpad Small, fast storage used in some computers in place of registers. Also called cache memory.

screen (1) A television-like output device that can display information. (2) A pattern of tiny dots used as shading in a graphic.

screen angle The angle at which a HALFTONE screen is printed.

screen capture (1) The transfer of the image on the current display screen into a graphics file. (2) A printout of the current screen display.

screen coordinates (1) The COORDINATE SYSTEM that defines the display screen. (2) An alternate name for device coordinates.

screen cursor An indicating symbol generated by the display hardware and moved by the user around the screen area. Its position on the screen can be made to correspond to the position of a hand-held input device, such as a mouse moved across a mouse pad.

screen dump (1) The process of transferring the information currently appearing on a display screen to a printer or saving it as a file on disk. (2) A "snapshot" of the screen.

screen fonts The bit-mapped representations of a printer font used to display the font on the screen. A screen font is designed to mimic the appearance of printer fonts when displayed on medium-resolution monitors.

screen generator A special utility program used to create customized screen displays.

screen image In computer graphics, a pattern of points, lines, and characters shown on the display surface of a display terminal.

screen overlay (1) A clear, fine-mesh screen that reduces the glare on a video screen. (2) A window of data that partially overlays another window of data.

screen position The physical location of graphic data on a visual display screen.

screen resolution A measure of the crispness of images and characters on a screen, usually specified in terms of the number of PIXELS in a row or column.

screen saver A program that produces moving patterns on the screen after a specified number of minutes without keyboard or mouse activity. Pressing a key on the keyboard or moving the mouse restores the screen. Screen savers are used to prolong the life of a monitor; they prevent one image from being burned into the screen phosphors. See also PHOSPHOR BURN-IN.

screen size A measure of the amount of information that a video display screen can display. Screens can be measured diagonally, as TV sets (usually a diagonal measure in inches), or by the number of vertical and horizontal dot or character positions. See RESOLUTION.

screen space The space defined by pixel coordinates.

screen update The process of changing screen contents to reflect new information.

script font A typeface that looks like fine handwriting or calligraphy.

scripts Framelike structures for representing sequences of events.

scroll To move information (graphics or text) up/down or right/left on a computer display screen.

scroll arrow An arrow displayed at the ends of each SCROLL BAR. Clicking or holding the mouse pointer on the scroll arrow causes the document in the window to move.

scroll bar In some types of graphical user interface, a vertical or horizontal bar at the side or bottom of a window that can be used with a mouse for moving around in a document.

scroll box A box that slides in a SCROLL BAR to indicate the relative position of a displayed document.

scrolling The vertical or horizontal movement of information (text or graphics) on a display screen in order to display additional information.

scrolling area An area on the screen in which scrolling takes place.

SCS Abbreviation for SOCIETY FOR COMPUTER SIMULATION.

SCSI Abbreviation for Small Computer Systems Interface. The SCSI is a general-purpose parallel interface designed for connecting one or more computers and one or more peripherals— a total of eight devices may be connected to one bus. It is an industry-standard interface for high-speed access to peripheral devices. Used extensively on the Apple Macintosh computer, SCSI's great advantage is its ability to chain together multiple devices on a single I/O card, each of which has a unique address.

sealed module A disk drive containing the disks, access arms, and read/write heads sealed together. Also called Winchester disk.

search (1) To examine a set of items for those that have a desired property or predetermined criterion, such as a particular name or graphic image. (2) A procedure for automated problem-solving in which a computer seeks a solution by selecting among various possible alternatives.

search and replace A software feature that finds a designated character sequence and replaces it with a new one. Important in word processing applications. See GLOBAL SEARCH AND REPLACE.

search key Data to be compared to specified parts of each item for the purpose of conducting a search.

search memory See ASSOCIATIVE STORAGE.

search tree A hierarchical arrangement of choices used in solving a problem through search.

secondary key A field used to gain access to records in a file; not required to be unique.

secondary storage A memory device that supplements the primary internal memory of a computer. Same as auxiliary storage. Contrast with MAIN STORAGE.

secondary-storage device A machine, such as a disk unit, mass storage device, or tape unit, that is capable of providing storage to supplement primary memory.

second-generation computers Computers belonging to the second era of technological computer development, when the transistor replaced the vacuum tube. Second-generation computers were prominent from 1959 to 1964, when they were displaced by computers using integrated circuitry.

second source A manufacturer who produces a product interchangeable with the product of another manufacturer.

secretary's syndrome A set of symptoms associated with prolonged sitting at a desk, including tight shoulders, tingling arms, stiff neck, tendonitis, and spinal misalignment.

secret key An ENCRYPTION key that must not be disclosed. If it is revealed, the security offered by an encryption algorithm is compromised. Not all encryption keys have to be kept secret. See PUBLIC KEY.

sectioning and paneling Computer-aided mapping functions that allow a cartographer to create new maps by joining a number of smaller-scale maps. These two functions trim extraneous data, allow maps with common boundaries to be merged, and correct small inconsistencies.

sector An area on a disk. Disks are usually divided into sectors and tracks. The address where data is stored is made up of the sector and track number. On most computers, a sector is the smallest unit of information sent between the disk drive and the CPU.

sector chart A pie chart.

sector method A method of organizing data on a disk in which each track is divided into pie-shaped sectors that hold a specific number of characters.

secure kernel A protected segment of a systems program.

security The state achieved by hardware, software, or data as a result of successful efforts to prevent damage, theft, or corruption.

security controls Methods to ensure that only authorized users have access to a computer system and its resources. See PASSWORD.

security files Back-up files for important and critical data and information.

security program A program that controls access to data in files and permits only authorized use of terminals and other equipment.

security specialist The person responsible for the physical security of the computer center and logical security for data resources.

seed A value used initially by an algorithm. For example, a random-number generating program may use a seed number (constant) to begin generating a series of random numbers.

seed filling Filling a bounded area with color by switching just one pixel (or very few pixels) to a chosen shade.

seek To position the access mechanism of a direct access device at a specified location.

seek time The time required for an access arm to position over a particular track on a disk.

segment **(1)** To divide a program into parts such that some segments may reside in internal storage and others may reside in auxiliary storage. Each segment will contain the necessary instructions to jump to another segment or to call another segment into internal storage. **(2)** The smallest functional unit that can be loaded as one logical entity during execution of an overlay program. **(3)** As applied to the field of telecommunications, a portion of a message that can be contained in a buffer of specified size.

segmentation A technique for dividing computer programs into logical, variable-length blocks.

segmented bar chart A bar chart made up of two or more segments positioned atop each other to represent elements of a whole.

select To pick out a group of records from a database according to specifications provided by the user; for example, to select all records with the year greater than 1991.

selection Choosing between alternatives.

selection sort A sort that selects the extreme value (smallest or largest) in a list, exchanges it with the first value in the list, and repeats with a shorter list.

selection structure One of three primary structures of a structured flowchart. Provides a choice between two alternative paths, based upon a certain condition. Also called decision structure and if-then-else. See SEQUENCE STRUCTURE and LOOP STRUCTURE.

selective erase   A graphics feature for deleting portions of a display without affecting the remainder or having to repaint the entire CRT display.

selector   In OBJECT-ORIENTED PROGRAMMING, an operation that accesses the state of an object but does not alter that state.

selector channel   In certain computer systems, an input/output channel that can transfer data to or from only one peripheral device at a time. Contrast with MULTIPLEXER CHANNEL.

self-adapting   Pertaining to the ability of a system to change its performance characteristics in response to its environment.

self-checking code   See ERROR-DETECTING CODE.

self-compiling compiler   A compiler written in its own source language and capable of compiling itself.

self-complementing code   A code with the property that the binary one's complement of the weighted binary number is also the number nine's complement in decimal notation.

self-correcting code   A numerical coding system in which transmission errors are automatically detected and corrected. Same as ERROR-CORRECTING CODE.

self-documenting language   A COMPUTER LANGUAGE that does not need comments or other documentation.

self-validating code   A code that makes an explicit attempt to determine its own correctness and then proceed accordingly.

semantic net   A knowledge representation scheme that organizes human knowledge into a weblike structure consisting of nodes—objects, concepts, and events—connected by links that specify the nature of the connections.

semantics   The study of the science of meaning in language forms. Pertains to the relationships between symbols and what they represent. See PROGRAMMING LINGUISTICS.

semaphores   The synchronization primitives used to coordinate the activities of two or more programs or processes running at the same time and sharing information.

semiconductor A crystalline substance, usually germanium or silicon, that conducts electricity when it is "doped" with chemical impurities. It is the material from which integrated circuits are made.

semiconductor device An electronic element fabricated from crystalline materials such as silicon or germanium that in the pure state are neither good conductors nor good insulators and are unusable for electronic purposes. When certain impurity atoms such as phosphorus or arsenic are diffused into the crystal structure of the pure metal, the electrical neutrality is upset, introducing positive or negative charge carriers. Diodes and transistors can then be implemented.

Semiconductor Industry Association (SIA) A consortium of semiconductor product producers formed to address the interests of the semiconductor industry and provide a collective voice for lobbying efforts.

semiconductor storage A memory device whose storage elements are formed as solid state electronic components on an integrated circuit chip.

semirandom access A method of locating data in storage that combines in the search for the desired item some form of direct access, usually followed by a limited sequential search.

sense (1) To examine, particularly relative to a criterion. (2) To determine the present arrangement of some element of hardware. (3) To read holes punched on a card.

sense probe An input mechanism that activates sensitive points on a visual display screen and thereby provides input to a computer.

sense switch A computer console switch that may be interrogated by a program. Very useful when debugging a large, complex program.

sensitivity The degree of response of a control unit to a change in the incoming signal.

sensors Devices to detect and measure physical phenomena, such as temperature, stress, heartbeat, wind direction, and fire. Sensors translate physical stimuli into electronic signals that may, for example, be input into computers.

separated graphics Graphics characters with spaces between them. When a set of characters with a space at one side and at the top or bottom is printed in adjacent positions, the spaces will separate the graphics characters.

separations Transparencies or pages used for color reproduction. Each separation is used to reproduce a particular color.

sequence The arrangement of items according to a specified set of rules; in numeric sequence, normally in ascending order.

sequence check A check used to prove that a set of data is arranged in ascending or descending order.

sequence structure One of three primary structures of a structured flow-chart, in which instructions are executed in order. See SELECTION STRUCTURE and LOOP STRUCTURE.

sequential Pertaining to the occurrence of events in time sequence, with little or no simultaneity or overlap of events.

sequential access The process of obtaining data from storage files in the order in which they were stored. Required with magnetic tape, which must be searched serially from the beginning to find any desired record. Contrast with DIRECT ACCESS.

sequential access storage device An AUXILIARY STORAGE DEVICE from which information is read in the order that it was written onto the device.

sequential computer A computer in which events occur in time sequence with little or no simultaneity or overlap of events.

sequential data set A data set whose records are organized on the basis of their successive physical positions, such as on magnetic tape.

sequential data structure A data structure in which one atom is immediately adjacent to the next atom. Also called contiguous data structure.

sequential device   A peripheral device from which data are read or into which data are written in order; nothing can be omitted.

sequential file organization   A file whose records can be accessed only sequentially.

sequential list   A list stored in contiguous locations. Also called dense list and linear list.

sequential logic   A circuit arrangement in which the output state is determined by the previous state of the input. Contrast with COMBINATION LOGIC.

sequential machine   A mathematical model of a certain type of sequential switching circuit.

sequential organization   The arrangement of data on a physical medium either ascendingly or descendingly by some key field.

sequential processing   Processing of files ordered numerically or alphabetically by key. Contrast with DIRECT ACCESS PROCESSING and RANDOM PROCESSING.

sequential storage   AUXILIARY STORAGE where data are arranged in ascending or descending order, usually by item number.

serial   **(1)** Pertaining to the sequential occurrence of two or more related activities in a single device. **(2)** Handling of data in a sequential fashion. Contrast with PARALLEL.

serial access   Descriptive of a storage device or medium in which there is a sequential relationship between access time and data location.

serial adder   An adder that performs its operations by bringing in one digit at a time from each of the quantities involved. Contrast with PARALLEL ADDER.

serial cable   A common term for a cable for connecting devices with serial ports (where each byte is sent, bit by bit, down a single wire).

serial computer   A computer in which each digit or data word bit is processed serially. Contrast with PARALLEL COMPUTER.

serial data   Data transmitted sequentially, one bit at a time.

serial form   The processing of data one bit at a time.

serial input/output   Data transmission in which the bits are sent one by one over a single wire. Contrast with PARALLEL INPUT/OUTPUT.

serial interface   An interface on which all the data moves over the same wire, one bit after the other. Contrast with PARALLEL INTERFACE.

serializability   The result of several users accessing data at the same time, which must be equivalent to that which occurs when they access the data one at a time.

serial machine   A computer that can process only one instruction at a time.

serial mouse   A MOUSE that connects to a computer's serial port.

serial operation   A computer operation in which all digits of a word are handled sequentially rather than simultaneously. Contrast with PARALLEL OPERATION.

serial port   Input/output port in a computer through which data are transmitted and received one bit at a time.

serial printer   A printer that receives information from the computer one bit at a time through a single wire. (One character equals eight bits). One or more additional wires may be necessary to exchange control signals. Serial printers print one character at a time and are designed to be connected to the computer's serial port.

serial processing   Reading and/or writing records on a file, one by one, in the physical sequence in which they are stored. See SERIAL ACCESS. Contrast with PARALLEL PROCESSING.

serial storage device   A SECONDARY STORAGE device on which data are stored one bit at a time.

serial transmission   A method of data transfer in which the bits composing a character are sent sequentially. Required for telephone data transfer. Contrast with PARALLEL TRANSMISSION.

Series/1   A series of MINICOMPUTERS from IBM Corporation, introduced in 1976.

serif   An ending stroke on the arms, tails, and stems of characters in certain typeface designs. Serif type styles are typically considered businesslike, formal, and authoritative.

serif face   A typeface that contains SERIFS, or finishing strokes.

server   (1) The central computer in a LOCAL AREA NETWORK (LAN); it is responsible for managing the LAN. The server is dedicated to serving devices attached to the network. (2) In OBJECT-ORIENTED PROGRAMMING, an object that never operates upon other objects, but that is only operated upon by other objects.

service bureau   An organization that provides data processing services for individuals or other organizations. See IMAGESETTER SERVICE BUREAU.

service contract   A contract with a computer dealer, computer store, or service company that ensures immediate repair of a computer system.

service programs   Programs that supplement the control programs of an operating system, such as language translators, utility routines, and programmer aids.

service representative   An individual who performs maintenance services for computer equipment or systems.

service window   The hours during the day or night that are covered by a maintenance agreement. Service provided outside the "window" is not covered by the contract.

servomechanism   A feedback control system.

session   The period of time during which a computer system operator works from a terminal at one sitting.

set   (1) To place a binary cell into the 1 state. (2) To place a storage device into a specified state, usually other than denoting zero or blank. (3) Any collection of related things. (4) In a relational database model, a collection of things. (5) In a network/hierarchical database model, a one-to-many relationship, the path by which one record type is connected to another.

SETL   A high-level language designed to facilitate the programming of algorithms involving sets and related structures.

setup   The arrangement of data or devices to solve a particular problem.

setup time   The time between computer runs or other machine operations that is devoted to such tasks as changing disk packs and moving forms and other supplies to and from the equipment.

shade   (1) In computer graphics, the quantity of black mixed with a pure color. (2) To give added dimension to an image by including changes in appearance caused by light and shadow.

shading   (1) Changing the brightness and color of parts of an image to simulate depth or otherwise enhance definition. (2) As applied to graphic objects, the way light reflects off a surface. (3) Emphasizing a given display group by changing the attributes of all other display groups in the same display field.

shading symbols   Block graphics characters that are part of some computer graphics built-in character sets. They provide different dot densities, giving the appearance of different levels of shading.

shadow mask   A metal plate with tiny holes positioned inside the CRT hardware. The electron beam passes from the electron gun through a hole in the shadow mask, which guides the beam and ensures its precise placement on the inside of the display surface.

shadow memory   In 32-bit computers, a portion of random access memory set aside for the storage of ROM routines during an operating session so that these routines can be executed at the microprocessor's fastest possible speed.

shadow printing   A style applied to text in which a duplicate of each character is shifted, often down and to the right, to create a shadow effect.

shape   Any area defined by line, color, tones, or the edges of forms. The visible configuration or outward form of something.

shape fill   The automatic painting-in of an area of a drawing, defined by user-specified boundaries.

SHARE   An organization of users of medium- and large-scale IBM data processing systems.

shared file   A direct access device that may be used by two systems at the same time; it may link two computer systems.

shared logic   The concurrent use of a single computer by multiple users.

shared memory   Memory accessed by two or more programs in a multi-tasking environment.

shared resource   A computer resource shared by more than one user or computer system.

shareware   Software that is passed around. The authors let users copy and share their programs freely, but retain the copyrights. Shareware provides income to its authors in the form of "contributions," much like public TV. Payment is strictly voluntary. Even though shareware is given away free, the maker hopes that satisfied users will voluntarily pay for it.

sharpen   To use an image-enhancement technique that enhances edges and details in an image.

sharpness   The clarity and quality of an image produced on a visual display device, digital plotter, printer, film recorder, or other device. See RESOLUTION.

Shatter   The first computer-generated comic book, published in 1984. The original work was drawn on an Apple Macintosh microcomputer with a monochrome paint program. The black and white output was hand-painted with an airbrush and traditional tools.

shattered image   An image broken into pieces to achieve a desired aesthetic effect through the use of computers and imaging software programs.

shear   In computer graphics, to slant an object along a specified axis.

sheetfed scanner   A scanner into which single pages are fed.

sheet feeder   A device that attaches to a printer, designed to automatically insert and line up single sheets of paper or envelopes in much the same way as an operator would perform the task. It usually sits above the printer platen and is operated either mechanically or electrically by the printer. See FRICTION-FEED.

shell   (1) An operating environment layer that separates the operating system from the user. The shell provides a graphical icon-oriented or menu-driven interface to the system in order to make it easier to use. (2) A high-level EXPERT SYSTEM framework. A shell is an expert system without the domain knowledge.

shield   A foil or braided-wire covering for a cable that prevents excessive noise pickup or radiation.

shielding   Protection against electrical or magnetic noise.

shift   To move the characters of a unit or information columnwise right or left. For a number, this is equivalent to multiplying or dividing by a power of the base of notation.

shift-click   To click the mouse button while depressing the shift key on the keyboard.

shift-key   The key on a computer keyboard that, when pressed, makes letters print as capitals instead of lowercase letters and allows some special characters to be printed. On many keyboards, it acts as a shift lock and must be pressed again to return to lowercase.

short card   In a MICROCOMPUTER, a plug-in printed circuit board that is half the length of a full-size accessory card or expansion card. Short cards plug into the microcomputer's expansion slots.

shortest operating time   A scheduling procedure for scheduling jobs that take the shortest amount of computer time first.

shutdown   The termination of electrical power to all or part of the computer system components, whether intentional or inadvertent.

SIA   See SEMICONDUCTOR INDUSTRY ASSOCIATION.

sidebar   A block of text or a graphic image placed to the side of the main body of text in a document.

side effect   A consistent result of a procedure that is in addition to the basic result.

SideKick™   A desktop accessory program that provides a computerized calculator, notepad, appointment calendar, and automated phone dialer. These features can be used alone or in combination with each other; some features can also be used with other software. Developed by Borland International, Inc.

sift   To extract certain desired items of information from a large amount of data. Compare SELECT.

sifting   A method of internal sorting by which records are moved to permit the insertion of other records; also called insertion method. Compare BUBBLE SORT.

SIG   Acronym for **s**pecial **i**nterest **g**roup, often a sub-unit of a professional organization. Made up of members with common interests, such as a "Computers in Education" SIG, a "Computer Graphics" SIG, or a "Computers in Medicine" SIG.

SIGGRAPH   A special interest group on COMPUTER GRAPHICS that is part of the Association for Computing Machinery (ACM). Each year SIGGRAPH holds an annual conference that has become a focus for the exchange of information regarding fundamental discoveries and the latest innovations in the field of computer graphics. The conference includes lectures, exhibits, films, and a computer art show.

sign   A term used in the arithmetic sense to describe whether a number is positive or negative.

signal   In communications theory, an intentional disturbance in a COMMUNICATIONS SYSTEM. Contrast with NOISE.

signaling rate   The rate at which signals are transmitted over a communications link.

signal-to-noise ratio   In data communications, the ratio of the (wanted) signal to the (unwanted) noise.

sign digit   A digit in the sign position of a word.

sign extension   Duplication of the sign bit in the higher-order positions of a register. Usually performed on one's complement or two's complement binary values.

sign flag   Flip-flop that goes to position 1 if the most significant bit of the result of an operation has the value of 1.

significant digit   Any digit that contributes to the precision of a number. The number of significant digits is counted beginning with the digit contributing the most value, called the most significant digit, and ending with the one contributing the least value, called the least significant digit.

sign-off   (**1**) The process of disconnecting from a time-sharing computer network. (**2**) The dissolution of any user/computer interface.

sign-on   (**1**) The process of getting connected to a time-sharing computer network. (**2**) The establishment of any user/computer interface.

sign position   The position at which the sign of a number is located.

silicon   A nonmetallic chemical element used in the manufacture of integrated circuits, solar cells, and so forth. It is a chemical element (atomic number 14, symbol Si) widely found in sand and clay.

silicon chip   A tiny portion of a silicon wafer with thousands of electronic components and circuit patterns etched on its surface.

silicon-controlled rectifier (SCR)   A semiconductor device that, in its normal state, blocks a voltage applied in either direction.

silicon disk drive   A drive that uses banks of RAM as a storage device.

Silicon Valley   The nickname for an area south of San Francisco noted for its large number of electronic, semiconductor, and computer manufacturing firms. Also known as Silicon Gulch.

silicon wafer   A silicon slice on which INTEGRATED CHIPS are fabricated. After fabrication, the wafer is cut into many individual chips, which are then mounted in dual in-line packages.

silk screen   A type of artwork that can be generated by a CAD/CAM system for printing component placement and/or identification information on a PC board.

SIMM   Acronym for SINGLE IN-LINE MEMORY MODULE, a module designed to add memory to a computer system. A special type of RAM chip that plugs into a socket on the computer's motherboard.

simplex   Pertaining to a communications link capable of transmitting data in only one direction. Contrast with FULL-DUPLEX and HALF-DUPLEX.

SIMSCRIPT   A high-level programming language specifically designed for simulation applications.

Simula   A language developed in the late 1960s for programming simulations. Simula included class and inheritance mechanisms and is considered to have influenced today's object-oriented languages. It was a forerunner of SMALLTALK.

simulation   The representation of certain features of the behavior of a physical or abstract system by the behavior of another system, such as the representation of physical phenomena by means of operations performed by a computer, or the representation of operations of a computer by those of another computer.

simulator   A device, computer program, or system that represents certain features of the behavior of a physical or abstract system.

simultaneous input/output   A process in which some computer systems allow new information to be input while other information is being output.

simultaneous processing   The execution of more than one program at the same time, each program using a separate CPU.

single address   See ONE-ADDRESS INSTRUCTION.

single-board computer   A computer that contains all its circuitry on one board, including the CPU, ROM, RAM, and peripheral interfaces.

single density   A method of storing data on a diskette. See DOUBLE DENSITY.

single entry   The unique point where execution of a program module begins.

single exit   The unique point where termination of a program module occurs.

Single In-line Memory Module (SIMM)   A module designed to add memory to a computer system. SIMMs are used in the Apple Macintosh line of computers.

single precision   Pertaining to the use of one computer word to represent a number. Contrast with DOUBLE PRECISION and TRIPLE PRECISION.

single-sided disk   A diskette with only one side used for reading and writing information. Contrast with DOUBLE-SIDED DISK.

single step   The operation of a computer in such a manner that only one instruction is executed each time the computer is started.

single-user computer   A microcomputer designed for use by one person; a PERSONAL COMPUTER.

site license   A license permitting a customer to make multiple copies of a piece of software and distribute them freely within the facility.

sixteen-bit chip   A microprocessor chip that processes information sixteen bits at a time. Contrast with EIGHT-BIT CHIP and THIRTY-TWO-BIT CHIP.

size   The physical magnitude of objects, forms, elements, and quantities.

sizing   The process of changing the size or shape of a window.

sketching A computer graphics technique in which a trail of lines is drawn or sketched along the path of the cursor.

sketch pad A working storage area displayed on a visual display screen that permits the operator to add and delete graphic or textual information easily before it is entered into permanent storage.

skew In computer graphics and optical scanning, a condition in which a character, line, or reprinted symbol is neither parallel with nor at right angles to the leading edge. See STAIRSTEPPING.

skip To ignore one or more instructions in a sequence of instructions.

skip factor In a computer graphics program, an increment that specifies how many data points the program should skip as it constructs a chart or graph.

slab Part of a WORD.

slack time See FLOAT.

slave A device controlled by another device.

slave tube A CATHODE RAY TUBE connected to another in such a way that both tubes perform identically.

SLD A slide file format for AutoCAD.

sleeve A protective envelope for storing a diskette.

slew To move paper through a PRINTER.

slewing A term describing the speed at which numerically controlled machine tools move from one position to another.

slice (1) The thin substrate resulting when a silicon ingot is cut; the wafer. (2) A special type of chip architecture that permits the cascading of devices to increase word bit size.

slide A photographic representation of a visual screen display.

slide show Computer-graphics software that displays graphics images in a timed sequence on the video display screen in a manner similar to a slide show.

slot (1) A single board position in a backplane. (2) In DATA COMMUNICATIONS, a unit of time in a multiplexed channel. (3) In ARTIFICIAL INTELLIGENCE, an element of a frame that is filled with descriptive information about a particular object or concept. (4) In OBJECT-ORIENTED PROGRAMMING, a respository for part of the state of an object; collectively, the slots of an object constitute its structure.

SLSI Abbreviation for SUPER LARGE-SCALE INTEGRATION.

slug (1) In DESKTOP PUBLISHING, a code inserted in headers or footers that generates page numbers when the document is printed. (2) In line printers, a metal casting that carries the image of a printable character. It prints by striking the paper.

small caps A font of capital letters that are smaller than the standard capital letters in that typeface.

Small Computer System Interface (SCSI) A general-purpose PARALLEL INTERFACE for high-speed access to peripheral devices.

small-scale integration (SSI) The class of INTEGRATED CIRCUITS that has the fewest number of functions per chip.

SmallTalk An OBJECT-ORIENTED PROGRAMMING language in which text is entered into the computer by using the keyboard, but all other tasks are performed using a mouse. SmallTalk systems are characterized by a high degree of pictorial interaction. SmallTalk was developed in the late 1970s by Alan Kay at Xerox Corporation's Palo Alto Research Center (PARC). It was used on Xerox's Alto computer, which was designed for it. SmallTalk has served as the forerunner of various computer languages and environments in use today. It was the first truly object-oriented programming language and environment.

smart Having some computational ability of its own. Smart devices usually contain their own microprocessors.

smart card   A credit card with a built-in microprocessor and memory that can be used as an identification or financial transaction card.

smart machines   Machines that use microprocessors as their control elements.

smart terminal   A terminal that contains some capacity to process information being transmitted or received, although not as much as an intelligent terminal. See LOCAL INTELLIGENCE. Contrast with DUMB TERMINAL.

smash   To destroy an area of storage by overwriting with another program.

SME   See SOCIETY OF MANUFACTURING ENGINEERS.

SMIS   Abbreviation for Society for Management Information Systems, a professional organization for fostering improved management performance and information exchange.

smooth   To apply procedures that decrease or eliminate rapid fluctuations in data.

smoothing   (1) Any image-enhancement technique in which the effect of noise in the original image is reduced. (2) Fitting together curves and surfaces so that a smooth, continuous geometry results.

smooth scrolling   Scrolling text without its jerking from one line to the next.

smooth shading   A shading method that blends colors smoothly across an object.

smudge   A feature of some graphics programs that blends colors or softens edges that are already in place in an image. The effect is supposed to resemble what would happen if someone ran a finger over an image made of wet paint.

SNA   Abbreviation for systems network architecture.

snapshot dump   A DYNAMIC DUMP of the contents of specified storage locations and/or registers performed at specified points or times during the running of a program.

snap, snap to   The automatic movement of a selected object or point to the nearest designated grid line, grid intersection, or connection point.

SNOBOL   Acronym for **str**ing-**o**riented sym**bo**lic **l**anguage, a unique language that provides complete facilities for the manipulation of strings of characters. SNOBOL was developed in 1962 by Ralph Griswold at Bell Laboratories and was the forerunner of languages such as LISP. Nowadays, the language is little used because the language statements do not provide for structured programming. However, the characteristics of SNOBOL make it suitable for artificial intelligence applications.

SO   Acronym for **s**end **o**nly, a designation used to indicate the send-only capabilities of equipment. Contrast with RECEIVE ONLY.

Society for Computer Simulation (SCS)   The only technical society devoted primarily to the advancement of simulation and allied technologies, notably those dealing with management, social, scientific, biological, and environmental problems; has a worldwide membership.

Society of Certified Data Processors (SCDP)   An organization that represents the interests and wishes of certified computer professionals, formed in 1971. Members control the positions, actions, and directions the organization takes.

Society of Manufacturing Engineers (SME)   A professional society of manufacturing engineers, industrial engineers, computer professionals, and others involved in manufacturing disciplines. SME has special interest groups (SIGs) for all areas of manufacturing. The Computer and Automated Systems Association (CASA) and Robotics International (RI) groups are very active in developing and promoting advanced manufacturing techniques and philosophies.

soft clip area   Limits of the area where data can be presented on a plotting device.

soft copy   Data presented as a display screen image, in audio format, or in any other form that is not HARD COPY.

soften   To use a filtering effect that decreases contrast in an image.

softer software   SOFTWARE that is very easy to use.

soft fails   Spontaneous changes in the information stored in computer memories due to noise bursts in microelectronic circuits caused by cosmic-ray particles.

soft font   A font that is downloaded from a computer to a printer from files stored on a disk.

soft hyphen   A conditional (nonrequired) hyphen printed only to break a word between syllables at the end of a line. Contrast with HARD HYPHEN.

soft keys   The keys on a keyboard that can have a user-defined meaning, so-called because their meaning can change from user to user or program to program.

soft return   A combination line feed/carriage return command, entered by a program containing the word wrap feature, to begin a new line within a paragraph. Unlike a hard return, it is conditional— the computer executes the command only when the current word doesn't fit in the line in progress.

soft sector   A method of marking sectors or sections on a disk by using information written on the disk; a method of determining positioning of data on the disk by software calculations rather than by physical monitoring of the disk. Contrast with HARD SECTOR.

software   The generic term for any computer program or programs; instructions that cause the hardware to do work. Contrast with the "iron" or HARDWARE of a computer system.

software base   Software available for a particular computer system. The broader the software base, the more versatile the computer system.

software broker   An individual who specializes in marketing software packages.

software command language   A HIGH-LEVEL LANGUAGE developed to work with an application, such as a database management program.

software company   A SOFTWARE HOUSE.

software compatibility   The ability to use programs written for one system on another system with little or no change.

software development   The creation of sets of programs that meet the requirements of a user.

software development tools   Programs used to develop, analyze, debug, and perfect software. These tools include compilers, editors, debuggers, linkers, optimizers, and libraries.

software documents   The written or printed material associated with computer equipment and software systems.

software encryption   The encoding or decoding of computerized data by using programming techniques rather than hardware devices such as scramblers.

software engineering   A term coined in 1967 by the Study Group on Computer Science of the NATO Science Committee to imply the need for software manufacture based on the types of theoretical foundations and practical disciplines traditional in established branches of engineering. Software engineering is concerned with the development and implementation of large-scale software systems on production-model computers. It encompasses a broad range of topics related to the controlled design and development of high-quality computer software, including programming methodology and management of software projects.

software flexibility   The property of software that enables it to change easily in response to different user and system requirements.

software gap   The relative difference between the costs of hardware and software.

software house   A company that offers both general software packages and specific software packages for sale to computer system owners. See PACKAGED SOFTWARE.

software librarian   The person in charge of a large collection of software (usually on disk packs, diskettes, or magnetic tapes) in a company. See CUSTODIAN.

software license   A contract signed by the purchaser of a software product in which he/she is usually made to agree not to make copies of the software for resale.

software maintenance   The ongoing process of detecting and removing errors from existing programs; done by maintenance programmers.

software monitor   A program used for performance measurement purposes.

software package   A prewritten program that can be purchased for use with a specific computer to perform a specific task. Usually includes the programs, stored on a storage medium (floppy disk, CD-ROM, and so on), and an operating manual.

software piracy   Copying of commercial or proprietary software without permission of the originator.

software portability   The ease with which a program can be moved from one computer environment to another. As third-party software becomes more prevalent in the computer industry, portability becomes a more valuable attribute.

software product   A vendor package comprising programs, data, documentation, and sometimes vendor assistance; also called programming product.

software protection   The resistance to unauthorized copying of software. See SOFTWARE PIRACY.

software publisher   A business that designs, develops, and distributes software packages.

software resources   Program and data resources that represent the software associated with a computing system.

software science   The discipline concerned with the measurable properties of computer programs.

software security   The protection of software assets such as user application programs, database management software, and the operating system.

software system The entire set of computer programs and their documentation, as used in a computer system.

software tools Programs that help programmers write other programs. Such tools include compilers, editors, debuggers, clip-art libraries, source-code libraries, and so on.

software transportability The ability to take a program written for one computer and run it without modification on another computer. See SOFTWARE PORTABILITY.

solarization In computer graphics, an effect achieved by changing the intensity levels in an image in a way that particularly brightens or transforms the middle levels.

soldered A term describing the way chips are placed on circuit boards. Chips are soldered onto the board with a melted metal that seals them securely in place. Today, some boards have snap-in chips, making it easier for end users to add and replace chips as necessary.

solicitation A request to vendors to submit bids for hardware, software, or services. See REQUEST FOR PROPOSAL and REQUEST FOR QUOTATION.

solid A black or one-color area on a printed page that contains no artwork, text, or patterns.

solid font mechanism The printing element on a printer, such as a DAISY WHEEL PRINTER, that produces solid characters.

solid modeling A mathematical technique for representing three-dimensional images and cross-sections of solids. Unlike wireframe and surface modeling, solid modeling systems ensure that all surfaces meet properly and that the object is geometrically correct.

solid state The generic name given to integrated circuits and other electronic systems containing no moving parts as part of their prime functions.

solid state device A device built primarily from solid state electronic circuit elements.

S-100 bus The standard means of interconnection between some older microcomputers and peripheral equipment, so named because popularity made it standard and it has 100 electrical contacts.

son file   See FATHER FILE.

sonic pen   A pencil-shaped device using sound to select a screen location.

SOP   Acronym for **s**tandard **o**perating **p**rocedure, the status quo.

sort   To arrange data into a new sequence according to a logical system.

sort effort   The number of steps needed to order an unordered list.

sorter   A program that sorts data.

sort generator   A program that generates a sort program for production running.

sorting   The process of arranging data according to a logical system.

sort/merge program   A generalized processing program that can be used to sort or merge records in a prescribed sequence.

SOS   Abbreviation for **s**ilicon **o**n **s**apphire, the process of fabricating integrated chips on layers of silicon and sapphire.

sound   Any wave motion in air that is detected by the ear. Most computers have commands that enable sounds to be generated, ranging from simple beeps to multichannel music with harmony.

sound chip   The integrated circuit that executes sound instructions. Microcomputers use specialized sound chips that are microprocessors in their own right. A distinguishing feature of these chips is their ability to synthesize sound effects.

sound hood   A device that fits over a printer during use to dampen noise; also called acoustical sound enclosure.

source   **(1)** One of three terminals or electrodes of a field effect transistor; the origin of the charge carriers that flow past the gate to the drain. **(2)** A disk, file, or document from which data is taken or moved.

Source (The)   An information utility service available to subscribers. It allows users with microcomputers and modems to play games, access databases, check flight schedules, post messages, receive and send electronic mail, read newspaper wire services, and do a host of other things. Personal computer users can use The Source network via a common telephone hookup. It is operated by The Source Telecomputing Corporation.

source code   Symbolic coding in its original form before being processed by a computer. The computer automatically translates source code into a code it can understand.

source computer   The computer used to translate a SOURCE PROGRAM into an OBJECT-ORIENTED PROGRAM.

source-data automation   The process whereby data created while an event is taking place is entered directly into the system in a machine-processable form. See TRANSACTION PROCESSING.

source disk   The disk from which a file or program is copied. Contrast with TARGET DISK.

source document   Any original document from which basic data is extracted, such as an invoice, a sales slip, or an inventory tag.

source language   Any low-level language, such as assembly language, or any high-level language— such as BASIC, PASCAL, or COBOL— in which a source program is written.

source media   Checks or other source documents from which raw data is derived. Compare INPUT MEDIA and OUTPUT MEDIA.

source module   The original form in which a program is entered into an input device by a user or programmer prior to being translated into machine language. Also called source program.

source program   A program as originally coded, before being translated into machine language. It is converted to a machine language program by a COMPILER, INTERPRETER, or ASSEMBLER.

source program listing   A printed version of a program as the programmer wrote it.

source register   A register that contains a data word that is being transferred.

source statement   A single statement in the source code of a program.

SPA   Abbreviation for **S**ystems and **P**rocedures **A**ssociation, a professional organization whose purpose is to promote advanced management systems and procedures through seminars, professional education, and research.

space   (1) One or more blank characters. (2) The state of a communications channel corresponding to a binary zero.

spacebar   At the bottom of a keyboard, the long, narrow key that generates spaces. When pressed once, it causes a space to be placed into the text at the insertion point.

space figures   In computer graphics, a set of points that may have one, two, or three dimensions, such as cubes, spheres, and pyramids. Sometimes called solids, solid geometrical figures, or solid shapes.

spaghetti code   A program written with poor structure and very little discernable logic flow. The term was first used by Edsger Dijkstra. It often implies an excessive use of the GOTO statement.

span   The difference between the highest and lowest values in a range of values.

spanning tree   A subgraph of a graph with two properties: that it is a tree, and that it contains all the nodes of the original graph.

sparse array   An array in which most of the entries have a value of zero.

spatial   Having the attributes of two- or three-dimensional space.

spatial data management   A technique that allows users access to information by pointing at pictures on a display screen representing databases, document files, or any category of information.

spatial digitizer   A device often used in computer graphics to simulate three-dimensional objects; a three-dimensional scanner.

spatial resolution   The number of PIXELS used to represent an image from side to side and top to bottom.

spec   Abbreviation for SPECIFICATION; more often, specs.

special character   A graphics character that is neither a letter, a digit, nor a blank; for example, a plus sign, equal sign, asterisk, dollar sign, comma, period, and so on.

special function key   The key on a keyboard to control a mechanical function, initiate a specific computer operation, or transmit a signal that would otherwise require multiple key strokes.

Special Interest Group (SIG)   Any special group within an organization that holds meetings, sponsors exhibits, and publishes documents related to some special interest, topic, or subject. For example, the Association for Computing Machinery (ACM) has more than 30 SIGs. These groups elect their own officers, set their own dues, and are self-supporting.

Special Libraries Association (SLA)   An international organization of libraries and information specialists that promotes the establishment of resource centers for various interest groups such as banks, museums, and law firms.

special-purpose   Being applicable to a limited class of uses without essential modification. See DEDICATED. Contrast with GENERAL-PURPOSE.

special-purpose computer   A computer designed for solving only a few selected types of numerical or logical problems. Uses range from automobiles, cameras, and home appliances to monitoring flights of space vehicles. Contrast with GENERAL-PURPOSE COMPUTER.

special-purpose programming language   A programming language designed to handle one specific type of problem or application.

specification   A detailed description of the required characteristics of a device, process, or product.

specification sheet   A form used for coding RPG statements.

specific DSS   A decision support system (DSS) that solves a specific problem.

specs   Specifications.

SpectraColor   A color paint program for the Commodore Amiga computer.

speech processing   The field of ARTIFICIAL INTELLIGENCE whose goal is to recognize and synthesize spoken human speech.

speech recognition   The process of presenting input data to the computer through the spoken word; the discrimination of speech sounds by a computer.

speech recognition device   A device that accepts the spoken word through a microphone and converts it into digital code that can be understood by a computer.

speech synthesis   The computer generation of sound that resembles human speech. The synthesis is accomplished through the use of stored sounds and algorithms.

speech synthesizer   A device that converts numerical code into recognizable speech, which is played over a loudspeaker; a peripheral that converts output signals into an artificial human voice that "speaks." See DIGITAL SPEECH.

speech understanding systems   ARTIFICIAL INTELLIGENCE programs whose goal is to understand human speech.

speed of light   The speed at which light travels—186,284 miles per second. A limiting factor in the speed of data transmissions within and between computers and peripherals.

spelling checker   A computer program, usually associated with word processing, that compares typed words against a word list and informs the user of possible spelling mistakes. A sophisticated spelling checker can have a base dictionary of well over 100,000 words and can provide the user with the ability to create special-purpose dictionaries of words not included in the base dictionary.

spider configuration   A type of distributed system in which a central computer system is used to monitor the activities of several network computer systems.

spike   A sharp-peaked, short-duration voltage transient; a brief sudden surge of electricity. A spike that affects the power supply of a computer can wipe out data. Spike suppressors can be inserted between the computer and the 120-volt AC receptacle to reduce this problem.

spindle   An axle for mounting a disk or reel of MAGNETIC TAPE.

Splash!   A paint program for IBM-compatible microcomputers.

spline   In computer graphics, a piecewise polynomial with at least first-order continuity between the pieces. A mathematically simple and elegant way to connect disjoint data points smoothly; hence, it is used not only for generating smooth curves and surfaces between sparse data points, but also for smooth motions between parameters sparsely located in time, such as those used to describe the key-frames in an animation.

spline curve   See B-SPLINE CURVE.

split screen   A display screen that can be partitioned into two or more areas (windows) so that different screen formats can be shown on the screen at the same time. It implies that one set of data can be manipulated independently of the other.

splitting a window   The act of dividing a window into two or more panes.

spooler   SOFTWARE that coordinates the movement of data between a file and the printer.

spooling   The process of storing information in a special area of memory or a disk in preparation for being sent to the printer. The spooler is typically used to speed up the apparent throughput of a computer system.

spooling program   A program that temporarily stores input or output in auxiliary storage to expedite processing.

spot   In referring to the output of an imagesetter or film recorder, the smallest element that can be written. Also called pixel or dot.

spot color   The use of one or more extra colors on a page to highlight specified page elements. Colors are usually specified as PMS codes.

spot size   In vector displays, the diameter of the focused electron beam of the display surface.

spray can   One of the capabilities found in several computer graphics systems. A spray can provides the computer graphics artist with a method of shading or "spraying" an area with a specific pattern or color.

spraying   A feature of a paint program mimicking the action of a spray gun by painting a fine pattern of pixels.

spread   In computer graphics, enlarging the width of lines in an image to overlay gaps between the line and an adjoining fill area.

spreadsheet   A program that uses a matrix consisting of rows and columns to perform calculations on numerical data. Spreadsheets are widely used in most businesses to perform both simple and complex financial computations.

spreadsheet analysis   An analysis of data that uses a spreadsheet made up of values and formulas.

sprites   Small, high-resolution objects that can be moved independently of other text or graphics on the monitor. They can change color and size and move in front of or behind other objects on the monitor. Used to create animated sequences.

sprocket holes   Equally spaced holes on both edges of continuous forms for use by a TRACTOR-FEED MECHANISM to feed paper through a printer.

SQL   See STRUCTURED QUERY LANGUAGE.

squash and stretch   In computer graphics, the technique of exaggeration of a drawing; the distortion given to a normal reaction to make it more forceful.

squeezer   The person who lays out the LSI circuit in its original "large" form.

SRAM   Abbreviation for **s**tatic **r**andom-**a**ccess **m**emory, memory chips that can hold data stored in them without requiring a regular clock signal. SRAM chips are more expensive and hold less data than DRAM chips, but they can work faster.

SSI   Abbreviation for **S**MALL-**S**CALE **I**NTEGRATION.

ST   A PERSONAL COMPUTER series from Atari Corporation. The Atari ST family of personal computers are high-performance personal computers with capabilities for computer graphics in color.

stack   A sequential data list stored in internal storage. Rather than addressing the stack elements by their memory locations, the computer retrieves information from the stack by popping elements from the top (LIFO) or from the bottom (FIFO). See PROGRAM STACK and STACK POINTER.

stack pointer   A register used to point to locations in the stack. Incremented by one before each new data item is pulled or popped from the STACK, and decremented by one after a word is pushed onto the stack. See POP and PUSH.

stacks   A term given to a "stack" of cards (information displayed on-screen) created through HYPERCARD.

staffing   Hiring and training workers.

staircasing   A characteristic of lines drawn on dot matrix screens that makes them appear jagged rather than smooth. The degree of staircasing depends on the angle at which the line is drawn (horizontal and vertical lines do not exhibit staircasing) and the resolution of the screen. Finer screens exhibit far less staircasing than coarse ones. Synonymous with ALIASING.

stairstepping   A rough or "stairstep" appearance in a line or curve that should be smooth.

stair-steps   See ALIASING and ANTIALIASING.

stand-alone   A term descriptive of a single, self-contained computer system, as opposed to a terminal that is connected to and dependent upon a remote computer system. A stand-alone device can operate by itself, requiring no other equipment.

stand-alone graphics system   A graphics system that includes a microcomputer or minicomputer, storage, video display terminal, and other input/output devices.

stand-alone program   A self-contained program, such as a word processing or spreadsheet program.

stand-alone system   A self-contained computer system that can work independently, not connected to or under the control of another computer system. A stand-alone system contains all the hardware and software a user requires.

standard   (1) A guide used to establish uniform practices and common techniques. (2) A yardstick (or meterstick) used to measure performance of any computer system function. May be laid down by a statutory body or simply created by a major manufacturer's practice. See ANSI.

standard cell   A technique for designing integrated circuits where predefined functions such as processing elements and memories are obtained from libraries and used in the design process.

standard interface   The standard physical means by which all peripheral devices are connected to the central processing unit, such as a standard form of plug and jack. See RS-232C.

standardize   To establish standards or to cause conformity with established standards.

Standard Pascal   A version of the PASCAL programming language that is described in the Pascal User Manual and Report by Kathleen Jensen and Niklaus Wirth.

standards enforcer   A computer program used to determine automatically whether prescribed programming standards and practices have been followed.

standby equipment   A duplicate set of equipment to be used as backup if the primary unit becomes unusable because of malfunction.

standby time   **(1)** The period between placing an inquiry into the equipment and the availability of the reply. **(2)** The period between the setup of the equipment for use and its actual use. **(3)** The period during which equipment is available for use but is not being used.

Star   A workstation from Xerox Corporation that introduced the desktop user interface in 1981. Although the Star was not successful, it was the inspiration for Xerox's subsequent machines and Apple's Macintosh microcomputer.

star network   A network configuration consisting of a central host computer and satellite terminals that connect to the computer to form a star pattern. The remote terminals may be geographically widespread.

start bit   **(1)** A bit or group of bits that identifies the beginning of a data word. **(2)** A bit indicating the beginning of an asynchronous serial transmission. Contrast with STOP BIT.

start/stop symbol   An oval symbol used to indicate the beginning and end of a FLOWCHART.

startup   The process of setting computer system devices to proper initial conditions and applying appropriate electrical power.

startup disk   A DISKETTE that contains the information to start the computer system.

startup screen   A graphics file that, when placed in the System Folder on an Apple Macintosh computer, is displayed when the computer is turned on. Any bit-mapped graphic image can be used as a startup screen. For example, users can display a fish, a tree, or even a picture of a favorite movie star.

state   **(1)** A condition of bistable devices used to represent binary digits. By definition, such devices can have only two states; the state of a switch describes whether it is on or off. **(2)** In OBJECT-ORIENTED PROGRAMMING, one of the possible conditions in which an object may exist.

statement   An expression of instruction in a COMPUTER LANGUAGE.

statement label   A line number or symbol of a statement in a source-language program.

state-of-the-art   A phrase pertaining to the very latest technology; at the forefront of current hardware or software technology.

static   Not moving or progressing; stationary; at rest.

static analysis   An analysis of a program performed without executing the program.

static binding   A binding in which the name/class association is made when the name is declared (at compile time) but before the creation of the object that the name designates. In OBJECT-ORIENTED PROGRAMMING, binding denotes the association of a name with a class.

static dump   A storage dump performed at a particular point in time with respect to a machine run, often at the termination of a run. See POST-MORTEM DUMP. Contrast with DYNAMIC DUMP.

staticizing   The process of transferring an instruction from computer storage to the instruction registers and holding it there, ready to be executed.

static memory   Memory that retains its programmed state as long as power is applied. It does not need to be refreshed, and does not require a clock. See NONVOLATILE STORAGE.

static RAM   Memory that doesn't need to be refreshed many times a second, as is required with DYNAMIC RAM. It does not lose its contents as long as power to the computer is on. Once the computer puts a value into a static memory location, it remains there. Abbreviated SRAM.

static typing   In OBJECT-ORIENTED PROGRAMMING, the addition of types to each object at compile time.

station   One of the input or output points on a data communications system. Synonymous with workstation. See TERMINAL.

statistics   The branch of mathematics that collects information and tabulates and analyzes it.

status   The present condition of a system component.

status report   An analysis of actual project costs and time expended against the plan, with variances calculated and displayed.

stem   In typography, the main vertical stroke of a character.

step   (1) To cause a computer to execute one instruction. (2) One instruction in a computer routine.

stepped motor   A mechanical device that rotates by a fixed amount each time it is pulsed. Often used in disk drives and digital plotters.

stepwise refinement   The process of breaking major program modules down into lower-level components.

steropsis   The dimensional perception resulting from two different views of the same image.

stick model   A model made of lines, or vectors. For example, in dancing applications, the limbs of a person are converted into lines so that the dance steps can be observed and studied.

stickup initial   In DESKTOP PUBLISHING, an enlarged initial letter at the beginning of a paragraph that rises above the top of the first line.

stippling   (1) In computer graphics, the technique of applying color or tone as a mass of small dots made with the point of a fine brush, a drawing instrument, or the paintbrush facility of a computer paint program. (2) Filling a region with a stipple, or a pattern of dots.

stitch   To combine several images, especially side-by-side strips made by hand scanners, into a single image.

stochastic process   Any process dealing with events that develop in time or space and that cannot be described precisely, except in terms of probability theory.

stop bit   (1) A bit or group of bits that identifies the end of a data word and defines the space between data words. **(2)** A bit indicating the end of an asynchronous serial transmission. Contrast with START BIT.

stop code   A specific control character.

stop key   In WORD PROCESSING, a control that terminates or interrupts an operation.

storage   Descriptive of a device or medium that can accept data, hold it, and deliver it on demand at a later time. The term is preferred over memory. See AUXILIARY STORAGE, INTERNAL STORAGE, PROM, PROTECTED STORAGE, RAM, and ROM.

storage allocation   The assignment of specific programs, program segments, and/or blocks of data to specific portions of a computer's storage. Sometimes called MEMORY ALLOCATION. See PROGRAM STORAGE.

storage block   A contiguous area of INTERNAL STORAGE.

storage capacity   The number of items of data that a storage device is capable of containing. Frequently defined in terms of computer bytes (Kbytes or Mbytes).

storage device   A device used for storing data within a computer system, such as a hard disk, floppy disk, magnetic tape, or optical disc.

storage dump   A printout of all or part of the contents of the internal storage of a computer. Often used to diagnose errors. Also called MEMORY DUMP. See POST-MORTEM DUMP and SNAPSHOT DUMP.

storage fragmentation   A condition in which there are many scattered areas of storage that are too small to be used productively.

storage key   An indicator associated with a storage block or blocks; it requires that tasks have a matching protection key to use the blocks. See PRIVILEGED INSTRUCTION and STORAGE PROTECTION.

storage location   A position in storage where a character, byte, or word may be stored. Same as CELL.

storage map   A diagram that shows where programs and data are stored in the storage units of the computer system. Also called MAP.

storage partitioning The subdividing of storage into independent sections.

storage pool A group of similar storage devices; disk drives in a computer installation are collectively referred to as the disk pool.

storage protection Protection against unauthorized writing in and/or reading from all or part of a storage device. Generally implemented automatically by hardware facilities, usually in connection with an operating system. Sometimes called memory protection. See STORAGE KEY.

storage tube An electron tube into which information can be introduced and from which it can be extracted at a later time. Used in FIRST-GENERATION COMPUTERS.

storage unit See STORAGE DEVICE.

store (1) The British term for storage. (2) To place in storage.

store-and-forward In DATA COMMUNICATIONS, the process-handling messages used in a message-switching system.

stored-program computer A computer capable of performing sequences of internally stored instructions and usually capable of modifying those instructions as directed by them. Same as digital computer.

stored-program concept The storage of instructions, as well as data values, within the internal storage of a computer. The instructions can thus be accessed more quickly and may more easily be modified.

storyboard Preliminary sketches or diagrams made in panels to suggest the sequence of action and dialogue for movies, TV ads, and so forth.

straight-line code The repetition of a sequence of instructions by explicitly writing the instructions for each repetition. Generally, straight-line coding requires less execution time and more storage space than equivalent loop coding. Contrast with LOOP CODE.

straight-line drawing A GRAPHICS IMAGE composed of only straight lines.

streaming cartridge A type of cartridge tape drive that records whole tracks of a cartridge at one time, rather than stopping and starting for individual blocks. Used primarily for backup of hard disk drives.

street price   The current price of a computer product at a computer store, mail order business, or other retail business. The street price is often considerably lower than its retail price. It is an average price charged by dealers around the country. See LIST PRICE.

STRESS   Acronym for **St**ructural **E**ngineering **S**ystem **S**olver, a problem-oriented language used for solving structural engineering problems.

stress testing   Ensuring through trial operation that a program or system will continue to perform reliably in spite of data inaccuracies and extraordinary data volumes.

stretch   In computer graphics, a graphics aid that enables the user to automatically expand a displayed entity beyond its original dimensions.

strikethrough   A line drawn through a selected range of text. Marking text in this manner indicates that the text is to be deleted at some future time.

string   A connected sequence of characters or bits treated as a single data item. The word "windsurfer" is a string of ten characters.

string handling   The ability of a programming language to operate on strings of characters.

string length   The number of characters in a string.

string manipulation   A technique for manipulating strings of characters.

string processing languages   Programming languages designed to facilitate the processing of strings of characters.

string variable   A string of alphanumeric strings.

stringy floppy   A computer storage device that holds a magnetic tape, called a wafer. The enclosed wafer tape is thinner, narrower, and faster than conventional cassette tapes.

strobing   A peculiar jitter effect that results in computer animation when an object is moved too fast and leaves a representative trail behind it.

stroke (1) In computer graphics, a line created as a vector. (2) In DATA ENTRY, a keystroke. (3) In PAINT PROGRAMS, a "swipe" of the paintbrush made when creating a graphic image. (4) In printing, the weight, or thickness, of a character.

stroke beam In computer graphics, a technique for displaying information on a CRT that directs the beam from point to point on the display screen. The beam traces only the points required to display the desired information.

stroke display An alternative name for a CRT vector display.

stroke writer A vector graphics terminal that represents objects on a screen by a series of lines (vectors).

stroke writing A graphics picture-generating technique in which a beam is moved simultaneously in X and Y directions along a curve or straight path in much the same way as in an Etch-A-Sketch™ children's toy.

strongly typed language A COMPUTER LANGUAGE that requires the declaration of all variables as to their type.

structural description A description of an object based on its components and the relationships among them.

structural design (1) The overall organization and control logic of processing. (2) In ARTIFICIAL INTELLIGENCE, an approach to expert system design that consists of reducing a problem to a set of subgoals. A module is designed for each subgoal.

structure (1) The organization or arrangement of the parts of an entity; the manner in which a program is organized. The design and composition of a program. A STRUCTURED PROGRAM is one in which the purpose of the program can be found easily by reading the listing, and the main part of the program can be used as an index to find the details of how actions are carried out. (2) In OBJECT-ORIENTED PROGRAMMING, the concrete representation of the state of an object.

structure chart A design tool for documenting the organization or program modules and the control logic that relates them to one another. The graphic representation of TOP-DOWN PROGRAMMING.

structured analysis   The examination of a complex problem by breaking it down into simple functions.

structured approach   In SYSTEMS ANALYSIS, a set pattern of steps from a logical design of a system to a physical design.

structured coding   A method of writing programs with a high degree of structure.

structured data   Data generated in a byte/character format that is stored as organized information such as textual data.

structured decisions   Decisions for which policy can be set in advance.

structured design   A methodology for designing programs and systems through top-down, hierarchical partitioning and logical control structures.

structured English   An approach to languages that is based on replacing symbols with recognizable English words.

structured flowchart   A method of representing problem solutions in terms of three flowcharting structures: the sequence structure, the selection structure, and the loop structure.

structured graphics   See OBJECT-ORIENTED GRAPHICS.

structured program flowchart   A FLOWCHART embodying many of the principles of STRUCTURED PROGRAMMING.

structured programming   A programming technique used in the design and coding of computer programs. The approach assumes the disciplined use of a few basic coding structures and the use of top-down concepts to decompose main functions into lower-level components for modular coding purposes. It is concerned with improving the programming process through better organization and programs, and with better programming notation to facilitate correct and clear descriptions of data and control structures.

Structured Query Language (SQL) A RELATIONAL DATABASE LANGUAGE developed by IBM Corporation. SQL allows users to present near-English queries to the database manager in order to view the database in a variety of different ways.

structured walkthrough A formal review process in which a designer or programmer leads one or more members of the development team through a segment of design or code.

structure knowledge One of three types of knowledge found in diagnostic EXPERT SYSTEMS. It is the knowledge of the parts the expert system is to diagnose.

STRUDL Acronym for **Stru**ctural **D**esign **L**anguage, a programming language used for the design and analysis of structures.

stub A routine that contains no executable code. A dummy-program module.

stub testing A top-down module testing process that involves using a small dummy-program module inserted and called in a larger program at the location of and in lieu of another routine.

Studio/8™ An Apple Macintosh paint program that supports color.

Studio/1™ An Apple Macintosh graphics program that combines black-and-white painting, scanning, and animation with a computer slide-show capability.

Studio/32™ A powerful Apple Macintosh paint program that supports 32-bit full color, giving computer artists virtually unlimited colors and tools to work with.

style A variation in the appearance of a typeface (for example, italic, bold, shadow, outlined, normal).

style sheet In WORD PROCESSING and DESKTOP PUBLISHING, a file that contains formatting instructions but not text. Style sheets contain such information as margin sizes, column widths, paragraph indentation, spacing, fonts, size, and style. Applying a style sheet to text automatically formats the text according to the style sheet's specifications.

stylus In computer graphics, a pointer operated by placing it in a display space or a graphics tablet. To draw a point, the user touches the stylus (also called a pen) tip to the surface of the graphics tablet. The stylus and graphics tablet are preferred drawing devices for artists.

subclass In OBJECT-ORIENTED PROGRAMMING, the refinement of a class into a more specialized class.

subdirectory A file that lists the names of other files and is displayed in a disk directory. This system allows files to be classified together to save space in a disk directory. A directory within another directory.

sublaptop A hand-held or pocket-size portable MICROCOMPUTER, weighing as little as one pound.

submenu An additional set of options related to a prior menu selection.

subprogram The segment of a program that can perform a specific function. It can reduce programming time when a specific function is required at more than one point in a program. If the required function is handled as a subprogram, the statements for that function can be coded once and executed at the various points in the program. SUBROUTINES and FUNCTIONS may be used to provide subprograms.

suboptimized system A system in which at least one subsystem is not integrated with other subsystems, resulting in a less-than-optimal performance by the overall system.

subroutine A subsidiary routine within which initial execution never starts. Executed when called by some other program, usually the main program. Also called subprogram. See CLOSED SUBROUTINE, OPEN SUBROUTINE, and NESTED SUBROUTINE.

subroutine reentry The initiation of a subroutine by one program before it has finished its response to another program that called for it. May happen when a control program is subjected to a priority interrupt.

subschema   The logical organization of data required for a particular program; an individual user's partial view of the database.

subscript   (1) An integer value, appended to a variable name, that defines the storage elements composing an array or a matrix. (2) In noncomputer typefonts, a letter or digit written below and to the right of a symbol to distinguish it from variations of the same symbol, such as Q_a and Q_b. Contrast with SUPERSCRIPT.

subscripted variable   A symbol whose numeric value can change, denoted by an array name followed by a subscript, such as CHESS(2,4) or A(7). See SUBSCRIPT and VARIABLE.

subset   Any set contained within another set.

subtraction   In computer graphics, a method of combining two objects into one. The subtracted object "carves away" the overlapping portion of the second object.

substrate   In microelectronics, the physical material on which a circuit is fabricated. Silicon is the most widely used substrate for the manufacturing of chips.

substring   A portion of a character string.

subsystem   A system under the control of the main system. A microcomputer might serve as a data collection subsystem for the mainframe.

suite   A set or group of closely related or interacting programs.

summarizing   The process of reducing a mass of data to a manageable form.

summary report   A management information system report limited to totals or trends.

Sun Microsystems, Inc.   A manufacturer of network-based, high-performance workstations founded in 1982.

SuperCalc   A SPREADSHEET for IBM-compatible microcomputers from Computer Associates. It was one of the first spreadsheets in the early 1980s. Several enhanced versions of the spreadsheet have been released.

superclass In an OBJECT-ORIENTED PROGRAMMING inheritance hierarchy, a more general class that stores variables and methods that can be inherited by other classes.

supercomputer The largest, fastest, and most expensive mainframe computer available. Used by businesses and organizations that require extraordinary amounts of computing power.

superconducting computers High-performance computers whose circuits employ superconductivity and the JOSEPHSON EFFECT to reduce cycle time.

superconductor An ultra-fast electronic circuit.

superimposition **(1)** In computer graphics, the combination of two separate drawings into a single drawing. **(2)** The laying of one image or portion of an image over another.

super large-scale integration The use of ultra-high-density chips that contain millions of components per chip.

supermini Any of a group of minicomputers that have the fastest processing speeds available at a given time.

SuperPaint™ An Apple Macintosh graphics program that combines drawing and paint capabilities.

superscript A letter or digit written above and to the right of a symbol to denote a power or to identify a particular element of a set, such as the 3 in x^3. Contrast with SUBSCRIPT.

Super 3D An Apple Macintosh graphic program.

Super VGA A high-resolution video display standard for IBM microcomputers and compatibles.

supervisor The part of the operating system that schedules and coordinates the execution of other programs.

supply company A company that offers a number of supplies that may not be produced and distributed by computer manufacturers, such as printer paper, printer ribbons, and diskettes.

support The help and verbal advice that a vendor supplies a customer.

support equipment All the machines that make it possible to get data and programs into the CPU, get processed information out, and store data and programs for ready access to the CPU.

support library A library that contains complete programs and subroutines that have already been developed, tested, and documented.

suppress To eliminate leading zeros or other insignificant characters from a computer printout. See ZERO SUPPRESSION.

suppression The elimination of some undesired components of a signal.

surface A set of points; usually undefined in geometry. There are plane surfaces such that a straight line joining any two of its points lies completely in the plane, and there are curved surfaces of which no part is a plane. A surface may consist of plane and curved surfaces.

surface modeling A display method used by some computer-aided design (CAD) programs that gives on-screen constructions the appearance of solidity.

surface of revolution The figure resulting from the rotation of a curve around a fixed axis set at a specified angle.

surge A sudden sharp increase in voltage; also called spike.

surge protector A device that protects electrical equipment from being damaged by short surges of high voltage by filtering them out. A computer or other device is plugged into the surge protector, which itself is plugged into a standard electrical outlet. See LINE SURGE.

surging A sudden and momentary changing of voltage or current in a circuit.

suspend To halt a process in a manner that allows resumption, perhaps by a system interrupt.

swapping **(1)** In VIRTUAL STORAGE, bringing a new page into internal storage from auxiliary storage and replacing an existing page. **(2)** In a network system, bringing the program into internal storage or storing it on a storage device. **(3)** Transferring out a copy of what is in internal memory to auxiliary storage while simultaneously transferring into internal memory what is in auxiliary storage. **(4)** The process of exchanging one item for another, as in swapping floppy disks as needed, in and out of a single drive.

swarm   Several program bugs.

sweep   In computer graphics, movement along an arc around a given center point.

sweeping   In computer graphics, generating a surface implicitly by moving a curve over a trajectory.

swim   A situation in which the images displayed on a video display screen move due to some hardware instability or defect such as a slow refresh rate; undesirable movement of an image on a video display screen.

switch   **(1)** In PROGRAMMING, a point at which a program may branch to one or more different program statements, depending upon the conditions of specified parameters at that point. **(2)** Physical or electronic means of changing the state of a component or device, such as an on/off toggle switch.

switched lines   Data communication lines that connect through telephone switching centers to a variety of destinations. Contrast with LEASED LINES and DEDICATED LINES.

switching algebra   The name given to BOOLEAN ALGEBRA when it is applied to SWITCHING THEORY.

switching circuit   A constituent electric circuit of switching or digital systems. Well-known examples of such systems are digital computers, dial telephone systems, and automatic inventory systems.

switching theory   The theory applied to circuits that have two or more discrete states.

Swivel 3D   An Apple Macintosh 3-D graphics program that can be used to create, manipulate, and render complex objects.

symbol   (1) A letter or mark representing quantities, relations, or operations. (2) In ARTIFICIAL INTELLIGENCE, an entity chosen to represent a person, object, concept, operation, relationship, or attribute of an object in the world.

symbolic address   An address, expressed in symbols convenient to the program writer, that must be translated into an absolute address (usually by an assembler) before it can be interpreted by a computer. Contrast with EXPLICIT ADDRESS.

symbolic coding   Coding in which the instructions are written in nonmachine language, using symbolic notation for operation codes and operands.

symbolic debugger   A debugger that allows the programmer to trace the values of variables in a program by requesting a particular symbol or name from the source code.

symbolic device   A name used to indicate an input/output file, such as SYSDSK to specify a magnetic disk unit. Compare SYMBOLIC I/O ASSIGNMENT.

symbolic editor   A system program that helps computer users in the preparation and modification of source-language programs by adding, changing, or deleting lines of text.

symbolic I/O assignment   The name used to indicate an input/output unit, such as PTR used to specify a printer. Compare SYMBOLIC DEVICE.

symbolic language   A PSEUDOLANGUAGE made up of letters, characters, and numbers that are not the internal language of the computer system.

symbolic logic   A discipline that treats formal logic by means of a formalized artificial language whose purpose is to avoid the ambiguities and logical inadequacies of natural language.

symbolic modeling   The technique of representing a body of symbolic knowledge in a computer program so that the program can draw conclusions and answer questions about the body of knowledge.

symbolic name   See NAME.

symbolic processing   Processing that distinguishes artificial intelligence programming from other types of programming; formal reasoning with symbols. The manipulation of symbols using strategies and heuristics, as opposed to the manipulation of numbers or the use of algorithms.

symbolic programming   (1) Using a SYMBOLIC LANGUAGE to prepare computer programs. (2) An alternate name for artificial intelligence. The advantages of the term symbolic programming are that it avoids the futuristic connotations and the inevitable comparisons with human beings.

symbolic table   A table for comparing a set of symbols to another set of symbols or numbers; for example, in an assembler, the symbol table contains the symbolic label address of an assembled object program.

symbol manipulation   The recognition, assembling, and modification of symbols. The thrust of artificial intelligence has been to use symbols to make inferences, and this is the core of symbol manipulation.

symbol processor   (1) A COMPUTER that manipulates symbols as well as numbers. (2) An alternate name for a computer.

symbol string   A string consisting solely of symbols.

symbol structure   A DATA STRUCTURE made up of symbols.

symbol table   A list of names used in a program with brief descriptions and storage addresses.

Symphony™   A software package that provides word processing, database management, spreadsheet, data communications, and graphics.

sync character   A character transmitted to establish character synchronization in synchronous communications.

synchronization   An adjustment of the chronological relationships between events, either to cause them to coincide or to maintain a fixed time difference between them.

synchronization check   A check that determines whether a particular event or condition occurs at the proper moment.

synchronous communications   A method of exchanging data at very high speeds between computers. It involves careful timing and special control codes. Contrast with ASYNCHRONOUS COMMUNICATIONS.

synchronous computer   A computer in which each operation starts as a result of a signal generated by a clock. Contrast with ASYNCHRONOUS COMPUTER.

synchronous network   A COMPUTER NETWORK in which all the communications channels are synchronized to a common clock.

synchronous operation   The operation of a system under the control of clocked pulses.

synchronous transmission   Data transmission in which the bits are transmitted at a fixed rate. Transmitter and receiver both use the same clock signals for synchronization. Contrast with ASYNCHRONOUS TRANSMISSION.

synergy   The concept that the whole is greater than the sum of its parts.

synonyms   **(1)** Records with duplicate disk addresses. **(2)** Two or more keys that produce the same table address when hashed.

syntactical form   In PROGRAMMING, the syntax that must be followed in the writing of a program.

syntactic ambiguity   A program in the field of NATURAL LANGUAGE understanding that refers to the possible multiple interpretations a sentence can have.

syntactic analysis   The study of the structure of the sentence, which is important in natural language processing.

syntax   **(1)** The rules governing the structure of a language and its expressions. All assembly and high-level programming languages possess a formal syntax. **(2)** The order in which the symbols in an expression are arranged. **(3)** The rules that specify the use of symbols in an expression.

syntax error In a COMPUTER PROGRAM, an error in the syntax, or vocabulary, of a program.

synthesizer An output device that generates and processes sound automatically. Some synthesizers include microprocessors, which are used as controlling devices. A voice synthesizer can produce sounds that closely resemble a person speaking, a musical instrument, and so on.

sysgen A contraction for **sys**tem **gen**eration, the process of installing or transferring an OPERATING SYSTEM.

SYSOP Acronym for **sys**tem **op**erator, the person who operates an electronic bulletin board.

system A composite of equipment, skills, techniques, and information capable of performing and/or supporting an operational role in attaining specified management objectives. Includes related facilities, equipment, material, service personnel, and information required for its operation to the degree that it can be considered a self-sufficient unit in its intended operational and/or support environment.

system acquisition The phase of the systems development life cycle in which equipment, software, or services are acquired from vendors.

system analyzer A portable device that can be used as a trouble-shooting unit for field service of complex equipment and systems.

system board The main CIRCUIT BOARD of a MICROCOMPUTER. Also called MOTHERBOARD and BACKPLANE.

system chart A type of flowchart. See SYSTEM FLOWCHART.

system commands Special instructions given to the computer when one operates in the conversational time-sharing mode. They direct the computer to execute programs (RUN), list them (LIST), save them (SAVE), and do other similar operations.

system diagnostics A program used to detect overall system malfunctions.

system disk The disk that contains the OPERATING SYSTEM and other SYSTEMS PROGRAMS that are necessary to start the computer.

system failure A malfunction of the hardware or systems software within a computer system.

system flowchart The graphic representation of an entire system or portion of a system consisting of one or more computer operations. Composed of interconnected flowcharting symbols arranged in the sequence in which the various system operations are performed. Essentially an overall planning, control, and operational description of a specific application. Contrast with PROGRAM FLOWCHART. See DATAFLOW DIAGRAM and FLOWCHART.

system folder In an Apple Macintosh environment, the folder that contains the System File and the Finder, the two components of the Macintosh's operating system.

system follow-up The continuing evaluation and review of a newly installed system to see that it is performing according to plan.

system generation (SYSGEN) The process of initiating a basic system at a specific installation. Involves modifying the generalized operating system received from the vendor into a tailored system meeting the unique needs of the individual user.

system implementation The final phase in the creation of a new system. During this phase a system is completely debugged, and it is determined whether it is operational and accepted by the users.

system installation The activities by which a new system is placed into operation.

system interrupt A break in the normal execution of a program or routine that is accomplished in such a way that the usual sequence can be resumed from that point.

system level (1) A description of the interface or connection that runs between computer subsystems such as the main board and disk controller or between parts of a multiprocessor computer. (2) An operation that is performed by the operating system or some other control program.

system librarian The person in a computer operations area responsible for managing data files and programs stored offline on disks, tapes, and other types of storage media.

system loader A supervisory program used to locate programs in the system library and load them into the internal storage of the computer.

system maintenance An activity associated with keeping a computer system constantly in tune with the changing demands placed upon it.

system operator A person who runs an ELECTRONIC BULLETIN BOARD.

system priorities Priorities established to determine the order in which information system projects will be undertaken.

system programmer (1) A programmer who plans, generates, maintains, and controls the use of an operating system with the aim of improving the overall productivity of an installation. (2) A programmer who designs programming systems. Contrast with APPLICATIONS PROGRAMMER.

system reset An operation that occurs whenever a computer is fooled into thinking that it was turned off and turned on again.

systems analysis The examination of an activity, procedure, method, technique, or business to determine what must be accomplished and how the necessary operations may best be accomplished by using data processing equipment.

systems analysis and design The process of developing a system design to meet a new need or to solve a problem in an existing system.

systems analyst One who performs SYSTEMS ANALYSIS.

systems approach An approach to PROBLEM SOLVING that views problems or activities as systems that must be managed.

systems design Specification of the working relationships between all the parts of a system in terms of their characteristic actions.

systems development The process of studying a problem or opportunity area, designing a system solution, and acquiring the resources necessary to support and implement that solution.

systems development life cycle   The process consisting of the five phases of systems development: preliminary investigation, systems analysis, systems design, system acquisition, and system implementation.

systems engineer   One who performs systems analysis, systems design, and/or systems programming functions.

System 7™   (1) An OPERATING SYSTEM for the Apple Macintosh computer. System 7 expands the Macintosh capabilities by including an upgraded finder, file sharing capability, truetype fonts, inter-application communications, and virtual memory. (2) An IBM Corporation MINICOMPUTER system, introduced in 1967–70.

systems house   A company that develops hardware and/or software systems to meet user requirements.

systems manual   A document containing information on the operation of a system. Sufficient detail is provided so that management can determine the dataflow, forms used, reports generated, and controls exercised. Job descriptions are generally provided.

systems programmer   One who understands the interaction between the application software and the systems software on a specific computer system. See SYSTEM PROGRAMMER.

systems programming   The development of programs that form operating systems for computers. Such programs include assemblers, compilers, control programs, and input/output handlers. Contrast with APPLICATIONS PROGRAMMING.

systems programs   Programs that control the internal operations of the computer system, such as operating systems, compilers, interpreters, assemblers, graphics support programs, and mathematical routines. Contrast with APPLICATIONS PROGRAMS.

systems resource   Any resource of a computer system that is under the control of the operating system.

systems security   Technical innovations and managerial procedures applied to hardware and software (programs and data) to protect the privacy of an organization's records and its customers.

systems software   Programs that run a computer system and aid the applications programmer in doing his/her task.

systems study   An investigation to determine the feasibility of installing or replacing a business system. See FEASIBILITY STUDY.

systems synthesis   The planning of the procedures for solving a problem.

systems testing   Testing of a series of programs in succession to make sure that all programs, including input and output, are related in the way the systems analyst intended.

system testing   The testing of all programs that make up a system in the sequence in which they will be executed.

System/32-System/38   MINICOMPUTER systems introduced by IBM Corporation: System/32 was released in 1975; System/34 was introduced in 1977; System/38 was introduced in 1978; and System/36 was introduced in 1983.

System/3   A MINICOMPUTER introduced by IBM Corporation in 1967-70.

System/370   A family of compatible MAINFRAMES introduced by IBM Corporation in 1970, replacing the older System/360 mainframes.

System/360   A series of MAINFRAMES introduced by IBM Corporation in 1964. It was the first family of compatible computer systems ever introduced, and its appearance marked the beginning of third-generation computing.

tab   The carriage control that specifies output columns.

table   The collection of data in a form suitable for ready reference. The data are frequently stored in consecutive storage locations or written in the form of an array of rows and columns for easy entry. An intersection of labeled rows and columns serves to locate a specific piece of information. Tables are useful for holding tabular data, such as the data found in spreadsheets.

table look-up   The procedure for using a known value to locate an unknown value in a table.

table plotter   See FLATBED PLOTTER.

tablet   In computer graphics, a locator device with a flat surface and a mechanism that converts indicated positions on the surface into coordinated data.

tabulate   (1) To print totals. (2) To form data into a table.

tagged image file format (TIFF)   A common file format used to store BIT-MAPPED GRAPHICS. TIFF simulates gray-scale shading.

tail   A special data item that locates the end of a list.

tailor-made   Describing a program specially written for one particular task, business, or set of people. Tailor-made programs are usually commissioned by an individual customer and not sold to anyone else.

talking computer   A computer system that uses a speech synthesizer to produce speech.

tandem computers   Two or more computers connected together and working on the same problem at the same time.

Tandy Corporation   A leading manufacturer of personal computers and electronics. In 1977, Tandy introduced one of the first personal computers, the Radio Shack TRS-80 Model I. Several other TRS-80 models were developed, and in 1984, Tandy started building IBM-compatible micro-computers. Today, Tandy markets a variety of microcomputer systems through their company-owned Radio Shack stores.

tangible benefit   A benefit to which a specific dollar amount can be assigned.

tape   A strip of material that may be punched or coated with a magnetically sensitive substance and used for data input, storage, or output. Data are usually stored serially in several channels across the tape, transversely to the reading or writing motion. See MAGNETIC TAPE and PAPER TAPE.

tape backup   A mechanism that reads and writes information on magnetic tape to provide a copy of a user's data in case of an accident. The TAPE CARTRIDGE or cassette is capable of holding at least 20 MB of data.

tape cartridge   See MAGNETIC TAPE CARTRIDGE.

tape cassette   A sequential access storage medium used in older microcomputer systems for digital recording.

tape deck   See MAGNETIC TAPE UNIT.

tape drive   See MAGNETIC TAPE DRIVE.

tape handler   See MAGNETIC TAPE UNIT.

tape label   Usually the first record on a magnetic tape reel, containing such information as the date the tape was written, identification name or number, and the number of records on the tape.

tape librarian   The person responsible for the safekeeping of all computer files, such as programs and data files on magnetic tapes, floppy disks, and microfilm.

tape library   A special room that houses a file of magnetic tape under secure, environmentally controlled conditions. See DISK LIBRARY and DATA PROTECTION.

tape mark   A special code used to indicate the end of a tape file.

Tape Operating System (TOS) An operating system in which the programs are stored on MAGNETIC TAPE.

TARGA Acronym for **T**ruevision **A**dvanced **R**aster **G**raphics **A**dapter, a file format created by Truevision for image capture boards; compatible with NTSC standards.

Targa board A video graphics board from Truevision that is used in high-resolution graphics applications.

target disk A disk to which a program or file is copied. Contrast with SOURCE DISK.

target language A language into which some other language is to be properly translated. Usually has the same meaning as OBJECT LANGUAGE.

target printer A specific PRINTER selected for printing a job.

target program Same as object program (see OBJECT-BASED PROGRAMMING).

tariff In data communications, the published rate for a specific unit of equipment, facility, or type of service provided by a communications common carrier.

task An element of work that is part of getting a job done, such as the loading of programs into computer storage.

taxonomy The classification of objects as to how they are alike and different.

tax planning and preparation package A software package that keeps track of tax records throughout the year and determines the effects of different financial decisions.

TB Abbreviation for TERABYTE.

TCP/IP Abbreviation for **T**ransmission **C**ontrol **P**rotocol/**I**nternet **P**rotocol, a networking protocol with broad support deriving from its ability to connect disparate hosts.

teacherless learning Learning using intelligent COMPUTER-ASSISTED IN-
STRUCTION programs.

tear-off menu A screen MENU that can be moved off its primary position,
relocated to any part of the display screen, and kept active.

technical writer A person who prepares proposals, training manuals,
reference manuals, programming manuals, books, and reports associated with computer equipment and software or other technical fields.

technology (1) The knowledge and methods used to create a product.
(2) Activities that are directed toward the satisfaction of human needs
that produce alterations in the material world.

technology transfer The application of existing technology to a current
problem or situation.

telecommunications The transfer of data from one place to another over
long distances, using telephone lines, microwaves, and/or satellites. See
DATA COMMUNICATIONS and TELEPROCESSING.

telecommunications package A group of programs that allows a PER-
SONAL COMPUTER user to communicate with other users, computers, and
databases.

telecommunications specialist A person responsible for the design of
data communications networks.

telecommuting Working at home with telecommunications between office and home.

teleconference A conference among people remote from one another
who are linked by telecommunications devices. Considered an alternative
to travel and face-to-face meetings, a teleconference is conducted with
two-way video, audio, and, as required, data and facsimile transmission.

telecopying Long-distance copying. Same as FACSIMILE.

telematics The convergence of telecommunications and automatic information processing.

telemeter To transmit data by telecommunications facilities; for example, data can be telemetered from a satellite and recorded at a ground station.

telemetry   The transmission of data from remote measuring instruments by electrical or radio means; for example, data can be telemetered from a spacecraft in outer space and recorded at a ground station on Earth.

Telenet   A communications network that enables many varieties of user terminals and computers to exchange information.

teleprocessing   The use of telephone lines to transmit data and commands between a remote location and a data processing center, or between two computer systems; the combined use of data communications and data processing equipment. See TELECOMMUNICATIONS.

telesoftware   Computer programs sent by telephone line or television as part of the teletext signal.

teletext   A one-way communications medium used in some videotex services. Images, each constituting a single frame of TV data in a special, compressed format, are transmitted in a continuous sequence. Users indicate which frames they would like to see by interaction with the decoding units in their local TV sets.

television receiver (TV)   A display device capable of receiving broadcast video signals (such as commercial television) by means of an antenna. Can be used in combination with a radio-frequency modulator as a display device for several microcomputers. See VIDEO MONITOR.

Telex   A telegraph service provided by Western Union.

Telpak   A service offered by communications common carriers for the leasing of wideband channels between two or more points.

template   **(1)** A plastic guide used in drawing geometric flowcharting symbols. **(2)** In COMPUTER GRAPHICS, the pattern of a standard, commonly used component or part that serves as a design aid. Once created, it can be subsequently traced instead of redrawn whenever needed. **(3)** In a SPREADSHEET program, a worksheet that has already been designed for the solution of a specific type of problem. **(4)** A plastic sheet placed over keyboard keys to help the user remember the tasks performed by each key. **(5)** In PAGE LAYOUT and WORD PROCESSING programs, a predesigned page format used by loading the file, adding the text and/or graphic images, and printing.

template matching   A technique in which a computer identifies objects by comparing shapes derived from the digitized image with stored prototype patterns.

temporary storage   In PROGRAMMING, storage locations reserved for intermediate results. Synonymous with WORKING STORAGE.

temporary variable   A variable that is used to store a value temporarily.

Tempra   An image-editing program for IBM PC-compatible microcomputers operating in MS-DOS.

ten-key pad   A separate set of keys numbered 0 through 9 on a keyboard that allows easy entry of numbers. Similar to a CALCULATOR KEYPAD.

ten's complement   A number used to represent the negative of a given value. It is obtained by subtracting each digit from a number containing all 9's and adding 1; for example, 654 is the ten's complement of 346 and is obtained by performing the computation $999 - 346 + 1$. Synonymous with true complement. Compare ONE'S COMPLEMENT, TWO'S COMPLEMENT, and NINE'S COMPLEMENT.

tera   A prefix meaning one trillion.

terabyte (TB)   Specifically, 1,009,511,627,776, or 2^{40} bytes. More loosely, one thousand gigabytes, one million megabytes, one billion kilobytes, or one trillion bytes. Used to measure capacities of high-capacity data storage.

term   The data structure of a logic program; for example, a constant, variable, or compound term. It is the smallest portion of an expression to which a value can be given.

terminal   A keyboard/display or keyboard/printer device used to input programs and data to the computer and to receive output from the computer.

terminal emulation (**1**) The ability of a personal computer to act, generally via modem, as a terminal to a host system. (**2**) A situation in which special software makes a computer behave as though it were a terminal connected to another computer.

terminal error An error of sufficient consequence that the program cannot continue. See FATAL ERROR.

terminal node A node that ends a path.

terminal stand A wood or metal stand designed to support a computer terminal.

terminal symbol An oval flowcharting symbol used to indicate the starting point and termination point or points in a procedure.

terminator In a NETWORK, a device used to signify the end of the series.

ternary (**1**) Pertaining to a characteristic or property involving a selection, choice, or condition in which there are three possibilities. (**2**) Pertaining to the numeration system with a radix of 3.

terrain modeling In computer graphics, generating realistic-looking natural surfaces, most often through the use of fractals.

terrestrial microwave station A ground station that receives, amplifies, and transmits microwave signals.

tessellate In computer graphics, to subdivide a surface into a collection of smaller geometric forms.

test data Data especially created to test the operation of a given program. Usually, one or more hand-calculated or otherwise known results will be associated with test data so that the program under testing may be validated. Data known to be invalid are also used as test data. See TESTING.

test driver A program that directs the execution of another program against a collection of test data sets.

testing The examination of a program's behavior by executing the program on sample data sets, including both valid and invalid data, in an effort to explore all possible causes of misbehavior. See DEBUG, PROGRAM TESTING, STRESS TESTING, and SYSTEMS TESTING.

test plan A general description of what testing will involve, including specification of tolerable limits.

test run A run carried out to check that a program is operating correctly. During the run, test data generate results for comparison with previously prepared results.

Texas Instruments, Inc. A manufacturer of semiconductors and computer equipment.

text Words, letters, and numbers that express the information to be conveyed. Contrasted with GRAPHICS, which are shapes, lines, and symbols.

text composition In DESKTOP PUBLISHING, evenly spaced lines, usually set in the same type size and style.

text editing A general term that covers any additions, changes, or deletions made to electronically stored material.

text editor A computer program used to manipulate text; for example, to erase, insert, change, and move words or groups of words. The manipulated text may be another computer program.

text file A file containing information expressed in text form. Same as DATA FILE.

text formatting (1) The process of controlling the appearance of a document so that it will look good on paper. (2) The output generated by computer software that closely resembles the galleys set on conventional composing machines.

text generation The process of constructing meaningful text using a computer.

text graphics Graphic images created by combining ASCII characters.

text letter A TYPEFACE that looks like early brush-stroke lettering.

text processing   The manipulation of alphabetic data under program control.

text system   A collection of hardware and specially written software used together to manipulate textual information. See WORD PROCESSING.

textual   Composed entirely of text, without graphic images or other data.

texture   In computer graphics, any 2-D pattern used to add the appearance of complexity to a 3-D surface without actually modeling the complexity.

texture mapping   In computer graphics, the application of graphic representations of surface textures to objects.

text window   An area on some computer graphics systems display screens within which text is displayed and scrolled.

TGA   A bitmap format for images created on high-resolution video boards. Due to their resolution, these files can be very large. Because they can have up to 16 million colors, the palette often has to be compressed before the files can be used. See TARGA.

thematic map   A map specifically designed to communicate geographic concepts such as the distribution of densities, relative magnitudes, gradients, spatial relationships, movements, and all required interrelationships and aspects of the Earth's distributional characteristics. Computer-aided design systems facilitate the use of thematic maps by allowing the quick assignment and identification of both graphic and nongraphic properties.

theorem   A statement that can be proved; the conclusion of a valid argument.

theorem prover   A program that starts with a goal and searches for implications whose conclusions will unify with the goal. A theorem prover has a database consisting of a set of axioms. Its inference mechanism makes inferences that lead to the satisfaction of the goal.

theorem proving   The branch of artificial intelligence involved in using computers to prove mathematical and logic theorems.

thermal printer   A nonimpact printer that uses a paper treated to form a dark image when exposed to heat. Black, blue, and purple image papers are common. The print head consists of an array of resistive elements (thin or thick film) that moves across the paper printing serially, or an array of elements in which the paper moves past, printing an entire line at a time. To print, the head normally must be in contact with the paper.

thermal wax-transfer printer   A nonimpact printer that uses heat applied by pins to melt colored wax onto paper to create an image.

thesaurus program   With a WORD PROCESSING PROGRAM, a program that provides a list of synonyms and antonyms for a word in a document.

thick and thin   In computer graphics, the weight of a line, or its graphic quality.

thin film   Computer storage made by placing thin spots of magnetic materials on an insulated base (usually a flat plate or wire); electric current in wires attached to the base is used to magnetize the spot.

thin window display   A one-line display used on keyboards, pocket computers, and so on. Usually an LCD or LED display.

third-generation computers   Computers that use integrated circuitry and miniaturization of components to replace transistors, reduce costs, work faster, and increase reliability. Introduced in 1964 and still the primary technology for digital computers. Compare FIRST-GENERATION COMPUTERS, SECOND-GENERATION COMPUTERS, FOURTH-GENERATION COMPUTERS, and FIFTH-GENERATION COMPUTERS.

third-party vendor   A company that specializes in obtaining equipment from manufacturers or original owners. The equipment is then leased or sold to another company.

thirty-two-bit chip   A CPU chip that processes data 32 bits at a time. Contrast with EIGHT-BIT CHIP and SIXTEEN-BIT CHIP.

thrashing   Overhead associated with memory swapping in a virtual memory system. Also called churning.

threaded   Pertaining to a program consisting of calls to several separate subprograms.

threaded tree   A TREE containing additional pointers to assist in the scan of the tree.

three-dimensional array   An array that provides a threefold classification: row, column, and layer.

three-dimensional digitizer   A piece of digitizing equipment for taking coordinate data directly from a physical three-dimensional object.

three-dimensional graphics (3-D)   GRAPHIC IMAGES in three dimensions—height, width, and depth. A three-dimensional image is rendered on a two-dimensional medium; the third dimension, depth, is usually indicated by shading or by means of perspective.

three-point perspective   In COMPUTER GRAPHICS, representations drawn in perspective so as to show height, width, and depth.

threshold   A predefined level used by a scanner to determine whether a pixel will be represented as black or white.

throughput   A measure of the total amount of useful processing carried out by a computer system in a given time period.

throughput crime   A COMPUTER CRIME that involves modifying software so that the data it processes are manipulated differently from the original intent.

thumbnail layout   In DESKTOP PUBLISHING, a quickly drawn sketch that shows the major elements in a document.

thumbwheel   A device for positioning an input cursor; consists of a rotatable wheel that controls the movement of that cursor in one axis. Normally, thumbwheels are found in pairs, one controlling vertical cursor movement, the other horizontal movement.

Thunderscan   An inexpensive high-resolution scanner that replaces the ribbon cartridge in an Apple ImageWriter printer and converts photographs and printed images into data that can be stored on a disk.

thyration   See SCR.

thyristor   A bistable device comprising three or more junctions. See SCR.

tie-breaker   Circuitry that resolves the conflict that occurs when two central processing units try to use a peripheral device at the same time. See CONTENTION.

tie line   A leased communications channel.

tie mark   Any marking along a scale to indicate values. Can be used to denote points between identified numerical values.

TIFF   Acronym for tagged image file format, which is basically a standardized header (tag) defining the exact data structure of the images to be processed. A common bit-mapped file format. The TIFF format will handle gray-scale shading and images with a resolution up to 300 dpi.

TIFF-24   A version of the tagged image file format (TIFF) that encodes 24 bits of information for each point in the image.

tightly coupled   A term describing computers that are dependent upon one another.

tile   A single sheet or portion that can be combined with others to form an oversize page, or to split a page into such sections.

tiled   A term describing objects displayed side by side.

tiled windows   A screen display divided into nonoverlapping windows.

tiling   In computer graphics, the filling of an object with a design or pattern instead of a solid cover. Tiling is used to cover defined areas of the screen with particular images.

tilting screen   A video display screen that can be angled back and forth from top to bottom for easier viewing—one result of ERGONOMICS.

time-delay   A MODEM feature that allows a computer to call another computer and transfer a file at a future time.

time-division multiplexing (TDM)   The merging of several bit streams of lower bit rates into a composite signal for transmission over a communication channel of higher bit-rate capacity. See CONCENTRATOR.

time log Logging of how a COMPUTER SYSTEM was used during a specified time period, such as 24 hours.

timer A computer's internal clock.

time-sharing A method of operation in which a computer facility is shared by several users for different purposes at (apparently) the same time. Although the computer actually services each user in sequence, the high speed of the computer makes it appear as though the users are all handled simultaneously.

time-slice A small fraction of a computer's total execution time that is allocated to a terminal in a time-sharing system.

time slicing The allotment of a portion of processing time to each program in a multiprogramming system to prevent the monopolization of the central processing unit by any one program.

Times Roman An attractive and easy-to-read SERIF FONT that is included as a built-in font with many LASER PRINTERS.

timing diagram In OBJECT-ORIENTED PROGRAMMING, part of the notation of an object diagram, used to show the dynamic interactions among various objects in an object diagram.

tint screen A uniform screen pattern used for visual effect in a layout.

TIPS An imaging program for IBM-compatible microcomputers.

title bar In a graphics environment, the line of text at the top of a window that indicates the name of the application or file in that window.

toggle (**1**) A keystroke that turns a function of a program on or off. (**2**) A device having two stable states. (**3**) The ability to go back and forth between two distinctly separate functions on a CRT.

token (**1**) A symbol representing a name or entity in a programming language. (**2**) A group of bits, such as eight 1's, used in some bus networks to signal network access by a particular station. (**3**) A physical object, sometimes containing sophisticated electronics, which is used to gain access to a system. Some tokens contain a microprocessor and are called "intelligent tokens."

token sharing network A LOCAL AREA NETWORK in which a bit pattern, called a token, determines which user on the network can send information.

tonal range In computer graphics, the spread between the lightest and darkest parts of an image.

tone In computer graphics, the degree of tint and shade in color.

toner A very fine black powder that is fused to paper in laser printing; the equivalent of black ink.

toner cartridge In a LASER PRINTER, the disposable container that holds the electrically charged dry ink and drum used in creating an image on the paper.

tone value In computer graphics, a characteristic of all colors, according to whether they are light or dark. Tone value is that quality which distinguishes a light color from a dark color.

tool (1) An object or icon used to perform operations in a computer program. Tools are often named either by what they do or by the type of object on which they work. (2) In some computer systems, an applications program. (3) In ARTIFICIAL INTELLIGENCE, an INFERENCE ENGINE, a user interface, and procedures for entering knowledge.

toolbox A group of icons that perform such functions as pointing, cropping, drawing, and so forth.

toolkit A collection of programs designed to aid a programmer in the development of software.

tool palette A collection of on-screen functions that are grouped in a menu structure for interactive selection.

top-down approach See STRUCTURED APPROACH.

top-down design An approach to writing a structured program in which the program is divided into blocks or modules that are written individually and then combined into the final program.

top-down development Architectural discipline for computer program development wherein the high-level functions are coded and tested in an outline form early in the development process. Lower-level detail is added and tested progressively. From specifications and interfaces the complete package is constructed beginning with the highest levels of control, such as job control languages and operating system services, progressing to program control modules, and extending to successively more detailed levels of program modules in a hierarchically descending structure.

top-down programming A programming method that begins with the most general statement of a program and divides it into increasingly detailed sets of routines.

topology The physical layout of a computer network; the interconnection of devices and communication channels into a network configuration.

TOPS An inexpensive and easy-to-use LOCAL AREA NETWORK that allows up to 32 computers to be connected in a single local network, allowing the sharing of drives, files, and printers.

torus In computer graphics, a surface or solid generated by the revolution of a circle or other conic section about an axis; for example, a solid ring of circular or elliptic sections, a doughnut-shaped surface.

TOS An operating system for the ATARI ST microcomputer. TOS controls how the computer operates the GEM Desktop, the MOUSE, and any peripheral devices the user connects to the computer.

touch pad An INPUT DEVICE with which the user may enter information through a pad that is sensitive to pressure.

touch-sensitive screen A display screen on which the user can enter commands by pressing designated areas with a finger or other object. This method takes advantage of an individual's natural instinct to point.

touch-sensitive tablet A input device that converts graphics and pictorial data into numerical form for use by a computer. Graphic data can be generated by pressing the tablet with a stylus.

touch-tone telephone   A push-button telephone used in teleprocessing systems.

tower configuration   A floor-standing cabinet that is taller than it is wide.

trace   (1) The scanning path of the beam in a RASTER DISPLAY. (2) An electrical pathway on circuit boards that connect electronic components.

tracing routine   A routine that provides a time history of the contents of the computer operational registers during the execution of a program. A complete tracing routine would reveal the status of all registers and locations affected by each instruction each time the instruction is executed.

track   (1) The path along which data are recorded on a continuous or rotational medium, such as magnetic tape or magnetic disk. (2) To follow or record the moving position of a video display cursor, stylus, mouse, or other input device.

track ball   A device used to move the cursor around on a computer display screen. Consists of a mounting, usually a box, in which is set a ball. As the user spins the ball, the cursor moves at the speed and in the direction of the ball's motion. The housing is stationary, as opposed to the mobile mouse unit.

tracking   Moving a CURSOR or predefined symbol across the surface of the visual display screen with a light pen, electronic pen, track ball, or mouse.

tracking symbol   The small symbol on a video display screen that represents the position of the cursor.

tractor-fed printer   A printer through which paper with holes along its edges is fed by sprocket wheels within the device.

tractor-feed mechanism   A pair of pin-studded belts that rotate in unison and pull paper, punched with marginal holes, into a printer. See PIN-FEED and CONTINUOUS FORMS. Contrast with FRICTION-FEED.

tradeoff   The balancing of factors in a computer system.

traditional programming   Programming using procedural languages such as BASIC, C, or PASCAL. Such languages support program construction based on determining the sequence of procedures that act on a separate set of data.

traffic intensity   The ratio of the insertion rate to the deletion rate of a queue.

trailer record   A record that follows a group of records and contains data pertinent to the group.

trainer   A person who provides education to end users about a particular program, system, or technology.

training manual   A manual designed to be used while learning to use a computer system or program.

trajectory   The motion of a ROBOT.

transaction   An exchange of one value for another. In a cash sale, cash is exchanged for merchandise.

transaction code   One or more characters that form parts of a record and signify the type of transaction represented by the record.

transactional data   DATA that are created in a transaction that requires a consumer to reveal his or her identity.

transaction file   A file that contains all changes to be made to the master file, including additions, deletions, and revisions.

transaction processing   Activities related to the processing of transactions as they occur.

transaction screen   A screen in a personal budgeting software package that prompts the user to enter actual income and expenses.

transaction trailing   In DATABASE MANAGEMENT SYSTEMS, the creation of an auxiliary file that traces all file updates.

transborder   A term describing data communications between computer systems located across national borders.

transcribe   To copy from one external storage medium to another. The process may involve conversion.

transducer   Any device or element that converts an input signal into an output signal of a different form.

transfer   (1) To copy or read, transmit, and store an item or block of information. (2) To change control. See BRANCH, CONDITIONAL TRANSFER, JUMP, and UNCONDITIONAL TRANSFER.

transfer address   See ENTRY POINT.

transfer rate   The speed at which accessed data can be moved from one device to another. See ACCESS TIME and SEEK TIME.

transform   To change the form of data without changing its meaning. See CONVERT.

transformation   In computer graphics, one of the modifications that can be made to the placement or size of an on-screen image. The three basic transformations are translation, scaling, and rotation.

transformer   An AC device used in computer power supplies to reduce 115 volts 60 Hertz to a lower, more suitable voltage usable by computer equipment.

transient   (1) A term describing a phenomenon caused in a system by a sudden change in conditions that persists for a relatively short time after the change. (2) A term describing a momentary surge on a signal or power line that may produce false signals and cause component failures.

transient error   The type of error that occurs only once and cannot be made to repeat itself.

transient program   A program that does not reside in the computer system's main memory. When needed, the computer reads the program from a disk or tape. Contrast with RESIDENT PROGRAM.

transistor   A semiconductor device used for controlling the flow of current between two terminals. Transistors were developed at Bell Laboratories during World War II and used for the first time in second-generation computers.

transistor-transistor logic (TTL) A family of integrated circuits characterized by relatively high-speed and low-power consumption. Logic circuits based on bipolar devices, usually low-power Schottky circuits that are fast but expensive because gold-plated Schottky diodes are required on every TTL bus input.

translate To change data from one form of representation to another without significantly affecting the meaning.

translating In computer graphics, moving all or part of a display image on a display space from one location to another without rotating the image.

translation In computer graphics, the movement of an image to a new position on the screen. Under translation, every point in the image moves in the same direction with the same speed at any given instant.

translator A computer program that performs translations from one language or code to another. See ASSEMBLER, COMPILER, INTERPRETER, and TRANSLATION.

transmission The sending of data from one location and receiving of data in another location, usually leaving the source data unchanged. See DATA TRANSMISSION.

transmission facility A communications link between remote terminals and computers, such as communication lines, microwave transmission lines, communications satellites, lasers, telephone lines, fiber optics, and waveguides.

transmission time The actual time needed to transfer data to or from a disk.

transmit To send data from one location and to receive the data at another location.

transparency The clarity of a program. The degree to which an artificial intelligence program is understandable.

transparent A term describing any process that is not visible to the user. For example, the details of how a file is stored on tracks and sectors are transparent to the user.

transponder A device in a communications satellite that receives a transmission from Earth, amplifies the signal, changes the frequency, and transmits the data to a receiving earth station.

transpose To interchange two items of data.

transputer A 32-bit RISC chip used for PARALLEL PROCESSING.

transversal The execution of each statement of a program for debugging purposes.

trap A programmed conditional jump to a known location, automatically executed when program execution reaches the location where the trap is set. See INTERRUPT.

trapdoor A breach created intentionally in an information processing system for the purpose of later collecting, altering, or destroying information.

trapping A hardware provision for interrupting the normal flow of control of a program while transfer to a known location is made. See INTERRUPT.

traverse adjustment A computer-aided mapping feature that automatically distributes corrections through any surveying traverse to eliminate the error of closure, and to yield an adjusted position for each traverse station.

tree A connected graph with no cycles. Also called TREE DIAGRAM. See FOREST.

tree diagram The pictorial representation of the logical structure of a program or system. See LEAF, NODE, and ROOT.

tree network A network in which a hierarchy of nodes provides control and communication. Can be represented on paper as the inverse of a family tree. The apex of the network, or top of the tree, represents the primary control for the network, but certain levels of control may be delegated down to intermediate branches. See NETWORK TOPOLOGIES.

tree sort   A sort that exchanges items treated as nodes of a tree. When an item reaches the root node, it is exchanged with the lowest leaf node. Also called heap sort.

tree structure   An alternate term for hierarchical structure, a form of DATABASE organization.

trend line   The calculated extension of a data series for the purpose of predicting trends beyond known data.

triad   (1) Any group of three, such as three bits, bytes, or characters. (2) In a color CRT, one set of red, green, and blue phosphors.

triangulate   In computer graphics, to subdivide a polygon into triangles to simplify rendering.

trichromatic   Three-colored. In COMPUTER GRAPHICS, trichromatic generally refers to the three primary colors (red, green, and blue) combined to create all others.

trigger   (1) A concept referring to the execution of procedures as a part of an object-oriented database. A trigger is a procedure that is automatically activated whenever a predefined condition arises. Triggers are like methods, but they are not encapsulated along with the local data on which they operate. (2) The button on a joystick.

trigonometry   The branch of mathematics dealing with the relations of the sides and angles of triangles, including the various algebraic functions of these relations. In a right triangle, the basic relationships are called trigonometric functions. Trigonometric functions are represented as library routines in many programming languages.

trilogy   A language which is a combination of logic, procedural languages, and database languages. It is similar to PROLOG.

triple   A record, or row, in a relational database model.

triple click To press and release the mouse button three times rapidly in quick succession.

triple precision The retention of three times as many digits of a quantity as the computer normally uses. See PRECISION. Contrast with SINGLE PRECISION and DOUBLE PRECISION.

tristate logic A form of transistor-transistor logic in which output stages or input and output stages can assume three states. Two are normal low-impedance 1 and 0 states; the third is a high-impedance state that allows many tristate devices to time-share bus lines.

tristimulus values Relative amounts of three primary colors combined to create other colors.

trochoid In computer graphics, the curve made by any point on the edge of a circle rolling like a wheel.

Trojan horse A term describing a crime in which a computer criminal places instructions in someone else's program that will allow the program to function normally but also to perform illegitimate functions.

tron A popular high-tech suffix, such as in *datatron* and *cyclotron*.

troubleshoot To try to find a malfunction in a hardware unit or a mistake in a computer program. Synonymous with DEBUG. See BUG, DEBUGGING AIDS, and TEST DATA.

TRS-80™ The first family of personal computers from Radio Shack, a division of Tandy Corporation. The TRS-80 Model I was one of the first personal computers.

True BASIC A structured version of the BASIC PROGRAMMING LANGUAGE. Developed in 1983 by the inventors of the original BASIC language, John Kemeny and Thomas Kurtz. True BASIC is a version of BASIC that does not require line numbers and that includes advanced control structures that make structured programming possible.

true color (1) A term describing graphics systems that are usually equipped with at least 24 bits per pixel; this translates to a total palette range of 16.7 million colors. **(2)** Color systems in which the color information in the image is used directly to create the output color rather than as an index to a table of colors in a palette.

true complement An alternate term for TEN'S COMPLEMENT and TWO'S COMPLEMENT.

truncate **(1)** To reject the final digits in a number, thus lessening precision; for example, 3.14159 truncates the series for π, which could conceivably be extended indefinitely. **(2)** To cut off any characters that will not fit into an allotted space.

truncation error An error due to truncation. Contrast with ROUND-OFF ERROR.

trunk A direct line between two telephone switching centers.

truth table A systematic tabulation of all the possible input/output combinations produced by a binary circuit.

T-switch An electrical switch that allows the user to change the connections between computing equipment just by turning the dial on a switch. T-switches are useful for sharing infrequently used or expensive peripheral devices such as a laser printer.

TTL Abbreviation for TRANSISTOR-TRANSISTOR LOGIC, a medium/high-speed family of logic integrated circuits.

tunnel diode An electronic device with switching speeds of fractional billionths of seconds. Used in high-speed computer circuitry and memories.

tutorial disk A FLOPPY DISK provided with PERSONAL COMPUTER software that demonstrates the use of the software.

turbo A trade name for hardware and software that implies high speed.

Turbo C A COMPILER for the C programming language from Borland International.

Turbo Pascal A very popular variation of the PASCAL programming language. Turbo Pascal provides an integrated package that includes an editor, compiler, and linker. The language was designed in 1984 by

Philippe Kahn of Borland International and closely follows the definition of standard Pascal. In addition to the standard, Turbo Pascal includes a number of extensions to the language.

Turbo PROLOG   An implementation of the PROLOG programming language, developed by Borland International, Inc. for use on microcomputers.

TURING   A programming language developed in 1982 by R.C. Holt and J.R. Cordy at the University of Toronto, whose primary design goal was to eliminate some of the inadequacies of the PASCAL programming language. Turing runs under the UNIX operating system.

Turing's test   A game to determine whether a computer might be considered to possess intelligence, developed by British mathematician Alan Turing. Participants include two respondents (a computer and a human) and a human examiner who tries to determine which of the unseen respondents is the human. According to this test, intelligence and the ability to think would be demonstrated by the computer's success in fooling the examiner.

turnaround form   An output document that serves as an input medium during a subsequent phase of processing.

turnaround time   (1) The time it takes for a job to travel from the user to the computing center, to be run on the computer, and for the program results to be returned to the user. (2) The time spent between transmissions in data transmission using a half-duplex channel.

turnkey system   A prepackaged, ready-to-use computer system containing all the hardware, software, training, and maintenance support needed to perform a given application. All the prepared system needs is the "turn of the key."

turn off   The act of turning off (powering down) a computer system.

turn on   The act of turning on (powering up) a computer system.

turtle   A robot that moves about on the floor, or a shape that moves about on the screen. Both types are used to demonstrate programming, and can draw a trail showing where they have been.

turtle graphics   Graphics accomplished by a simulated robot that have been incorporated into LOGO and other computer languages. Used to teach geometry and computer graphics concepts.

tutorial   A hardware or software training manual; can be a printed document or recorded in magnetic form on a disk or tape.

tutorial program   A computer program that explains new material and then tests the user's retention.

TV terminal   A common television set used as a computer output device. See VIDEO MONITOR and TELEVISION RECEIVER.

tweak   To fine-tune or adjust a piece of equipment; to enhance. To make final small changes to improve software performance.

tweaking   In CAD, a modelling technique in which the user "tweaks" a control dial, causing a selected shape to elongate on the screen.

tweening   See IN-BETWEENS.

twinkle box   An input device consisting of optical sensors, lenses, and a rotating disk, capable of determining the three-dimensional position of a light-emitting object by angular light sensing.

twisted wire   A data communications medium that consists of pairs of wires twisted together and bound into a cable. Used to transmit information over short distances.

two-alternative decision   In programming, a decision that results in one of two possible actions; one action is taken by the program if a certain condition is true, and another action is taken if that condition is false.

two-dimensional array   An arrangement consisting of rows and columns. See MATRIX. Contrast with ONE-DIMENSIONAL ARRAY.

two-dimensional graphics (2-D)   A graphic image in two dimensions—height and width.

two-pass   A term describing an operation or program that has to manipulate its data twice. It partially accomplishes its purpose on the first pass through the data. The operation is completed in the second pass through the data.

two-point perspective   In computer graphics, perspective viewed when an object is observed from an angle. There are two vanishing points.

two's complement   A method of representing negative numbers. A positive or negative binary number is changed to the opposite sign by changing all 1's to 0's and all 0's to 1's, then binarily adding 1. Synonymous with true complement. Compare ONE'S COMPLEMENT, NINE'S COMPLEMENT, and TEN'S COMPLEMENT.

type ahead   In WORD PROCESSING, a feature that prevents the loss of characters when the operator is typing faster than the computer can display characters on the screen.

typeface   A collection of letters, numbers, and symbols that share a distinctive appearance (for example, Helvetica, Times Roman, Bodoni, Schoolbook, Courier, and Palatino).

typeface family   A group of typefaces that include the normal, bold, italic, and bold-italic variations of the same design; a related group of type fonts.

type font   A complete set of characters in a consistent and unique typeface.

typematic   Any keyboard character that repeats for as long as it is pressed.

typeover   The ability of an impact printer to strike a character more than once to produce a boldface effect on the printed copy. See OVERSTRIKING and SHADOW PRINTING.

typeover mode   See REPLACE MODE.

typeset quality   Printer resolution of 1,200 to 2,540 dots per inch.

typesetting   The production of camera-ready copy on a laser printer (low-quality typesetting) or an imagesetter (high-quality typesetting).

type size   The size, in points, of a typeface.

type style   The weight (such as normal or bold) or posture (such as italic) of a font.

type table   A file used by certain OCR programs that contains character shapes for a particular font. The program refers to the type table when recognizing that font.

typing   In OBJECT-ORIENTED PROGRAMMING, the enforcement of the class of an object, which prevents objects of different types from being interchanged.

typo   In DESKTOP PUBLISHING, a typesetting or clerical error in producing typed copy.

typography   The science and art of designing typefaces and of composing printed works.

— U —

UCSD Pascal A high-level programming language developed largely by the Institute for Information Science at the University of California, San Diego, under the direction of Kenneth L. Bowles. It contains a number of extensions to Standard Pascal, particularly ones that handle graphics and character strings.

UCSD p-system A program development system created by Kenneth Bowles at the University of California at San Diego (UCSD). It includes an operating system, a text editor, and compilers for FORTRAN, Microsoft BASIC, and Pascal.

ultrafiche Microfiche holding images reduced a hundredfold or more.

ultra-large-scale integration The process of placing millions of integrated circuits on a single chip. Abbreviated ULSI.

UltraPaint™ An Apple Macintosh graphics program that combines black-and-white painting, color painting, gray-scale image editing and object drawing.

ultraviolet light Light with rays shorter than those of visible light but longer than X rays. Used to erase data or instructions stored in an ERASABLE PROM. Once the EPROM has been erased, it can be reprogrammed by using a PROM programmer.

unary See MONADIC.

unattended operation Data transmission and/or reception without an operator.

unblocked record A physical record that corresponds to one logical record.

unbundled Pertaining to services, programs, training, and so on sold independently of computer hardware by the hardware manufacturer. Contrast with BUNDLED.

unconditional jump   A program transfer that takes place whenever the instruction that specified it is executed.

unconditional transfer   In program control, an instruction that always causes a branch away from the normal sequence of executing instructions. Contrast with CONDITIONAL TRANSFER.

uncontrolled loop   A program loop that does not reach a logical end.

underflow   **(1)** A condition that arises when a computer computation yields a result smaller than the smallest possible quantity the computer is capable of storing. **(2)** A condition in which the exponent plus the excess become negative in a floating-point arithmetic operation.

underline   To format a selection of text so that the text is printed with a line slightly below it.

undersizing and oversizing   In computer graphics, graphics editing tools for the systematic reduction or enlargement, respectively, of the areas in a layout.

undo   A command that undoes the effect of the previous command and puts the text or graphics back the way it was. Some programs provide multiple undo levels, letting users take back commands given in the past.

unfragmented   A hard disk that has most of its files stored in consecutive sectors rather than spread out over the disk. Such an arrangement allows more efficient reading of data with less time required to move the read/write head to gather the information.

unibus   A high-speed data communications BUS structure shared by the CPU, internal memory, and peripherals.

uninterruptable power supply   A battery-operated device that supplies a computer with electricity in the event of a brownout or blackout.

union   In computer graphics, a method of combining two objects into one, with the objects being "fused" into a single object.

unipolar   Having one pole. Contrast with BIPOLAR.

Unisys   A computer company formed in 1986 as a merger of the Burroughs

Corporation and the Sperry Corporation, both large mainframe manufacturers. Unisys continues to emphasize the product lines of both companies, and in addition, has introduced several new mainframe, minicomputer, and personal computer products.

unit Any device having a special function, such as the arithmetic-logic unit, central processing unit, or disk unit.

unit position The extreme right position of a field, especially an integer numeric field.

universal asynchronous receiver/transmitter An integrated circuit device that receives serial data and converts it into parallel form for transmission, and vice versa.

universal identifier The standard multidigit number assigned to an individual to be used in verifying her or his identity.

universal language Any programming language available on many computers, such as PASCAL, COBOL, and BASIC. Same as COMMON LANGUAGE.

universal product code (UPC) A bar code developed to identify products and manufacturers of products. The code is to be read by OPTICAL CODE READERS.

UNIX™ An easy-to-use operating system developed by Ken Thompson, Dennis Ritchie, and coworkers at Bell Laboratories. Since the UNIX operating system is very easy to use, its design concept had a great influence on operating systems for microcomputers. UNIX is widely used on a great variety of computers, from mainframes to microcomputers.

unpack To separate short units of data that have previously been packed. Opposite of PACK.

unpopulated board A circuit board whose components must be supplied by the purchaser. Contrast with POPULATED BOARD.

unset To change the value of a bit (or a group of bits) to binary 0.

unstructured data Storage of retrievable information that is not organized into bytes or characters and customarily stored as a sequential bit stream representing pixels that must be reconstructed in its entirety to achieve intelligible results.

unstructured decisions   Decisions for which policy cannot be set in advance.

up   The state of a computer system that is currently operating.

up-and-running   A term used to indicate that a computer system or peripheral device has just been put into operation and is working properly.

UPC   Abbreviation for UNIVERSAL PRODUCT CODE.

update   (1) A software update usually occurs whenever a minor change has been made to the software. Updates are often free to registered owners of the software. (2) To make data files more current by adding, changing, or deleting data.

upgrade   (1) A software upgrade usually occurs whenever new features or major enhancements are added to the software. The cost for upgrades to registered owners of the software is usually substantially lower than the retail price for the product. (2) To reconfigure a computer system to increase its computing power; for example, to upgrade a microcomputer system with a faster and larger hard disk.

upload   To transfer information (files) from a smaller computer to a larger computer.

uppercase   Capital letters. All VCTS have the capability of using these. Contrast with LOWERCASE.

uptime   The period of time that equipment is working without failure. Contrast with AVAILABLE TIME and DOWNTIME.

upward compatible   A term used to indicate that a computer system or peripheral device can do everything that the previous model could do, plus some additional functions. See COMPATIBILITY.

usability   The worth of a system as evaluated by the person who must use it.

user (1) Anyone who owns or utilizes a computer for problem solving or data manipulation. (2) Anyone who requires the services of a computer system. Also called end user.

user-defined function Any function that has been defined by the user.

user-defined key A computer keyboard key that has a predefined function or whose function can be changed by a program. The function is performed by the computer whenever the key is depressed.

user-friendly The term applied to software and/or hardware that has been designed to be easily used, without the user having to remember complex procedures. Very easy for the inexperienced person to use.

user group A group of computer users who share the knowledge they have gained and the programs they have developed on a computer or class of computers of a specific manufacturer. They usually meet to exchange information, share programs, and trade equipment.

user involvement The involvement of users in the systems development life-cycle process.

user number A number or combination of letters and numbers that identifies a computer user for accounting purposes.

user-oriented language See PROBLEM-ORIENTED LANGUAGE and PROCEDURE-ORIENTED LANGUAGE.

user profile Information used as a part of a security system, such as the user's job function, areas of knowledge, access privileges, and supervisor.

user's manual The document describing how to use a hardware device, software product, or system.

user terminal See TERMINAL.

utility A program that helps the user run, enhance, create, or analyze other programs, programming languages, operating systems, and equipment.

utility programs Computer programs that provide commonly needed services, such as transferring data from one medium to another (disk to tape) and character conversion. Vendors of large computer systems commonly supply a set of utilities with their systems.

utility server   A device that allows everyone on a network to use several peripheral devices.

utility software   Software that controls a computer's daily housekeeping operations.

utilization statistics   The measure of a computer's performance based on the time log.

—— V ——

V   A prefix to indicate virtual, meaning capabilities that substitute for some real device or feature that isn't really there; for example, Vdisks—the emulation of disk drives in memory; VM—the emulation of memory on disks; and Vslots—the emulation of slots through interface ports.

VAB   Acronym for **V**oice **A**nswer **B**ack, an audio response device that can link a computer system to a telephone network, thus providing voice response to inquiries made from telephone-tape terminals.

vaccine   A program designed to counter the effects of a virus program.

validation   The examination of data for correctness against certain criteria, such as format (patterns of numbers, spaces, and letters), ranges (upper and lower value limits), check digits, and equivalent entries on a master file.

value   **(1)** Any constant or quantity stored in a computer's memory. **(2)** In a SPREADSHEET, data consisting of a number representing an amount, formula, or function.

value-added network   A system in which a carrier leases communication lines from a common carrier, enhances them by adding improvements such as error detection and faster response time, and then leases them to a third party.

value rule   A spreadsheet formula that tells the program how to calculate a cell's value.

vanishing point   In computer graphics, the place where parallel lines seem to come together in a perspective drawing.

vantage point   In computer graphics, the position from which an object or scene is viewed.

vaporware   Slang for announced software that may never materialize. In other words, a program promised by a publisher but never released.

VAR   Abbreviation for **v**alue-**a**dded **r**eseller, a person or company that buys equipment at a discount from manufacturers, combines it into systems or adds software, and then sells it to end customers.

variable A quantity that can assume any of a given set of values. For example, in a BASIC program that states PRINT A, B, C, the variables A, B, and C represent the actual values that will be printed. See SUBSCRIPTED VARIABLE. Contrast with CONSTANT.

variable-length record A record in a file in which records are not uniform in length. Contrast with FIXED-LENGTH RECORD.

variable name An alphanumeric term that identifies a data value in a program. The term can assume any of a set of values.

variable word length A term describing a machine word or operand that may consist of a variable number of bits, bytes, or characters. Contrast with FIXED WORD LENGTH.

VAX The designation for a family of 32-bit minicomputer systems manufactured by Digital Equipment Corporation. VAX machines were introduced in 1977 and range from desktop personal computers to large-scale mainframes.

Vbase An OBJECT-ORIENTED DATABASE.

VDL Abbreviation for **V**ienna **D**efinition **L**anguage, a language for defining the syntax and semantics of programming languages.

VDT Abbreviation for **V**IDEO **D**ISPLAY **T**ERMINAL, an input/output device consisting of a display screen and an input keyboard. Synonymous with CRT TERMINAL.

VDU Abbreviation for **v**isual **d**isplay **u**nit, a peripheral device on which data are displayed on some type of screen.

vector **(1)** A list of numbers all of which are expressed on the same line, such as a single column or row. **(2)** A quantity having magnitude and direction, as opposed to scalar value. **(3)** In COMPUTER SCIENCE, a data structure that permits the location of any item by the use of a single index or subscript. **(4)** A type of CATHODE RAY TUBE on which graphic data are represented by lines drawn from point to point rather than by illumination of a series of contiguous positions, as on a RASTER DISPLAY device. **(5)** In PLOTTING, an element of a line connecting two points. **(6)** In computer graphics, a line drawn in a certain direction from a starting point to an ending point.

vector font   A font in which the characters are drawn in arrangements of line segments rather than arrangements of curves or bits.

vector graphics monitor   A monitor that generates pictures by drawing numerous straight-line segments (vectors) on the screen.

vector image   An image defined as a series of straight-line vectors. The beginning and ending points of each line are stored and later adjusted as the image is sized.

vector pair   Data points that make up the opposite ends of a vector.

vector processor   A processor that performs simultaneous high-speed calculations on numerical elements. Vector processors are used extensively in systems that require intensive graphics operations.

vendee   A person or business that purchases a hardware or software system.

vendor   **(1)** A company or business entity that sells computers, peripheral devices, or computer-related services. **(2)** Any supplier from whom a vendee may purchase material.

Venn diagram   A diagram that uses circles and ellipses to give a graphic representation of logic relationships.

Ventura Publisher   A DESKTOP PUBLISHING program for IBM-compatible microcomputers and Apple Macintosh computers from Ventura Software, Inc. The program provides typeset-quality desktop publishing.

verification   The process of comparing information on a disk, tape, or punched card with the correct information.

verify   **(1)** To determine whether a data processing operation has been accomplished accurately. **(2)** To check data validity.

version   A specific release of a software product of a specific hardware model. Usually numbered in ascending order. For example, DOS 5.0 is a later version of a disk operating system than is DOS 4.1 or DOS 3.3.

verso   The left-side (even-numbered) page in a two-sided printing of a book or document.

vertex   (1) The point where two sides of an angle meet. (2) The highest or lowest point on a graphed line.

vertical   Going up or down.

vertical applications   Programs designed for specific professions or to do specialized kinds of work. Dentists can purchase applications, for example, that are designed expressly to manage a dental practice, such as scheduling, billing, ordering supplies, and so forth. There are hundreds of vertical applications available.

vertical axis   The Y-AXIS in a Cartesian coordinate system.

vertical justification   See LEADING.

vertical market   A market consisting of a group of similar customers.

vertical market software   Software for a group of similar customers such as printers, dentists, artists, or doctors.

vertical recording   Technology that strives to stand magnetic bits of information on end instead of side by side on a disk as they are today. Using this technology, several billion bytes of information could be stored on one disk.

vertical scrolling   The ability of a system to move up and down through a page or more of data displayed on the video screen. See SCROLLING.

vertical software   Specialized applications software that is designed for a particular discipline or activity. Examples include software that controls a spacecraft and simulates the game of blackjack.

very-high-level language   A FOURTH-GENERATION PROGRAMMING LANGUAGE.

very-high-speed integrated circuit (VHSIC)   An integrated circuit that performs operations at a very high rate of speed.

very large scale integration (VLSI)   The process of placing a large number (usually between 100,000 and 10,000,000) of components on one chip.

vesicular film   A coating for optical disc platters that permits the raising of small bumps on the surface instead of the pits used in standard CD-ROM discs for recording data. Bumps, unlike pits, can be flattened out to make an optical disc erasable and thus rewritable.

VGA   Abbreviation for **v**ideo **g**raphics **a**rray, an IBM high-resolution video display standard for its personal computers. VGA displays images at 640 pixels horizontally by 480 pixels vertically. This color bit-mapped graphics display standard was introduced by IBM Corporation in 1987 with its PS/2 computers.

VHSIC   See VERY-HIGH-SPEED INTEGRATED CIRCUIT.

video   A visual display, especially on a VIDEO DISPLAY TERMINAL.

video buffer   The memory on a video adapter used to store the data waiting to be shown on the video display.

video digitizer   An input device that converts the signal from a video camera into digital form and stores it in computer storage, where it can be analyzed or modified by the computer. See DIGITIZER.

videodisc   An OPTICAL DISC used to store video images and associated audio information.

video disk   A read-only form of secondary storage, usually a laser or optical disc.

video display page   A portion of a computer's video buffer that holds one complete screen image.

video display terminal (VDT)   A device for entering information into a computer system and displaying it on a screen. A typewriterlike keyboard is used to enter information. See CATHODE RAY TUBE, DISPLAY, and SCREEN.

video game machine A microprocessor-controlled machine designed principally for running commercially produced cartridges and disks that contain games and educational programs.

video graphics Computer-produced animated pictures.

video graphics board A video display board that generates text and graphics and accepts video from a camera or video recorder.

video input camera A video camera that converts images (photographs, real-life situations, drawings, and so forth) into dot-by-dot images in a computer's memory. The digitized images may be shown on a display screen or printed on paper by a graphics printer.

video monitor The device on which images generated by the computer's video adapter are displayed.

video page In WORD PROCESSING, the amount of text that can actually be seen on the screen at one time.

VideoPaint™ A powerful Apple Macintosh paint program.

video RAM (VRAM) A special type of DYNAMIC RAM (DRAM) used in high-speed video applications.

video signal An electronic signal containing information specifying the location and brightness of each point on a CRT screen, along with timing signals to place the image properly on the screen.

videotex An interactive electronic information system that includes news, electronic mail, shopping, banking, weather, and stock reports services.

vidicon The tube inside a TV camera that converts the image of a scene into an electrical signal.

view (**1**) To display information on a computer display screen. (**2**) The display of a graphical image from a given perspective. (**3**) In CAD programs, an image of a 3-D graphics model as it would be seen from a particular viewpoint. (**4**) In DATABASE SYSTEMS, a way of presenting the contents of a database to the user, not necessarily the same as the way the fields and records are stored in the database.

viewdata   Same as VIDEOTEX.

viewing pipeline   In computer graphics, the process by which picture data are translated from user input to the screen display.

viewport   A process that allows a user to place any selected picture in a chosen location on a video display screen. Compare WINDOW.

view volume   In computer graphics, the space in which objects are seen to exist in a three-dimensional display.

vignette   In computer graphics, an irregular shape to a graphic image without square edges to frame it.

virtual   Appearing to be rather than actually being, as in virtual storage.

virtual address   In virtual storage systems, an address that refers to virtual storage and must, therefore, be translated into a real storage address when it is used.

virtual function   In OBJECT-ORIENTED PROGRAMMING, a special member function that is invoked through a base class reference or pointer and is bound dynamically at run time.

virtual image   An image that has been copied into a computer's memory but that is too large to be displayed all at one time on the screen. Methods such as scrolling and panning are used to bring unseen portions of a virtual image into view.

virtual machine   The illusion of having many copies of the existing computer running simultaneously.

Virtual Machine (VM)   A functional equivalent of an entire computer. VM is IBM Corporation's implementation of this concept in their mid-size to large-scale systems.

virtual memory   Storage that is actually provided on a disk drive or other mass storage device but appears to programs to be part of the main memory of the computer. Thus, the programs seem to use more main memory than is actually provided.

Virtual Storage Access Method (VSAM) A highly efficient mass-storage device (disk) file access system for IBM mainframe systems.

virus A computer program that can wreak havoc on a system either by destroying data or simply gumming up the works. It is called a virus because it acts like a biological virus does in a human (but the computer virus is not actually a live organism). Viruses usually enter via shareware or public domain programs, though there have been reports of viruses being carried by commercial software.

visible page The image that is being displayed on the screen.

VisiCalc™ The first electronic spreadsheet, introduced in 1978 for the Apple II microcomputer.

vision recognition A method for processing pictorial information by computer. For example, an artificial intelligence computer can recognize a TV image of a horse and say (or print out), "It is a horse." Recognizing images is a very complex process for machines. See IMAGE PROCESSING.

visual display A visual representation of data such as a picture or diagram drawn on a display screen or a diagram produced by a plotter.

visual operating system An operating system that relies on icons, selected by a mouse, for giving commands to the computer.

visual page A visual representation consisting of one or more stored screen display files.

visual programming A way for programmers to interact with software and the programs they construct. The term indicates a new dimension added to programs and software systems, namely the ability to gain different insights and new ways to deal with software through visual and graphical means.

visual texture In computer graphics, surface variety that can be seen but not felt with the fingers.

visual thinking The art of problem solving with visual imagery.

VLDB Abbreviation for **v**ery **l**arge **d**ata**b**ase, a database distributed among multiple computers with different database management systems.

VLSI Abbreviation for **v**ery **l**arge **s**cale **i**ntegration, microchips that typically have more than 250,000 components each. VLSI methods allow thousands of integrated circuits to be placed on each chip and keep production costs relatively low. As VLSI technology improves, both a CPU and its memory may eventually be located on a single chip.

VM See VIRTUAL MACHINE.

vocabulary Codes or instructions that can be used to write a program for a particular computer.

voice actuation Control of the computer by spoken commands.

voice communications Transmission of sound in the human hearing range. Voice or audio sound can be transmitted either as analog or digital signals.

voice grade A term describing computer-to-computer links that employ the lines used in normal telephone communications.

voice input An input device that permits a human voice to be used as input to a computer. Also called speech recognition.

voice mail Messages spoken into a telephone, converted into digital form, and stored in the computer's memory until recalled, at which time they are reconverted into voice form.

voice output An audio response device that permits the computer to deliver output by the spoken word. The range of uses includes computer-assisted instruction and self-service gas stations. See PHONETIC SYSTEM.

voice recognition system A system designed to recognize and understand the voice and vocabulary of the user.

voice response COMPUTER OUTPUT in spoken form.

voice synthesis The ability of a computer to use stored patterns of sounds within its memory to assemble words that can be played through a loudspeaker.

volatile A term referring to the loss of data in semiconductor storage when the current is interrupted or turned off.

volatile file Any file in which insertion of new records or deletion of old records occurs at a high rate. Access time is critical.

volatile storage A storage medium whose contents are lost if power is removed from the system. See DYNAMIC RAM. Contrast with NONVOLATILE STORAGE.

volatility When a file is processed, the percentage of records added or deleted, an important parameter in designing a database.

voltage Electrical pressure. High voltage in a computer circuit is represented by 1; low (or zero) voltage is represented by 0.

voltage regulator A circuit that holds an output voltage at a predetermined value or causes it to vary according to a predetermined plan, regardless of normal input-voltage change or changes in the load impedance.

voltage surge A surge in electricity that can destroy a computer's hardware or memory.

voltage surge protector See SURGE PROTECTOR.

volume A physical unit of a storage medium, such as a diskette, hard disk, disk pack, or tape reel, capable of having data recorded on it and subsequently read.

von Neumann architecture Standard computer design based on stored programs and sequential processing.

von Neumann bottleneck The constraints in calculation ability brought about by the von Neumann architecture, which dictates one step at a time.

von Neumann machine A machine that consists of a central processing unit (CPU) and memory. The CPU fetches, executes, and returns. It treats data and programs in the same way. Most current computers are based on the von Neumann machine. Contrast with PARALLEL COMPUTERS.

voxel   In COMPUTER GRAPHICS, short for volume element. A voxel is a three-dimensional element that describes the data in a volumetric structure. It can be thought of as a "solid pixel."

VRC   Abbreviation for **v**ertical **r**edundancy **c**heck.

VS   Abbreviation for VIRTUAL STORAGE.

VSAM   See VIRTUAL STORAGE ACCESS METHOD.

vulnerability   Weaknesses in a computer system that pose security hazards.

wafer   A thin, circular disk on which many integrated circuits are fabricated and subsequently diced up into individual chips. It is a slice, approximately ¹⁄₃₀ inch thick, from three to six inches in diameter.

wait state   (1) A condition in which the CENTRAL PROCESSING UNIT is idle, not executing instructions. (2) A condition that occurs when a processor runs faster than its memory chips can retrieve data, thereby forcing the processor to wait periodically. Fast computers have no wait states, while slower computers have one or two wait states.

wait time   The time during which a program or computer waits for the completion of other activities.

walkthrough   A process in which one or more individuals "play computer" and follow the logic of a program through the steps performed by the computer in executing a program.

Wallis filter   An image processing enhancement technique.

WAN   Acronym for WIDE AREA NETWORK, a network of geographically distant computers and terminals.

wand   A hand-held optical device that can read and identify coded labels, bar codes, and characters.

Wang Laboratories   A major manufacturer of computers founded in 1951 by Dr. An Wang. In 1970, Wang introduced its first word processing system. Eight years later it was one of the largest suppliers of small business computers and word processors.

warm   In computer graphics, referring to color images that have a reddish tint. Those that are more blue are referred to as cool.

warm boot   The process of fooling the computer into thinking that its power has been turned off although power is still on. Contrast with COLD BOOT.

warm start   Same as WARM BOOT.

warm-up time   The interval between the energizing of a device and the beginning of the application of its output characteristics.

Warnier-Orr   A method of program design that uses top-down methods. Braces or curly brackets are used to indicate how the details of each step are arranged.

warning message   A diagnostic message produced by a COMPILER to alert the user to a nonfatal error.

warping   In computer graphics, the transformation of an image in a complex manner that may result in the image being twisted and enlarged in some areas and reduced in others.

warranty   Limited protection for hardware and software products, similar to warranties for most consumer products.

Water Color   A RASTER-based paint program designed to emulate the watercolor process operating in MS DOS. The program emulates standard artist tools.

WATS   Acronym for **W**ide **A**rea **T**elephone **S**ervice.

WCCE   Abbreviation for **W**orld **C**onference on **C**omputers in **E**ducation.

weakly typed language   A COMPUTER LANGUAGE that does not require the declaration of variables as to their type.

weed   To discard currently undesirable or needless items from a file.

weight   The variation in the heaviness of a typeface.

What if?   (1) The premise on which most electronic SPREADSHEET programs operate. New values may be substituted to determine the resultant effect on other values. (2) In ARTIFICIAL INTELLIGENCE, a term used in EXPERT SYSTEMS. The process is as follows: once a set of data has been entered, questions have been answered, and a conclusion has been reached, a portion of the data of answering a question is changed to see how the conclusion would be altered.

wheel graph   An alternate name for PIE CHART.

wheel printer A LINE PRINTER with a printing mechanism that contains the printing characters on metal wheels.

white noise A continuous noise produced over all audible frequencies to "fill in the gaps" between discontinuous office distractions such as printers, keyboards, and footsteps.

white space (1) A character that does not result in a printed number, letter, or symbol, e.g., space or tab. (2) The portion of the page not printed. A good page design involves the use of white space to balance the areas that receive text and graphics.

wholeness The degree of complexity of an EXPERT SYSTEM.

whole number A positive number without a fractional part, such as 84 or 22.0 or 0 (the only nonpositive whole number); a positive integer or zero.

wide area network (WAN) A data communications network designed to serve an area of hundreds or thousands of miles. WANS are generally implemented by linking together several remote local area networks (LANS) through the use of gateways and bridges over dedicated telephone lines.

wideband In DATA COMMUNICATIONS, a channel wider in bandwidth than a voice-grade channel. Same as BROADBAND. Compare NARROWBAND.

widow The last line of a paragraph sitting alone at the top of a page of text. Considered undesirable in all forms of printing. Compare with ORPHAN.

wild card A method of file-naming conventions that permits an operating system to perform utility functions on multiple files with related names, without the programmer or user having to specify each file by its full, unique name.

wild card search In WORD PROCESSING, a search for a word when only part of the word is known.

Winchester disks A particular form of hard disk in which several disk platters and their associate heads are sealed inside an enclosure. This enclosure is then kept as airtight as possible to exclude dust.

window   A portion of the video display area dedicated to some specified purpose. Special software allows the screen to be divided into multiple windows that can be moved around and made bigger or smaller. Windows allow the user to treat the computer display screen like a desktop where various files can remain open simultaneously.

window area   In SPREADSHEET SOFTWARE, the portion of the screen that contains the window onto the worksheet.

windowing   The act of displaying two or more files or disparate portions of the same file on the screen simultaneously.

windowing software   Programs that enable users to work with multiple on-screen windows. The Apple Macintosh Finder, Microsoft Windows, and the OS/2 Presentation Manager are all examples of windowing environments.

Windows™   A graphics-based operating environment for IBM-compatible microcomputers from Microsoft Corporation. It runs in conjunction with DOS. Some of the graphical user interface features include pull-down menus, multiple typefaces, desk accessories, and the ability to move text and graphics from one program to another via a clipboard.

windows environment   Any OPERATING SYSTEM or program that provides multiple windows on screen. Microsoft Windows, Presentation Manager, and Finder are examples of windows environments.

windows program   A program written to run under Microsoft Windows.

window-to-viewport mapping   The transformation of primitives from the world coordinate system to the device coordinate system.

wire chart   The primary end-product of a CAD/CAM wiring diagram system, which generates it automatically. A wire chart lists all devices, connections, and properties in a wiring diagram indicating physical locations of devices and connections, as well as the optimum wiring order for each connection to be made.

wireframe graphics A computer-aided design technique for displaying a three-dimensional object on the CRT screen as a series of lines outlining its surface. The skeletal form of an image created by a vector graphics display.

wire-frame model In computer graphics, a display of a three-dimensional object composed of separate lines that resemble strands of wire joined to create a model.

wire pairs Wires twisted together in an insulated cable that is frequently used to transmit information over short distances.

wire wrap A type of circuit board construction. Electrical connections are made through wires connected to the posts that correspond to the proper component leads.

wiring diagram (1) A graphic representation of all circuits and device elements of an electrical system and its associated apparatus or any clearly defined functional portion of that system. A wiring diagram may contain not only wiring system components and wires but also non-graphic information such as wire number, wire size, color, function, component label, pin number, and so forth. (2) An illustration of device elements and their interconnectivity as distinguished from their physical arrangement. (3) A drawing that shows how to hook things up. Wiring diagrams can be constructed, annotated, and documented on a CAD system.

wizard An experienced HACKER.

WMF Abbreviation for **W**indows **M**etafile **F**ormat, a common graphics file format for applications that run under Microsoft Windows.

word A logical unit of information; a group of bits, characters, or bytes considered as an entity and capable of being stored in one storage location. Compare KEYWORD.

Word See MICROSOFT WORD.

word length The number of bits in a word, usually 8, 16, 32, or 64.

WordPerfect™ A full-featured WORD PROCESSING program for IBM-compatible microcomputers, Apple Macintosh, and other computers.

word processing (WP) A technique for electronically storing, editing, and manipulating text by using an electronic keyboard, computer, and printer. The text is recorded on a magnetic medium, usually floppy disks; the final output is on paper. Words and letters are manipulated electronically, making it easy to copy and edit text.

word processing center A central facility that contains the word processing equipment and personnel that prepare written communications for an organization.

word processing operator An individual who operates word processing equipment.

word processing program Software that guides the computer system in writing, editing, and formatting text. Same as word processor.

word processing system An information processing system that relies on automated and computerized typing, copying, filing, dictation, and document retrieval. Increasingly used in modern offices.

word processor A computer program that provides for manipulation of text. Can be used for writing documents, inserting or changing words, paragraphs, or pages, and printing documents.

WordStar™ The first full-featured word processing program for IBM-compatible microcomputers. It was introduced in 1978 by WordStar International. WordStar gave sophisticated word processing capabilities to personal computer users at significantly less cost than the dedicated word processing machines of the time. Several different versions of the program are available today.

word wrap The feature that automatically moves a word to the beginning of the next line if it will not fit at the end of the original line. It is found in word processing and page layout programs.

workbench A programming environment in which hardware and software items are shared by several users.

working drawing   In building design, a detailed layout of a component with complete dimensions and notes, approved for production. It can be generated by a CAD/CAM system.

working storage   Same as TEMPORARY STORAGE.

Works   See MICROSOFT WORKS.

worksheet   In SPREADSHEET SOFTWARE, the grid that contains the actual labels and values.

worksheet area   See WINDOW-AREA.

worksheet window   The portion of the worksheet visible on-screen.

workspace   A loosely defined term that usually refers to the amount of internal storage available for programs and data and allocated for working storage.

workstation   A configuration of computer equipment designed for use by one person at a time. This may have a terminal connected to a computer, or it may be a stand-alone system with local processing capability. Examples of workstations include a stand-alone graphics system and a word processor.

work year   The effort expended by one person for one year, a term used to estimate the personnel resources needed to complete a specific task.

World Conference on Computers in Education (WCCE)   An international computer education conference sponsored by the International Federation for Information Processing and the American Federation of Information Processing Societies, held every four years in a different country. See NATIONAL EDUCATIONAL COMPUTING CONFERENCE.

world coordinates   In computer graphics, a coordinate system that is scaled so that user-defined objects can be represented in units appropriate to the application, such as inches, meters, and miles. Each object in a picture is first described in its own model coordinates, and all are then mapped into world coordinates.

world space   In computer graphics, the three-dimensional coordinate space where objects interact to make scenes.

worm   A destructive routine in a program that is designed to corrupt information on a disk. A worm differs from a virus in that it cannot replicate itself or attach itself to other programs. A worm usually exists as a program in its own right.

WORM   Acronym for **w**rite **o**nce/**r**ead **m**any, a term that describes storage devices upon which data, once written, cannot be erased. WORM drives write data by burning holes into the surface of a special type of disk. The disks last for decades. This indelible record is highly desirable in fields that require permanent, unalterable storage of important documents.

WPG   A WordPerfect graphics file format.

WPM   Abbreviation for **w**ords **p**er **m**inute, a measure of data transmission speed.

wraparound   **(1)** The continuation of an operation, such as a change in the storage location from the largest addressable location to the first addressable location. **(2)** A visual display cursor movement from the last character position to the first position.

wraparound type   Type that wraps around a graphic image in a body of text.

write   **(1)** The process of transferring information from the computer to an output medium. **(2)** To record data in a storage device. Contrast with READ.

write-enable ring   The plastic ring that must be placed on a tape reel before information can be recorded on the tape. Compare WRITE-PROTECT RING.

write head   A magnetic head designed to write data onto the media. Contrast with READ HEAD. Compare READ/WRITE HEAD.

write-inhibit ring   A plastic ring used to prevent data from being written over on magnetic tapes. Same as WRITE-PROTECT RING.

write-protect **(1)** To mechanically prevent a 3.5-inch diskette from being written to. To write-protect a disk, a user moves the write-protect tab in order to see through the write-protect notch, or so that the tab is at the bottom position in the notch. **(2)** To protect 5.25-inch diskettes from the possibility of undesired recording of data by application of a gummed tab over the write-protect notch. An uncovered write-protect notch will allow writing to the diskette.

write-protect ring A plastic ring that, when removed from the back of a tape reel, prevents writing on the tape. Also called WRITE-INHIBIT RING. See FILE-PROTECTION.

WYKIWYL Acronym for **w**hat **y**ou **k**now (by using a colleague's hardware/software) **i**s **w**hat **y**ou **l**ike (and often end up buying).

WYSIWYG Acronym for **w**hat **y**ou **s**ee **i**s **w**hat **y**ou **g**et, describing word processors that generate screen images that are identical in position and type appearance to the final document, as opposed to those that show the formatting or special type requested only when the document is printed.

—— X-Y-Z ——

X-axis   On a coordinate plane, the horizontal axis. Contrast with Y-AXIS and Z-AXIS.

XENIX   A variation on the UNIX operating system created by Microsoft Corporation for use on microcomputers.

xerography   A copying system that depends on an image formed from electrostatic charges. Powdered ink is attracted to the charged parts of a surface and then fused onto paper. The method is the basis for most office copiers and laser printers.

x-height   The height of lowercase letters without ascenders and descenders.

Xmodem   A method of transmitting data to another computer through modems. It transfers data in packages of 128K.

XOR   Acronym for exclusive **or**.

XT   The first IBM Personal Computer that included a hard disk, introduced in 1983. XT stands for extended technology.

X-Windows   A graphical user interface for Unix, developed at MIT, that many firms have made a standard.

X-Y chart   A form that allows plotting of one data series against another, without a time axis. Often used to determine if there is a correlation between two series, with the direction, slope, and curvature of the line showing the relationship.

x-y matrix   A group of rows and columns. Used as a reference framework for two-dimensional structures, such as 2-D graphics images, charts, tables, mathematical graphs and plots, digitizer tablets, digital plotters, and display screens.

X-Y plotter   An output device that draws points, lines, or curves on a sheet of paper based on X and Y coordinates from a computer. See PLOTTER.

X-Y-Z coordinate system   A three-dimensional system of Cartesian coordinates that includes a third (Z) axis running perpendicular to the horizontal (X) and vertical (Y) axes.

Y-axis   On a coordinate plane, the vertical axis. Contrast with X-AXIS and Z-AXIS.

YIQ   A color model designed for the Macintosh II microcomputer. It stresses luminance as a component of color.

Ymodem   A method of transmitting data to another computer through modems. Transfers data in packages of 1,024K, which makes it faster than the Xmodem transmission protocol. See also XMODEM.

yoke   That part of the electron beam deflection system used for addressing a video display.

yon plane   In computer graphics, the back clipping plane that defines a finite view volume. Graphic entities straddling this boundary are clipped in the Z-axis.

zap   **(1)** A command in many electronic SPREADSHEET programs that irretrievably erases all information on the spreadsheet. **(2)** To delete a file or clear a screen accidentally.

Zapf Chancery   A typeface developed by Hermann Zapf, a German typeface designer, and owned by the International Typeface Corporation (ITC). It is included as a built-in font with many POSTSCRIPT laser printers.

Zapf Dingbats   A set of decorative symbols developed by Hermann Zapf, a German typeface designer. Zapf Dingbats are used for decorative purposes in a document. The typeface is included as a built-in font with many POSTSCRIPT laser printers.

Z-axis   On a coordinate plane, the axis that represents depth. Contrast with X-AXIS and Y-AXIS.

Z-80   Zilog-80, an eight-bit microprocessor from Zilog Corporation that was widely used in many early microcomputer systems.

zero A numeral normally denoting lack of magnitude. In many computers, there are distinct representations for plus and minus zero.

zero flag A flip-flop that goes to logic 1 if the result of an instruction has the value of zero.

zeroize To initialize a program with zeros, or to fill spaces in memory with zeros.

zero suppression The suppression (elimination) of nonsignificant zeros in a numeral, usually before or during a printing operation. For example, the numeral 00004763, with zero suppression, would be printed as 4763. It is commonly used in pagination so that early pages of a report will be numbered 1, 2, ... rather than 01, 02, ... or 001, 002, ...

zone bits Special bits used along with numeric bits to represent alphanumeric characters in ASCII and EBCDIC codes.

zoom To view an enlarged (zoom in) or reduced (zoom out) portion of a page on-screen.

zoom box A box symbol that appears in the right corner of some program windows. Clicking in the zoom box causes the window to expand to fill the entire screen or to contract to a smaller size; clicking it again returns the window to its original size.

zooming Changing of a view on a graphics display by either moving in on successively smaller portions of the currently visible picture or moving out until the window encloses the entire scene.